Public
Sociology

Public Sociology

Research, Action, and Change

Philip Nyden
Loyola University Chicago

Leslie Hossfeld
University of North Carolina Wilmington

Gwendolyn Nyden
Oakton Community College

Los Angeles | London | New Delhi
Singapore | Washington DC

Los Angeles | London | New Delhi
Singapore | Washington DC

FOR INFORMATION:

Pine Forge Press
An Imprint of SAGE Publications, Inc.
2455 Teller Road
Thousand Oaks, California 91320
E-mail: order@sagepub.com

SAGE Publications Ltd.
1 Oliver's Yard
55 City Road
London EC1Y 1SP
United Kingdom

SAGE Publications India Pvt. Ltd.
B 1/I 1 Mohan Cooperative Industrial Area
Mathura Road, New Delhi 110 044
India

SAGE Publications Asia-Pacific Pte. Ltd.
33 Pekin Street #02-01
Far East Square
Singapore 048763

Acquisitions Editor: David Repetto
Editorial Assistant: Maggie Stanley
Production Editor: Catherine M. Chilton
Copy Editor: Pam Suwinsky
Typesetter: C&M Digitals (P) Ltd.
Proofreader: Annette R. Van Deusen
Indexer: Diggs Publication Services
Cover Designer: Bryan Fishman
Marketing Manager: Erica DeLuca
Permissions Editor: Karen Ehrmann

Image #1: ©iStockphoto.com/TommL

Image #2: ©iStockphoto.com/track5

Image #3: ©iStockphoto.com/pixdeluxe

Image #4: ©iStockphoto.com/asiseeit

Image #5: ©iStockphoto.com/VladKol

Image #6: ©iStockphoto.com/DIMUSE

Printed in the United States of America

Library of Congress Cataloging-in-Publication Data

Nyden, Philip W.

Public sociology: research, action, and change / Philip Nyden, Leslie Hossfeld, Gwen Nyden.

p. cm.
Includes bibliographical references and index.

ISBN 978-1-4129-8263-4 (pbk.)

1. Sociology—Methodology. 2. Sociology—Research. 3. Applied sociology. 4. Social change. I. Hossfeld, Leslie H., 1961- II. Nyden, Gwendolyn E. III. Title.

HM511.N93 2012 301.01—dc22 2010050142

This book is printed on acid-free paper.

11 12 13 14 15 10 9 8 7 6 5 4 3 2 1

Contents

Foreword

C. Wright Mills famously defined the sociological imagination as linking personal troubles to public issues. He thought it was sufficient to trace personal misfortune to social forces and people would throng the political arena. Thus, knowing that unemployment was not the result of bad luck or individual sloth but of the operation of the labor market, workers would demand state protection against unemployment. Knowing that domestic violence was conditioned by male power, women would demand laws and services that would empower women.

Knowledge, Mills assumed, was power. Maybe. But not in quite the sense he intended. Faced with those daunting forces beyond their control, but forces certainly within their intellectual grasp, the dominated throw up their hands in despair, paralyzed by their impotence rather than empowered by their understanding. Sociological imagination may expose social structure as the source of our malaise, but it is not sufficient for political action. We also need a *political imagination* to turn personal troubles into public issues, which is precisely what suffuses this collection of public sociologies edited by leading figures in this field. Whether they are writing about community development, environmental justice, access to education and health, overcoming inequalities, or tackling crime, the authors are found not only in the classroom but also in the trenches of civil society (or in the classroom as a trench of civil society), exercising their political imagination in galvanizing the public will. Outside a few elite research universities—those rapidly disappearing islands of insularity—carrying sociology into the community is neither rare nor controversial. In fact, for the authors of these case studies, and so many others, it is a way of life that needs to be made more known, more public.

An effective political imagination depends on an organic connection between sociologists and their publics. But such "organic" public sociology is not just a form of sociological practice suited to the social justice foundations of sociology; rather it is an essential intervention, necessary to save the university under siege from state and market. Bereft of public funds, the university is rapidly becoming a capitalist machine, servicing corporations with research and demanding escalating fees from students-become-consumers. Living in a fool's paradise, we have been accustomed to take for granted public funding of universities. Those days are definitively gone. In the end we may have to accept the corporatization of the university, in which everything is reduced to the bottom line, but for now we can put up a fight, building and extending collaborations with communities, themselves under assault. This book shows we still have a choice, albeit one that is rapidly receding, to defend the public university—public in the sense of being accountable to broad public interests. In this regard sociology leads the way in alliance with other academic disciplines. It has, after all, its roots and its standpoint in civil society, defending the latter's integrity against the predatory state and the tyrannical market. Thus, in defending civil society sociology is not only defending its own existence, but that of wider humanity too.

Michael Burawoy
University of California, Berkeley

Foreword

Community-based service organizations are in continual motion. Our speed and adaptability create numerous benefits. We respond quickly to changing needs, we modify services midstream when we discover a more effective strategy, and we can launch new programs with little notice to bring new funding to our communities.

But operating in hyperdrive leaves little time for reflection, planning, or deeper learning. Every day, we add to our unexamined stockpiles of information. Too often, that means unique and valuable data go to waste—data that could have led to better results, transferable lessons for other organizations, or headway on broader, systemic problems.

Fortunately, partnerships with academic institutions to engage in applied research can unlock the potential of that unprocessed knowledge. The methods, discipline, and perspective of research and evaluation expand our decision-making tools from gut reactions to conscious analysis. They let us integrate relevant information about our regions, or see small changes over time, or uncover correlations that lie beneath the surface. In our case, at STRIVE, a nonprofit job training program in Chicago, an ongoing partnership with Loyola's Center for Urban Research and Learning led to research and program evaluations that yielded expanded staff development, improved retention for hard-to-serve clients, and a new model for clients' career advancement.

At the same time, researchers gain unique benefits from this access to field data and immediate application of findings. They get information long before it appears in official statistical reports or administrative records. They can see in real time the impact of applying proposed revisions to service models. And ultimately, when evaluating their recommendations, they can apply the critical test: Will they work?

Together, this collaboration between universities and communities is the remarkable realm of sociology in action.

Steven Redfield
Coro National

Foreword

Public sociology. It has been done. It is being done. And you can do it. This timely book explains what it is and cites important historical examples. The book also provides dozens of contemporary cases demonstrating how public sociology "gets put into play." I hope the readers can find themselves in these examples and "just do it."

As the authors of these chapters and case studies point out, the majority of people who call themselves sociologists work in academia. However, all the people who have advanced degrees and even all who take undergraduate sociology courses have the opportunity to use what they have learned in the public arena. I got my "Invitation to Sociology" from Peter Berger in his book of that title back in the early 1960s. In it he said that sociology is an attempt to understand in a disciplined way the "world taken for granted" that we all live in. That understanding is the beginning. Making a difference is the real challenge of public sociology. The challenge is beautifully laid out in these pages.

I spent 20 years in departments of sociology in three major universities and 20 years in a large private foundation. I concur with the authors that doing public sociology requires intentionality, persistence, and sometimes courage. Each organization—especially the academy—has its own set of expectations. And sometimes it requires effort to connect with the world outside. Any discipline spends a lot of effort differentiating itself from others, sociology perhaps more than others. In my experience that process can lead to insularity and inward thinking. Public sociology helps us break out, but we must be intentional.

One chapter refers to public sociology as "crossing boundaries." My metaphor is building bridges. Bridges require firm foundations at both ends; they are built to last; and they go both ways. Public sociology must not only have a permanent foundation in the academy (or your organization), but also in the community. And it is not a one-time affair. Knowledge, even wisdom, exists at both ends of this bridge and must flow both ways. I have had colleagues suggest that doing research with community "waters down the research." To the contrary, it makes the findings richer and more relevant.

In 20 years at a foundation, I never began a sentence with "As a sociologist." But, I never examined a proposal without thinking of the project as a test of a null hypothesis. We never called grant making research, but I always considered every report and every publication a contribution to a continuing intellectual dialogue. Some seem to think that public sociology is somehow less rigorous than other kinds. I have found that it takes more theoretical and methodological sophistication. And while results may not find their way to the top disciplinary journals, true practitioners do contribute to the dialogue in appropriate written vehicles and in organizational and public policy.

Public Sociology: Research, Action, and Change confirms and reinforces my experiences. I highly recommend it to teachers, grad students, and practitioners.

Dan E. Moore
GivingInsight

Acknowledgments

Pine Forge Press and SAGE Publications would like to acknowledge the following reviewers:

Mary Gatta
Rutgers University

Toby A. Ten Eyck
Michigan State University

Kathy S. Stolley
Virginia Wesleyan College

1

Public Scholarship, the Sociological Imagination, and Engaged Scholarship

The purpose of this book is to highlight the variety of ways in which sociology "gets into play," bringing about social change in community settings, assisting nonprofit or social service organizations in their work, influencing local, regional, or national policy, informing the general public on key policy issues through media publications or visibility, and creating research centers that develop and carry out collaborative research involving both researchers and practitioners in all facets of the research process. When sociologists are actively engaged with audiences outside of academia in identifying issues, researching those issues, and disseminating results, the process of connecting sociology to those publics is most obvious.

Defining Public Sociology

Although there is a long history of sociologists and social scientists working outside the walls of academia—some dating back to the 19th century—the most recent movement to connect sociology to the interests, needs, and concerns of organizations, communities, and individuals outside the university has been framed by discussion of "public sociology." Michael Burawoy, president of the American Sociological Association (ASA) in 2004, has been a significant leader both in recognizing the importance of engaged scholarship outside of the university and in facilitating the work of sociologists engaged in public scholarship. The ASA annual meeting organized around the theme of public sociology in 2004 was the best-attended national meeting to date. The increased presence of graduate students and younger sociologists was notable. Burawoy defines *public sociology* as a

> sociology that seeks to bring sociology to publics beyond the academy, promoting dialogue about issues that affect the fate of society, placing the values to which we adhere under a microscope. What is important here is the multiplicity of public sociologies, reflecting the multiplicity of publics—visible and invisible, thick and thin, active and passive, local, national and even global, dominant and counter publics. The variety of publics stretches from our students to the readers of our books, from newspaper columns to interviews, from audiences in local civic groups such as churches or neighborhoods, to social movements we facilitate. The possibilities are endless. (Burawoy, 2004, p. 104)

Burawoy further distinguishes between "traditional" and "organic" public sociologies. Traditional public sociology includes scholarship and professional activity that is driven by interests and priorities of the discipline. Although not done in conjunction with any organizations or movements, the products of such scholarship may have significant relevance for those outside of academia. Work on educational inequality, persistent racial and ethnic income inequities, gender differences in career development, effective leadership styles in large organizations, or the new role of tourism in local community identity may be motivated by interests within the discipline of sociology. As Burawoy puts it, "The traditional public sociologist instigates debates within or between publics, although he or she might not actually participate in them" (2005, p. 7). However, all of these research areas are of considerable relevance to various groups outside the university. Insofar as sociologists who have done this work write op-ed columns for local newspapers, testify at government hearings, speak to community groups, consult with organizations about their work, or report on their research through blogs, web pages, and other Web-based media, they are engaged in a form of public sociology.

EXPERT TESTIMONY

Gregory Squires, a faculty member at George Washington University and national expert on racial and ethnic discrimination in housing and housing-related financial services (such as mortgage loans and home insurance), has presented testimony before congressional committees in addition to serving as an expert witness in many court cases. He also serves on the board of the Woodstock Institute, a nationally recognized policy research organization focusing on fair lending and financial service industry reform.

What impact has your congressional testimony had?

It is difficult to answer this specifically and concretely. I do not think that anyone can point to a particular piece of testimony that was given as the cause of a particular law that was eventually passed or regulation that was eventually promulgated. But the reality is that before any legislation is considered, a hearing record is developed. In the course of congressional debate, proponents point to that hearing record as part of the evidence as to why they are proposing their legislation.

It is rare, if ever, that a particular statement actually causes a legislator to change his or her mind. But in the absence of a compelling hearing record, it is unlikely that any significant legislation or regulation will be enacted. In the case of my recent testimony on how racial segregation in U.S. cities has opened the door to subprime lending [where some groups are forced to pay higher loan or mortgage rates], a major financial services reform bill was passed a few months later. I suspect that my testimony may not be 100 percent responsible for that! But in the absence of hundreds of people like me testifying, at the dozens of hearings on financial services issues held over the past five years, I suspect that we might not have gotten this bill.

Are you giving voice to communities typically not heard by policy makers?

That has been the intent. Ever since I worked in the Chicago Regional Office of the U.S. Commission on Civil Rights, I have tried to consciously conduct research projects for which the findings would provide evidence for people who are trying to ameliorate various forms of discrimination. So I pay attention to what government law enforcement agencies are looking at, what nonprofit advocacy groups are doing, and I try to figure out a way that I can do research that will give these groups additional ammunition. This was my approach when I worked with community groups in Chicago while at the commission and with neighborhood organizations in Milwaukee when I taught at the University of Wisconsin–Milwaukee; in Washington, D.C., I have been more involved with national organizations, most of which are umbrella organizations for local groups.

Distinct from this traditional public sociology is organic public sociology. This represents a more collaborative approach to research in which boundaries between researcher and practitioner, scholar and activist, or university and community are more permeable. It is a sociology that more explicitly recognizes the value of both university-based knowledge (e.g., outcomes from research done by academic sociologists responding to interests of the discipline) *and* community-based knowledge (e.g., awareness of community practices and histories). Burawoy explains that in organic public sociology, "The sociologist works in close connection with a visible, thick, active, local and often counterpublic. . . . Between the organic public sociologist and a public is a dialogue, a process of mutual education" (Burawoy, 2005, pp. 7–8). Organic public sociologists often find themselves working in very dynamic environments in the middle of heated community debates, conflicts between organizational managers and staff, disputes between elected officials and grassroots organizations. Although such public sociologists have sometimes been dismissed as having crossed over to the other side and having not been objective in their research, that is generally far from the truth.

Immersing oneself in the world outside of one's discipline does not mean that one drops the discipline's standards of research. It does mean that one becomes more aware of the complexities of these outside worlds—the complexities with which nonsociologists and nonacademics are intimately familiar. Truly listening to the perspectives of outside publics and using these perspectives in shaping research add to the quality of sociological research. Entering into unfamiliar communities or organizations with preconceived perspectives and notions created solely by research in the discipline and shaped solely by other sociologists is more likely to produce research that misses the mark than is the research informed by publics. As the expression goes, "A mind is like a parachute; it doesn't work unless it is open." Similarly, sociology does not work effectively if is not open to considering perspectives of publics outside the field.

It is in concert with publics that some of sociology's most valuable contributions to the broader society can be enhanced. The critical eye that undergraduate sociology majors and graduate students develop is of significant value in the everyday world in sorting through layers or organizational rules and regulations or taking seemingly random community social interactions and making sense of them. C. Wright Mills wrote of the "sociological imagination" as a perspective that can produce clearer thinking, can liberate, and can facilitate social change:

> The sociological imagination enables its possessor to understand the larger
> historical scene in terms of its meaning for the inner life and the external career

of a variety of individuals. It enables that person to take into account how individuals, in the welter of their daily experience, often become falsely conscious of their social positions. Within that welter, the framework of modern society is sought, and within that framework the psychologies of a variety of men and women are formulated. By such means the personal uneasiness of individuals is focused upon explicit troubles, and the indifference of publics is transformed into involvement with public issues. (Mills, 1959, p. 5)

From a different perspective, symbolic interactionist Herbert Blumer describes something similar to Mills's "sociological imagination." Blumer (1969) talks about sociologists' skills in systematically uncovering societal conventions and practices that obscure social processes from common view. He explains that much of his own work as been "to lift the veils that cover . . . group life. . . . The veils are not lifted by substituting, in whatever degree, preformed images for firsthand knowledge. The veils are lifted . . . by digging deep . . . through careful study" (p. 39). As Burawoy states, sociologists' ability to clear away some of the fog and place issues in clear focus is at the heart of the work of organic public sociologists: "The project of such public sociologies is to make visible the invisible, to make the private public, to validate these organic connections as part of our sociological life" (2005, p. 8).

There is an activist thread in the work of many public sociologists, past and present. Alfred McClung Lee, a past president of the American Sociological Association and founder of the Association for Humanist Sociology, speaks on the need for sociology to be proactive in connecting to the world around us:

> The great challenge of social science is the development and wide dissemination of social wisdom and social-action techniques that will enable more and more people to participate in the control and guidance of their groups and their society. In meeting this challenge, social science stimulates and nurtures the fuller development of individual potential. (1973, p. 6)

This is not suggesting that sociologists take up positions on the front lines of social movements and political battles. However, it is suggesting that it is not sufficient to just "do sociology"; there is a need to more actively work with others outside the field and outside of academia in seeking positive change.

We do not pretend that public sociology is the be-all or end-all of engaged scholarship, nor do we want to suggest that this work was not being done before Michael Burawoy came along and named it in 2004, before the ASA created the Task Force on Public Sociology in 2004 (ASA Task Force, 2005), or before the American Sociological Association established the Sociological Practice and Public Sociology Section. In some ways this is repackaging current and past work in the field. Certainly the work of James Coleman on educational policy (Coleman et al., 1966), William Foote Whyte and his colleagues on community efforts to preserve jobs (Woodworth, Meek, & Whyte, 1985), or Seymour Martin Lipset (Lipset, Trow, & Coleman, 1977) on union democracy would fit under the public sociology umbrella. Similarly, work variously described as action research, participatory action research, participatory evaluation research, and collaborative research, among other grassroots approaches, also fit—particularly into the organic public sociology model (Gaventa, 1991; Stoecker, 2005; and Strand, Marullo, Cutforth, Stoecker, & Donohue, 2003).

The accomplishments of Burawoy's leadership in getting the field of sociology to recognize the importance of public sociology should in no way diminish the efforts of many who have worked under these different banners. There are some who argue that traditional academics might even learn something from these well-established participatory research traditions—as one sociologist put it, this might be the time to teach "academic dogs and cats new tricks" (Felt, Rowe, & Curlew, 2004). In this book we do not assume that we know it all, nor do we suggest that there are not other well-established approaches to go about research that brings about effective community-based change. We do seek to broaden research horizons, learn from others, and make sociology the dynamic field that it can be.

Mainstream or Marginal?

The public sociological projects included in this book do not represent outliers from mainstream sociology. The case studies represent the kind of work that many sociologists do on a regular basis. It is why many of us went into sociology in the first place. Most of us did not go into sociology so that we would spend the rest of our lives reading Weber, Durkheim, and Marx; rather we wanted to do something with our training. Even within public sociology, most of the work is best classified as organic public sociology. As Burawoy observes, "The bulk of public sociology is indeed of an organic kind—sociologists working with a labor movement, neighborhood associations, communities of faith, immigrant rights groups, human rights organizations" (Burawoy, 2005, pp. 7–8). Indeed, historically a number of sociologists routinely worked in polling, industrial sociology, labor relations, and other fields outside of the academy. The growing call for a more relevant sociology in the late 1960s in response to more activist students and younger faculty had its influence on the field. In the 1980s, the shrinking job market for sociologists pushed the profession to work with publics outside of academia (Freeman & Rossi, 1984). Recognition that the field needs to be responsive to the outside world if sociology is to remain vibrant and viable continues to fuel support for engagement outside of the academy today.

There is a distinct grassroots character to much of public sociology and certainly most of the projects outlined in this book. If one reads only the "top" journals in the field, one might miss the bulk of work going on within sociology. Whether it is working with graduate and undergraduate students on one of the community-based projects described in this book or directly with local organizations, engagement is a natural extension of the sociological enterprise. If we do not actively connect our sociological work to the needs of the broader society, the long-term health of the field will be threatened. Connection to the broader public and to consumers of our research, whether made traditionally or organically, is vital to the continued vibrancy of our field.

This is not to say that all is well for public scholarship in academia-world. There is significant resistance from a number of directions. The reward system for professors in most colleges and universities is slanted toward outcomes valued by the discipline. More than one sociology department has a "point system" in which faculty have to excel if they are to get tenure, better salaries, and other rewards. Publishing in sociology journals may be valued more than publishing in policy journals. A peer-reviewed published article that will ultimately be read by 200 fellow sociologists may be weighted much more heavily than a local policy report read by 2,000 community residents and leaders who are seeking solutions to reduce youth crime. The central focus of the discipline is the quality of the methodology, the strength of the sociological analysis, and discipline-based publication. Points are typically not rewarded for documenting that your research has contributed to improved education in local schools, less poverty in a neighborhood, more affordable housing, less racial profiling by the police, or more employment opportunities. Those promoting public sociology are not attempting to diminish the importance of quality research; rather they are trying to *add* positive impact on the local community and broader society as one measure the discipline uses in evaluating research quality.

Just as they are trying to meet the challenges of pressing problems in the world around them through their research, the contributors to this book have not been fazed by resistance to public scholarship within their departments or within the field. In subsequent chapters we talk more about strategies for surviving as a public sociologist within academia. We also show that not all public sociologists work in universities. Historically, some of the most prominent public sociology was done by people who were outside of academia or who spent a substantial amount of time outside of universities. W.E.B. DuBois and Jane Addams are two such examples from the 19th and early 20th centuries.

Although we have included examples of both traditional and organic public sociology in our case studies, this book has a distinctly grassroots orientation. A few years ago, the University of California Press published a book entitled *Public Sociology: Fifteen Eminent Sociologists Debate Politics and the Profession in the Twenty-First Century* (Clawson et al., 2007). Many of these scholars, from Francis Fox Piven and William Julius Wilson to Barbara Ehrenreich and Orlando Patterson, offer valuable perspectives from their years of scholarship, policy work, and activism. However, the more than 30 sociologists writing in this book do not pretend to be "eminent" sociologists. We are more the rank-and-file of public sociology who represent a growing sector of the field. A year ago Michael Burawoy visited the Center for Urban Research and Learning at Loyola University Chicago, a collaborative university–community research center directed by Phil Nyden. After talking with faculty, graduate students, and community partners, Burawoy remarked, "I just write about public sociology, you are doing it." For public sociology to survive, we need advocates, eminent established scholars, *and* the front-line public sociologists along with their community partners.

Focus on Active Sociology

This book emphasizes actions and connections. This is not armchair sociology in which self-proclaimed public sociologists just write articles suggesting what government, corporations, communities, or others "ought to do." We are interested in the *active* connections to publics and users of the research, not a passive research process. We do not shy away from getting into the thick of community controversies and policy debates and having a significant presence in settings outside of university walls. We do not retreat from interacting with various community groups, advocacy organizations, or government agencies under a false guise of objectivity that says you have to stay at arm's length from "interest groups in your research." Public sociologists actively engaged in the community can just as easily maintain top ethical and research standards as can the sociologist studying secondary datasets and not directly immersed in the community.

Moreover, the claim that engaged sociology has the inherent danger of being biased and too political because the researcher gets too close to various interest groups is a red herring. *All* research is political. Sociologists' choices of what to research and how to research it are very political decisions. One sociologist may decide to study how to create more effective corporate management strategies to increase worker productivity. Another sociologist may study the impact of discrimination on workers in the same company. Both may be legitimate topics for sociological research, but the outcomes of the two research projects will have different implications for increased corporate control versus worker rights. The difference between these two orientations is a political difference.

How research is done is also a political decision. One sociologist may choose to do his research from afar, using existing datasets and other secondary information rather than interacting with any of the individuals, communities, or organizations active in the issue being studied. This approach is a political decision—a decision to stay at arm's length from those being studied and not seek their direct input in research design or in interpreting data. A second sociologist may decide to immerse herself in the field with an openness to discover social practices that she could not anticipate before entering the field. That choice is a political decision to give community members or staff in an organization more direct voice in the research.

The two sociologists described in the example are making political decisions. One is more willing to work with data collected by surveys designed by sociologists and coded by sociologists with limited input from publics. The second sociologist may assume that the discipline does not know everything, that people in the community have valuable knowledge that needs to be gathered, and that there is a complexity of everyday life that gets overlooked by the numbers in the databases. The end results of both research projects may be valuable, but the different ways in which the two sociologists go about their work does represent a political orientation—one favoring more reliance on sociologist-produced knowledge and the other being more open to the knowledge and perspectives of community members in influencing the direction of the research.

Clearly the character of a particular sociology department factors into this political environment. The extent to which a junior faculty member perceives senior colleagues as supportive or not supportive of public sociology will affect his or her decision to pursue such sociology. It will also affect the kind of research that students do, particularly graduate students as they decide on thesis and dissertation topics. This means that the new faculty member's decision regarding what department to apply to for a job and the prospective graduate student's decision regarding which M.A. or Ph.D. program to apply to have consequences for the kind of sociology they will pursue in their careers. Of course, the ups and downs of job markets and the competitiveness of the graduate program application process also factor into this equation and are not completely in the control of the job candidate or prospective graduate student.

Even the decision to become a sociologist is a political decision. In a society where we look to individual explanations for human behavior before we look to the role of social structures, social institutions, or social class, the choice to become a sociologist rather than a psychologist is a political decision. Sociologists often find themselves swimming against the stream in a society that likes to focus on individual initiative, leadership ability, and intelligence, as factors explaining success.[1] A sociologist's analysis of racial discrimination, social class boundaries, or unequal educational opportunities often challenge existing practices and can make powerful individuals or institutions uncomfortable.

Our book grows out of our direct experience doing public sociology, establishing research centers or networks that engage in public sociology, work within the American Sociological Association to institutionalize public sociology in the field, and teaching in the college classroom. The book presents a broad range of sociology projects. In some cases these are interdisciplinary projects, since solutions to social problems are often multifaceted and do not fit into disciplines as defined by universities. We hope that this book will be of value to undergraduate students, graduate students, faculty, policy makers, and activists. For students we try to illustrate how engaged social science projects are developed, what impact they have, and the broad areas in which social science has had an impact. For established sociologist researchers inside and outside of academia, we provide a broad picture of the field in which public sociologists work and seek to encourage more public sociology work to keep our field dynamic and responsive to the world around us. To policy makers and community activists, the book gives examples of those places where sociology is responsive to and addresses their needs. We hope this encourages more connections between our field and those working to improve the quality of life in our many communities.

References

American Sociological Association Task Force on Institutionalizing Public Sociologies (ASA Task Force). (2005). *Public sociology and the roots of American sociology: Re-establishing our connections to the public.* Interim report and recommendations to the ASA Council. Available at http://pubsoc.wisc.edu/tfreport090105.pdf

---

[1]Similarly, the assumption that an individual's own shortcomings are the cause for failure is endemic in American society. William Ryan's book *Blaming the Victim* (1976) documents this bias quite well.

Blumer, H. (1969). *Symbolic interactionism*. Englewood Cliffs, NJ: Prentice-Hall.

Burawoy, M. (2004). Introduction. In M. Burawoy, W. Gamson, C. Ryan, S. Pfohl, D. Vaughn, C. Derber, & J. Schor, Public sociologies: A symposium from Boston College. *Social Problems*, 51(1), 103–130.

Burawoy, M. (2005, February). 2004 presidential address: For public sociology. *American Sociological Review, 70*, 4–28.

Clawson, D., Zussman, R., Misra, J., Gerstel, N., Stokes, R., Anderton, D. L., & Burawoy, M. (Eds.). (2007). *Public sociology: Fifteen eminent sociologists debate politics and the profession in the twenty-first century*. Berkeley, CA: University of California Press.

Coleman, J. S., Campbell, E. Q., Hobson, C. J., McPartland, F., Mood, A. M., Weinfeld, F. D., et al. (1966). *Equality of educational opportunity*. Washington, DC: U.S. Government Printing Office.

Felt, L. F., Rowe, P.M., & Curlew, K. (2004). *Teaching academic dogs and cats new tricks: "Re-tooling" senior academic researchers for collaborative community-based research*. Paper presented at the Researching the Voluntary Sector Conference, Sheffield, UK. Retrieved from http://www.envision.ca/pdf/cura/DogsCats.pdf

Freeman, H. E., & Rossi, P. H. (1984, August). Furthering the applied side of sociology. *American Sociological Review*, 49(4), 571–580.

Gaventa, J. (1991). Toward a knowledge democracy: Viewpoints on participatory research in North America. In O. Fals-Borda & M. A. Rahman (Eds.), *Action and knowledge: Breaking the monopoly with participatory action research*. New York, NY: Apex.

Lee, A. M. (1973). *Toward humanist sociology*. Englewood Cliffs, NJ: Prentice Hall.

Lipset, S. M., Trow, M. A., & Coleman, J. S. (1977). *Union democracy: The internal politics of the international typographical union*. New York, NY: Free Press.

Mills, C. W. (1959). *The sociological imagination*. New York, NY: Oxford University Press.

Ryan, W. (1976). *Blaming the victim*. New York, NY: Vintage.

Stoecker, R. (2005). *Research methods for community change: A project-based approach*. Thousand Oaks, CA: Sage.

Strand, K., Marullo, S., Cutforth, N., Stoecker, R., & Donohue, P. (2003). *Community-based research and higher education: Principles and practices*. San Francisco, CA: Jossey-Bass.

Woodworth, W., Meek, C., & Whyte, W. F. (Eds.) (1985). *Industrial democracy: Strategies for community revitalization*. Beverly Hills, CA: Sage.

2

Crossing Boundaries in 21st-Century Research

Sharing Knowledge and Collaborating Between University and Community

Challenging established ways of doing things and questioning individuals in decision-making positions is not easy. It often creates opposition and sometimes can make life uncomfortable for university faculty or students. However, universities and scientific disciplines have been built on the premise that existing knowledge must be continually challenged with new ideas and new findings. Even though most academic colleagues agree with this intellectual premise, practicing what we preach (or teach) is not always so easy. A faculty member who has invested a career in researching and writing on a particular substantive area may not take kindly to new ideas critiquing his or her past work. A field that has long-established traditions of recognizing only the knowledge and research credentials of Ph.D.-trained sociologists might have difficulty with suggestions that research done in collaboration with community experts may represent a research methodology that can add to existing, more discipline-based knowledge. This chapter looks at how some forms of public sociology and collaborative research can challenge the ways things have been done in our field. It also makes the case for crossing the academic–community boundaries as a way of stimulating creativity, challenging old ideas (on both sides of the boundary), and strengthening our knowledge base.

Moving Beyond the Cult of the Expert

The cult of the expert endemic to modern society has created a misleading notion that the community knows little and researchers, scholars, and professionals know most everything. Certainly the training that a Ph.D. sociologist receives does create an expertise and knowledge base that those who have not undergone such training do not have. Certainly universities are well organized to engage in research, information gathering, and analysis. They frequently have used this privileged position to place university researchers on pedestals above the average citizen. But specialized knowledge in statistics, advanced research methodologies, or a substantive area does not give the researcher a right to claim an exclusive license over knowledge production.

Long-term community residents, community leaders, businesspersons, and nonprofit organization staff all have considerable knowledge, albeit not always organized or analyzed. We should not confuse the skills and expertise to collect and analyze information with knowledge itself. In increasingly complex societies, one needs to tap multiple perspectives and multiple knowledge sources to understand the full picture. Our understanding of the world around us takes not only the skills of the sociologist but the knowledge and perspectives of those outside of our field and outside of academia. This complementary view is apparent in many of the public sociology projects described in this book.

Translational Research

Related to the cult of the expert, in the academic world there is also a pecking order in which "original" research—work that produces new findings— is valued more highly than "translational" research—work that organizes existing research reports and disciplinary knowledge and communicates relevant findings to practitioners or activists trying to solve ongoing problems. Within academic culture the favoring of original research can become dysfunctional for the broader society. If the link between original research and policy or programmatic applications is not made, then how relevant is the discipline to the needs of broader society? In the health field, the National Institutes of Health (NIH) recognized a crisis when basic biological and medical research was taking as much as 10 and 15 years to get into the hands of doctors and other health professionals treating patients! One researcher found that because of this gap, only one-half of patients in the United States were receiving medical services recommended by up-to-date research findings (McGlynn et al., 2003). In response, NIH created new offices of translational research to address this gulf between researcher and the ultimate consumer public. Other government agencies have set up similar divisions; for example, the U.S. Department of Housing and Urban Development (HUD) now has a Research Utilization Division.

Within sociology there is a similar gap between original research and translational research. While a delay in getting findings into the public's hands may not be as life-threatening as the delay in getting the latest cancer treatment innovations into medical doctors' offices, the delay in understanding the ineffectiveness of job training in getting people into jobs during a recession or the lack of communication about successful domestic violence reduction strategies can have negative consequences for the broader society's economic recovery or the physical and mental health of family members who are victims of ongoing domestic violence. The need for more translational research also has implications for the field of sociology itself. If original research, however high-quality and relevant to solving pressing social problems, does not get into the hands of policy makers, practitioners, and the general public, the field of sociology can slip into irrelevance in the eyes of university administrators, elected officials shaping public university budgets, and research funders. The movement within the field of sociology to promote public sociology is both a movement to connect sociology to those who can benefit from the research and a movement to protect the viability of the field itself.

Translational research can be of as much value in facilitating communication inside academia among different professionals and experts as it can be in the communication of research to publics outside the research world. In academic worlds, where disciplines or specialists within a discipline keep to themselves, researchers do not always clearly communicate among themselves. Therefore, in this world of non-communicating silos, it is not surprising that cooperation between professionals and the general public is a radical step. In 2002, the American Sociological Association (ASA) took its own significant step toward translational research by creating *Contexts*, a quarterly magazine targeted both to sociologists and to general audiences outside the field.[1] Each issue carries articles on recently published research reports as well as coverage of recent contributions that sociological research has made in a number of policy fronts. For example, volumes have included pieces on increasing equitable access to quality public education, ageism in the workplace, Mexican immigrant integration into American society, and the social foundations of the global economic market collapse.

---

[1]More information on *Contexts* can be found at http://www.contexts.org.

Herbert Gans, one of the best known sociologists of the past 50 years, recognizes the need to write for broader audiences and train students to research and write for nonsociologist audiences:

> Sociology should provide the same kind of training and career advancement for the [public sociology] research and writing I have advocated as for contributions to theorizing, methodological work and empirical studies that contribute to the disciplinary "literature." Students and professors must be encouraged, funded, and otherwise rewarded for work on topics and issues that are relevant, useful, and accessible to people outside the disciplines. Then the editors, reviewers, and other gatekeepers who publish the general magazines and books serving the lay public may pay more attention to sociology than they do now. (2010, p. 88)

Some research can be best referred to as "passive translational research," a sort of write-it-and-they-will-come kind of research results. In many cases authors and publishers do not go out of their way to get their research into the hands of audiences outside the immediate discipline. Although an article may be published in the *American Sociological Review*, *Social Forces*, or the *American Journal of Sociology*, it remains largely inaccessible, or at least off the beaten track, to leaders of social movements, staffs of elected officials, and even the media. Publishing research does not mean that people will use it, particularly if they do not have easy access to university library accounts that provide students and faculty—but not the general public—with free access to journal articles. Although *Contexts* is a step in the right direction, it still is more passive than active in getting the information out.

The ASA has worked to market the magazine and get it onto library shelves. The association has a public relations department that actively contacts media outlets in an effort to give new research reports public visibility. However, this is generally focused on national studies authored by prominent sociologists. There are few discipline-driven efforts connecting the thousands of sociologists who do work at local or regional levels. Universities do provide some connections, but this is not consistent across the country. This begs the question, Are there efforts in the field to more actively connect with nonsociologists not only in disseminating research results but also in including publics in the research process?

Collaborative Research

Increasing numbers of sociologists and interdisciplinary research centers are pursuing collaborative research that brings together researchers and practitioners, researchers and activists, as well as universities and communities in all phases of the research process. On one level, this is nothing new. Participatory action research, participatory evaluation research, and action research models have all involved nonsociologists in the conceptualization of research questions and the design of research. In some cases nonsociologists have been involved in data gathering, data analysis, report writing, and dissemination. In effect, this research includes the consumers of the research actively into the research process itself. It is research done with a constituency from day one.

Michael Burawoy labeled this "organic" public sociology, although clearly the tradition predates his promotion of the term *public sociology* by many decades. In the 1930s, educational philosopher and activist John Dewey advocated for connecting knowledge to action and criticized the isolation of higher education from the communities they should be serving (Benson, Harkavy, & Puckett, 2007). Jane Addams, a sociologist by training, studied and mapped Chicago's poor communities in the late 19th and early 20th centuries. The work of Addams and Hull House, the settlement house she helped to found, is credited with saving thousands of infants' and children's lives by identifying both the needs for better nutrition and sanitation and the strategies to overcome these problems (Deegan, 1988).

Although in recent years much has been written by academics about participatory action research (Maguire, 1987; Park, Brydon-Miller, Hall, & Jackson, 1993; Whyte, 1991), it was the work of pioneers like Jane Addams, W.E.B. DuBois, and Saul Alinsky that established connections between research and action before discipline-based researchers took up the mantel. Indeed, Addams, DuBois and Alinsky were at the margins of academia or battled traditional academics at points in their careers. In their book, *Community-Based Research and Higher Education*, Kerry Strand and her coauthors document the different historical threads of community-based research over the past century, emphasizing that this tradition has been as strong outside of academia as it is inside academia (Strand, Marullo, Cutforth, Stoecker, & Donohue, 2003). For example, the community-based participatory research used by the Highlander Center in Tennessee helped to shape and direct the successful gains of the civil rights movement and has also been active in documenting and challenging the activities of coal companies in perpetuating deadly working conditions for underground coal miners and destroying the mountains of Appalachia through strip mining.[2] The Institute for Community Economics (ICE) and the National Housing Trust have worked with local communities and low-income residents in shaping alternative housing ownership models, such as land trusts, to

---

[2]A series of working papers related to community change and organizing are available on the Highlander Center's website: http://www.highlandercenter.org/r-b-working-papers.asp.

address the continuing housing crisis in the United States.[3] Similarly, the Institute for Community Research (ICR) has long been in the forefront of participatory research on health and mental health issues, particularly in the area of youth.[4] In all of these cases, research was done by a combination of community activists and university-trained researchers.

Growing Support for Engaged Research Nationally and Internationally

During the past two decades there has been increased support for research and teaching that actively engages with the community outside the university and outside the discipline. In the 1990s the federal government established an Urban Community Service Program in the U.S. Department of Education as well as a Community Outreach Partnership Center (COPC) program at HUD. Although both of these early programs have since ended, they did provide millions of dollars of support to get university–community partnerships off the ground; many of these initiatives are still going strong today. Among the publications produced over the years of HUD's COPC program is a blueprint for applied research and community change (Silka, 2006). Private foundations, most notably the Ford Foundation, the John D. and Catherine T. MacArthur Foundation, the McCormick Tribune Foundation (now McCormick Foundation), the Kellogg Foundation, and the Bonner Foundation have at various times funded significant initiatives encouraging the formation of researcher–practitioner networks and projects. The pool of government and private funding has had a positive impact on the work of public scholars in the academy.

Professional organizations as well as discipline-based publications have been more active in their support of public scholarship. In addition to recent efforts of the American Sociological Association to institutionalize public sociology, journals (e.g., *The American Sociologist, Social Problems, Sociological Quarterly, Journal of Urban Affairs, Humanity and Society, Journal of Sociology and Social Welfare, Environmental Science and Technology,* and *Journal of General Internal Medicine*) have either dedicated special issues to public scholarship research outcomes or become more welcoming of individual articles reporting on community-based research.

---

[3]More information on ICE and the National Housing Trust is available on their website: http://www.nhtinc.org/ice.php.

[4]More information on ICR is available on its website: http://www.incommunity research.org.

New journals have emerged with a dedicated focus on community-engaged scholarship (e.g., *Gateways: International Journal of Community Research and Engagement* and the *Journal of Higher Education Outreach and Engagement*).

Not surprisingly, some of the richest territory for public scholarship is in fields that have always focused on applying knowledge and influencing policy. Most notable have been efforts in the public health field. In addition to the collaborative university-community scholarship within schools of public health and related journals, one of the most active research-practitioner–community activist networks in the United States is in this field. Community-Campus Partnerships in Health (CCPH) has been a leader in promoting collaborative research and changing the way in which universities and researchers do research.[5]

At the international level, a number of networks have served to promote researcher–public connections in research development and dissemination. Among the more activist and politically explicit movements is the action research or participatory action research movement, particularly based in emerging nations of Latin America, Africa, and Asia—areas particularly characterized by extreme inequalities. This research is first and foremost organized to democratize control and production of information and arm the general population with knowledge needed to end inequality and auto-cratic control in their societies. Paulo Freire, the Brazilian educator and scholar-activist, is most associated with this form of public scholarship. As Freire wrote, "If I perceive the reality as the dialectical relationship between subject and object, then I have to use methods for investigation which involve the people of the area being studied as researchers; they should take part in the investigation themselves and not serve as the passive objects of the study" (Freire, quoted in Park et al., 1993, p. 34).

More recently, a "science shop" movement has emerged in Europe. Started in the Netherlands in the 1970s, it has since spread throughout Europe and other countries around the world. Science shops are typically formal units within universities that actively link the work of faculty and students to community and government needs, although a few have been established independently from universities. While many of the early science shops were in the natural sciences, during the past three decades they have expanded into the social sciences. Now loosely organized through the inter-national LivingKnowledge network, science shops address everything from water quality, flooding, and the impact of agricultural pesticides to afford-able housing, domestic violence, and youth homelessness.[6]

---

[5]More information is available on CCPH's website: http://www.ccph.info/.

[6]More information on the LivingKnowledge network and conferences is available at http://www.scienceshops.org/.

In recent years, the European science shop movement has been enhanced by funding from the European Union (EU). Just as the EU has been working to unify political and economic institutions in its membership countries to increase efficiencies, it has recognized the need to unify research and policy efforts between scientists and the broader public. Whether it is members of local communities affected by such matters as pollution and housing market trends or policy makers developing new policies for local and national governments, the EU has recognized that societal resources are more efficiently used if knowledge is shared. The EU wants to make active interaction between researchers and the general public more the rule than the exception. Discussing a 2003 conference sponsored by the European Commission, organizers were emphatic about the need for researchers to end their isolation:

> Conditioned by a narrow and dogmatic scientific training, many scientists never learned to communicate among plural perspectives. They have felt uneasy about accepting and managing uncertainty, complexity, and value commitments, and they have reduced knowledge assessment to peer review of narrow technical issues. Now the public is demanding transparency, openness, and public participation in science policy. (Vaz & Pereira, 2006, p. 10)

The best way of understanding the new trend in collaborative research is to look at two models of collaborative university-community research centers and processes that bring together sociologists and the broader communities outside of academia. Although the two discussed here are both established research centers, there are many more informal networks of researchers and activists working together in many regions of the United States.

The Loyola University Chicago Center for Urban Research and Learning

The Loyola University Chicago Center for Urban Research and Learning (CURL) was established in 1996 and grew out of a process that consciously brought together university and community partners in tackling pressing policy issues in Chicago—particularly those facing low-income communities, communities of color, and other marginalized groups.[7] CURL does not do research *on* the community; rather it does research *with* the community. It recognizes knowledge in the university and in the community. It takes a broad view of what constitutes "the community,"

---

[7]More detailed information on CURL, its research publications, and its structure are available on its website: www.luc.edu.

including smaller community-based organizations and neighborhood networks as well as local government and larger social service organizations in its definition.

CURL is adding chairs at the research table using effective time-proven methods to enhance intellectual creativity. Universities and disciplinary-based professional gatherings have been proven methods of developing new ideas and giving guidance to fellow researchers as they design research, collect data, and analyze results. In some cases the gathering may just be a casual conversation in the hallway about a research question. In other cases, it may be a faculty member presenting an idea at a brown-bag lunch with other faculty and students. The discussion with colleagues at such occasions taps into their expertise and provides guidance to the faculty member as the research moves ahead. Similarly, presentations at professional meetings and comments back from peer reviewers on manuscripts submitted for publication serve as guides to faculty doing research and analyzing results. Yes, there may be differences of perspective and argument, but that is seen as a positive in the university environment.

SETTING A GRADUATE EDUCATION PATH FOR PUBLIC SOCIOLOGY

Julie Hilvers is currently a full-time predoctoral fellow at the Loyola University Chicago Center for Urban Research and Learning (CURL).

During my first few weeks of a traditional sociology M.A. program at the University of Cincinnati, my professor asked me, "What do you want to do with a graduate degree in sociology?" I described my research interests in urban neighborhoods and access to resources, and then described the then-current struggle to save the only grocery store in a low-income neighborhood in Cincinnati. I related that I wanted to apply my research about the devastating impact of losing grocery stores in urban neighborhoods to work with those who were organizing to save the grocery store. Apprehensively, I expressed concern that I might be in the wrong field. My professor responded, "That's public sociology!"

I began exploring public sociology and traveled to Chicago to visit CURL. I was excited about the range of projects taking place at CURL, all with the overall goal of improving Chicago communities. I saw the center as an opportunity to combine my interest in community activism with my sociology career interests. The fact that research was conducted in collaboration with community groups and other partners also attracted me to CURL.

I transferred to the sociology Ph.D. program at Loyola University and began working as a graduate fellow at CURL. At the center, I have had the opportunity to apply the research training I received through my sociology coursework. I have worked on a range of projects—primarily program evaluation research—in areas including gentrification, homelessness, and workforce development. With the CURL research teams, I have worked on every stage of the research process, from conceptualizing research questions with community partners to data collection and analysis, report writing, and dissemination.

At present, I work as project director of an evaluation of Chicago's 10-Year Plan to End Homelessness. During research meetings with our project partners, who include the Chicago Alliance to End Homelessness (an umbrella organization including homelessness service providers, consumers, and funders) and the City of Chicago, it is exciting to see how the community partners aim to utilize research findings for programmatic and policy objectives in an effort to end homelessness.

My work at CURL has prepared me for a career in public sociology. I have honed my research and evaluation skills, gained experience in project management, and learned how to build and maintain relationships with community partners. I have also discovered a variety of career options in applied research. I continue to explore career directions, including regional policy advocacy organizations such as Chicago Metropolis 2020, sustainable technology centers such as the Center for Neighborhood Technology, philanthropic organizations such as United Way, and university research centers conducting engaged research.

While job postings advertising "Public Sociologist Needed!" are few, my combined sociological training and practical research experiences at CURL have opened up a broad range of career options.

What CURL is doing is bringing community partners to this research table. The center is harnessing the creative tensions between researchers and community practitioners. CURL does not defer to the community, and its research is not community driven. Rather it invites both community and university input at all stages of research, from conceptualization and designing the methodology to collecting and analyzing data. Report writing and dissemination of results is also a collaborative process. The research skills and standards set by the discipline and the experience and perspectives of community members are a powerful combination that can produce high-quality research.

Collaborative Research Teams

Central to CURL's work is its collaborative research teams. A fully developed team will include faculty members, graduate research fellows, undergraduate fellows or undergraduates from an urban studies seminar run by CURL; community partners or community fellows; and CURL staff. The research process taps into the perspectives and creativity of *all* participants and provides an effective way of managing community and university resources. Teams are also an effective way of integrating university and community resources—from use of graduate and undergraduate student time to efficiently integrating expertise of faculty and community organization staff.

Although the dominant model of university-based research centers has faculty at the core, true to CURL's collaborative mission *both* faculty and community partners help frame the research. They are always "on call" during the research process. Generally, graduate students are at the center of the teams. They manage day-to-day work, coordinate (and mentor) undergraduate fellows, communicate with faculty and community partners as needed, and work with other CURL full-time staff. Given the costs of buying out portions of faculty members' salaries and the limited time that faculty and already overtaxed community leaders have, engaging graduate students in coordinating the research process effectively extends the research capacity of faculty and community leaders.

Collaborative research teams also provide unparalleled practical learning environments for students. CURL staff often talk about throwing graduate students into the "deep end" of research as a way of teaching them to "swim." The availability of 15 or more colleagues at the center in any given day means that there is lots of guidance and advice always available to provide a helpful hand. Graduate students have thrived in this environment.

Guidance comes in many forms. In addition to consultation with other team members and regular team meetings (typically weekly meetings for active projects), graduate students and other team members work in an environment that encourages an exchange of knowledge and exposure to different perspectives—perspectives that are not always available in traditional academic research settings. During the academic year, CURL schedules regular Friday morning seminars in which CURL researchers present on their research; faculty outside the center talk about community-related issues; community leaders discuss new programs; leaders of advocacy organizations describe current initiatives; and other collaborative researchers talk about community-based participatory research approaches.

Other Informational, Creative, and Think Tank Meetings

In addition to opportunities for mentoring and idea generation provided at the Friday morning seminars, CURL holds monthly meetings, led by graduate students, on substantive or technical aspects of current research projects. These may include topics like what constitutes research ethics; how to convince the institutional review board that community input in research design is part of the process; how to integrate existing community organization data into the research model; or how to manage undergraduate team members. CURL also schedules bimonthly "idea meetings" in which staff and students can bring up possible new research ideas emerging out of current research projects, new ideas that might be suggested by policy, or community-based issues with which CURL is aware by virtue of its regular contact with community groups.

Although staffing and fellowships fluctuate with the number of research projects, in a typical year, CURL has eight full-time staff members, four faculty fellows, two community fellows, 10–12 funded graduate students, 25 paid undergraduate fellows, and another 35 undergraduate students working one day a week in conjunction with an urban studies seminar. Funding comes either from CURL's endowment or from stipends or salary built into various research grants.

To provide a more level playing field in collaborative research, CURL has always worked to build in compensation for community partners. While this can take the form of paying for community organization office space or other project expenses, it most often means salary support for staff members involved in the research team. CURL offers community fellowships that range from $5,000 to $10,000 in a given year. In a few projects CURL has built in full-time community positions.

The collaborative research team approach effectively integrates community knowledge and university knowledge. The perspectives of community leaders as well as the knowledge of longtime community residents, along with the more traditional academic input, inform all stages of the research. These are not perspectives that can easily be understood through surveys and focus groups. They are perspectives that are needed even before effective research approaches can be crafted. Community members *are* at the research table in CURL's research teams.

The teams have also institutionalized community–university knowledge building through an organic process in which learning is happening in multiple directions. Faculty learn from community members, community members learn from faculty, and faculty can learn from students. Just as the outcomes of collaborative policy research have tied community and university knowledge together in positively affecting the quality of life in local communities, the collaborative team process has demonstrated to all involved that everyone has knowledge and that everyone can have a voice.

Variety of Research Projects

CURL does not have a particularly substantive research specialty. The center has completed research on topics as varied as what produces stable racially and ethnically diverse communities (Nyden, Lukehart, Peterman, & Maly, 1998) and the impact of a new inner-city Wal-Mart on small businesses in Chicago's low-income African American community (Davis et al., 2009). A number of projects have focused on youth-driven participatory action research. One project, completed in cooperation with a high school in a diverse suburban community, engaged students in a study of race-based and ethnic-based friendship groups in the high school. With access and perspectives that adult researchers, teachers, and administrators would not have had, students produced a study that contained valuable insights—many that had not been apparent to adult leaders in the school or community. A research report to the local school board and other elected officials was well received.

In some cases the projects have been translational research, pulling together existing data and research and getting them into the hands of those who can effectively use them in their work and policy making. In cooperation with Hull House and the City of Chicago Human Relations Commission in 2003, CURL completed a study of persistent gaps in racial and ethnic equity in Chicago (City of Chicago Human Relations Commission, Jane Addams Policy Initiative, and the Center for Urban Research and Learning). Taking a page from the Urban League's annual publication, *State of Black America*, CURL gathered a large amount of existing research data from federal, state, county, and city agencies as well as a broad range of research done by academic-based researchers and journalists to paint a current picture of the state of race/ethnic relations in Chicago. CURL did not gather original data but rather pulled together information from all of these sources and organized them by policy areas, such as education, health care, criminal justice, employment, and housing. In addition to both hard copies and Web-based versions of the report, CURL worked with its community partners in making presentations to a variety of audiences such as city government leaders, foundation leaders, corporate leaders, health care providers, and others.

This has been one of the most widely used reports that CURL has produced, underscoring the importance of translational research in helping to guide social change and policy making.

Another area of CURL research has been evaluation research. This has included evaluating citywide programs as well as individual organizational programs. A two-year, National Institute of Justice–funded project was completed in cooperation with the City of Chicago Mayor's Office on Domestic Violence. The first large-city study of its kind, it produced valuable information reinforcing the need to continue the city's innovative Domestic Violence (DV) Help Line, which has been used by thousands of victims to connect to needed services. Unlike more passive referral services, the help line directly follows up with victims after DV incidents and connects them with needed services through three-way conversations, making sure the connection is made and the link to follow-up services put in place. The research was particularly important in keeping the help line as a distinct referral service rather than blending it into the citywide, nonemergency 311 system, where DV advocates feared it would be watered down and much less effective in extracting victims from violent living situations. A more detailed discussion of this report and another CURL report are included in Case Studies 1.2 (Nyden, Davis, & Edlynn) and 7.3 (George) in this book.

Funding

Although CURL now has close to a $10,000,000 endowment and an annual budget of more than $1,000,000, its origins lie with the unfunded efforts of community activists and academics. In the late 1980s and early 1990s a multi-university and multi-community–based organization collaborative research network set the stage for CURL's development. The Policy Research Action Group (PRAG) developed out of the interests of already-connected activist university faculty and community leaders.[8] A combined $20,000 grant from the John D. and Catherine T. MacArthur Foundation and the Joyce Foundation funded an initial conference examining research needs and priorities in Chicago communities. Out of this working relationship grew a strong regional network that attracted additional funding for research on issues ranging from the impact of gentrification on low-income

---

[8]More information on PRAG (which existed from 1989 to 2007) is available at www.luc.edu/curl/prag and covered in Nyden et al. (1998), chapter 2 (Effective Models of Collaboration).

communities to workforce development. Its university–community collaborative research approach opened the doors to research funding that neither community-based organizations nor universities could get separately. The more than $6,000,000 in funding it attracted in six years got the attention of university administrators. This set the stage for Loyola University to seek further funding for its own center, ultimately attracting more than $20,000,000 in grant and endowment money.

The Wilmington Housing Authority–University of North Carolina Wilmington Community Campus

In contrast to CURL, the Wilmington Housing Authority–University of North Carolina Wilmington (WHA–UNCW) Community Campus is much smaller in scale and much newer. The groundwork for this initiative began in 2005 as a determined effort to provide services and resources to economically disadvantaged communities in Wilmington, North Carolina. At that time, the director of the University of North Carolina Wilmington (UNCW) Public Sociology Program was seeking hands-on experience for public sociology undergraduate and graduate students, looking for opportunities to conduct research *in* and *with* the community. The idea of a community campus where community, students, and faculty could partner and work together addressing critical issues facing resource-poor neighborhoods began to take shape.

DEVELOPING STUDENT COMMITMENT TO PUBLIC SOCIOLOGY

Kim Lancaster is an M.A. in public sociology candidate at the University of North Carolina Wilmington and holds a B.A. in public sociology.

When I first started working toward my degree in sociology, I thought that I understood what sociology was all about. However, I realized I was mistaken when I started my public sociology seminar and practicum. My eyes were open to the potential that I have in "doing" sociology on a daily basis and making an impact in the community. The public sociology program at the Community Campus at Hillcrest gave me the opportunity to apply the research methods and concepts that I had previously only read about in textbooks.

Having a community-based research and internship experience allowed me the opportunity to see and feel how research can make a difference and affect the greater community. As an undergraduate intern in the program at the Community Campus at Hillcrest, I interviewed and surveyed parents and guardians of children who participated in programming at the campus. The goal of my research was to see how the parents and guardians defined involvement in their child's education. By working in the community, I was able to foster relationships with the children and the parents. Once I became a familiar face, more residents of Hillcrest were willing to speak with me and participate in my research.

The research that is completed by public sociology students is not just written up and forgotten about. We presented our research to the Wilmington City Council and members of the community. This research has been used to help improve, implement, and/or create programming to meet the needs of the greater community. Findings from our research have helped us create a community garden and nutrition program, as well as a new parenting class, and have led to improvements to the afterschool programming held at the Community Campus. In addition, our research has directly affected changes to Wilmington's public bus system by disseminating our findings that previous bus routes were not accessible to low-income families. Our presentation to the Wilmington City Council helped elected officials see the need for change.

The rich community-based research experience I had as an undergraduate led me to enroll in the M.A. in public sociology program at UNCW, where I am studying community and university partnerships and how the collaboration at the Community Campus at Hillcrest can become a model for other programs. As a graduate assistant in the program, I serve as the WHA-UNCW Community Campus coordinator; I plan, organize, and oversee all programming, look for funding opportunities and write grants, build relationships with community partners, and oversee new public sociology students' internship and research projects. I know that the Community Campus is making a difference in many people's lives, and I feel fortunate to play a role in its success.

It took almost three years of meetings to lay the foundation from which the community campus emerged. There was tremendous support from top administration at UNCW to see the partnership come to fruition. The director of the Public Sociology Program and the vice chancellor of public service hosted a series of meetings during this period, bringing together representatives from the nonprofit sector, WHA administration and residents, faculty from across the university, health and human service practitioners, community college administrators, grant writers, law enforcement representatives, graduate and undergraduate students, university information technology administrators, and community organizers.

Some early concerns stemmed from WHA residents who were tired of being "researched." Over the years the university had conducted its fair share of surveys "on" residents, only to disappear once the data had been collected. Residents were particularly irritated by the lack of communication and collaboration with researchers; they were also tired of being subjects of research. Having everyone at the table during these many months of planning helped shape the focus of the partnership and build the much-needed trust that had been lacking for many years. The physical presence of the university at a public housing community helped residents see that a sustainable, long-term partnership was possible.

With special assistance from the vice chancellor for public service at UNCW and key partners at Wilmington Housing Authority, the WHA-UNCW Community Campus opened its doors at the Hillcrest Public Housing Community in May 2008; a memorandum of understanding was signed by the UNCW chancellor and the executive director of the Wilmington Housing Authority. While the community campus is based at one public housing community in Wilmington, its outreach and service covers all seven public housing neighborhoods in Wilmington as well as all low-income residents in the area.

Creating a Structure and Finding Funding

The structure of the WHA-UNCW Community Campus is still taking shape after two years of operation. With the state budget crisis affecting both the university and public housing, funding is a continual struggle.

An immediate concern was to secure funding to hire a community campus coordinator. In the first year, WHA had a small amount of money to hire a part-time coordinator. Since then, the UNCW public sociology M.A. program has committed a graduate assistantship position to serve as campus coordinator. This position manages more than 18 programs at the community campus, writes grants, oversees public sociology interns, coordinates research projects at the center, and develops new partnerships in the community. An advisory board was created consisting of the WHA director, WHA residents, WHA staff, a member of the WHA board of directors, the UNCW public sociology director, the UNCW vice chancellor of public service, UNCW students, and the Community Campus Coordinator. This group meets monthly to address funding needs, operational concerns, and programming.

Substantial *in-kind* start-up funding has been provided from both the university and housing authority. UNCW Information and Technology

Services Department (ITSD) installed computers and printers at the community campus; the housing authority provides funding for wireless access. WHA maintains the community campus building and covers operational expenses. IBM donated three KidSmart computers and $14,000 for technology needs at the community campus. The partnership has secured close to $100,000 in small-grant funding, and both UNCW and WHA are actively pursuing grants, including a federal Fund for the Improvement of Postsecondary Education (FIPSE) grant.

Numerous university departments offer programs at the community campus: music, art, gerontology, social work, school of education, and information technology; almost all of the programs that are offered to residents have research agendas attached to them. In addition, the WHA-UNCW Community Campus partners with community agencies to offer programming to residents. These include GED classes and career pathways courses taught by the local community college faculty; DREAMS Center for Arts Education, a nonprofit arts program for children offering dance, pottery, and art classes; a college counseling program; and a nutrition and community garden program provided by the Southeastern North Carolina Food Systems Program.

Research Projects

The UNCW Public Sociology Program has been based at the community campus from day one: Students have offices at the community campus, and all classes are held on site. Public sociology undergraduate students devote two consecutive semesters to working at the community campus as interns and researchers. Over the course of two semesters, students identify critical social issues, design a research protocol to investigate these issues, and carry out research. Students work directly with residents to frame the research agendas and program development. At the end of the two-semester course, students disseminate their findings through presentations to the Wilmington City Council, Wilmington Housing Authority board of directors, and other community stakeholders and at academic conferences.

Some of the research projects have focused on food security needs for low-income residents, EBT (electronic debit transfer food stamps) card use at the local farmers' markets, and public transportation bus routes that meet low-income users' daily needs. In 2010, the Wilmington City Council voted to take action on research findings from the students' research, in particular, revamping public transportation bus routes in the city.

Another research project involved a needs assessment of low-income residents in a high-crime area of Wilmington. A team of graduate students, faculty, and public housing residents carried out the research, interviewing residents and service providers. The findings were disseminated to a newly formed New Hanover County Blue Ribbon Commission Taskforce on Youth Violence. Recommendations from the report were instrumental in creating the Youth Empowerment Zone, a new program modeled on the successful Harlem Children's Zone.

Faculty and students from other university departments conduct programs and research at the community campus. Several successful programs have included a Direct Instruction Reading Program for children ages four to seven to address the significant gap in reading achievement scores between Black and White students in the county. The program is based at the community campus and involves faculty from the UNCW Public Sociology Program and the School of Education and a partnership with local schools. Volunteer WHA residents and UNCW graduate and undergraduate students receive seven hours of direct instruction training and become tutors in the program. Tutors monitor progress and conduct and disseminate research findings to the county school board. Other university departments, such as gerontology, social work, and the School of Education have worked directly with residents on research projects and programming for low-income residents.

The model for research at the WHA-UNCW Community Campus is still taking shape. The university has recognized the value of providing students with opportunities to participate in scholarly engagement. Public housing residents and administrators have recognized the value in partnering with the resource-rich university in addressing the vital needs of residents. Both have adopted an approach that recognizes and values the knowledge that each brings to the table. Taking a cue from the early formative meetings, all partners are keenly aware of the problems that arise when people feel they are being researched *on* instead of working *with* researchers. The work at the community campus has kept this concern at the forefront of all its planning, ensuring that residents are part of every step along the way.

Building Community Capacity

Early on, the public sociology interns identified a literature on building community capacity by Chaskin (2001) that they felt resonated with the work that was taking place at the WHA-UNCW Community Campus. They presented their literature review to the local public housing authority's resident advisory board for input.

In this work, community capacity is conceptualized as the relationship among human capital, organizational resources, and social capital used to solve problems and improve a community (Chaskin, 2001). According to Chaskin, this involves four key elements: (1) a sense of community, (2) a level of commitment, (3) the ability to solve problems, and (4) access to resources. Social agency is a critical component in building community capacity. Chaskin goes on to identify four core strategies to building community capacity: (1) leadership development, (2) organizational development, (3) community organizing, and (4) fostering collaborative relations among organizations. Residents agreed that this framework best fits the spirit of the collaborative partnership that is growing at the community campus, and in many ways, this is the underlying model that shapes and informs the work of the WHA-UNCW community partnership. Results from a recent evaluation of the community campus programming suggest that the partnership is moving in that direction (Lancaster et al., 2010).

In 2010, the WHA-UNCW Community Campus received the National Association of Housing and Redevelopment Officers (NAHRO) Award of Merit in Housing and Community Development. While the honor of receiving national recognition is rewarding, the partners stay grounded in the reality that the road ahead is a long one and that much work still needs to be done.

Building Blocks of Public Sociology

From translational research to collaborative research, there is no set formula for engaging in public sociology. There are certainly differences in the reach of the research of public sociologists. Individual sociologists—whether faculty or students—can make significant contributions to the field itself and to communities around them. As both the CURL and WHA-UNCW descriptions demonstrate, establishing larger centers and networks—particularly when the university actively integrates this into its ongoing teaching and research mission—has the potential to create a permanent home for public scholarship. Recognizing that it is not always feasible to create centers and larger networks, our next chapter looks at how to start up public sociology on smaller scale and how this can be built into larger, more sustained efforts.

References

Benson, L., Harkavy, I., & Puckett, J. (2007). *Dewey's dream: Universities and democracies in an age of education reform*. Philadelphia, PA: Temple University Press.

Chaskin, R. J. (2001). Building community capacity: A definitional framework and case studies from a comprehensive community initiative. *Urban Affairs Review, 36,* 291–323.

City of Chicago Human Relations Commission, Jane Addams Policy Initiative, and the Center for Urban Research and Learning. (2003). *Minding the gap: An assessment of racial disparity in metropolitan Chicago.* Chicago, IL: Loyola University Center for Urban Research and Learning.

Davis, J., Merriman, D., Samayoa, L., Flanagan, B., Baiman, R., & Persky, J. (2009). *The impact of an urban Wal-Mart Store on area businesses: An evaluation of one Chicago neighborhood's experience.* Chicago, IL: Loyola University Chicago Center for Urban Research and Learning.

Deegan, M. J. (1988). *Jane Addams and the men of the Chicago School, 1892–1918.* New Brunswick, NJ: Transaction.

Gans, H. (2010, Spring). Making sociology more socially useful. *Contexts, 9*(2), 88.

Lancaster, K., Carrier, L., Dick, J., Dodson, E., Geen, H., Glovas, J., et al. (2010, Fall). Building community capacity in resource poor neighborhoods: Community–university partnerships. *Explorations: The Journal of Undergraduate Research and Creative Activities for the State of North Carolina,* 128–150.

Maguire, P. (1987). *Doing participatory research: A feminist approach.* Amherst, MA: University of Massachusetts School of Education, Center for International Education.

McGlynn, E. A., Asch, S. M., Adams, J., et al. (2003). The quality of health care delivered to adults in the United States. *New England Journal of Medicine, 348*(26), 2635–2645.

Nyden, P., Lukehart, J., Peterman, W., & Maly, M. (Eds.). (1998). Neighborhood racial and ethnic diversity in U.S. cities, *Cityscape, 4*(2), special issue.

Park, P., Brydon-Miller, M., Hall, B., & Jackson, J. (Eds.). (1993). *Voices of change: Participatory research in the United States and Canada.* Westport, CT: Bergen and Garvey.

Silka, L. (Ed.). (2006). *Scholarship in action: Applied research and community change.* Washington, DC: U.S. Department of Housing and Urban Development.

Strand, K., Marullo, S., Cutforth, N., Stoecker, R., & Donohue, P. (2003). *Community-based research and higher education: Principles and practices.* San Francisco, CA: Jossey-Bass.

Vaz, S. G., & Pereira, A. G. (2006). Introduction.. In A. G. Pereira, S. G. Vaz, & S. Tognetti (Eds.), *Interfaces between science and society* (pp. 8–14). Sheffield, UK: Greenleaf.

Whyte, W. F. (1991). *Participatory action research.* Newbury Park, CA: Sage.

3

Starting Up and Sustaining Public Sociology Projects

W hile we recognize that there is a broad variety of public sociology projects, we present here a basic guide for students, faculty, and community partners focusing on developing and sustaining public sociology projects. Public sociology can include anything from working with an environmental group to identify health problems in a local community to working with local government to develop strategies to attract more private employers to their city. While we touch on all kinds of public sociology, our focus here is on research (original and translational) and collaborative researcher–practitioner/activist activities that fit comfortably under Burawoy's "organic sociology" category. We use our own experience in organizing and doing public sociology and also draw from the case studies in this book.

It would be ideal to have hundreds of interdisciplinary centers and networks like the Loyola University Chicago Center for Urban Research and Learning (CURL) and the Wilmington Housing Authority–University of North Carolina Wilmington (WHA-UNCW) Community Campus. However, rather than talking more about established centers and networks, we focus on how public sociology projects—large and small—can get off the ground. Often it is one faculty member or a small group of faculty, or a student or a group of students, who may initiate a modest project with little or no funding or university support. This chapter is targeted to sociologists at this starting point.

Identifying Projects and Partners

There is no website with a universal list of public sociology projects that need doing. Identifying a project and potential research partners outside the university is a process that combines researchers' personal interests and skills with community research and information needs. What are the critical issues in the broader community that need more analysis? Is there an organization, network, or movement that needs this analysis and is ready to use the outcomes of the research? When is the information needed? Can the researchers deliver the information in time? What resources are needed to do the research, and are they available? Does the project have the potential to produce peer-reviewed publications, student research papers, or dissertations? From the point of view of the community partner, does the project represent the first step in a research relationship that may be a more substantial source of valuable ongoing information? What is the potential for funding if the initial project is successful?

More often than not, public sociology projects do not start with a cold call to an individual or organization outside the university, asking "Do you need my help?" Research projects typically grow out of existing relationships between sociologists and publics. These relationships may be anything from a passing conversation at a community meeting to two years of volunteering with a nonprofit organization. Santa Clara sociologist Laura Nichols's partnership with San Jose housing/homelessness specialist Fernando Cázares began when she responded to an email that he had sent to members of the Santa Clara Collaborative on Housing and Homeless Issues (Case Study 1.1).

Public sociologists are typically more civically engaged than the average citizen—or average academic, for that matter. Although areas of specialized interest may vary—one sociologist may be interested in addressing domestic violence while another may be concerned about the lack of affordable housing—public sociologists are typically in tune with community issues, political events, and social policy issues that supplement knowledge drawn from the field of sociology. Keeping on top of the news in the local community through print, TV, and Web-based media is one way of maintaining a general understanding of current and emerging community issues and a way that a sociologist may best fit in with his or her skills. *Community* may be the physical community or neighborhood, but it could also be a community of interests, such as people addressing health care issues or HIV/AIDS or a local coalition attempting to get city government to pass an ordinance requiring developers to pay into an affordable housing fund before building new developments.

Engagement in community activities facilitates the face-to-face contact that both adds to this understanding of ongoing issues and creates credibility in the eyes of community leaders. It gives the potential researcher the opportunity to "ask around" about potential projects and gives him or her ideas about emerging research needs. In many ways this is not much different from the conversations that sociologists have with each other over lunch in the department lounge or in the hotel lobby during a regional or national association meeting. The only difference is that the sociologist is talking with someone *outside* the field and including this input in defining research.

WORKING WITH THE ACADEMY:
A COMMUNITY PERSPECTIVE

Rev. Mac Legerton is the executive director of the Center for Community Action, Lumberton, North Carolina.

In my 35 years of working with the academy, there is one area of community practice that needs the most work. While good planning, development, communication, research, and evaluation skills are all important, these are technical skills that relate to instrumental learning. In working with the academy, the greatest challenge is never the skills that academics bring to community partnerships. The greatest challenge is always the *approach* to practice and the often unconscious assumptions and perspectives toward community that hinder the effectiveness and success of the partnerships and projects. An important insight is this:

> Approach working in community with the same eyes that you view yourself. You are led to public sociology with a perspective of your own resourcefulness that you bring, or desire to bring, to the aid of community. Approach and come to know the community in the same way: with all its resourcefulness and resiliency.

It is neither the public service sector nor the private economic sector that holds our communities together and sustains them. The glue of community is our people and how we informally give to and support each other. Build your partnerships and community practice on these relationships and mutual support in our grassroots communities. See and come to understand the relational bonds and culture that lie within and between our grassroots people. Government service programs and private sector jobs—both for- and nonprofit—come and go. Community needs and issues also come and go and are continually changing. Our people and our resiliency remain, and are, vibrant.

(Continued)

(Continued)

Focus on building and contributing to the resourcefulness and equity of our communities. Driven by grants and the major theories of community program development, our communities are most often perceived and approached from the aspect of *need, lack, deficit*, or *problem*. The assumption is that the solution that is needed must come from the outside and will help meet an unmet need, right a terrible wrong, and build capacity where competency is lacking. The assumption is that the community needs what academics have to offer. Imagine going into any personal relationship in your life with this perspective and ask yourself, How would these—often unconscious—assumptions be a barrier to building effective relationships and processes, meeting relational goals, and achieving mutual outcomes?

Public sociology practice results in an authentic relationship between community and academy partners when our grassroots communities are respected and honored and our resources and resourcefulness are recognized and engaged. When practiced, this honoring and respect of community is imbued in all aspects of project development, planning, implementation, and evaluation. Working effectively together, public sociology is transformative: both community and academic partners increase the breadth and depth of self- and cultural understanding, knowledge, influence, and impact in and on grassroots and professional communities, institutions, systems, and cultures. In the end, this reciprocal gift is the most significant outcome and the most that we in community can ask and mutually accomplish.

It is my hope that the experience of community-based research and practice will accomplish more than just equip undergraduate and graduate students with new knowledge and skills for a lifetime. It is my dream that the experience will be so life changing and fulfilling that graduates will consider living and working in our grassroots communities for a lifetime, either within universities and colleges or within nonprofit or government settings. We need more people who are formally trained to make commitments to live and practice in high-poverty areas across urban and particularly rural America. For students in higher education, public sociology is a window into our world. There's a door carved in the wall right next to that window. With a combination of persistent effort and patient trust, this door of lifelong learning, deep meaning, broad purpose, and significant impact will open.

It is critical that public sociologists and students of public sociology get outside of their day-to-day environments, their comfort zones. Given the inherent boundary-crossing character of public sociology, faculty and students need to go outside the secure walls of their universities and immediate circles of friends in seeking partners. Engaging in conversations with community leaders, policymakers, social service agency staff, and community residents in general often adds perspectives and dimensions to a research project that would not be there if we limited our conversations to colleagues in the discipline. Discovery and innovation frequently come when we are confronted with new ideas, different ways of doing things, and different ways of looking at a problem. While certainly valuable, talking with or partnering with fellow sociologists about an emerging research project does not always allow us to fully develop all facets of the research. Approaching individuals and leaders outside our circles of friends or professional colleagues can feel awkward at first. It is a bit like diving in the deep end of the pool when you are just learning to swim. This does not mean that we just look at a few websites and send a few emails to find folks outside the university that might want to collaborate on research. It means visiting communities, attending community meetings, talking to people in relevant organizations, and meeting with government officials and policy leaders in shaping research directions.

When we engage in research with people outside our everyday circles of colleagues and friends, we often gain new insights into community and organizational life. We gain a better picture of decision-making processes. We start to understand key issues or obstacles facing communities and organizations. If we are hoping to make contributions to positive social change, engaging with partners outside of the discipline provides a better view of potential problem-solving innovations. Equally as important are insights about how these innovations might be put into practice. Innovations and good ideas alone do not bring about change. Understanding organizational, community, and broader societal power structures and histories provides valuable guidance when working with nonacademic partners in creating blueprints for change. However, without an understanding of power structures and decision-making processes, research outcomes may just sit there unused. They are added to the library of good ideas and good intentions—a library where contributions gather dust rather than serve as useful social change tools.

Community-based research partners tend to have a better map of who has power, points of resistance, and the history of past attempts to bring about change. This knowledge can be used to shape the focus of the research, the methodologies, and how data are analyzed and presented. It can increase the likelihood that research outcomes not only address the needs of a community or organization but are made more consumable by publics. Working with the Center for Community Action, University of North Carolina Wilmington (UNCW) sociologist Leslie Hossfeld and her students provided research upon which the Southeastern North Carolina Food Systems Program was built; this movement challenges the power of industrial agriculture by supporting local farmers in developing a sustainable local food economy in the region (Case Study 6.3). Peter Callero's students at Western Oregon University who get involved in the tenants union learn important lessons about the role of social movements in challenging the power of local landlords (Case Study 8.1).

Keep in mind that there is a broad range of publics with which you can work. In addition to a large variety of nonprofit organizations (ranging from social service agencies and health care providers to cultural institutions and some media outlets), there are government agencies, chambers of commerce, foundations, religious organizations, social change coalitions, and advocacy groups. Large organizations may have dedicated research offices; smaller organizations do not, but they have even greater needs for partners on various research fronts. While local foundations focus on funding service delivery, innovative projects, and research, some—particularly community foundations that focus on local or regional issues—are often interested in matchmaking researchers with organizations in need of research.

If you are interested in working on a particular issue area but are not sure what the options are, there are both knowledgeable individuals and more formal networks that can help you locate organizations and initiatives related to your area of interest. For students, a logical starting point is to identify a faculty member who not only is interested in the subject but is engaged in this work with outside organizations, either through a research relationship or work outside his or her academic role. This faculty member may be someone outside your department; a faculty in an environmental sciences program may be excited to have a sociologist aboard in a project examining community attitudes about a cleanup of a local toxic dump. Melissa Swauger's dissertation topic was on the relevant factors and conditions that influence how adolescent girls think about their futures. She wanted to use focus groups to collect her data and needed to recruit a sample. Through a former coworker, she heard about "Gwen's Girls," a girl-centered organization in Pittsburgh. While her initial contact with Gwen's Girls was to find study participants, Melissa was soon volunteering at the agency, giving back in the form of doing a needs assessment, developing career exploration curriculum, and serving on the steering committee of a regional coalition of agencies that work with adolescent girls (Case Study 4.2).

Ideally, if there is either a university or independent research center that focuses on an area of interest to you, whether you are a faculty member or student, contacting them about existing or developing research opportunities is a logical step. Although there may be opportunities for funded positions, most likely there will not. However, getting your foot in the door gives you the chance to prove yourself and positions you well for future opportunities. Affiliation with centers also gives you a built-in support network—one that can be of value to faculty looking for supportive colleagues as your career develops and also of value to students looking for public sociology research projects down the road. For junior faculty, connecting with a research center and applying for research grants through a center can give you instant credibility, because the reputation and accomplishments of the center are already known to community partners and funders. You are effectively connecting yourself to the *collective résumé*—the sum total of projects completed, articles published, reports completed, and changes made as a result of the work of center researchers and practitioners and activists over the years. This gives you a tremendous boost in your public sociology career.

The independent research centers outside the university, often focused on a particular policy issue, should not be overlooked. They are most likely to be found in larger cities and metropolitan areas, but regional centers can be found in midsized cities and rural areas as well. For example, in Chicago, the Woodstock Institute is nationally known for its work on banks and lending practices. Other small centers, such as the Center for Economic Policy Analysis in Chicago, are often very interested in volunteer help on their research projects. The Center for an Urban Future in New York City has worked closely with *City Limits* magazine in completing policy-oriented reports and investigative journalism projects that are routinely published in the magazine. PolicyLink, in Oakland, California, has an experienced staff with research, policy, and community organizing experience.[1] Cities like Washington, D.C., are brimming with independent policy research centers that have a national focus. Many of these organizations are listed on social change and social justice jobs websites like Good Works (goodworksfirst.org), Jobs for Change (jobs.change.org), or Idealist.org. Even though you may not be looking for a job, such lists are good maps to potential research partners in your region.

The coordinator of the university's service learning program or a local coalition of nonprofit agencies may be another source of information. One caution to public sociologists: Be aware of the need to manage the amorphous boundary between service learning and research, particularly social change-oriented research. A service learning program coordinator may be

---

[1]In 2009 the parent company of the Center for an Urban Future and *City Limits* spun off the magazine to a separate entity. Both are still functioning. *City Limits*'s website is www.citylimits.org; the center's website is www.nycfuture.org. PolicyLink's website is www.policylink.org.

more oriented to connecting students to volunteering at a homeless shelter than in working with a local homeless coalition collecting the data to establish the case that more permanent housing is needed. Both are legitimate needs, but the latter would be a better match for a prospective researcher. These are not disconnected activities: a possible route to a public sociology project is first doing volunteer work and getting familiar with the community, organizational staff, and issues; then, second, discussing possible research projects once you have a working relationship with the organization, staff, and community members.

For faculty, service learning can represent a trap that undermines professional credibility. In its discussion of tenure and promotion guidelines, the American Sociological Association Task Force on Public Sociology was adamant in distinguishing public sociological research and "service." Too often work with organizations outside the discipline—even substantial, rigorous research—gets pushed aside on a faculty member's evaluation form to the service category. In most departments and universities, service is not as heavily valued as research. Service gets you a pat on the head and some attention from the university public relations office, but it does not always get you points from faculty colleagues considering you for tenure and promotion. So this word of caution has less to do with using service learning offices for contacts and more with making sure that research that you complete is viewed by your colleagues as serious sociology.

Negotiating the Research Project

The dominant model of academic research is the "lone ranger" model: a faculty member comes up with her own idea, develops the research project on her own, collects and analyzes the data on her own, and writes the single-authored article for submission for a peer-reviewed journal. There is no negotiating with a nonacademic partner about the focus of the research. There is no process of building credibility and trust in the eyes of partners outside the field. She is her own boss, sets her own priorities, and works according to her own timetable. Or at least she sets priorities consistent with the interests of the discipline and within the academic timetable.

This parallels the controlled environment of the typical classroom. A faculty member organizes knowledge into weekly topics and readings, creates a syllabus to guide the class, and fits all of this into a nicely packaged 14-week semester. Yes, there are frameworks and requirements established by departments and colleges to govern classes, but faculty typically have a significant amount of autonomy in shaping teaching a course.

This one-person-rules approach does not always fit well in public sociology projects. In working with partners outside of academia, there can be complex organizational bureaucracies to negotiate, different leaders and constituent priorities, and even amorphous leadership structures in the case of social movements or emerging community-based initiatives. You are not automatically trusted because you are a Ph.D. sociologist and have an impressive curriculum vitae. In fact, in some contexts this can be a liability until you earn your trust among community organization staff or local residents.

Depending on the nature of the initial contact with outside organizations, there is often a negotiation process as to what is to be researched, how it is to be researched, and what outcomes will be. In some cases, when outside organizations have a very specific research project in mind, there is less negotiation. This is more typical of request for proposal processes, when the organization actually has some money in hand to pay for the research. Frequently, particularly in the case of community-based organizations or smaller nonprofits, when there are limited or no funds available to support the research, there is a negotiation process between researchers and organizational staff.

Both researchers and community-based collaborators may have wish lists of research that they want to do. A process of "laying your cards on the table" in terms of interests, needs, and resources is a productive first step. A faculty researcher may be interested in the policy area but looking at something that can both contribute to the community and provide the basis for a published peer-reviewed article down the road. The faculty member has resources in terms of his time, access to students interested in doing research, and university resources such as computers, meeting space, and the expertise of other faculty. The community partner may have needs to better understand changes in community demographics or the effectiveness of their programs. Such information may be critical for continued government or private funding. The organization also has resources in the form of an understanding of practices in the local community, staff expertise, and access to volunteers who can assist on the research project (and even be more successful interviewers and focus group leaders given the credibility that they have in the eyes of other residents). In the course of such initial discussions, it might be the researcher's fourth idea on his top-five wish list and the community organization's number two idea on its wish list that provides the match.

Once a research idea is negotiated, negotiating work plans and schedules can be as important as the substance of the research itself. Academic timelines are often out of synch with timelines outside of colleges and universities. The rest of the world does not function on a semester or quarter schedule. Organizing public sociology work to avoid early and late-semester time crunches is not always possible. More often than not, community partners have an urgent need for the work to be completed. It might be connected to a local political battle, such as preserving affordable housing that might be threatened with redevelopment into luxury condominiums. It might be related to evaluating the effectiveness of an early childhood education program so that government or private funding can continue. Randy Stoecker's work with the Community Shares of Wisconsin, which began in one semester but then carried over for two more semesters, highlights some of the challenges of trying to fit the community partner's timeline with the university calendar (Case Study 8.3).

In negotiating public sociology projects outside the university, time flexibility and respect for the community's urgent needs is important. This is when centers, department-wide efforts, or at least faculty networks can play an important role. The ability to manage a team of researchers, including students and faculty, over multiple semesters greatly increases the ease of doing public sociology and meeting community timelines. Thinking outside of a timeline constrained by a semester-to-semester schedule is vital in sustaining organic public sociology projects. Students may be an important part of research teams, but the ability to coordinate student work over multiple semesters is a key to success (through piecing together fellowships or making sure that new students get recruited to replace students who did the work on the project last semester).

Building Trust and Credibility

In addition to making the initial contacts, coordinating schedules, and meeting community deadlines, building trust and credibility among community partners is central to successful public sociology. What have you done for this community before? What have you done for this organization? What impact has your work had? What skills and resources do you have that the community or organization does not have? In some cases individual faculty can build up this positive community reputation over time. If you look at the careers of most active public sociologists, this trust-building and credibility-building process plays a significant role in developing the careers outside of academic circles. While skills and experience play a key role, the normal currency of the discipline—numbers of publications, papers presented, academic promotions, and scholarly awards—do not necessarily mean access or success in the community. Rather your ability to understand community needs, your talents in communicating with broader audiences outside of academia, and your long-term commitment are measures of a good researcher in the community's eyes.

The difficulty in gaining instant credibility and trust often makes the first steps for a junior faculty member or a student difficult. The difficulty is compounded by colleagues telling you to wait until you have the dissertation done, or you have received tenure, so that you don't diminish your discipline-based work and credentials. However, delaying your community engagement is typically not personally satisfying (doing such engaged research may very well be why you entered the field in the first place) and more often than not, when you delay your community work, it does not ever happen. The wait-until-next-year approach does not generally work.

What *does* work is seeking out centers, established researcher networks, or established faculty with whom you can connect in your work. It is the collective résumés of such centers and networks or the established track record of the established researcher that can serve as the incubator for new scholar development. Shedding the lone ranger approach to academic research and joining with researcher teams and networks is a common, effective strategy for emerging public sociologists to get their careers going. Not only can you get instant credibility and trust by stepping under the existing collective résumé of the center or network—the sum total of years of past work by multiple engaged scholars—but you gain access to a network that can guide your research, open new doors for research, and provide credible support when, in the case of students, looking for jobs or, in the case of faculty, seeking tenure and promotion.

Making University–Non-University Connections More Routine

Implicit in the previous discussion is that creating working relationships with publics outside the discipline does not come naturally to academic-based sociologists. Although this will always be an issue when people function in different worlds with different cultures, rewards, and work expectations, there are strategies that can make the connecting process more routine. Following are a few ideas that can more efficiently identify mutual interests on an ongoing basis. These ideas can help to establish connections for a broader segment of faculty and students and make the process more seamless, so that you are not feeling like you are always diving into cold water.

Establish Working Groups on Substantive or Methodological Issues

Convening a group of academics, practitioners, and community members to discuss mutual interests and research needs can be an effective way of identifying potential research projects, building trust among prospective partners, and even identifying funding possibilities. In essence this is a process of sharing university knowledge and community knowledge. These can be done as one-time two-hour "think tank" meetings or as multiple sessions over time. This has been a highly effective technique that the Center for Urban Research and Learning has used over the years. At a minimum, participants can gain an understanding of the different needs and perspectives in a particular policy or service area, for example, domestic violence prevention, creating community diversity, early childhood education, or youth violence. More often than not, such discussions lead to ongoing research connections among some of the participants.

Set Up Regular University-Community Seminars

In conjunction with the meetings just described, regular seminars can be held at which faculty, students, and community partners participate in informal seminars reporting on faculty research, community initiatives, policy research, and developing issues. In addition to providing a way to broaden your perspective on various work and emerging issues, it is an effective way of building regular communication between university and community. It also raises awareness about community issues among university colleagues and increases the legitimacy of engaged social science activities. It is not unusual for faculty attending seminars to express surprise at the knowledge and insights of nonacademic presenters.

Develop a Request for Proposal Process

Assuming that your department, university, or consortium of universities can guarantee some regular resources to research ideas emerging from the community—resources such as x amount of faculty time, x number of graduate fellows or x number of undergraduate interns—then a modest request for proposal (RFP) process to offer your department's services to the community can be highly productive. Distributing a call for two-page community proposals on emerging needs that could benefit from additional research is an effective way of starting new research initiatives. It has the advantage of capturing emerging needs and trends in the community through the eyes and ears of people on the front lines. It also allows the university to get in on the ground floor on new issues—often issues that funders are ultimately very interested in supporting via research grants (particularly grants to university–community research partnerships).

Set Up an Advisory Committee for Engaged Research Projects

When collaborative research projects do take place, it is often helpful to create an advisory committee consisting of those faculty, students, and community members directly involved in the project along with other faculty and community leaders who may have an interest in the issue. Formally integrating community and university voice in the research project and establishing working relationships among individuals beyond the project itself is a proven way of building a positive reputation and trust in the broader community. This opens the door for future research projects as well.

Make Sure That Past and Present Research Relevant to the Community Are Visible

Descriptions of both collaborative research projects and other research that may be relevant to policy or other community issues should be visible to those outside the university. Web pages are the logical location for this. Including both descriptions and copies of reports or articles helps to demonstrate your department's or university's track record of engaged research and implicit willingness to work with nonacademic partners on research projects. This also suggests that someone should be monitoring university research for such community-relevant research. This is typically the job of the media relations office, but when trying to build more cooperative research relationships with various publics, faculty (and possibly government and community relations offices) also need to be involved in this process.

Examples of this can be found among the case studies. The youth research that Barry Checkoway has profiled in Case Study 4.3 is posted on the Youth Dialogues on Race and Ethnicity website, hosted by the University of Michigan School of Social Work.[2] Peter Dreier (Case Study 5.1) directs the Urban & Environmental Policy Institute at Occidental College; that center's website provides details on programs and lists all the staff publications.[3] The Center on Alcohol Marketing and Youth, Johns Hopkins Bloomberg School of Public Health, directed by David Jernigan (Case Study 5.2) includes research reports, fact sheets, examples of advertisements (to provide a

---

[2]http://www.ssw.umich.edu/public/currentProjects/youthAndCommunity/dialogues.html

[3]http://departments.oxy.edu/uepi/index.htm

context for the center's reports), and descriptions of successful community campaigns against marketing alcohol to youth.[4] Finally, Leslie Hossfeld's work with the Southeastern North Carolina Food Systems Council (Case Study 6.3) is posted at that group's website; in addition to research, there is a list of partners and programs as well as practical information for growers and consumers.[5]

Do Not Forget Past Research Partners and Consumers of Research Outside the University

Regular communication with past and current partners not only keeps them on top of developments within the university but sustains positive relationships that can lead to new research projects. Moreover, such non-academic leaders or activists can be valuable resources in class presentations and in serving on university advisory committees. Keeping the attention of past partners can also make them think of you when new projects or funding opportunities arise.

Funding

In starting up public sociology projects, the issue of funding invariably comes up early in the conversation. If it is assumed that funding is needed *before* work can start, efforts can stall immediately. Looking at the case studies in this book, as well as the very early beginnings of centers and networks described in the last chapter, strong interest in demonstrating the relevance of sociology to publics outside the university and engaging in research with publics outside the university is an initial driving force. Yes, funding is ultimately valuable in sustaining larger research initiatives and developing ongoing community-engaged centers or faculty networks. However, foundations, government agencies, and private donors generally look for a track record and commitment to research before providing substantial funding. The bottom line of effective sociology is the impact it has on policy, on the quality of life in local communities, and on organization effectiveness, among other things. As demonstrated in all of the case studies, interest in social justice, community change, policy change, and contributions to the broader community is what drives most public

---

[4]http://camy.org/

[5]http://www.feastsoutheastnc.org/

sociologists. As much as they may be effective in writing successful grant applications, it is not purely money that keeps them committed to this work.

Having said this, it is clear that funding is important to sustaining public sociology research. What often is not understood by university administrators, including chairs of sociology departments, is that public sociology—particularly university-community collaborative research—provides greater access to larger funding opportunities than does research developed by and for the discipline. While there are sources of funding that focus just on sociology—for example, certain programs in the National Science Foundation—far greater sources of funding are available to work on issues such as educational reform, affordable housing, youth engagement, community safety, reduction of obesity, effective job training, and community economic development. These are all areas that have received substantial attention from sociological research over the years. The ability to tie research track records (on the part of an individual or on the part of the field historically) to organizations engaged in work in these specific areas is the winning combination that has helped to fund sociological research in the past. This is the secret to funding success for many university-community collaborative projects. Research with a constituency, research with publics built into the research process itself, often gives public sociologists an edge in getting funding. Vandana Kohli received a large grant to explore the motivational and technological dimensions of teen pregnancy prevention. Among the many outcomes of the project, she notes that receiving the grant increased the university's reputation in the local area, leading to more local grants that dealt with children's health issues. Securing this first large grant also improved the institution's sense of its own capacity to handle large-scale grants (Case Study 6.1).

There Is No Simple Formula for Public Sociology Success

The purpose of this chapter has been to plant some seeds among readers—whether they are undergraduates, graduate students, faculty, or community leaders—about ways to get started in public sociology work or enhance the work you are already doing. There is no simple formula for getting started in public sociology. Different orientations of colleges and universities call for different approaches; different communities call for different working relationships; different regions of the country call for different entry points for sociologists working with relevant leaders and organizations outside of the university. The approaches suggested here may help you develop a stronger public sociology presence in your department or college. The case studies that follow provide multiple variations on how to start and sustain public sociology work in a broad range of substantive areas. Undoubtedly, those just starting out in engaged sociology will develop even more successful approaches to strengthening the collective contributions of public sociology.

4

Career Guide for Public Sociologists

With Roberta Spalter-Roth and Susan Ambler

Throughout the history of sociology, as a profession and as a discipline in the United States, sociologists have done public sociology and applied research as well as worked in courts, health and welfare organizations, social policy-oriented foundations, marketing firms, and government agencies. Despite this, the career model and career training for sociologists has almost exclusively been geared toward traditional academic work. As Michael Burawoy (2005), a former president of the American Sociological Association (ASA), put it, "There is one dominant career model in sociology (as well as in other social sciences)—consisting of standardized courses, regimented careers, intensive examination, the lonely dissertation, and the refereed publications—all captured on the all-powerful CV" (p. 5).

This chapter provides alternatives to this dominant career model. We offer practical information on how to build a career in public sociology, from setting your educational trajectory to finding public sociology work inside and outside of academia.

Getting Started: How Do You Get the Training and Education You Need to Be a Public Sociologist?

Whether you decide to have a career inside or outside the academy, your training in public sociology will take a similar path. Developing a skill set and finding opportunities to participate in engaged scholarship are your primary goals, whether you focus on a B.A., M.A., or Ph.D.

Bachelor's Degree in Sociology

Many of you reading this book are undergraduate students majoring in sociology. You are excited by sociological concepts, want to change society, and like the idea of engaging with various publics and taking your sociological skills outside the academy. Yet, you may not be finding resources in your department to help you carve out a career as a public sociologist. You are probably asking, What do I do with a bachelor's degree in sociology? Do I need to continue into graduate school? What are my options?

For students currently in a community college with plans to go on to a four-year institution to get a B.A., these questions are also relevant. Although much of the more specialized undergraduate work in the major takes place in junior and senior years, community college students can create a solid foundation by seeking out professors who offer service learning opportunities and internships. Since 1994, the American Association of Community Colleges (AACC) has been assisting in the development of service learning programs in the more than 1,200 associate degree-granting institutions in the United States. This means that students at many of these colleges have opportunities to gain significant experiences outside the classroom.[1]

If you are a B.A.-bound student, it is important that you recognize the skills you will obtain in your undergraduate sociology program and figure out how to emphasize these when looking for work. This may sound obvious, but if you ask an undergraduate sociology major what their "skill set" is for employment, they may be hard-pressed to provide an answer.

A recent publication by the ASA entitled, "What Are They Doing With a Bachelor's Degree in Sociology?" found that many sociology majors believe they did not receive beneficial guidance from either their departments or their university career counseling centers on marketing their skills (Spalter-Roth & Erskine, 2006; Spalter-Roth & Van Vooren, 2008). Since there are very few jobs labeled "sociologist," and probably fewer labeled "public sociologist," it is important to become attuned to the skills you are learning in your undergraduate degree and be able to draw attention to these skills on the job search.

---

[1]For more information on AACC's service learning initiative and the community colleges that have been particularly active in this work, see the association's website: http://www.aacc.nche.edu/Resources/aaccprograms/horizons/Pages/default.aspx

The typical undergraduate sociology curriculum emphasizes methods, data analysis, and theory. In addition, there are a host of substantive courses needed to fulfill the major requirements. From these courses you learn both hard skills and soft skills. Hard skills include data analysis, computer skills, statistical software skills, ability to develop evidence-based arguments, and other research skills (Spalter-Roth & Van Vooren, 2010). The soft skills include sociological explanations about social issues, inequalities in race, class, gender, and so forth, how small groups work, and viewing society from a critical perspective (Spalter-Roth & Van Vooren, 2010). These skills are applicable in many work settings; being able to articulate and convey what these skills entail is essential to finding employment. Results from an ASA survey in 2007 showed that students who were made aware of these skills, included them on their résumés, and discussed these in job interviews were more likely to find jobs that mirrored what they learned in their sociology programs (Spalter-Roth & Van Vooren, 2008). In addition, the ASA reported that if students participated in out-of-classroom applied activities that "increased their human and social capital (through internships, service learning projects or attendance at job fairs) . . . they were likely to be highly satisfied with their jobs" (Spalter-Roth &Van Vooren, 2010, p. 3).

B.A. programs that emphasize public sociology typically provide community-based research and work opportunities that give students experience in using their sociological skill sets outside the classroom. It is important to take advantage of these opportunities, as you will gain firsthand experience in using the tools of the discipline, and you will actually do sociology rather than just read about it. Seek out courses that have experiential or applied learning components. Consider internship experiences that include research requirements as well as work experience. Ideally these opportunities will arise within your own department, but it may be that you will need to search for opportunities across campus. If this is the case, look for internship or experiential learning projects that bring together participants from multiple disciplines in which you can apply your skills as a sociologist and work collaboratively with others from diverse disciplines. The goal is to build your human capital during your undergraduate program, developing and strengthening both the hard and soft skills of the discipline by actively putting sociology into play.

There are additional skills you will need to develop to become a public sociologist. A great deal of public sociology work is done in the community, and public sociologists often work in teams with community partners who represent diverse backgrounds and interests. Learning to work as a team member with different constituencies is vital. Equally important is developing the skill of networking: meeting people, connecting on issues, and working together almost always leads to new contacts and potential new partnerships and initiatives. In the ASA report discussed earlier, 57.2% of B.A. sociology graduates surveyed indicated they wished they had learned networking skills in their undergraduate career, appreciating the importance of this skill only *after* graduation (Spalter-Roth & Van Vooren, 2010). You can gain experience early on in your career by identifying community organizations that appeal to your worldview and volunteer in such a way that utilizes the skills you are learning from the discipline.

Since so much of community work is grant-funded, learning how to write grants is extremely valuable. Look for grant-writing workshop opportunities, often offered by your grants office on campus or sometimes available in your community or through a community college. This is the skill that students at all levels wish that they learned in their sociology programs. If there is an opportunity to work with a faculty member or community partner in developing and writing a grant, this experience can provide an excellent introduction to grant development strategies and writing. Grant writing is not easy and frequently involves trial and error to learn how to be a successful grant writer. The earlier you can gain experience doing this, the better.

Public sociologists are deeply concerned about disseminating their research findings beyond the academy. To do this, you will need to learn how to present information for nonacademic audiences—something easier said than done. The academic world has a way of writing that is very different from that of the general public. Being able to write and speak for lay audiences is a necessary skill for public sociologists. Leading workshops, making community presentations, writing research briefs for lay audiences, or writing op-ed pieces for newspapers are some of the ways in which public sociologists disseminate their research. Learn how to visually present data and research findings in such a way that a nonsociologist or nonacademic can understand it. Learn how to convey sociological information to nonacademic audiences in simple language, through public presentations and writing styles that break down the academic jargon to get your message across to multiple publics. Dennis Meredith's *Explaining Research: How to Reach Key Audiences to Advance Your Work* (2010) provides useful insights for the public sociologist at any educational level. Gaining experience in translating sociology for general audiences can never start too early.

Resources for Students

There are many professional resources available to you as you move along in your career as a public sociologist. The ASA is an excellent resource for all sociologists, at whatever stage of their careers. The research department of the association has developed an extensive portfolio describing trends in sociology, career information and employment projections for sociologists, and other resources useful for students. The ASA has nearly 50 sections divided by specific areas within the discipline. The section devoted to public sociology is called "Sociological Practice and Public Sociology";[2] it provides resources for students, practitioners, and faculty. ASA membership is very affordable for students, and the resources and networking opportunities are extremely valuable. In addition to the ASA, there are other national, regional, and state professional sociology associations that have annual meetings at which you can network with others and gain experience presenting your research.[3] Many of these organizations have specific outreach to undergraduate and graduate students. These include

- Sociologists for Women in Society
- Association of Black Sociologists
- Rural Sociological Society
- Association for Applied and Clinical Sociology
- Association for Humanist Sociologists
- Southern Sociological Society
- Mid-South Sociological Association
- Eastern Sociological Society
- Midwest Sociological Society
- Pacific Sociological Association
- Southwestern Sociological Society
- North Central Sociological Association

Finding Graduate Programs: What Graduate Program Fits Best?

Generally speaking, the curricula of sociology graduate programs across the United States indicate an underlying assumption that being a sociologist means being an academic. This is true of master's as well as doctoral programs. This may seem especially peculiar for the master's-granting institutions, given that for most of their M.A. graduates, without a doctorate degree the likelihood of teaching at a university and following the traditional academic career model is very slim.

---

[2]See http://www.asanet.org/sections/SPPS.cfm

[3]A list of state, regional, international, and other related associations is available on the ASA's website: http://www.asanet.org/about/Aligned_Associations.cfm

Part of the reason for the dominant focus on academic career models in graduate sociology departments is that there is a general lack of knowledge among faculty of careers in research, policy, community, and other applied settings. A survey of sociology Ph.D.s finds that 85% claim they were not encouraged to pursue nonacademic careers, and nearly two-thirds (63%) said that they had not had an opportunity to interact with nonacademic sociologists as part of their graduate school training (Spalter-Roth, Thomas, & Levine, 2000). In the words of one Ph.D. sociologist employed in the U.S. federal government: "The discipline needs to reduce snobbery and acknowledge that careers outside the academy are not only personally fulfilling, but are crucial to the development of the field" (Spalter-Roth, 2008, p. 6). As you will read throughout this chapter, this view may ultimately prevail as 21st century sociology increasingly embraces a more engaged scholarship and recognizes that careers in applied, research, and policy settings are key to a robust and relevant profession.

A New Type of Graduate Program

If the traditional academic track career model is so pervasive, how do we mentor and professionalize the students who are not seeking the teaching, research, and service model of the academy yet view themselves as sociologists in professional nonacademic settings? The University of North Carolina Wilmington (UNCW) wrestled with this question. In 2005 the university received funding from the Council of Graduate Schools to develop a professional M.A. program in sociology. In 2007, UNCW launched the first program in the United States focusing on public sociology, creating a degree that prepares students for sociology outside academia. The focus is on providing the professional tool kit that is needed to work as a sociologist outside the academy.

The curriculum drew heavily from a report of the ASA Research Division, *Beyond the Ivory Tower: Professionalism, Skills Match and Job Satisfaction in Sociology* (Spalter-Roth, 2007a). This research was based on a survey of Ph.D. sociologists employed in applied, research, and policy positions outside the academy asking about their job satisfaction and what skills they used in their current profession. While this research was based on Ph.D. graduates, it proved to be an important guide in determining the skills nonacademic sociologists use in their employment. Respondents to the ASA survey were mostly found in private, not-for-profit, and government sectors, areas in which master's students find jobs (Spalter-Roth, 2007a).

Findings from *Beyond the Ivory Tower* identify the essential skills for non-academic sociologists: grant writing, program evaluation, visual presentation (how to present data to nonacademic audiences), and policy analysis. Respondents from the ASA survey said that graduate programs needed to provide more information about nonacademic careers, more mentoring and networking outside the academy, greater skills development in communicating to lay audiences, more opportunity for interdisciplinary collaborations, and grant-writing skills.

Using this information, the UNCW public sociology director created a graduate course of study that provides students with both the skill sets they need as sociologists outside the academy and opportunities to put these into practice with various publics. The curriculum includes skill development that focuses on these nine areas:

1. Writing for lay audiences

2. Grant writing

3. Collaborating with other disciplines

4. Evaluation research methods course

5. Extended discussion of the differences between academic culture and the cultures of community and not-for-profit organizations

6. Networking outside the academy

7. Dissemination of scholarly research

8. Basic demographic skills and visual presentation of data

9. Internship experience culminating in a thesis-like paper

Since the creation of the UNCW program, other master's programs added an applied, professional, or public track to their curriculum. A 2008 ASA survey examined the characteristics of free-standing sociology master's programs. Of these programs, more than half (53%) reported that their programs offered an applied, professional, or public track as an alternative to a traditional master's program that prepared students for a Ph.D. in sociology. These programs were more likely to require internship programs, to employ faculty members who have nonacademic experience, to appoint an outside advisory board, and to offer online courses. As a follow-up to this survey, ASA tracked students who began their master's degrees in 2008. One year later, the majority of those who are employed full time are in one of three types of positions. The first is research occupations, in which students apply methods including evaluation, survey, field, and policy research. The second occupation is coordinating or managing programs, including those directed at families, college students, communities, consumers, and voters. The third occupation is case work and counseling. Nearly half of respondents reported that their jobs are closely related to their sociological studies. The most frequently reported job skill is "working with people" (71%). Grant writing was the skill that most respondents (57%) wished they had learned. About a third wished they had had better access to career counseling, and nearly 30% wished they had participated in an internship program. All of these findings suggest that there need to be more applied programs, and that more should follow the UNCW model.

It is not uncommon in M.A. programs to hear students express their dislike for academia yet their love for the discipline. They get enjoyment from sociology and use the theory, methods, and data analysis to understand the social world. However, they seek employment outside of academia in "real-world" settings; they have no interest in pursuing Ph.D.s and becoming professors.

This new type of graduate program will prepare M.A. graduates with a skill set that will enable them to work in sociologically informed ways in employment outside academia, with multiple publics, in collaboration with others from various disciplines. There are many such programs being developed, and older programs are being revamped to address needs of the M.A. sociology graduate in the 21st-century labor market. The ASA is the best source of information on these new programs. The annual *Guide to Graduate Departments of Sociology* as well as direct inquiries can provide up-to-date information on graduate programs with a specific focus on public sociology.

Ph.D. Programs

There are only a handful of Ph.D. programs in the United States that provide specific training and career guidance for becoming a public sociologist. Nevertheless, this does not mean that you cannot carve out a public sociology niche in a traditional academic program.

Regardless of whether you want to follow the traditional career model or the public sociology career model, the Ph.D. is an intense and often lonely endeavor. As you have read throughout this book, there are very real tensions between the dominant career model of academia and the public sociology career model. You will have to navigate these, as there will most likely not be a lot of information and support within your program for public sociology work, and you may even be told that you should not pursue this type of work.

As one graduate student said:

> To try to carve out my place in the field as a public sociologist has been difficult with no real direction here. To have to go elsewhere and take time and

energy to find that for myself, and to have to make a case about how it could fit into my schedule has been stressful and detracts from my coursework and research. I just hope I'll find a way to make it work and to receive the training I'll need to feel comfortable calling myself a public sociologist, especially at the PhD level. (Leslie Hossfeld's correspondence with graduate student)

This feeling of frustration is a very real one. Despite this, you *can* survive as a public sociologist in a traditional, academically oriented world. While training and advising related to the various facets of public sociology is partially the function of individual departments, sociology graduate students and junior faculty themselves need to make informed career choices, obtaining effective mentoring inside and outside of their departments and managing their professional development as sociologists.

One of the first steps you need to take is to find allies on the faculty that are engaged in community work. Look at both the undergraduate and graduate coursework in your program to see which faculty incorporate experiential learning into the curriculum. Read through faculty web pages to find out who is working with community groups or publishing on social issues in the region. You may have to look outside the department to faculty in other disciplines who are working on community-based projects; joining a multidisciplinary research team is an excellent way to find others across campus who may serve as mentors or as sounding boards for your community engagement. Connect with centers and institutions on campus that may be conducting research or partnering with community agencies that address critical issues in your area. There may be research projects based at these centers that would welcome a sociological perspective on their research teams.

Begin making connections and expanding your networks within the community by developing community relationships. As you reach out and begin identifying public sociology initiatives, keep in mind that the projects that develop should be projects that work *with* community partners—a horizontal model that values the knowledge base of all those at the table. In contrast to the more conventional, vertical, top-down research model typically conducted by academics *on* communities, public sociology is informed by, and reacts to, the needs of community-based organizations, social movement networks, and a variety of other public agencies; sociologists collaborate *with* various publics in the production of new knowledge. As your networks and partnerships grow, your opportunities to do public sociology work will expand exponentially. From this, you will be building your experience base and creating a track record that will help advance you in your career.

It is important to remember as you move through your Ph.D. program that high-quality public sociology research upholds the same rigorous methodological standards as conventional academic sociology. Sociology is founded upon a tradition of quantitative and qualitative methods. All academic and professional sociologists are trained in these techniques, and the same techniques pertain whether research questions are investigated ultimately for other sociologists or for the broader public. Having said this, you should keep in the forefront of your mind, particularly in programs that follow a traditional academic model, that public sociology *is* critical to the vitality of our field— it is no less than *and* no better than conventional sociological research. Both are indispensable to the vitality of our discipline.

The next section in this chapter explains research findings from Ph.D. public sociologists employed outside academia and the skills these sociologists use in their careers. This information is important for all public sociology graduate students, whether they continue in the academy or not.

Career Paths for Nonacademic Public Sociologists

The fact that only one-third of sociologists are employed outside institutions of higher education suggests that the academic career path is the dominant route for doctoral degree recipients. Concerned about the lack of information for graduate students who have no access to sociologists in research, policy, and applied settings and who are discouraged from pursuing these jobs, Roberta Spalter-Roth of the ASA conducted a study of 600 sociologists outside the professoriate who were employed in applied, research, and policy positions. Spalter-Roth's (2007b) findings shed light on the careers of nonacademic sociologists and help graduate students consider career options outside the professoriate by getting a clearer picture of what this type of work entails.

What do nonacademic sociologists do? Sociologists employed outside the professoriate work in a variety of sectors and occupations that affect their job satisfaction. They use a variety of sociological skills and perspectives on their jobs and work in a variety of substantive areas. Relatively few respondents had the job title of "sociologist." Instead, the largest group, about 25%, is categorized as research analysts, research associates, and statisticians. The next largest group is categorized as executives and administrators, followed by research and social scientists. The smallest category (17%) is research directors.

Where do they work? They are most likely to work in the nonprofit sector (36%), closely followed by employment in the government sector, and least likely to work in the for-profit sector (18%). The largest group of respondents applies disciplinary concepts and methods to the analysis of heath and health care issues (28%). They are most likely to be employed in the nonprofit sector and hold a wide array of positions in centers for research on substance abuse, health disparities, cancer prevention, epidemiology, maternal and child health, HIV prevention, and health care policy. The largest group of these health care specialists does evaluation research, followed by epidemiological research. Other kinds of public policy issues and programs of nonacademic sociologists include environment, defense, food policy, population, social services, and education. A small number address issues and programs in the justice system, international relations, and economic development.

What sociological skills do they use? Nearly three-quarters reported using sociological perspectives, drawing upon disciplinary literature, and applying theory and methods in their work. For example, one executive director of a nonprofit think tank stated:

> The field of HIV/AIDS has come to recognize that the global pandemic cannot be understood or addressed without examining the underlying social forces that contribute to risk, transmission, access to services, etc. Sociological knowledge is essential for identifying the contextual factors that affect the epidemic and people's relative risk. (Spalter-Roth, 2008, p. 6)

These nonacademic sociologists reported using sociological concepts, perspectives, and frameworks including power relations, social construction, marginalization, globalization, assimilation, structural change, and social-ization. Concepts such as social roles, social forces, contextual factors, insti-tutional practices, structures, stratification, discrimination, social networks, and relationships between micro and macro levels are part of the theoreti-cally informed conceptual repertoire that these sociologists bring to issues such as health disparities, international law making, community services, school performance, neighborhood contexts, and family formation.

They use methodological skills that they learned in graduate school, but they also report that they were not well trained in a variety of skills that they need on the job. More than three-quarters report a strong match between the research design skills that they learned and those they use on the job: 63% reported using the statistical analysis skills, 55% used the survey meth-ods skills, and 46% used the programming and statistical software skills they learned in graduate school. More important, they report the lack of visual presentation skills (with more than 60% reporting this lack), grant-writing skills, program evaluation skills, and policy analysis skills.

What does the job entail? The great majority of these sociologists describe their jobs in terms of what Spalter-Roth calls "professional characteristics," using specialized knowledge obtained through academic qualifications, a set of ethics, and a degree of autonomy and control over their work. For example, close to 90% agree that their jobs are somewhat or strongly related to sociology, suggesting that they practice in the specialized field that they mastered in graduate school. About 70% supervise other workers and therefore have some autonomy and control over their work flow, and about 73% consider research ethics and scientific integrity as an important feature of their jobs. More than half (56%) describe their work as resulting from their own curiosity and expertise, another measure of autonomy, as well as client needs (understanding that the client can be the federal government, a foundation, or a nonprofit organization), and an additional 26% said that their research is driven only by their own curiosity.

Do they like doing this kind of work? More than half the sociologists Spalter-Roth studied were highly satisfied with their jobs, but a somewhat smaller percentage was highly satisfied with the economic security of their jobs. Few reported that they were very dissatisfied. Spalter-Roth found that the greater the amount of time spent working on research, the greater the overall job satisfaction. Those sociologists who responded that research activities took up most of their time or were a prominent part of their job are 14% more satisfied than those who spend less time doing research. The more people supervised others, a measure of autonomy and control, the greater the overall satisfaction. Using sociological perspectives and literature in their daily work, to form hypotheses and typologies or to solve interpretative problems, increases overall satisfaction by 10% compared to those who do not use sociological perspectives for these purposes. Sociologists employed outside of the academy experience as much satisfaction with the professional characteristics of their jobs as did those employed in the academy.

What can we learn from nonacademic sociologists? When survey respondents were asked about their recommendations for improving the graduate school curriculum in order to make it friendlier to jobs outside the professoriate, the number one improvement suggested was for more information and "less snobbery" about jobs outside the professoriate. In short, they felt they were looked down upon by their academic colleagues and did not learn all the skills they needed to work outside of academia.

We learn from nonacademic sociologists that jobs in policy, research, and applied settings can provide high levels of satisfaction. To receive the training needed to work outside the academy, graduate students need to develop networks with nonacademic employers, link up with policy makers, decision makers, and community leaders, and develop partnerships with outside organizations. Sociology as a profession and a discipline might gain more status, or at least more jobs, if there were more than a single career model, and sociologists applauded the diversity of sociological work throughout the economy.

ENJOYING SUCCESS OUTSIDE THE ACADEMY

Roberta Spalter-Roth is the research director of the American Sociological Association and has extensive experience working in applied settings outside of academia.

I should note that I had biases, based on my own career experiences, when conducting this study of nonacademic Ph.D.s. I left a position in the academy in a huff when I was not allowed to use grant monies to reduce my course load so that I could do research at the Institute for Women's Policy Research in the early 1990s. Although my academic position promised lifelong job security, it also promised a life of continuous assessments and evaluation of my teaching (that I admit was not fabulous); attending faculty meetings fraught with personal agendas for distributing all-too-scarce resources; low pay; and well-meant, and probably correct, advice to write scholarly papers rather than policy papers, research briefs, and technical reports on issues of welfare reform, family leave policies, unemployment insurance, and health care.

In contrast, I loved conceptualizing and doing policy research, and more recently, science policy research. During the 20-odd years that I have been doing research in the U.S. government (briefly) and the nonprofit sector, I have used the theories, concepts, and methodological skills that I learned in graduate school (although, as the respondents to the survey suggest, more experience with graphics, fund-raising, and statistical methods would have helped). Some of the concepts that I have developed (such as work/welfare cycling) have become part of the sociological tool kit, and my current work at the American Sociological Association has a high use value. Nonetheless, because success in sociology is still defined as a tenured position, preferably in a "top 10" research university, many academics are limited in their curiosity about life in research, policy, or applied shops. In turn, nonacademics may have limited ability to participate in discussions of capturing the best new Ph.D.s, academic politics, and departmental prestige hierarchies. The result, I have found, are fewer dinner invitations from academics and great annoyance at my lack of status.

Working as a Public Sociologist
Within the Academy

Applying for a job is a time consuming and sometimes lengthy process. Just ask any Ph.D. student on the job market and you will learn immediately how arduous it can be. You will need to devote time to constructing a cover letter and curriculum vitae (CV) that describes who you are and your career objectives. Of course the job market fluctuates depending on university budgets and when positions open. Two excellent resources for job listings are the ASA Job Bank and the *Chronicle of Higher Education*; both provide a current, monthly list of sociology jobs in academic and nonacademic settings. You will also see notices on association listservs and learn about jobs through word of mouth. The greater your networks, the more job opportunities you will hear about! The job advertisement will tell you a lot about what the institution is looking for. If it clearly states public, applied work, then you know there will be support for your public sociology work. You should obviously apply to departments that are looking for your substantive areas whether or not they request public sociology skills. Your CV and cover letter should address your dissertation and how you will expand your research agenda in your substantive area at the institution to which you are applying. Take care to tailor your cover letter to the particular needs and interests of each department; these targeted letters are much more effective than using the same letter for all applications.

PUBLIC SOCIOLOGIST AS TEACHER FIRST

Susan Ambler is a sociologist at Maryville College in Tennessee, a small liberal arts college that emphasizes teaching. She describes how, over time, she carved out a niche in her department in which she has brought together teaching, research, and service.

We need to look beyond mere contributions to the discipline and focus on the communities around us. Public sociologists have a responsibility to work with groups with less power in our society, similar to what Frances Fox Piven, a former president of the ASA and well-known scholar-activist, argues:

Sociologists need to devote our attention and our knowledge skills to the expressed needs of the poor and the working class rather than to the comfortably well off, to racial minorities and especially African Americans, to women more than men, to those without legal residence instead of those with legal residence and citizenship, to the marginalized and down-and-out of all descriptions. (2007, p. 163)

As a faculty member at a liberal arts college that provides only undergraduate education, my primary focus is teaching. Faculty members are evaluated first and foremost on the basis of their teaching performance and second on the basis of faculty development, which includes attending and presenting at sociology conferences, conducting research, and writing articles, or books. This, of course, reverses the order of priorities for a faculty member working at a research-focused university. What this means is that much of the public sociology I do is in the context of teaching and mentoring students in their development as sociologists.

My approach to public sociology has included three components: (1) teaching courses with a project that involves students in community organizations or with community residents; (2) working with local community organizations or agencies to assist or collaborate with them about their research needs; and (3) collaboratively developing a regional organization, Just Connections, that serves to network college faculty, staff, students, and grassroots organizations with common social justice interests.

When I first began doing public sociology I felt somewhat isolated when I faced issues that came up when working with community organizations or teaching public sociology. Just Connections was a response to a feeling of isolation inside academia and the need to find allies outside the college—allies who could provide guidance on community needs and respond to ideas on how to improve college-community collaboration.

Juggling teaching demands and the need to finish research projects has also been a challenge. In the context of teaching, this often means finishing projects that students began but remained incomplete when they finished the semester's work. Finding the time to analyze and then write collaboratively with the organization about the multiple oral histories has been difficult with a heavy teaching load. I am now more deliberate about saving time in the summer for writing as well as obtaining grants to fund released time for writing during the semester.

There are resources that public sociologists sometimes overlook in their own institutions. Administrators who are involved in university outreach often are seeking opportunities to feature university-community partnerships and the faculty engagement outside the university. Institutional mission statements often emphasize regional engagement and service to the broader community. Make an effort to draw attention to your research if it aligns with a university

(Continued)

(Continued)

or college mission statement by working with your university media office to promote your work. Often sociologists squirm at the idea of "marketing" public sociology work, however, it is not at all about being boastful. Rather it is about increasing the visibility of the engaged work, the social issue, *and* the expansion of networks that may result from publicizing the public sociology activities and outcomes more widely. This also brings positive attention to your department and the university, which in turn may create recognition and status for your program. From this, you begin carving out your niche in the department and the university, creating a public sociology research agenda that is recognized by your community and peers.

You should certainly include your community work and public sociology as it relates to your research agenda. When you get the interview, highlight how your public sociology work fits into the traditional academic environment and the expectations of the department. Do not try hiding your public sociology interest. If you intend to have an academic career with a strong interest in public sociology, you want to find a department that is happy to have you. Being in a department where you regularly have to defend your career interests is not nearly as enjoyable as working in a department where you receive support for your work

Working With Your Department and University

Your job as a faculty member will be to divide your labor into three areas: teaching, research, and service. This is the universal model for all academics across all disciplines. The amount of time you devote to each area will be determined by your department and the type of university or college where you work. Many faculty view these as separate, often disconnected categories that cover the work they must do to receive high marks on their annual reviews. One of the best strategies for a public sociologist is to combine these three hats and wear them on your one head! Granted, this sounds like a daunting undertaking—but the more you can blend these three areas of your work into one, the more fluid and seamless your public sociology research, teaching, and service will become. Both Susan Ambler's and Leslie Hossfeld's reflections in the sidebars in this chapter address distinct issues facing public sociologists in academia.

Getting Published and Getting Tenure

The cornerstone of the traditional academic model is getting published so that you get tenure. It cannot be stressed enough how important this element is in moving along in your academic career. Public sociologists focus on dissemination of their findings to broader publics affected by their research, but public sociologists in the academy simply cannot neglect publishing in peer-reviewed journals. Consider the policy reports, evaluation and assessment projects, and other non-peer-reviewed publications you have written and determine whether and how these can be translated into academic publications; many can be. Consider the handful of disciplined-based peer-reviewed journals that are geared to public and applied sociology as well as the traditional outlets for peer-reviewed publications.

LEARNING IS A TWO-WAY STREET

Leslie Hossfeld

My Ph.D. had a small public sociology component, and I had worked with community organizations throughout graduate school. I certainly didn't go onto the job market describing myself as a public sociologist, but my CV illustrated my work and research interest in the community. My first job was at a small state teaching university. My intention in my new job was to continue working as a public sociologist, but I was unsure how to start out. It was interesting how it evolved. I had reached out to a community organization that worked on social justice issues in the region and began meeting with the director to establish a relationship and see how I could fit with their projects. At the same time, I was teaching a social problems class in the evening; many of the students were nontraditional students returning to college.

One night I was lecturing on job loss and economic restructuring when I realized, through discussion and comments, that a large portion of my students were displaced textile workers—the very people I was describing in my lecture! The tables quickly turned and now I was the student, learning about their lives and what happens when work disappears. When I told this to the community organization director, who was well aware of the crisis in job loss in the area, he suggested we do something about it. What developed was a year-long job-loss project that involved community organizing, research, and a social action component to address economic recovery in our region.

(Continued)

(Continued)

I began integrating the job loss project into two of my classes, and students helped with the research, community organizing, and dissemination of the findings. We turned the report into a peer-reviewed journal article. My teaching was enhanced by bringing sociology to life for my students; students felt engaged in the subject matter they were learning as they were actively involved in the research process. We published the research, and the service to the community was extensive. I saw the beauty in weaving together teaching, research, and service; it is a model I follow to this day.

Bear in mind that public sociologists work, in collaboration with various publics, in the production of new knowledge that can be translated into academic publications. The production of new knowledge is the foundation of the traditional academic model. Public sociology is research based in that it draws on and disseminates: (1) existing knowledge and findings from sociological literature and/or (2) new research findings based on data gathered and analyzed using professionally accepted sociological methods. In some cases conceptualization and completion of other facets of research may be done by sociologists in collaboration with nonsociologists. While informed by input of nonsociologists, such research upholds the accepted standards of rigorous research.

The ASA Task Force on Institutionalizing Public Sociologies worked diligently to create a guide entitled *Standards of Public Sociology: Guidelines for Use by Academic Departments in Personnel Reviews*, which is available on the task force's website (http://pubsoc.wisc.edu). The guide provides direction for the academic department in evaluating public sociology research and serves as a template for creating your public sociology portfolio. You should certainly include your policy reports and nonacademic publications in your portfolio along with the peer-reviewed journal articles. In addition, it will be important to obtain letters of support from both inside and outside the academy that describe the influence and impact of your research on the public.

An excerpt from the guide provides this foundation:

The foremost standard of public sociology is that it is grounded in scholarship of a sociological nature. Public sociology entails sharing sociologically based knowledge with publics outside the academic setting. It may involve the translation of existing sociological theory and research findings for use by broader audiences (e.g., through research reports completed for specific organizations or publication of op-ed columns and other forms of public media commentary). It also may involve the transmission of new research findings—gathered in the academic arena or in cooperation with a research institute (in or outside the academy), a public agency, or other non-academic organizations.

As you work inside the system identifying yourself as a public sociologist, you indeed change the system in terms of its recognition of public sociology.

The case studies in this book are from public sociologists both inside and outside academia. They provide rich detail on doing public sociology, including the difficulties, successes, partnerships, and collaboration, funding challenges and contributions of putting sociology into play. Throughout all of these cases, you will hear, either directly or indirectly, the great satisfaction in doing public sociology and the ultimate fulfillment in realizing the promise of our discipline.

References

Burawoy, M. (2005). 2004 presidential address: For public sociology. *American Sociological Review, 70,* 4–28.

Meredith, D. (2010). *Explaining research: How to reach key audiences to advance your work.* New York, NY: Oxford University Press.

Piven, F. F. (2007). From public sociology to politicized sociologist. In D. Clawson, R. Zussman, J. Misra, N. Gerstel, R. Stokes, D. L. Anderson, & M. Burawoy (Eds.), *Public sociology: Fifteen eminent sociologists debate politics and the profession in the twenty-first century* (pp. 158–166). Berkeley, CA: University of California Press.

Spalter-Roth, R. (2007a). *Beyond the ivory tower: Professionalism, skills-match and job satisfaction in sociology.* Research brief. Washington, DC: American Sociological Association.

Spalter-Roth, R. (2007b). Sociologists in research, applied and policy settings: Bringing professionals in from the cold. *Journal of Applied Sociology, 1*(2), 4–18.

Spalter-Roth, R. (2008, August). *Sociologists in applied, research and policy settings: Satisfaction outside the professoriate.* Unpublished conference paper. Annual Meeting of the American Sociological Association, Boston, MA.

Spalter-Roth, R., & Erskine, W. (2006). *What can I do with a bachelor's degree in sociology? A national survey of seniors majoring in sociology.* Washington, DC: American Sociological Association.

Spalter-Roth, R., Thomas, J., & Levine, F. (2000). *New professionals inside and outside the academy.* Washington, DC: American Sociological Association.

Spalter-Roth, R., & Van Vooren, N. (2008). *What are they doing with a bachelor's degree in sociology?* Washington, DC: American Sociological Association.

Spalter-Roth, R., & Van Vooren, N. (2010). *Mixed success: Four years of experiences of 2005 sociology graduates.* Washington, DC: American Sociological Association.

CASE STUDIES 1

Equitable Community Development

One consequence of urban growth and development in the second half of the 20th century has been significant inequalities within cities and metropolitan areas. Investments in some urban and suburban communities were matched by disinvestment in others. Social science research has documented that this disinvestment is linked to a host of social problems and that disinvested communities have few resources with which to address these problems. Within this context, public sociologists, often with the help of local universities, are able to work with residents of disinvested communities to find solutions, as the case studies in this first section demonstrate.

Similar to many other regions around the country, the uneven development of affordable housing, combined with a loss of skilled jobs paying a living wage, has contributed to both a housing crisis and a homelessness problem in Silicon Valley in California. The first case study describes a homelessness research project. A group of public officials and service providers were interested in developing new policies and programs to meet the needs of the homeless, especially those who were overnight riders on a local bus, but the group lacked factual data. San Jose's development specialist Fernando Cázares approached Professor Laura Nichols about having Santa Clara University students collect the needed information as part of a project for an applied research class. For three nights students like Angelica Rodriguez rode the bus, interviewing the riders and hearing firsthand about their experiences. As the case study shows, these students not only had the opportunity to apply the skills they learned in the classroom but also gained an understanding of how their findings would inform the work of local policy makers and might lead to social change.

PARTNERSHIPS FROM THE PERSPECTIVE OF THE COMMUNITY

The partnership between Laura Nichols, professor of sociology at Santa Clara University, and Fernando Cázares, former housing development specialist with the City of San Jose, began with an email. In the spring of 2007, Cázares wanted to survey homeless persons during a local service delivery event, but he needed help. So he sent an email to the Santa Clara Collaborative on Housing and Homeless Issues, a network of local researchers and practitioners. Nichols responded with an offer to have her students do a survey, analyze the data, and write up a report with their findings. Cázares immediately accepted the offer; thus began the partnership.

A few months later, Cázares turned to Nichols for help again. A working group made up of transit officials, municipal staff, and service providers had been meeting to talk about the problems of the unhoused who rode a regional bus—coined "Motel 22" among homeless persons and service providers—throughout the night instead of seeking shelter beds. Before the group could begin to address the needs of this population, they needed more information about these riders, but no agency had the designated resources to conduct the survey. Cázares proposed that Nichols and her students do another survey, an idea to which the others readily agreed. Not only did she have a university affiliation that provided credibility and institutional expertise, but more important, her services were free.

The students' research helped filled an information vacuum (see Case Study 1.2). Yet Cázares is not sure that the study led to any longer-term changes in how service providers collaborated to reach this somewhat isolated population, which was something he had hoped would come out of the partnership. During the initial working group discussions, it was clear that each agency official defined the issue from his or her own institutional limitations, whether statutory or the result of precedence. Whenever a new idea was raised, there was usually someone who would reject it because "we've never done it that way" or "it is beyond our scope of authority, resources, or role." Cázares thought that a campus–community partnership would overcome some of these challenges and together they would be able to explore new ideas. Working with Nichols and the students to design and implement the survey gave these officials, many of whom had been strangers to one another previously, a better understanding

(Continued)

(Continued)

of their respective realities and relationship to the issue. It offered them a chance to collaborate toward a single goal: producing a more complete and accurate picture of the "Motel 22" riders.

While creating partnerships can be mutually beneficial, Cázares sees challenges. Because of this partnership he was invited to a regional conference on campus–community collaboration where he discovered that he was probably the only practitioner in attendance. By the same token, he acknowledged that the academic professional is often not included in discussions among practitioners. When discussions about social problems occur in such vacuums, both the academic and the practitioner lose something. The academic has a set of rigorous research tools that can provide insight to practitioners' deliberations about the design and implementation of effective policies and services; the practitioner has the firsthand experience with the problem that can test the applicability of a given theory in the real world. The academic sees that sometimes the practitioners get caught up in rules and regulations, protocols, or present way of doing things, and they become jaded. By asking the tough questions, the academic gets the practitioner to step outside the box and think about social and policy issues in a new light. When both partners are present at all the conversations, they each add something valuable to the effort to solve problems. Further, in entering into a partnership, each must be realistic and intentional about the mutual and relative gains of the students, professor, the nonprofit service organizations, and ultimately, the people whom these participants are seeking to help.

The second case study presents a research project on the processes of gentrification and displacement, a focus of much local policy debate for the past few decades. The authors describe how a research team from the Center for Urban Research and Learning (CURL) at Loyola University Chicago worked with the City of Chicago Commission on Human Relations to document the impact of reinvestment on different racial, ethnic, and economic groups in the city. The research focused on two neighborhoods experiencing gentrification, one Latino and one African American; the team interviewed community leaders to measure their perceptions about the impact of the gentrification process. The project's findings showed that the gentrification process, and the tension generated by this process, was different in the two communities. In the African American community, the tensions were along class lines, as gentrification centered around trying to attract middle-class African Americans back to the neighborhood by capitalizing on its historic cultural and artistic roots. In the Latino community, tensions fell along both ethnic and class lines, as middle-class Anglo households displaced working-class Latino households. The research enhanced the Commission on Human Relations' understanding of the dynamics of gentrification in the city. It was also of interest to policy makers wanting to increase the presence of the African American middle class in the city and played a small part in the eventual passage of the city's inclusionary zoning ordinance.

The third and the fourth case studies provide examples of strategies for resisting disinvestment and gentrification. Small businesses in inner-city neighborhoods can contribute to a stronger local economy and reduce the risk of economic decline because they have the potential to add wealth and employment to inner-city neighborhoods. While these businesses are often provided with technical assistance in their initial phases, they are rarely supported over the long run, and many ultimately fail. In the third case study, Daniel Monti describes a program in Boston that provided resources and support to existing inner-city businesses as a strategy for getting them on a faster track to success. Monti and his team of researchers studied the participants using a mix of research methods. One of the interesting findings was that many of these businesses reflected a "hybrid enterprise" that combined "doing well" in business with "doing good" in the community. However, a significant challenge for these businesses is finding a good balance between making a profit and helping the community. The researchers documented that the program helped the entrepreneurs sharpen their focus and come up with better business plans that combined their dual missions, thus increasing their odds of succeeding.

The final case study in this section focuses on a unique campaign in one Chicago community to resist gentrifying forces. The work of a group of dedicated community residents highlights the potential of art to play a central role in resource mobilization and community investment for historically marginalized neighborhoods. In the course of conducting a survey of art activity in 10 low-income neighborhoods in Chicago, Diane Grams learned about the cooperative effort of a network of cultural leaders, administrators, bureaucrats, and arts participants in Bronzeville, a mid-South Side African American neighborhood, to wrest control of reinvestment activities from the "downtown growth machine." This case illustrates that communities can create an "ethnically driven stability machine" that operates in their interests, not those of some outside investors. Art that is made in the community, and that documents the rich cultural and social history of a community, can bring the community together, empowering residents and contributing to neighborhood stabilization in the face of gentrification threats.

Case Study 1.1. Educating About Homelessness: A University–City Government Research Partnership[1]

Laura Nichols, Fernando Cázares, and Angelica M. Rodriguez

Truth be told, the 12th floor of the city hall in the 10th largest city in the United States was the last place Laura expected to find community-based research projects for her undergraduate applied sociology students. And she certainly would have never guessed that three months later she would find herself on the bus with her students at 2 a.m., participating in one of the most ambitious applied research projects her students have undertaken in the community.

Until then, projects for the applied course had come from struggling nonprofit organizations in need of program evaluations, needs assessments, grant writing, and community-based asset mapping. But Laura wanted to expose students to and determine the plausibility of undergraduates doing work that could potentially affect policy. So she met up with Fernando, who at the time was a development specialist at the Homeless Services Division in the City of San Jose's Housing Department. This was not the first time she had worked with him; a year earlier students in her Sociology 1 class had helped to collect data at an event he ran, Project Homeless Connect.

In this case study Laura speaks from her perspective as the instructor of the Applied Sociology course in which undergraduate students learn how social science research can be applied in organizations, communities, and to policy. Fernando provides his view as a city-level policy maker and service provider often stymied by bureaucracy and specialized service provision.

---

[1]The authors thank the applied sociology students for their work on the projects as well as the riders who shared their experiences. This project was part of the California Campus Compact-Carnegie Foundation Faculty Fellows: Service-Learning for Political Engagement Program, funded by The Corporation for National and Community Service, Learn and Serve America, and the Ignatian Center at Santa Clara University. Opinions, points of view, and any mistakes are the authors' alone.

And Angelica gives the perspective of an undergraduate student who was part of the class that term.

Defining the Issues

Homelessness has been a persistent problem in the United States for decades. This is certainly the case in Silicon Valley in California, which has some of the highest housing prices in the United States, uneven development of affordable housing, and a piecemeal provision of resources despite sincere attempts to coordinate funding and services. Large cities that provide both funding and direct services are often asked to address problems that are bigger than their geographical domains. One such issue in our county that has been discussed in the local press is the practice of unhoused persons riding a 22-mile all-night bus line (Bus 22) that traverses city and county lines.

In early 2007, at the request of the public transportation authority, a group of public officials and homeless service providers began meeting to discuss the overnight use of buses for shelter. Attendees began drawing lines and entrenching perspectives early in the process: Transportation officials said that homeless riders caused problems for other riders and that buses "are not shelters"; shelter and other service providers said they were doing their jobs, which, based on their funded scope of services, did not include having staff work overnight on buses that cross city and county lines; cities and counties were constrained by their geographic and service boundaries; and a representative of the transit workers union was at the table to make sure that any policy changes would not negatively influence bus operators.

While there was consensus that the issue was multifaceted and that there was a lack of factual or sound information about the riders who were unhoused, inertia emerged, driven by an apparent lack of funds in city and county social service programs and limited outreach staff. After countless meetings with no movement, Fernando asked the group if they would support a survey of riders to help them in going forward. The group agreed, and Fernando began to look for ways to implement such a project with no funds or staff support. Laura and Fernando met to discuss a potential partnership.

The Class and Projects

The Applied Sociology class is a 10-week required course for junior and senior sociology majors at a private Jesuit university of 5,000 undergraduates. The course uses a systems-level approach to introduce students to research and careers at the individual, organizational, community, and policy levels. The biggest component of the course is a number of group research projects for local organizations that students work on all quarter. In the past 10 years, applied sociology students have conducted 35 projects for free at the request of and in partnership with community organizations. These have included program evaluations of literacy programs, needs assessments for a hot meals program and a grassroots political action organization, community-based asset mapping for a new transitional housing program, among many others.

Program evaluations, needs assessments, and marketing are often ongoing needs of nonprofits. So when classes present themselves as ready to provide such work, agencies often change their priorities so they can seize such opportunities. In contrast, in the policy realm timing matters, and it matters a lot. Therefore, organizing a class on an academic calendar with the hope that the research produced from it can contribute to policy becomes a challenge.

This particular quarter there were five community-based research projects, with four of the five requested by Fernando and related to homelessness.[2] The projects included the development of a public education campaign, data analysis and the creation of fact sheets on subpopulations within the homeless population, data collection on the bus, and analysis and distribution of the bus data. On the first day of class, students ranked their project preferences. The most challenging to implement during the 10-week quarter was the bus project.

Because the bus project was different than the rest, in that it required intensive training before data collection and that students spend hours at night on the bus, only those who ranked that project as their first choice would be chosen to participate. If too few students signed on, the project would not occur. More than 75% of the 34 students in the class wanted to work on the bus project. This allowed Laura to assign students who had the most community-based experience and research skills.

Besides coordinating the logistics of collecting data on a moving bus, much work was done to address potential safety issues as well as to properly train students to collect such data. The campus human subjects committee asked for clarification not about the potential harm to those being surveyed but rather the student data collectors. The transportation authority provided trainers, staff on the ground during data collection, and $5 gift cards for respondents. The union supported the project, and bus operators were

---

[2]The fifth project was an on-campus project requested by the Office of Sustainability and studied the green and not-so-green practices that took place in offices across campus.

informed of the study and welcomed surveyors on their buses over the three nights of data collection.

The partnership with Fernando provided access to a whole group of guest speakers who spoke to the class about policy and service provision. A panel of persons who had ridden the bus route for shelter also trained the students on how to collect data on the bus as well as educated the whole class about the realities of being homeless.

For Angelica and other students in the class, the project provided an opportunity to actually do something with all of the skills and knowledge they had been acquiring. On the first night of data collection, one junior told Laura, "I finally feel like a college student." Although many students had done direct service and volunteering through high school and college, this was the first time students had the opportunity to work on something that could potentially contribute to social change. It also allowed the students to more deeply explore their futures as civically engaged citizens beyond the individual level of direct service.

The data collected by the students included field notes from observations and recollections of conversations with riders that students wrote up after each night of data collection, as well as data from 49 usable surveys. The findings were analyzed and summarized in a final report and presentation. Later, Laura created a two-page research brief on the findings that is posted on the City of San Jose's website and has been widely distributed.[3]

The results showed that nearly half of those surveyed had been using the bus for shelter for many years, riding the bus throughout the year, regardless of season (Nichols & Cázares, 2010). The study also revealed that a significant portion of unhoused riders qualified as long-term or chronically homeless,[4] a high-priority group both federally and locally, and highlighted that any effort to respond to chronically homeless persons in the county ought to include a targeted outreach and service response to unhoused riders on Bus 22. The study also gave voice to the riders themselves. Representatives from the transportation authority and county social services attended the students' final project presentation and heard the students talk about the people they met on the bus. The riders became real people whose experiences and situations could no longer be ignored in policy discussions on the topic.

---

[3]http://www.scu.edu/cas/sociology/staff/upload/Bus22ExecSummaryFeb08draft3 .pdf.

[4]http://www.hud.gov/offices/cpd/homeless/chronic.cfm.

Educating Publics With Limited Resources

Besides the findings from the study, this case also magnifies how universities can help address policy and community issues when there are limited resources, voices are missing from the process, and jurisdiction becomes an issue. Universities such as Santa Clara University supersede city and county boundaries. And one of the greatest assets that universities have is a critical mass of social science students who are eager for experience (Strand, Marullo, Cutforth, Stoecker, & Donohue, 2003). Further, students are often viewed by the public as nonthreatening, in need of guidance, and as wanting to give back to the community. One of the trainers who spoke to the class gave a public "Thank you" to the student volunteers he had met while staying at local shelters.

This goodwill toward students helped in data collection. Wrote one student in his field notes, "When we approached people the reaction we received varied from person to person. Most people I encountered were very willing and happy to help us with the survey and welcomed us to sit next to them. . . . Riders who did participate in the survey were very willing to continue conversation with us (after taking the survey). These conversations ranged from policy talk about homelessness to simple conversation about school and the bus." Said one rider to a student, "Thank you for doing this. This is definitely a subculture that needs to be known about. You guys are doing a great job." Another said, "I am really happy that you guys are doing this research. . . . It is people like you who will make a change in the world we live in."

In addition, many students have grown up in the communities where the class research takes place. Students may have stronger ties to and familiarity with the community than faculty and even agency or government staff do. In addition, a class often includes students with many different language abilities, a need and extreme asset in community-based research. Wrote one student in her field notes, "I asked one of the riders I had seen sleeping on one part of the route if I could ask him some questions, but he told me that he didn't speak English. He told me this in Spanish, so I immediately established rapport with him in Spanish." Finally, because of growing service learning requirements in high schools and colleges, many students already have experience with direct service organizations as well as interacting across and within race, class, and age.

While the university calendar does not always correspond to the policy needs in communities, enriching partnerships that benefit students and the community can be developed, as was illustrated in this research on homelessness. And these data can be used to bring voices—voices often left out of policy making—to the conversation.

References

Nichols, L., & Cázares, F. (2010). The mobile shelter system: Public transportation as shelter. *Journal of Social Policy.*

Strand, K., Marullo, S., Cutforth, N., Stoecker, R., & Donohue, P. (2003). *Community-based research and higher education.* San Francisco, CA: Jossey-Bass.

Case Study 1.2. The Differential Impact of Gentrification on Communities of Color in Chicago

Philip Nyden, Julie Davis, and Emily Edlynn

The cycle of community reinvestment and displacement of low-income residents is a process present in cities throughout the United States, Europe, and other developed nations. It has been well documented in numerous studies (Dreier, Mollenkopf, & Swanstrom, 2001; Nelson, 1988; Palen & London, 1984; Schill & Nathan, 1983; Smith & Williams, 1986). Also referred to as gentrification and displacement, it has been the source of considerable policy debate in Chicago at both community and citywide levels.[5] Displacement—particularly when it takes place as communities are being revitalized—can move low-income populations further away from the very housing, educational, and employment opportunities that could ameliorate the problems of past social and economic exclusion.

Because community reinvestment was often seen as increasing racial and ethnic inequalities, the City of Chicago Commission on Human Relations approached the Loyola University Chicago Center for Urban Research and Learning to examine the impact that gentrification has on different racial, ethnic, and economic groups in Chicago. The commission routinely receives complaints from residents and elected officials about increased racial and ethnic tensions in some communities experiencing reinvestment. Because many city development policies are predicated on the assumption that community investment is always a positive, the commission felt a need to look at this process more closely.

---

[5]The use of the terms *gentrification* and *reinvestment* can have different meanings to different people. In a meeting with the staff of the Commission on Human Relations early in the research process, we were advised to use the term *gentrification* in our interview and focus group questions. Since developers and those uncritical of the gentrification and displacement cycle are more likely to use the term *reinvestment*, it was felt that use of this term might be perceived as biased by respondents. However, in the report itself we use the two terms interchangeably.

The Center for Urban Research and Learning

The Loyola University Chicago Center for Urban Research and Learning is an innovative, nontraditional collaborative university–community research center that only completes research when community partners are involved in all or most phases of the research. Described in more detail in Chapter 2, CURL recognizes the need to combine the knowledge and perspectives of both university and community partners. Without these combined perspectives, we are typically missing half of the picture in understanding issues facing local communities.

Exclusively discipline-driven research agendas do not always hit the target in providing information and insights for current, pressing community issues. In working with community partners, CURL has been able to both pull relevant information from past discipline-driven research and add information that is relevant to the community's immediate policy concerns. In the case of research on gentrification and displacement, much has been written within the field. However, the specific concerns of the Human Relations Commission around current racial and class tensions have not been the focus of the majority of this work. Moreover, unlike academics, who are completing an end product that will be of interest to fellow sociologists, community leaders are interested not only in the information but how it might fit into policies and neighborhood-level solutions. When community partners are involved in shaping the research and typically participate as respondents in focus groups, interviews, and surveys created by this collaborative process, research "data" have policy ideas and solutions imbedded in them. It is this natural link between research and solutions that has characterized much of CURL's research.

The Study[6]

As is typical of CURL projects, we enlisted a team of researchers that included faculty, graduate students, undergraduates, and community partners. The primary researchers included two sociologists (Nyden and Davis) and a psychologist (Edlynn). Among the others involved in the project— particularly helping in community-based interviews and focus groups—were three undergraduate students (psychology and sociology majors), three graduate students (two sociology students and one community psychology

---

[6]The full study (Nyden et al., 2006) is available on the Center for Urban Research and Learning website: http://luc.edu/curl/pdfs/HRC_Report.pdf.

student), and a recent sociology Ph.D. recipient who was working on fair housing issues in Chicago. Because there was a need to establish credibility and rapport in diverse communities, the diversity of the team was also important. The team included African American, Latino, Asian, and White Anglo members, which bolstered credibility both with our primary partner—the Human Relations Commission—and with interviewees during the research itself.

Although we provided a general demographic picture of citywide gentrification and displacement trends, we focused our report and interviews on two specific areas of Chicago—the predominantly Latino West Town and Humboldt Park community areas northwest of Chicago's central business district and the primarily low-income African American mid-South Side comprised of four Chicago community areas: Grand Boulevard, Douglas, Oakland, and Kenwood. Both of these areas were identified by city officials and researchers as the city's current gentrification "hot spots" (Zielenbach, 2005).

In particular, the study measured perceptions of community leaders about the impact of the gentrification process. We interviewed or included in focus groups 68 business leaders, community-based organization executive directors, social service agency staff, religious leaders, and others who were familiar with daily life in the two communities studied. These are people on the "front line" of community activities; they are among the most perceptive of social and economic changes in their communities. They are also aware of how residents perceive, interpret, and react to the changes that are going on around them.

Findings

Gentrification and displacement in West Town/Humboldt Park have taken on a distinctively Latino versus non-Latino debate. Puerto Rican culture has defined the neighborhoods since the in-migration of Puerto Ricans in the 1960s. Residents describe a block-by-block gentrification process that they liken to removing their community piece by piece: "I call it erosion because that Puerto Rican character, the Latino character in this area is being eroded. There are huge, huge, huge areas of Humboldt Park that are gone, that are lost to us through gentrification. There are whole neighborhoods here" (West Town community leader). The cohesiveness of the Latino community is viewed as threatened.

In the mid-South communities, initiatives to preserve African American historical institutions in Bronzeville have become a focus of community leaders and economic development proposals. These are not necessarily linked to plans to reduce residential displacement (which has already occurred) but rather are connected to economic reinvestment that preserves Chicago's African American historical roots on the South Side. Bronzeville emerged as one of the most visible African American communities in the United States after the Great Migration of African Americans from the South to northern cities. Located 2 miles south of Chicago's downtown, Bronzeville served as a hotspot for African American arts, culture, and society in the 1920s and later, claiming historical figures such as Langston Hughes, Nat King Cole, Louis Armstrong, and Lorraine Hansberry as residents (Diane Grams's case study in this same section discusses the use of Bronzeville's rich cultural history in its current redevelopment). Although the building of large, high-rise public housing developments in the 1950s and 1960s provided more affordable housing in the area, the large number of buildings and deterioration of tenant screening and management ultimately contributed to economic decline in the broader community.

There were distinct differences between the gentrification and displacement processes in the two communities. In West Town/Humboldt Park those being displaced were very much aware of those displacing them. Current residents routinely saw the gentrifiers moving into the rehabbed or new houses as their neighbors left apartments where they may have lived for more than 10 or 20 years. Gentrifiers were typically middle-class, White Anglos, while those displaced were usually lower-income Latinos.

In contrast, the gentrification and displacement process in the mid-South Side communities happened over a 30-plus-year period. It was more of a depopulation, displacement, and then gentrification process. The opening up of suburban housing opportunities for middle-class African Americans after federal civil rights legislation in the 1960s led to an exodus of middle-class families who previously had few housing choices outside the neighborhood because of persistent discriminatory practices in exclusive White communities. In addition to this depopulation, persistent racial segregation, lack of infrastructure investment (e.g., schools, libraries, and streets), as well as deteriorating housing quality and eventual teardowns of previously desirable apartments and greystone houses, caused the community to be even less desirable and created a further exodus of working-class African Americans and even some low-income families. From the 1970s until the noticeable reinvestment after 2000, absentee landowners sat on the vacant lots left after the teardowns. In addition to this, after 2000, the Chicago Housing Authority (CHA) systematically tore down scores of high-rise buildings representing thousands of low-income housing units. However, many of those units had been vacant for as many as 10 or 15 years before the buildings were demolished. Ultimately, in the first decades of the 21st century, the available empty space, along with increased city infrastructure investment, the transformation of CHA properties to mixed-income developments, interest in creating an African American historical district, and the booming real estate market combined to open the doors to neighborhood redevelopment.

Since 2000, the gentrifiers, mostly middle-class African Americans, typically moved into new housing built on these long-vacant lots or into substantially rehabbed greystones that may have been vacant for years. In this community most of the gentrifiers and the displaced were obscured from each others' view by time. Those displaced in the 1960s and 1970s were long gone before middle-class gentrifiers started moving in during the early 2000s. This time gap eliminated the possibility of gentrifier/displacee tensions. Also, since both the gentrifiers and those displaced years earlier were African American, race was not a point of tension. If there was any tension, it revolved around social class differences.

Given these different histories of the two communities, the gentrification process was viewed differently by residents of both communities. In the African American mid-South Side it was seen as more of a positive process; many considered the revitalization process as long overdue. Although there were significant concerns over what was happening to displaced low-income African American residents, the prospects of a middle-class African American revitalization of the area's past heyday of Black culture was seen as a positive. In contrast, in West Town/Humboldt Park, where the ethnic dividing lines of Latino and Anglo were congruent with the visible gentrifier/displaced dividing line, the revitalization process produced stronger ethnic tensions and was perceived in a negative light by many people living in the community.

Our report raised a number of other issues. In both communities, the difficulties that communities face in countering outside forces that are reshaping neighborhoods when there is little input from current residents was apparent. In West Town/Humboldt Park, developers converted affordable apartments into market-rate condominiums. The process through which developers bought up rental properties to convert into new condominiums was largely done out of the sight of community residents. Even community-based organizations struggled to get information on housing sales and permit applications. When they did find out, it was often too late to seek avenues to preserve buildings as affordable rental properties.

On the mid-South Side, both the absentee landowners and the government represented forces outside the local community's reach. In the 1950s, construction of massive numbers of high-rise public housing buildings by the CHA on Chicago's South Side not only reinforced Chicago's racial divide but created the concentrated poverty that ultimately set the stage for whole-sale community deterioration. In the neighborhoods adjacent to the CHA developments, absentee slum landlords profited from inflated rents, build-ings were not maintained and ultimately were torn down, and outside land speculators bought up cheap vacant lots and sat on them for years with the plan to make money when the neighborhood came back (Hirsch, 1998). From the perspective of local residents, community organizations, and non-profit community development corporations, the current-day revitalization was seen as a positive in some ways. However, just as outside forces had helped to determine the community's fate more than 50 years before, similar outside forces were directing the community's comeback.

Outcomes and Impact of the Research

Since the project was developed at the request of, and in cooperation with, the City of Chicago Commission on Human Relations, there was a built-in user of the research from day one. Since the commission is called in to mediate many neighborhood disputes, particularly those with racist or ethnocentric overtones, the research added a social class dimension to the commission's understanding. Our close study of Humboldt Park helped to shed light on Latino/White non-Latino/African American tensions. This is particularly salient in a city where there has been a very large increase in the Latino population (a 38% increase from 1990 to 2000). The study of the mid-South Side, while not seeing racial tensions, did shed light on the social class dynamics and tensions within the African American community. This is also of interest to city policy makers who want to strengthen the presence of the African American middle class in the city and stem the decades-long flow from the city to suburbs.

A month before the final report was to be completed, there was a sugges-tion from the mayor's office that the report should not be released, given the volatile nature of the gentrification debate. This was in itself an indirect measure of both the impact of the study and political divisions within the city administration. Ultimately discussions between the commission and the mayor's office turned back the suggestion that the report be held back.

When it was released in January 2006, the report was immediately dis-tributed to all of Chicago's aldermen, who were in the final stages of debate on an inclusionary zoning ordinance. The ordinance would require that a certain portion of units in new multifamily construction be affordable in cases where the city had provided financial support or zoning variances for the project. There had been a multiyear battle by a coalition of community groups to pass this ordinance, but Mayor Richard M. Daley had resisted passage of an ordinance that would include a 25% set-aside for affordable housing units. However, in the aldermanic elections that had just taken place a few weeks earlier, it appeared that a veto-proof city council majority supporting the higher set-aside might be in place when the new city council was sworn in at the end of the month. With a more aggressive council about to take office, the mayor supported passage of an inclusionary zoning ordinance with a 10% set-aside for affordable units in new privately developed larger multi-unit buildings. Although our report (and its linkage of gentrification/displacement issues to racial and ethnic tensions) was only one of many in the consideration of the ordinance, it made a small contribution to the ultimate passage of the city's first inclusionary zoning ordinance late in January.

CURL was proactive in making sure the report got into the hands of a variety of community-based organizations. Arranging media coverage of the report and posting the full report on our webpage were two of the ways in which information was distributed. CURL also made a number of presentations to community organizations around the city, particularly in the specific communities studied. The report stimulated additional work with community partners, including a block-by-block analysis of apartment-to-condominium conversions in select neighborhoods.

As with other CURL projects, undergraduate and graduate students were actively involved in the research and writing that went into the report. They are listed as authors and researchers on the report. Perhaps more important, they became increasingly aware of how the research fit into ongoing community efforts to bring about equity in Chicago's neighborhoods. Watching the politics of the research—from the role of the commissioners in helping to frame the research questions, to the hesitancy of the mayor's office in releasing the report, to the new city council legislation—students recognized that they were among the players in Chicago policy making.

References

Dreier, P., Mollenkopf, J., & Swanstrom, T. (2001). *Place matters: Metropolitics for the twenty-first century.* Lawrence, KS: University of Kansas Press.

Hirsch, A. R. (1998). *The making of the second ghetto: Race and housing in Chicago 1940–1960.* Chicago, IL: University of Chicago Press.

Nelson, K. P. (1988). *Gentrification and distress cities: An assessment of trends in intrametropolitan migration.* Madison, WI: University of Wisconsin Press.

Nyden, P., Edlynn, E., & Davis, J. (2006). *The differential impact of gentrification on communities in Chicago.* Chicago, IL: Loyola University Chicago, Center for Urban Research and Learning.

Palen, J. J., & London, B. (1984). *Gentrification, displacement and neighborhood revitalization.* Albany, NY: State University of New York Press.

Schill, M. H., & Nathan, R. P. (1983). *Revitalizing America's cities: Neighborhood reinvestment and displacement.* Albany, NY: State University of New York Press.

Smith, N., & Williams, P. (Eds.). (1986). *Gentrification of the city.* London, UK: Allen and Unwin.

Zielenbach, S. (2005). Understanding community change: A look at low-income Chicago neighborhoods in the 1990s. *Neighborhood change in urban America* (vol. 4, pp. 1–11). Washington, DC: Urban Institute Press.

Case Study 1.3. Research in Action: The Case of InnerCity Entrepreneurs

Daniel Monti

The project discussed here, InnerCity Entrepreneurs (ICE), was the brain-child of the author.[7] ICE, as it was originally conceived, would bring together the owners of existing inner-city businesses to figure out how to take their enterprise to "the next level," not just economically but also in their larger contribution to the community. They would receive in-class training, mentoring from technical experts and owners of larger businesses, and networking opportunities that, it was hoped, would put them on a faster track to success. Business owners also agreed to have their experiences tracked for several years after they graduated from the program so that we could track the effects of the program and how attendees put into practice what they had learned.

The research team consisted of two faculty members from Boston University and two graduate students, one each from the School of Management and sociology department. Professor Candida Brush, now at Babson College, had contacts with the Kauffman Foundation and assumed

---

[7]The early training work was underwritten by the Citizens Bank Foundation of Boston. The research was supported by a grant from The Ewing Marion Kauffman Foundation, which is located in Kansas City. A good portion of this case study is drawn from the report our research team submitted to the foundation in 2005 (Brush, Monti, Ryan, & Gannon, 2005). Two academic papers based on findings from the first two cohorts of businesses going through the program have been pub-lished from the information we collected (Brush, Monti, Ryan, & Gannon, 2007; Monti, Brush, Ryan, & Gannon, 2007). In addition to the several hundreds of thousands of dollars contributed by these organizations, ICE received "in-kind" contributions from Boston University, Roxbury Community College, and many individual businessmen and women, lawyers, and other people with technical skills that our participants could make use of.

primary responsibility for composing and acquiring the grant. The graduate students were listed as coauthors on every published paper, and the student from the School of Management used data from our survey in her dissertation.

The Research

Our inner cities look and function differently from other types of places. Many of the entrepreneurs there are minorities; and many of these men and women face particularly difficult challenges. But it is critical that they succeed. In Massachusetts alone there are nearly 40,000 firms, 1 in 4 companies, headed by low-income urban entrepreneurs (Staley et al., n.d.). Many of these firms are micro-enterprises and sole proprietorships that could add significant wealth and jobs in inner-city communities if they succeed and grow.

The unique ecology of urban areas may make such places particularly vulnerable to job loss and economic decline if they are not bolstered by a strong local economy of their own. While we as a society seem to know this well, we haven't backed up our talk with actions that will keep urban economies strong. Much of the technical assistance provided to business-people, for instance, goes to new business start-ups, particularly those in declining neighborhoods. Many of these businesses fail. We provide little or no assistance to entrepreneurial ventures that have managed to survive and now are ready to grow.

Our research, and the ICE program, hoped to fill this gap in both knowledge and practice. The research was drawn from data collected on two cohorts of 29 entrepreneurs. Specifically, we examined individual, firm, and community factors that influence growth, drawing on both sociology and business management principles and employing a mix of survey and personal interview data collection methods.

Our study showed the relative importance of individual, firm, and community factors in driving the growth of inner-city enterprises. We found that the entrepreneur's involvement in the community was tied to his or her values, motives, and strategic actions. In these ways, community involvement had an impact on the growth of the venture. Most of the ICE entrepreneurs did not fit the classic profiles either of "traditional" businessmen and -women who were primarily, perhaps even exclusively, focused on the bottom line or of social entrepreneurs who use good business practices explicitly to do more social good. The ventures of many of the ICE participants were best described as "hybrid enterprises" or "business-and-community ventures" in that they reflected *both* the entrepreneur's need to focus on the bottom line and the socially minded activist's desire to make the community better.

The Findings

Who Were the InnerCity Entrepreneurs?

Entrepreneurs in the ICE program provided everything from advice to coffee cakes, the news and the means to print or publicize it, caterers, florists and balloonists, food providers and people who help children, limo services and people who repair automobiles after they've been dinged or damaged. In short, this sample of entrepreneurs provided a variety of goods and services for individuals and other companies inside Boston and some of the suburbs surrounding it.

The 29 entrepreneurs came from a variety of backgrounds. They were Black (seven men and five women) and White (nine men and five women). Three were Hispanic. Almost two-thirds of them were 45 years old or younger. Nearly 80% of them had at least four years of college to their credit.

Most of the entrepreneurs (62%) started their ventures from scratch. In all, 72% of the entrepreneurs described themselves as business leaders, while 55% described themselves as community leaders. Connecting their business and social missions could be rewarding. However, it was hard to do and could throw roadblocks in front of their plans to grow their ventures, as the men and women involved in the program readily conceded.

These entrepreneurs worked hard. Approximately 80% of them spent anywhere from 9 to 11 hours a day on the job, and nearly half of them worked at least six days per week. Interestingly, minority entrepreneurs spent significantly more time on community activities. Further, those who were deeply involved with their ethnic communities spent more time on community activities than did those who were not. Virtually all of the entrepreneurs indicated that they felt a personal obligation to give something back to the community (93%).

How Did InnerCity Entrepreneurs Organize and Grow Their Ventures?

This collection of entrepreneurs had its own ways of acting and organizing. The values and goals of any two ventures, while conventional by any reasonable standard, didn't line up the same way. In short, there was no single pattern to how the businesses were set up and run, or in the way their owners or managers made some bigger sense of what they were doing. In one sense, we should not have been surprised. They are, after all, *entrepreneurs*. And entrepreneurs have a habit of doing things their own way or at least finding novel ways of doing things that other people either ignore or never imagine putting together in the way entrepreneurs do.

The overwhelming majority of ventures run by ICE participants were small, with 70% having fewer than 10 employees. They did not have large staffs and, as a result, the lead people in the organization did most of the jobs. Of the businesses, 44% had annual sales of more than $500,000, while more than 25% posted revenues of more than $1,000,000. These businesses were on average four years old.

Minority entrepreneurs (66%) in this sample were significantly more likely to market their products to their racial or ethnic groups than did their White counterparts. Nearly 33% indicated that their customers were primarily from their ethnic or racial group. This doesn't seem to have had any bearing on the geographic breadth of their markets. ICE entrepreneurs were already reaching out *geographically*. It remains to be seen how quickly and well they will expand the *ethnic* or *racial* focus of their markets.

How Were Business and Social Goals of InterCity Entrepreneurs Reflected in Their Ventures?

Most of the ventures were not focused exclusively on the bottom line. Nor were they social enterprises in the sense that their owners were do-gooders who decided they had to market themselves more aggressively if they wanted to keep doing good. They combined a bottom-line mentality with a broader social mission in ways we had not seen before. We classified these as "hybrid enterprises" or "business–community ventures."

We know that what's going on in the Boston area isn't unique. But we cannot say with any certainty that the odd mixing of business and social goals we saw in this sample is an agreeable mutation that many more businesses are going to adopt in the future. What we can say with confidence is that this collection of ventures and entrepreneurs did not get this way as a result of taking the ICE program. They were already acting this way before they entered it. If anything, the program helped them to sharpen their focus and come up with better plans for how they can combine "doing good" with "doing well" in the future.

Notwithstanding all the "giving back" that their ventures did, we found no relationship between the number of organizations the entrepreneurs joined and the number of ways their ventures gave back to the community. More importantly, the payoff to entrepreneurs for being better joiners was not at all clear. Entrepreneurs who were officers in one or more of the groups outside of work reported that their ventures got attention by the media. However, merely being the member of an organization did not seem to increase the amount of attention the media gave their ventures or the recognition their ventures got from people in their immediate neighborhoods.

What Are the Challenges of InterCity Entrepreneurs' Hybrid Enterprises?

The dual mission of a hybrid enterprise affects many decisions the entrepreneurs make. It can sometimes create special challenges as well. For example, the owner and chief executive officer of one business admitted that developing local talent, as opposed to hiring experienced talent from outside the community, had slowed his business's growth. Yet, his mission was clear, and he believed strongly that he was doing the right thing. So, while he certainly wanted to grow, he continually negotiated a balance between his complementary economic and social missions.

It could be argued that business owners who are interested only in sustaining a modest income need not worry so much about these distinctions. However, those who want to grow a business in the inner city, particularly in communities with relatively weaker institutional infrastructures and more unstable economic situations, face a variety of challenges. For hybrid enterprises, a poor balance of social and economic missions can put the business at risk. Balancing them well can make the business thrive. Yet, as a business grows, the entrepreneur becomes less involved in every decision, perhaps making it more difficult to manage both missions well.

The primary finding of this study—that many inner-city entrepreneurs create ventures that incorporate both economic and social missions—has implications for public policy initiatives and management education. The findings seem to suggest that hybrids require creative and innovative strategies to manage growth in ways that support the complex nature of their dual missions. It is not just a matter of training inner-city entrepreneurs to be like their White suburban counterparts. Our findings suggest that we must recognize the embedded nature of entrepreneurs and their ventures in the social environment. Future research on hybrid ventures may help us expand or redefine our notions about who these entrepreneurs are, why they do what they do, and how we can measure their success.

Lessons Learned

ICE continues to work in the Boston area and has expanded its base to one other city in the Commonwealth of Massachusetts. For a variety of reasons it is unlikely that it will expand further. Foremost among them, however, is the time and expense involved in identifying and enrolling enough businesses to take the course every year. Another limitation of the program today is that the idea of mounting a serious and ongoing research effort of the entrepreneurs, their enterprises, and a larger role in the community has been abandoned. Money to conduct follow-up studies was not forthcoming, and the managing staff shifted its emphasis to tracking a couple of key business-related measures of success—such as how much new financing the business secures and how many new jobs it creates—and publishing a glossy scorecard that featured the major success stories from each class.

The failure to take the research and community contributions of the entrepreneurs more seriously was hotly debated. The fact is, we do not know much about inner-city entrepreneurs or the minorities and women who often struggle to build successful ventures in often difficult urban environments. Speaking both theoretically and practically, this is a serious omission. Inasmuch as minority- and woman-led enterprises are the key to economic prosperity in urban areas, learning more about who they are, how they grow their ventures, and how they relate to their communities has special significance—not just for them but for all of us.

References

Brush, C. G., Monti, D., Ryan, A., & Gannon, A. (2005). *Building ventures and expanding community ties: The case of InnerCity Entrepreneurs.* Kansas City, MO: Ewing Marion Kauffman Foundation.

Brush, C., Monti, D., Ryan, A., & Gannon, A. (2007). Building ventures through civic capitalism. *Annals of the American Academy of Political and Social Sciences, 613,* 155–177.

Monti, D., Brush, C., Ryan, A., & Gannon, A. (2007). Civic capitalism: Entrepreneurs, their ventures and communities. *Journal of Developmental Entrepreneurship, 12*(3), 353–375.

Staley, S. R., Husock, H., Bobb, D. J., Burnett, H. S., Creasy, L., & Hudson, W. (n.d.). *Giving a leg up to bootstrap entrepreneurship: Expanding economic opportunity in America's urban centers.* Policy study 277. Retrieved from http://www.pioneerinstitute.org/pdf/entre_legup.pdf.

Case Study 1.4. Art and Equitable Community Development

Diane Grams

Following Harvey Molotch's (1976) characterization of urban development as a "growth machine," urban sociologists have documented and critiqued the role of artists and arts institutions as complicit actors in the transformation of gritty urban neighborhoods into exclusive spaces for urban elites. However, this case study of art and community development in Bronzeville—an area on Chicago's South Side often considered to be the heart and soul of Black American culture—builds upon research highlighting the potential of art to be central to resource mobilization and community investment for historically marginalized groups (Drake & Cayton, 1945/1962; Gans, 1974/1999) as well as being symbolic of municipal commitment to equitable community development (Jacobs, 1961/1992; Hayden, 1995; Simpson, 1982). As shown in this case study, the cooperative efforts of networks of cultural leaders, administrators, bureaucrats, and arts participants constitute an "ethnically driven stability machine" (Grams, 2010) holding at bay pressure for wholesale displacement of racial and ethnic minorities from increasingly valued inner-city real estate, while attracting both municipal and private investment to restore the cultural reserves of long-neglected inner-city areas.

Community-Involved Research Design

This research began in 2001 as a grant-funded survey of small-budget art activity in 10 of Chicago's low-income community areas.[8] I was a former director of a small nonprofit community-based museum working for a Ph.D. in sociology, and my research partner was an African American poet and arts consultant, Michael Warr. We sought to identify and map the arts activities found within predominantly poor and working-class residential communities as well as assess how these activities might benefit these locales. This survey, funded by two foundations interested in supporting local cultural activity, had broad implications for community arts groups.

Our research process included taking an inventory of nonprofit and commercial arts organizations, publicized cultural events, and public displays in each locale. We also built a snowball sample of local residents and leaders to help us learn about these places from insiders' perspectives. The art producers involved in this study were a different sort than the bohemian artists who

---

[8]"Community area" refers to aggregates of census tracts demarcated as "communities" by early 20th-century researchers and adopted by the U.S. Census Bureau in 1930. The community areas initially surveyed (Grams & Warr, 2003) were: Logan Square, Kenwood, Oakland, Woodlawn, Grand Boulevard, North Lawndale, Rogers Park, Uptown, Little Village, and Humboldt Park. This case study focuses on Bronzeville, an area in Chicago's mid-South region encompassing the community areas of Kenwood, Oakland, Grand Boulevard, and Douglas.

produced in the more well-known art scenes in Wicker Park and Chicago's West Loop, the chic professionals who frequented the River North Gallery District, or the elites who patronized downtown cultural institutions.

Among those interviewed in Bronzeville were African Americans who lived and worked in this area once considered to be one of Chicago's most neglected ghettos. As activists, their roles in their community revealed much about local art. Among the study participants were advocates for Black culture, institutions, and cultural tourism; teachers in public schools and public park programs who infused arts opportunities into daily educational and recreational programs; public housing residents and staff from social service agencies who established after-school and park-based cultural programs where few such programs had previously existed; city bureaucrats and workers who took advantage of budgeting opportunities to support local cultural efforts; and artists, musicians, writers, gallerists, art collectors, representatives, and publishers. While some of these participants eked out a living through a traditional job while pursuing an interest in art from a home-based workspace, others held positions of power or knew people who did.

Neighborhood Interaction Provides the Nexus of Local Art Production

The study participants became research partners helping to identify how art emerged through local social histories, in local social spaces through locally significant artistic and organizational forms. Highlighting the fact that ethnic culture is not "new," they pointed to the activities of art networks whose efforts built upon ethnic cultures and community-oriented art production. We saw a range of activities that celebrated historical cultural practices of African Americans who once lived and worked in the historic inner-city neighborhood. As these activities were not designed as status symbols for the city's elite, nor were they shaped by the city's downtown cultural institutions, art production took on forms that reflected the shared interests and values of a local community. For example, murals, ethnic monuments, and ethnic landmarks reflected topics such as the importance of nuclear families, the value of public education, community solidarity, union brotherhood, civil rights, high school graduation, political involvement, and religious inspiration. Furthermore, regular events in artists' home studios and in art collectors' homes, as well as in commercial and nonprofit spaces, nurtured local aesthetic understandings of what art could be and should be.

In such locales, artists engaged in mural making, performances, parades, and public festivals that enable the community to validate and legitimize its own cultural practices. Among the pioneering art activists at work on

Chicago's South Side were William Walker and the artists of Organization of Black American Culture (OBAC) who painted *The Wall of Respect* (1967). The massive mural, once located in the heart of Bronzeville on Forty-Third Street and Langley Avenue, is often considered to be the first community-based mural in the United States because the artists actively engaged the local residents in the mural-making process. This process is framed as an aesthetic approach that is based upon an expectation of dialogue with the local community residents before, during, and after the art-making process. This interactive involvement bears similarities to historic forms of Black culture such as the call-and-response form of blues, jazz, and gospel music, the improvisation of break dancing, second lining, or hip hop, and narrative structures of oral histories linked to African and Caribbean cultures. The Chicago Mural Group, a nonprofit art organization founded by Walker and John Pitman Weber in 1970, was renamed the Chicago Public Art Group (CPAG) after muralist Jon Pounds took over leadership in 1983. It is among the well-established nonprofit arts organizations working today in partnership with municipal and civic groups to restore the now-historic activist murals from the 1960s and 1970s and to make new ones relevant to contemporary life.

This approach, which places neighborhood interaction as central to artistic production, is common to Black aesthetic practice, according to Patric McCoy, an African American art collector who cofounded Diasporal Rhythms, a nonprofit organization to promote collecting of art of the African Diaspora. McCoy refers to it as "a bottom-up, rather than a top-down approach" (interview with author); it is an aesthetic that is shared among people who can and do know each other and is validated by the community rather than relying on the sanctioning by experts from the downtown cultural institutions.

Art Enabling Cultural Ownership of Urban Space

The South Side area now referred to as Bronzeville has been a site of struggle since the early 1990s, when longtime residents, art advocates, community activists, community organizations, and social service agencies successfully organized against efforts of the downtown growth machine to expand its interests and control beyond the downtown city center. One of the visible outcomes of their early effort was a 1993 strategic plan by the Mid-South Planning Group[9] to "Restore Bronzeville." This document

---

[9]The Mid-South Planning Group (later renamed the Mid-South Planning and Development Commission) includes community organizations, development corporations, the City of Chicago, and historic preservation groups.

represents some of the knowledge and community resources mobilized to attract investment and interest in the South Side as a historic and cultural site important to African Americans.

Using art to empower a community, rather than to displace it, the network conceived of Bronzeville as a contemporary place and framed a redevelopment strategy to further attract the Black middle class back to the inner city. They would do it by restoring the historic early 20th-century "Black Metropolis" (Drake & Cayton, 1945/1962) that once dominated Chicago's mid-South region. The term bronzeville, a generic reference to any segregated, predominantly Black town or place in the post-Civil War United States, frames the narrative driving redevelopment. Chicago's Bronzeville was the place where a racially segregated, clearly circumscribed but economically diverse and culturally rich Black population was contained. It was a place where poor Blacks, middle-class Blacks, Black professionals, and Black entrepreneurs all lived together because restrictive covenants barred them from living anywhere else in Chicago. In the 21st century, Bronzeville would be restored as a culturally rich, economically diverse, and primarily Black place on Chicago's South Side (Grams, 2010). This brought access to the information, money, and skill needed to bring the power of culture back to the locale; moreover, it had the potential to end the historic property devaluation associated with the stigma of blackness.

Accessing more than $100 million in federal, state, and municipal funds, cultural advocates sought to transform the former ghetto into an urban center for African American culture through identification, landmarking, and mapping of historic sites such as the homes of author Richard Wright, author and activist Ida B. Wells, and musician Muddy Waters; landmarking, preservation, and restoration of the National Guard Armory for the Eighth Regiment (an all-Black unit whose history can be traced to the Civil War) and eight business buildings constructed by Black entrepreneurs from 1920 to 1945; the restoration and preservation of historic public murals painted by Black activists between 1970 and 2000; the construction of three new art facilities; renovation of the historic Sutherland Hotel on 47th Street; and the construction of the Public Art of Bronzeville on Martin Luther King Drive.

The impact of these efforts has been to mark the locale as a place of importance to Black history. According to Harold Lucas, the founder and director of the nonprofit Black Metropolis Convention & Tourism Council, art is more than a tourist attraction; it is a symbol of both the past and the future of this community. Lucas and Paula Robinson, managing partner of the Bronzeville Community Development Partnership, have led the way in making the case for Bronzeville for more than two decades. Together, through a series of community meetings seeking input on the name to be etched on the public art relief map embedded on King Drive, they spearheaded the initiative to formally designate the name "Bronzeville" for the area (Grams, 2010). Robinson is now president of the nonprofit Black Metropolis National Heritage Area Commission, established in 2008, which is seeking congressional designation for the area as a national heritage site.

Art played an important role in a larger community restoration project; it reified the cultural and political identity of a place where Blacks first settled upon arriving in Chicago from the southern United States, where they lived during segregation, and where many remained for nearly a century. By mobilizing the resources to embed knowledge within legitimate forms of political and cultural power, these art producers provide the foundation for locally based knowledge to become a form of cultural capital (Bourdieu & Passeron, 1990).

Outcomes of This Research

This research led to greater understanding of how art that is "made in a community," "represented a community," or is "community-based" can distinguish the local from the downtown urban culture while expanding the range of participants involved. When the nexus of art production is found in the interaction among neighbors, art activities fulfill a number of important civic purposes, including building social relationships, enabling access to resources, and stimulating civic dialogue. As such, art becomes an empowerment activity rather than an elitist one; rather than being an instrument of the urban growth machine, it is a tool for neighborhood stability. It serves broader social justice causes by providing members of racial and ethnic minority groups with opportunities to align their interests and assert rights to representation in both public and private space.

The project had a number of other outcomes as well. It resulted in a research report, *Leveraging Assets: How Small-Budget Art Activities Benefit Neighborhoods* (Grams & Warr, 2003), which has been cited by scholars and consultants throughout the United States and has spawned a number of student projects. It led to another grant-funded project to map arts audiences for 61 Chicago institutions (LaLonde et al., 2006), a class project entitled "Excavating Cultural Policy" (Grams, 2005), and a collaborative study of how nonprofit arts organizations are increasing arts participation (Grams & Farrell, 2008).

References

Bourdieu, P., & Passeron, J. C. (1990). *Reproduction in education, society and culture* (2nd ed.). Newbury Park, CA: Sage Publications.

Drake, S. C., & Cayton, H. R. (1962). *Black metropolis: A study of negro life in a northern city.* New York, NY: Harper & Row. (Original work published 1945)

Gans, H. (1999). *Popular culture and high culture: An analysis and evaluation of taste.* New York, NY: Perseus Books. (Original work published in 1974)

Grams, D. (2005). Excavating cultural policy. In W. Holt (Ed.), *Sociology of culture teaching guide* (pp. 126–130). Washington, DC: American Sociological Association.

Grams, D. (2010). *Producing local color: Art networks in ethnic Chicago.* Chicago, IL: University of Chicago Press.

Grams, D., & Farrell B. (Eds.). (2008). *Entering cultural communities: Diversity and change in the nonprofit arts.* New Brunswick, NJ: Rutgers University Press.

Grams, D., & Warr, M. (2003). *Leveraging assets: How small budget arts activities benefit neighborhoods in Chicago.* Report for the Richard H. Driehaus Foundation and the John D. and Catherine T. MacArthur Foundation. Retrieved from http://tulane.edu/liberal-arts/sociology/upload/Grams-and-Warr-2003-Leveraging-Assets-March-2003.pdf

Hayden, D. (1995). *The power of place: Urban landscapes as public history.* Cambridge, MA: MIT Press.

Jacobs, J. (1992). *The death and life of great American cities.* New York: Vintage Books. (Original work published 1961)

LaLonde, R., O'Muircheartaigh, C., Perkins, J., Grams, D., English, N., & Joynes, D. C. (2006). *Mapping cultural participation in Chicago.* Chicago, IL: University of Chicago, Cultural Policy Center.

Molotch, H. L. (1976). The city as a growth machine. *American Journal of Sociology, 82*(2), 309–330.

Simpson, C. (1981). *Soho: The artist in the city.* Chicago, IL: University of Chicago Press.

CASE STUDIES 2

Environmental Issues

Environmental catastrophes such as Hurricane Katrina and the recent BP Oil disaster in the Gulf of Mexico are disturbing reminders of the tenuous relationship between society and the environment. Environmental sociologists examine the social character of environmental issues and play a vital role in understanding and helping to solve environmental problems. They raise important questions regarding privilege and access to resources, and why some populations are more likely to be affected by environmental problems than others; they examine the role of corporations and industry in contributing to environmental crises, and how governments respond, or contribute to environmental injustices.

The public sociologists in this section offer three different perspectives on environmental sociology. The first case study describes the work of the Contested Illnesses Research Group (CIRG) based at Brown University. CIRG was established in 1999 and is an advocacy and action research group of interdisciplinary scholars. Two of their research projects are described in this section: one based in the community of Tiverton, Rhode Island, and the other in Richmond, California. In the Tiverton example, residents formed a community response organization after learning they lived in a community that was contaminated with manufactured gas plant waste. Through a community-based participatory research project that included undergraduate and graduate students, they worked together on legislative initiatives resulting in the passage of two state bills to redress environmentally contaminated communities. In the Richmond, California, example, CIRG partnered with four other organizations to carry out the Northern California Household Exposure Study, a research project that examined air and dust contaminants in two communities in northern California. Residents were actively involved in the research process and developed a strong sense of ownership in the project. Ultimately the Richmond community used CIRG's findings to successfully stop the expansion of an oil refinery in the area. The authors of this case study, Alissa Cordner, Alison Cohen, and Phil Brown, draw on their experiences and research to offer valuable lessons in doing public sociology.

When we think of Hurricane Katrina we seldom think about the displaced college students and faculty who were affected by the devastation. As the authors of the second case study describe, more than 50,000 college students, as well as faculty, staff, and administrators were forced to leave New Orleans due to campus closures. Anthony Ladd was one of those displaced faculty members; he ended up at Mississippi State University (MSU) while his university remained closed. While at MSU, he and Duane Gill decided to use the opportunity to understand the experiences of students affected by Katrina. They conducted a Web-based survey asking hurricane-affected students about their evacuation experiences, resource loss, trust in institutions, and the impact of displacement on their education. Their findings have been disseminated widely and used to inform and guide universities in becoming better prepared to serve students' needs and to become more "resilient institutions in the aftermath of disaster."

The last case study in this section describes the work of David Pellow of the Minnesota Global Justice Project (MGJ). Concerned about the environmental harm caused by global mining companies, MGJ joined a collaborative effort with two other nongovernmental organizations that were confronting environmental injustice in the nations of the global South. The three groups devoted their expertise to developing a guide for community organizers to use to retaliate against large mining companies' and governments' harmful environmental practices against indigenous communities. Pellow describes the process of creating the guide and his experience as the only academic on the team. He reflects on his training in social movement theory, resource mobilization, and collective action frames and the way his sociological background helped shape and inform the research. The publication, *Protecting Your Community Against Mining Companies and Other Extractive Industries: a Guide for Community Organizers,* has been circulated globally and has been well received. Pellow includes poignant excerpts from environmental activists from around the world who describe the significance of the research in helping communities in their struggle against environmental injustice.

Case Study 2.1. Public Sociology for Environmental Health and Environmental Justice

Alissa Cordner, Alison Cohen, and Phil Brown

For 11 years, our Contested Illnesses Research Group (CIRG) has conducted community-engaged public sociology research and service to work toward environmental health and environmental justice. Our diverse team of sociologists and environmental and public health scientists engage in public sociology by doing community-based participatory research (CBPR) and working toward community-identified policy goals. Our approach to social science overall is tied closely to advocacy and action in that we are committed to doing research for and with publics.

We discuss two of our initiatives that speak to the diversity of approaches possible in the field of public sociology: legislative initiatives and organizational support with the Environmental Neighborhood Awareness Committee of Tiverton (ENACT, n.d.), a community-based organization in Tiverton, Rhode Island, and science-informed policy advocacy with Communities for a Better Environment, a community-based organization working in Richmond, California.

Environmental Neighborhood Awareness Committee of Tiverton: Struggles Over Highly Contaminated Land

In August 2002, residents of Tiverton, Rhode Island, discovered that the ground they lived on was contaminated with manufactured gas plant waste (Handle, 2003). This explained the dark blue tinge of the soil and a petroleum smell discovered during a public works project. The Environmental Neighborhood Awareness Committee of Tiverton formed in response, to keep the community informed about ongoing efforts to remediate the contamination.

In May 2005, we, the Community Outreach Core (COC) of the National Institute of Environmental Health Sciences (NIEHS)-funded Brown University Superfund Research Program, began a formal partnership with ENACT to work toward our shared goals of remediating existing contamination and preventing future contamination (Senier et al., 2008). We have worked with ENACT on many activities over the years, including building organizational capacity, designing local education programs, and studying community responses to remediation. Here we present our partnership on legislative initiatives to prevent other Rhode Island communities from having Tiverton's experiences. So far, two state laws have been passed.

The first legislative initiative was the Environmentally Comprised Home Ownership (ECHO) loan bill, which made home equity loans of up to $50,000 available for homeowners living on or abutting a contaminated site. Tiverton residents had seen their property value drop precipitously when their soil was discovered to be contaminated and a moratorium on digging was levied for the area. They found themselves without practical hope of selling their properties, and the loss of this critical—and often only—source of wealth created large financial burdens for most residents. Here, our community-based approach to policy engagement led COC members, including undergraduate students, to draft the ECHO bill and also advocate for its passage. The ECHO bill moved rapidly through the legislative process: It was introduced in June 2006 and signed into law later that same summer (for more detail, see Senier et al., 2008).

The second legislative effort took place over the course of three legislative seasons and resulted ultimately in the passage of the Polluter Penalties Bill in 2009. This bill greatly increased the limit on daily fines that can be assessed on companies that neglect to comply with state pollution regulations from $1,000 per day to $25,000 per day. This dramatic increase put Rhode Island on par with neighboring states and was intended to deter polluting activities. While Tiverton residents benefited from the ECHO bill, they supported the Polluter Penalties Bill even though it did not apply retroactively and specifically did not apply to their community. This joint initiative between our research group and our community partners was motivated by our shared desire to protect other communities from having to experience what Tiverton residents did.

In working with ENACT, we were able to capitalize on our skills as social scientists, which included teaching and facilitating undergraduate and graduate student involvement through service-learning projects (including the work that led to the drafting of the ECHO home loan bill) and negotiating dialogue between different sectors (primarily state government and communities). In addition to these skills, we also were able to offer funding resources through our NIEHS grant, and we were able to draw on the connections and respect associated with being the top research university in the state. We worked actively to alleviate the tensions that could have arisen from the unequal power and resource dynamics between the university and the community by acknowledging and working through potential differences in strategic orientations and timelines; providing space for everyone to share ideas and concerns; helping community partners successfully access resources; and cultivating personal and social relationships with our community partners. Because we approached our work as a partnership, we were able to leverage our differences toward achieving shared goals.

Through our collaborations on the ECHO bill and the Polluter Penalties Bill, we were able to significantly influence state government to make state policies more protective for environmentally contaminated communities. Often, communities waiting for their lawsuits to be resolved do not know what else to do. Our partnership with ENACT allowed Tiverton residents to channel their energy and concern about their neighborhood into preventive actions that will help protect residents in the rest of Rhode Island from having Tiverton's story happen to them. These were initially seen as intermediate activities to work on while the lawsuit was underway, but these policy changes will likely have a broader impact than the lawsuit itself. Our team's sociology, anthropology, political science, geology, international relations, environmental studies, and public health backgrounds allowed for an inter-disciplinary, community-oriented approach to working on other initiatives. Our public sociology approach identified unintended outcomes of cleanup and led to the development of innovative policy solutions for contaminated communities.

Communities for a Better Environment: Household Exposure Study of Toxics

The Northern California Household Exposure Study is an example of how the research and outreach activities of a research group can logically build on each other, leading researchers and community partners to innovative and exciting research opportunities. The study was a collaborative research project that conducted household sampling of contaminants in two communities in northern California (Brody et al., 2009). It was the result of a long-standing, multidisciplinary collaboration among Brown University; the University of California at Berkeley; Silent Spring Institute, a research institute in Massachusetts focused on the links between women's health and the environment; Communities for a Better Environment (CBE), a commu-nity environmental justice organization working in Richmond, California; and Commonweal, an environmental health organization located in Bolinas, California. The goal of the project was to use community-based participa-tory research methods and dynamic community education to learn about patterns of exposure in homes and to communicate those patterns to indi-vidual participants and their communities.

The project grew out of the Silent Spring Institute Household Exposure Study, which sampled dust and air in homes on Cape Cod in Massachusetts in 1999 (Brody et al., 2007). In 2004 and 2005, research partners received funding from NIEHS and the National Science Foundation (NSF) to conduct a second Household Exposure Study in Richmond, an industrial area of California, in collaboration with CBE, which has long worked on environ-mental justice campaigns there. The California project involved sampling household air and dust from both inside and outside 40 homes in Richmond and 10 homes in Bolinas. Bolinas is a smaller, wealthier, and mostly White coastal town west of Richmond with no heavy industry; it was added to the study design after Richmond residents who attended a community meeting early in the study design process told us that they wanted to learn how their results would compare to a site with no heavy industry. Although we had planned to sample homes randomly, we found that many residents wanted to volunteer to have their homes tested. After discussing the sampling question with the full research team and an external advisory board, we developed a research plan that met the needs of scientists and community leaders alike: Half the homes would be randomly selected from the neighborhood, and the other half would be volunteers. If some volunteers were randomly selected, as happened, it would reduce the number of actual volunteers in the sample. Because of our commitment to public engagement and a belief that participants have a "right to know" their individual results, we worked with the community to develop guidelines for reporting study results back to communities and individual study participants. We also asked participants if they wanted to receive their individual-level results; 95% expressed a desire to receive their results.

After sampling the homes and processing the results, CBE staff met individually with each study participant to describe and discuss CBE's individual- and community-level results packets (for more detail about our report-back procedures, see Brody et al., 2009). In addition to communicating the results to individual study participants, we also communicated the results more broadly through community meetings held throughout the research process. We shared overall results in a panel format and then broke into smaller groups in which community members could ask more detailed questions and brainstorm how the results could be leveraged for policy purposes. Because we had been actively involved with community partners throughout the study, the results were seen as useful and important for people's lives. Participants spoke about the project with ownership and used *their* data in other public forums. For example, Richmond participants used their data at Richmond City Council and Planning Board meetings to successfully stop the proposed expansion of the Chevron oil refinery (Baker, 2009).

The involvement of many publics was central to every step of our research process. This study provides a formal example of CBPR, in which research is oriented to meet the needs of communities and all partners are involved at every stage of the research process. The study was directed to many different publics: organizations like CBE and Commonweal, the communities of Richmond and Bolinas, and study participants. We also see our research process as being influenced by, and relevant to, several broader publics, including refinery activists in the San Francisco area, environmental health activists in general, researchers in the environmental breast cancer movement such as Silent Spring Institute, and participants and researchers of other biomonitoring and household exposure studies. These different publics fundamentally affected how we conducted and disseminated our research. CBE members and community participants were actively involved in shaping our research plan. Meetings open to all Richmond residents allowed us to communicate our study process and results to the community as a whole and forced us to think about how to present our findings in ways that would be most useful for concerned residents, community leaders, and activists.

In essence, our research process depended on community participation, not just community input. Community partners were involved in every step of the research process, and academic partners were just as committed to this participation as were the community partners. This does not mean that CBPR projects are without tensions. On the community level, economic pressures and high levels of unemployment in Richmond came into conflict with environmental and health concerns when halting the refinery expansion coincided with refinery layoffs. Additionally, CBE sometimes felt torn between their multiple priorities and limited amount of time and resources, and they worried that spending more time on research activities might detract from time spent on community outreach activities. Researchers also had to balance time, resources, and different levels of involvement and commitment by different organizations. In the end, however, we believe that the strengths of this type of publicly oriented research far outweigh the added difficulties. The ideas and involvement of our publics improved our study design and implementation in many ways. In addition to examples discussed previously, being connected with a respected local organization meant that we had very high participation rates, even among randomly selected households.

The California project was firmly grounded scientifically, and we drew on sociology to inform our project design and methodology. Our research process was guided simultaneously by our desire to contribute to sociology and other academic disciplines and by our desire to conduct work that was relevant to the community concerns and policy goals of our nonacademic partners. We believe we have accomplished both of these goals. Our work has led to innovations in research ethics and report-back procedures, a new and increasingly important area of research that is responding to advances in biomonitoring and exposure science (Brody et al., 2007) as well as developing the concept of an "exposure experience," which describes the personal, lived experience of toxic exposure that results from low-level, daily life exposure (Altman et al., 2008). The report-back interviews were simultaneously useful for participants, who felt that the conversations alleviated some of their anxiety. These advances improve sociology's understanding of the embodied illness experience and also contribute to the field of environmental health.

Our work is also directly relevant to the construction of health and environmental policy, including locally, with Richmond residents using results from this study in addressing the proposed expansion of the Chevron refinery there; statewide, as California becomes the first to implement a statewide biomonitoring program that requires individual-level report-back of results; and nationally, as biomonitoring becomes increasingly widespread among academic and government studies (Morello-Frosch et al., 2009).

Five Lessons Learned

First, our public sociology serves *multiple publics*. Each project involves work done with and targeted to multiple publics. For example, with ENACT, our primary publics were ENACT members and neighborhood residents, even though not all neighborhood residents were actively involved in the remediation effort or related advocacy endeavors. Indirect publics include all Rhode Island residents, who can benefit from the statewide legislation enacted. For the Polluter Penalties Bill, we also served the needs of the Rhode Island Department of Environmental Management (DEM), which very much wanted this bill passed to give them more authority over industrial polluters. Our way of doing public sociology balances the competing and complementary needs of diverse groups of stakeholders. Some publics are directly involved in our research process; others are more important during outreach and dissemination phases; and some are indirect publics who may use or draw on our research but whose goals or experiences are not always central to our research process. This means, generally, that our work must be relevant and understandable both for the immediate community and academic partners with whom we work as well as for affected communities and the general public overall. Often our work includes media outreach: We invited journalists to community meetings in Richmond and received extensive press coverage in Rhode Island for a protest related to the passage of the Polluter Penalties Bill. Sometimes we work simultaneously with government and community-based organizations that have differences with each other (e.g., environmental organizations and state agencies in Rhode Island). This forces us to maintain separate relationships with each, while pressing for what we believe to be the best outcome and also encouraging the parties to deal with their disagreements. We also have to frame our approaches and commitments differently for funding agencies, university faculty and administrators, and our partners and reach compromises: We can't always have the most activist approach for all parties.

Second, our public sociology takes *multiple forms*. Sometimes, as our CBE work demonstrates, we are involved in formal CBPR partnerships, with community partners involved in and contributing to all stages of the research process. In other projects, like our work with ENACT, our work is directed by service and outreach goals or influenced by community needs in the form of an organizational partnership. And in other instances from work not discussed in this case study, the public sociology we do involves outreach or dissemination of findings (from our research or the research of others) without a formal partnership. But although our activities can take many forms, all types of public sociology depend on engaging with our multiple publics, so that our research and outreach is relevant to those most affected and helps build the organizational capacity of our community collaborators.

Third, our public sociology involves *long-lasting, dense networks of collaborative partners*. These connections take time, effort, and resources to develop and especially to maintain. This intensive engagement improves the research process in several ways. First, it builds trust between partners, because partners are familiar with each other and have gone through the research process together in the past (Birnbaum, Zenick, & Branche, 2009). Second, these networks improve the quality of work, because each collaborator has a unique set of skills and resources that he or she can bring to the table. For example, once Richmond residents had identified that they wanted to add a nonindustrial comparison community to the Household Exposure Study, research team members from Silent Spring Institute, Brown, and Berkeley were able to use their pre-existing relationships with Commonweal to link into a new research site relatively easily. Third, partners from previous projects can carry into new research projects, allowing for continuity between different collaborators and further feeding into the ability of all partners to communicate openly and work effectively with each other. For example, our partnership with ENACT developed through a Brown University connection to Toxics Action Center and the Center for Health, Environment and Justice, two resource centers for environmental health-oriented community-based organizations that had supported ENACT. In addition, ENACT members had initially approached the Brown Center for Environmental Studies to ask for help and dialogue about potential collaborations before the creation of this formalized partnership. Finally, these long-lasting collaborations can help all partners secure funding: Academic partners can assist community organizations with grant writing, and many sources of government or foundation funding require or prefer that academic researchers partner with local community organizations.

Fourth, our public sociology involves *raising new questions we would not otherwise know to ask*. Our work with CBE shows that engaging in public sociology and working with community partners strengthens the research process in dramatic and unpredictable ways. Researchers cannot know all the issues that are relevant or the questions that need to be asked unless they engage with and listen to those communities most affected by the phenomena at hand. For example, Bolinas was only added to the Household Exposure Study based on community interest, but having a comparison site proved quite useful in understanding universal exposures. Our engagement with community partners in California led us to new scientific innovations in the field of exposure science, led to further research topics (e.g., a new project on flame retardants), and ensured that our findings are relevant to the needs and concerns of the public. A huge part of doing relevant, rigorous sociology is knowing which questions to ask; by partnering with community groups, we learn about new research questions and methods. Our research process changes, adapting to local circumstances and needs and leading us into new, innovative, and fruitful avenues of research.

Fifth, our public sociology focuses on *building the capacity of community groups and recognizing the values of different skill sets*. A necessary component of successful public sociology is recognizing the diverse skills and capacities of different partners. For our environmental health research, we have found that it is essential to understand our partners' levels of scientific competence and literacy, to fill knowledge gaps identified by community partners, and to recognize that tensions are likely to develop as different partners balance different priorities (e.g., CBE's concerns about prioritizing science over community organizing). Along with recognizing the capacity of community groups to engage in scientific research, it is equally important to understand what all participants—academic researchers included—are able to contribute to the research project as a whole and to all other partners. In each collaboration we try to give back to the community groups as much as they give to us—to truly engage with them as partners. This perspective forces us to recognize that each partner has unique and valuable skills: For example, community partners can provide local knowledge, access, and experienced community leaders, while academic partners can provide scientific knowledge, political or organizational connections, and funding. Beyond identifying our distinct skills and assisting in the division of labor on a research project, focusing on the capacities of each collaborative partner focuses our attention on shared, common goals and adds to the capacities and skill sets of each group.

Public sociologists have endless publics and many possible outcomes to consider, which can lead to the proliferation of research methods. Regardless of the outcomes of interest or the publics involved—as seen in these two examples—these five key lessons should be integrated into all public sociology research to ensure rigor, relevance, and reach.

References

Altman, R. G., Brody, J., Rudel, R., Morello-Frosch, R., Brown, P., & Averick, M. (2008). Pollution comes home and gets personal: Women's experience of household toxic exposure. *Journal of Health and Social Behavior, 49*(4), 417–435.

Baker, D. (2009, June 9). Judge deals setback to Chevron refinery. *San Francisco Chronicle*, p. B-1.

Birnbaum, L. S., Zenick, H., & Branche, C. (2009). Environmental justice: A continuing commitment to an evolving concept. *American Journal of Public Health, 99*, S487–S489.

Brody, J. G., Morello-Frosch, R., Brown, P., Rudel, R., Gasior, R., Frye, M., et al. (2007). Is it safe?—New ethics for reporting personal exposures to environmental chemicals. *American Journal of Public Health, 97*, 1547–1554.

Brody, J. G., Morello-Frosch, R., Zota, A., Brown, P., Perez, C., & Rudel, R. (2009). Linking exposure assessment science with policy objectives for environmental justice and breast cancer advocacy: The Northern California Household Exposure Study. *American Journal of Public Health, 99*, S600–S609.

Environmental Neighborhood Awareness Committee of Tiverton (ENACT). (n.d.). *ENACT: The Environmental Neighborhood Awareness Committee of Tiverton.* Retrieved from http://www.enactri.org

Handle, L. (2003, March 5). Toxic soil worries owner of day-care center. *Providence Journal*.

Morello-Frosch, R., Brody, J. G., Brown, R., Altman, R. G., Ruthann A., & Rudel, C. P. (2009). Toxic ignorance and the right-to-know: Assessing strategies for biomonitoring results communication in a survey of scientists and study participants. *Environmental Health, 8*, 6. Retrieved from http:www.ehjournal.net/content/8/1/6

Senier, L., Hudson, B., Fort, S., Hoover, E., Tillson, R., & Brown, P. (2008). Brown Superfund Basic Research Program: A multistakeholder partnership addresses real-world problems in contaminated communities. *Environmental Science and Technology, 42*(13): 4655–4662.

Case Study 2.2. Learning From Disaster: Documenting the Impacts of Hurricane Katrina on Displaced College Students From New Orleans

Anthony E. Ladd and Duane A. Gill

This case study describes collaborative research to document the psychosocial impacts of Hurricane Katrina on the dislocated college students from New Orleans. Arguably one of the greatest disasters in U.S. history, Hurricane Katrina made landfall on the Mississippi–Louisiana state line on

August 29, 2005, killing more than 1,800 people, destroying up to 260,000 homes, and displacing more than a million people. Mississippi Gulf Coast communities bore the brunt of the winds and tidal surge, while New Orleans weathered the winds—but not the failure of its levees. The resulting flood inundated 80% of the city with up to 12 feet of water and revealed widespread social system failures as a root source of the disaster. The New Orleans Diaspora included some 50,000 college students, as well as faculty, staff, and administrators whose wind- and flood-damaged campuses were forced to close for the fall semester. Fortunately, colleges and universities across the country opened their admission doors to displaced students, and by mid-September, some 18,000 New Orleans students had relocated to more than 1,000 colleges and universities across the country.

As one of the many evacuees of the storm, the lead author of this chapter, Anthony Ladd, was invited to join a Visiting Scholars Program for displaced New Orleans faculty set up by Art Cosby and Duane Gill (second author) at Mississippi State University's (MSU) Social Science Research Center (SSRC). Five displaced scholars from New Orleans joined SSRC researchers to study the impacts of the disaster on college students—including MSU students. Compared to New Orleans colleges and universities, MSU was relatively unscathed. Nevertheless, Katrina passed over Starkville and the MSU campus as a tropical storm with wind gusts up to 76 miles per hour and torrential rains that forced cancellation of classes for two days, damaged buildings, and left parts of the local area without electrical power. Moreover, a number of MSU students were from the heavily damaged Mississippi Gulf Coast area and had families who were displaced by the hurricane.

The Katrina disaster provided a unique opportunity to engage in a type of public sociology. We wanted to understand the individual and collective experiences of our students by conducting research that our respective universities could use to improve preparedness in serving student needs after a disaster and increase institutional resilience. At the same time, we had an opportunity to contribute to the sociological study of disasters.

Research Design and Sample

We designed a Web-based survey to measure student impacts and needs in the aftermath of the Katrina disaster. Beginning with MSU, we developed a questionnaire that focused on storm and evacuation experiences; resource loss; satisfaction with the disaster response of government, media, social agencies, and the university; trust in institutions; levels of psychological stress; educational impacts; and other pertinent issues (Fee et al., 2006). We obtained institutional review board (IRB) approval and emailed surveys to the MSU student body (N = 15,889), receiving 3,140 in return (20%). After an initial analysis (see Gill et al., 2006), we revised the survey to consider the unique experiences of students from New Orleans universities and colleges.

We wanted to include as many New Orleans universities and colleges as possible, but disaster response priorities and logistics precluded most institutions from participating. In particular, it was extremely difficult to obtain IRB approval and access to student email addresses because key personnel were displaced. Our team included displaced faculty from three major New Orleans universities—Loyola University, University of New Orleans, and Xavier University—and they were instrumental in obtaining IRB approval from these institutions as well as access to computer files listing students' existing university email accounts, personal email accounts, and/or newly reported email accounts. Fortunately, these three institutions were fairly representative of the city's college student population.

In early November, nearly 27,000 Internet surveys were sent to registered students of the three universities. After a two-week period, two reminder emails were sent in one-week intervals, and data collection ended in mid-December. A total of 7,100 students (26%) responded with useable surveys. Overall, the sample characteristics were roughly proportionate to demographic profiles of each respective university, except that significantly more females than males responded (see Ladd, Marszalek, & Gill, 2006).

Psychosocial Impacts of Katrina

Mental health impacts were assessed using two standardized measures: the General Health Questionnaire (GHQ) and the Impact of Events Scale (IES). The GHQ (Goldberg, 1972) measures social dysfunction and depression in community settings and nonpsychiatric clinical settings (e.g., primary care or general practice). The IES (Horowitz, 1974) measures event-specific psychological stress based on the rationale that highly stressful events are likely to produce high levels of recurring, unintentional, distressing feelings and thoughts (intrusive stress), as well as high levels of intentional efforts to suppress these feelings and avoid reminders of the event (avoidance symptoms).

As we analyzed data from the New Orleans sample and compared it to the MSU sample, an amazing portrayal of our students' disaster experiences, impacts, and storm narratives began to emerge. Our data revealed that Hurricane Katrina created negative psychosocial reactions among both student groups. Compared to MSU students, however, New Orleans students experienced significantly higher levels of psychological distress as measured by the GHQ and IES (Gill, Ladd, & Marszalek, 2007). Specifically, New Orleans students reported levels of depression and loss of confidence that were three times that of MSU students. Further, more than one-fourth of the New Orleans students were in the severe range on the IES, while the majority of MSU students (60%) were in the subclinical range. Additional comparisons between the two groups indicated that New Orleans students experienced: (1) more fear and threat from the storm, (2) greater perceptions of human responsibility for the disaster, (3) greater economic and personal loss, (4) less satisfaction with disaster response, and (5) less trust in institutions.

Our data revealed that the levels of psychological stress experienced by New Orleans college students were influenced by their social vulnerability, disaster experiences, resource loss, perceptions of trust in disaster response institutions and organizations, and physical symptoms experienced during and after the disaster. As measured by the GHQ and IES, higher levels of psychological stress among displaced New Orleans students were associated with their degree of social vulnerability, traumatic disaster experiences, loss of resources, loss of social capital, and the number of physical symptoms they experienced. Our results lend support to previous studies examining levels of stress among college students affected by hurricanes, as well as research on the psychological and somatic impacts of natural and technological disasters.

Upon returning to New Orleans when universities and colleges reopened for the spring 2006 semester, many students continued to experience a prolonged series of secondary traumas that MSU students generally did not confront. These differential impacts between the two populations became magnified further in the coming months as many New Orleans students returned to find not only much of their flood-damaged city in ruins but their campuses grappling with infrastructure repairs, debt, reduced enrollments, and a host of future institutional uncertainties (see Gill, Ladd, & Marszalek, 2007). Under administrative declarations of "financial exigency" or other degrees of fiscal emergency, all New Orleans universities in our sample (and others) began to initiate draconian cuts in operating and salary budgets. Various degree programs and academic departments were discontinued, class offerings were reduced, assorted faculty and staff were either furloughed or terminated, and student activities were scaled back. Amid fears that even more stringent reductions might be forthcoming, a number of junior faculty left for positions at other institutions, some older faculty members took early retirements, and hundreds of students transferred to other universities to continue their educations.

Summarizing the devastation Katrina brought upon New Orleans universities, a report by the American Association of University Professors (AAUP) concluded these events constituted "undoubtedly the most serious disruption of American higher education in the nation's history" (American Association of University Professors, 2007, p. 61). Our research not only confirmed this assessment but revealed that the full range of impacts sustained by New Orleans college students were proxies for what many residents in communities along the Mississippi–Louisiana Gulf Coast experienced in the aftermath of Hurricane Katrina. Still, existing research has tended to view college students as a relatively unique group that is not representative of either the U.S. population or those typically victimized by disasters. Indeed, some studies have suggested that students are less likely than local residents to be affected by the direct impacts of hurricanes due to their greater socioeconomic resources and fewer obligations to family and community (Van Willigen, Edwards, Lormand, & Wilson, 2005). Our data, however, revealed that key elements of New Orleans student experiences— their psychological stress, lifestyle and lifescape changes, loss of jobs and resources, and feelings of recreancy (anger and frustration over the way governmental agencies failed to carry out their obligations)—resonated closely with accounts and impacts of other disaster survivors. We believe that, like the citizenry of New Orleans, most of these students will bear the mark of this historic storm and levee failure for the rest of their lives, no doubt remembering Katrina the way older New Orleanians remember Hurricanes Betsy and Camille from the 1960s.

Research Outcomes and Recommendations

Given the severity of Katrina's impacts and increased potential for prolonged disruption from future disasters, we have tried to serve the aims and values of public sociology by urging our university communities to work harder to improve institutional preparedness and mitigation procedures in the face of these growing hazards. Since 2006, we have disseminated our research findings through many venues (journal articles, book chapters, research monographs, conference papers, newspaper stories, campus presentations, invited lectures, etc.) and made the data available to our own university communities to assist them in becoming more resilient institutions in the aftermath of disaster. Toward this important goal, we specifically recommended a number of measures:

- Colleges and universities need to improve their telecommunications and information delivery technology to provide remote, off-campus backup systems that can be put into action in the event that their normal operating systems are damaged and/or without electricity.
- Colleges and universities should identify and work with other regional educational institutions to prepare for future campus evacuations that could result in hundreds of additional displaced students seeking temporary admission, housing, and other academic resources for at least one semester.

- Colleges and universities need to improve their social support and mental health counseling services to students who have been directly or indirectly affected by traumatic events.
- Colleges and universities need to improve their campus security capabilities and be prepared to convert dormitory facilities and other campus buildings to temporary shelters before and after a disaster strikes.
- Colleges and universities must make more financial assistance available to students who have lost jobs, income, cars, and housing after a disaster as well as provide collaborative opportunities for students to participate in local disaster relief efforts in the larger affected community.

The 2010 fifth anniversary of Hurricane Katrina and the lessons learned from the 2008 coastal evacuation for Hurricane Gustav are powerful reminders of the need for campus communities to become better equipped to deal with disasters. In light of scientific predictions for increased hurricane activity in the Gulf of Mexico, it seems certain that university disaster preparedness and resiliency will be tested many times in the future. To date, many universities in the region have adopted a number of the mitigation measures suggested previously, and every campus has improved its policies for disaster/emergency preparedness and recovery.

In addition to improving the resiliency of regional colleges and universities, our study has contributed to the evolving academic literature on Hurricane Katrina as well as the larger field of disaster research. Numerous books, articles, papers, and media reports on Katrina have emerged since the disaster; our work is unique in its focus on college students. Indeed, the disaster experiences and impacts captured in both our quantitative data and the thousands of qualitative student narratives we gathered constitute a rich and important contribution to the literature on the "Voices of Katrina." Given the significant psychosocial impacts and challenges our research has documented, we believe that social scientists must pay greater attention to the effects of disasters on university communities and how these events parallel other populations and institutions.

Conducted in the post-disaster period, when many displaced residents were struggling to make sense of the tragedy through a lens of personal grief and collective national trauma, our work shows students similarly grappling with their own "storm stories" and trying to reflect on what had happened to them and how it was likely to affect their education and future. Yet, after five years, the aftermath and legacy of Hurricane Katrina is still a day-to-day reality in New Orleans as well as much of coastal Mississippi. The traumatic events and memories surrounding this historic disaster—significantly compounded now by the 2010 BP Deepwater

Horizon explosion and oil catastrophe in the Gulf of Mexico—will continue to unfold for years to come and will forever reside in the hearts and consciousness of those who experienced it.

References

American Association of University Professors. (2007). Hurricane Katrina and New Orleans universities. *Academe, 93*, 59–126.

Fee, V., Edwards, J. F., Cross, G. W., Edwards, A. K., Gill, D. A., Wells-Parker, E., et al. (2006). *Student needs and impacts surrounding Hurricane Katrina: A survey of Mississippi State University students.* Mississippi State, MI: Mississippi State University, Social Science Research Center.

Gill, D. A., Ladd, A. E., Cross, G. W., Fee, V., Edwards, J. F., Marszalek, J., et al. (2006). Impacts of Hurricane Katrina on Mississippi State University students. In Natural Hazards Center (Ed.), *Learning from catastrophe: Quick response research in the wake of Hurricane Katrina* (pp. 373–402). Boulder, CO: Natural Hazards Center.

Gill, D. A., Ladd, A. E., & Marszalek, J. (2007). College students' experiences with Hurricane Katrina: A comparison between students from Mississippi State University and three New Orleans universities. *Journal of the Mississippi Academy of Sciences, 52*(4), 262–280.

Goldberg, D. P. (1972). *The detection of psychiatric illness by questionnaire.* London, UK: Oxford University Press.

Horowitz, M. J. (1974). Stress response syndromes: Character style and brief psychotherapy. *Archives of General Psychiatry, 31*, 768–781.

Ladd, A. E., Marszalek, J., & Gill, D. A. (2006, March 22–26). *The other diaspora: New Orleans student evacuation impacts and responses surrounding Hurricane Katrina.* Paper presented at the annual meetings of the Southern Sociological Society, New Orleans, LA.

Van Willigen, M., Edwards, B., Lormand, S., & Wilson, K. (2005). Comparative assessment of impacts and recovery from Hurricane Floyd among student and community households. *Natural Hazards Review, 6*(4), 180–190.

Case Study 2.3. Working for Global Environmental Justice: Channeling Privilege, Producing New Knowledge

David N. Pellow

Michael Kimmel and Abby Ferber define *privilege* as the experience of being a part of one or more social groups that benefit from inequality but rarely have to account for it because privilege is often culturally invisible (Kimmel & Ferber, 2010). I employ the concept of privilege here to frame my case study as to the role I played as a public sociologist working with environmental justice activists.

Scholars and activists have, since the 1970s, presented evidence that people of color, as well as poor, working-class, and indigenous communities face greater threats from pollution and industrial hazards than do other groups. Environmental threats include municipal and hazardous waste incinerators, garbage dumps, coal-fired power plants, polluting manufacturing facilities, toxic schools, occupationally hazardous workplaces, substandard housing, uneven impacts of climate change, and the absence of healthy food sources. Marginalized communities tend to confront a disproportionate volume of these threats—what researchers and advocates have labeled *environmental injustice* and *environmental racism*. These communities are also more likely to be affected by extractive industrial operations such as mining, large dams, and timber harvesting, as well as natural disasters like flooding, earthquakes, and hurricanes. We observe these patterns at the local, regional, national, and global scales, and the damage to public health, cultures, economies, and ecosystems from such activities is well documented. In response, community leaders have built social movements to articulate and demand environmental justice.

Environmental justice is a goal in which no community is unfairly burdened with pollution or other environmental harms and when social justice and ecological sustainability prevail. Environmental justice is the right to a decent, safe quality of life for people of all races, incomes, and cultures in the environments where we live, work, play, learn, and pray (Bullard, 2005). It is a vision that emphasizes accountability, democratic practices, equitable treatment, and self-determination. In other words, environmental justice challenges many of the inequalities and abuses associated with social privilege.

Minnesota Global Justice Project

As a university professor I have accepted the fact that I enjoy many social privileges. However, rather than feeling guilty about it or ignoring it and doing nothing, I choose to strategically use my privilege in ways that build bridges between universities and communities struggling for environmental justice. As the facilitator of the Minnesota Global Justice Project (MGJ), I work to connect social science research with grassroots politics, and I find inspiration from a number of sources. For example, a colleague of mine once stated, "Sustainable knowledge is one of the most important foundations of sustainable communities." I instantly understood her point and its implications for public sociology and social change. As Eyerman and Jamison

(1991) argue, "It is precisely in the creation, articulation, and formulation of new thoughts and ideas—new knowledge—that a social movement defines itself in society" (p. 55). If new knowledge is at the center of what constitutes a social movement, then public sociologists are in an ideal position to contribute to social change, since we make a living creating and sharing ideas with our students, colleagues, and the public.

In 2008 I joined a collaborative effort with two nongovernmental organizations (NGOs) dedicated to environmental justice with the goal of writing a guide for community leaders confronting threats from mining companies operating primarily in global South nations. The two NGOs are Global Response (GR) and DECOIN (*Defensa y Conservacion Ecologica de Intag/* Intag Defense and Ecological Conservation group). Since 1990, Global Response has worked in solidarity with indigenous and other global South communities whose ecological resources and political rights are at risk from the activities of transnational corporations and the international financial institutions that support them. This frequently involves threats from oil, gold, silver, and coal mining, timber harvesting, and hydroelectric dam construction. Global Response has members in more than 100 nations who write letters urging the key decision makers in these cases to dramatically transform their practices to ensure basic rights and sustainable practices or cease operations altogether. DECOIN is an organization based in the Intag cloud forest region of Ecuador. Its members have successfully expelled some of the world's largest mining companies from the area after having experienced enormous environmental harm to the land and human health. DECOIN has also successfully launched sustainable businesses to provide a decent and nonexploitative living for community members.

The extraordinary damage to ecosystems and human health associated with large-scale mining operations has been documented in the United States, Latin America, Europe, Africa, Asia, and the Arctic. Some of the problems include high rates of morbidity and mortality within the surrounding communities and the work force, fish kills, coral reef destruction, deforestation, soil erosion, and the poisoning of farmland (Gedicks, 1993, 2001; LaDuke, 2005). And when communities have fought back against large mining companies and governments, the response of these companies and governments often involves intimidation, imprisonment, torture, murder, rape, and other human rights violations.

Few written resources exist to assist community activists in their efforts to combat these practices, so Global Response, DECOIN, and the Minnesota Global Justice Project teamed up to produce such a tool. I knew the folks at both NGOs since I had previously served as a board member and actions committee member at Global Response; GR had worked directly with

DECOIN on a campaign years ago. I was delighted to join this effort as facilitator of the MGJ and as an activist-scholar who could bring concepts from social movement theory like collective action frames, resource mobilization, and political opportunity structures to a situation facing real people on the ground. These sociological concepts helped the team think through more systematically how resistance movements make known their concerns and most effectively work to realize them in the face of repression and uneven power relations among actors involved. And while the specific language and discourse of social movement theory may not appear in our final product, they informed the process from the beginning.

In March 2009 we completed our report, titled *Protecting Your Community Against Mining Companies and Other Extractive Industries: A Guide for Community Organizers* (Zorrilla, Buck, Palmer, & Pellow, 2009). I was the only professional academic working on the project, although I had assistance from a graduate student and an undergraduate student at my university. The other principal authors of the guide were three community activists. We worked together for many months gathering data and writing drafts. The resources for this project came from two sources: (1) in-kind support from the authors and staff members who volunteered much of their labor, and (2) funds from the Minnesota Global Justice Project that were used for the production and dissemination of the guide and to provide compensation for students and partial compensation for authors.

My social science training was most useful for (1) framing the issues of power and political opportunities for the guide, (2) researching case studies regarding social movement opposition to mining companies, and (3) assisting with writing the report. As a public sociologist, I viewed my role as someone who could bring a critical scholarly eye to the project while ensuring its accessibility to broader publics.

The guide contains several cases that detail how activists and residents can work to secure their communities in the face of predatory actions by transnational corporations seeking to siphon off local minerals. The range of activities we examine includes building alliances and coalitions; using the law and the political process; framing messages and using the media; organizing globally; and engaging in direct action. The guide features an in-depth discussion of common mining company tactics to split community loyalties and to encourage governments to allow access to mineral wealth, along with examples of how activists have challenged them. The final section of the report contains a list of resources with the names of nongovernmental organizations around the world working on mining justice campaigns, technical and legal information, and a smaller subsection on how grassroots activists can use the media to their benefit.

Impact of the Guide

The impact of the guide was immediate. Since it was released in 2009, activists in Europe, Canada, East and West Africa, Latin America, Asia, and the United States have used it in their campaigns and in their broader efforts to educate and enlist support from residents in affected areas. An activist from Sierra Leone told me, "My community is fighting a mine right now and this guide is a great help to us." When I was at the annual Earth First! Round River Rendezvous in June 2009, one of the event organizers told me, "A friend of mine who is an anti-mining activist said this was the single best resource on the subject he has ever seen."

TESTIMONIAL FROM "BRIANA"

"Briana," a community activist in Mexico, used the *Protecting Your Community Against Mining Companies and Other Extractive Industries: A Guide for Community Organizers* in her fieldwork. She sent us this testimonial, dated January 4, 2010.

After decades of clear cut logging, the average person one talks to in the [region] will say there is nothing one can do to stop such activities because the authorities are only interested in enriching themselves. This perception has been echoed when people are questioned about mining. Most worrisome is that a large portion of the population seems unaware that mining is coming to change their way of life forever.

When we began our project, the movement against mining was small and uncoordinated. People would come to our office individually or in small groups to ask, always in whispers, for information about the plans for mines in their communities. Specific information about timelines for initiating mining was, and for the most part continues to be, nearly impossible to obtain. Generally, people in the most remote areas tend to be fearful of confronting the authorities.

Our work began with meetings with key individuals and a group of indigenous doctors, all of whom were poised to organize resistance given their work and stated desire to protect the people and the watershed. We provided information about...the dangers of mining; the track record of transnational mining companies in terms of accidents, contamination and the outcome of lawsuits by aggrieved communities; and international treaties and agreements that protect the interest and welfare of indigenous communities where mining companies hope to operate. We also discussed nonviolent protest and legal channels for opposing the imposition of mining in the communities.

We organized a three-day event with 250 representatives from the communities and...people came from all over the [region] for the meeting, indicating that they were ready to organize themselves. Unfortunately people have received "warnings" about questioning plans for mines and the leader of a strong movement in one community where a mine already operates was jailed under questionable charges.

But this is fast changing....The guide, which Global Response generously provided, proved to be very important for this effort. We distributed over 100 copies. Copies of copies are being made by those who received our copies. The guide provides a cool-headed orientation on how to proceed with resistance via national and international legal systems. This is important so that people can proceed....The movement...is quickly gaining strength under the leadership of the Church. The priests are using the approach of empowering people so that they will lead their own response to threats to public health and common environs. We were glad to be able to feed information to the key people who are the appropriate ones to organize further. Now it is up to the people to stand firm for the better world we all work for.

I had to work under the radar, which meant not using my phone or email when these would have been the easiest and fastest ways to coordinate. We had to do everything face to face, which in this region practically means having to go look for people on market days and hope you find them. Despite my efforts to remain invisible, I was visited by people who wanted to check up on me. But all told, I believe that the collaboration was more effective than we'd hoped and we were able to surpass our goals. Thank you for your support and for caring about the people of [this region].

Martin, an activist who works with an organization to confront extractive companies exploiting native communities in Southeast Asia, also was pleased to use the guide. He offered to translate it into a local language, thus making it more accessible to residents:

Our work is focused on providing indigenous communities with information that they can use to organize, to see through company tactics, to think through alternatives, and generally to support them in making decisions about their own futures. We were excited to read your guide; the analysis, approach and language are very close to our own. Over the last 3 years we've been working on the issue of oil palm plantations in Indonesia. We are developing more written modules to accompany the community film we made about the plantations. We would like to translate your guide on company tactics into Bahasa

Indonesia. A lot of the guide is relevant to oil palm and to Indonesia and it would be immediately useful in the dissemination of information to communities. (Communication from "Martin," community activist in the United Kingdom, April 2009)

Martin indicated that his organization would raise the money for the translation and also told us that he would try to meet with some of us during a future trip to Ecuador.

While much of the feedback on the guide has been positive, the authors expected that sooner or later the mining industry would get hold of the document and respond. It didn't take long. In early 2010 a documentary that was financed in part by North American mining corporations active in Ecuador contained a segment that was critical of the anti-mining movement in that nation, specifically targeting Carlos Zorrilla and the sections of the guide he authored. The documentary argues that the guide distorts facts and encourages extreme tactics to oppose mining operations. Zorrilla and I, along with the other authors of the guide, are considering our response at the time of this writing, but one thing is clear: We have touched a nerve and produced a document that has threatened at least one aspect of power relationships between global South communities and transnational corporations.

Thoughts on Privilege and Public Sociology

As a North American university–based scholar, I have the privilege of considerable resources at my disposal. As an activist-scholar studying and working with environmental justice leaders in the United States and globally, I have had amazing experiences collaborating with people outside of academia to produce new knowledge in the service of social change. In that sense, I like to think that I am using my privilege in a productive way and, in some small measure, challenging the social relations that create and legitimate gross hierarchies among nations, communities, humankind, and ecosystems. The production of new knowledge is a critical goal that public sociologists pursue, and we should never underestimate its value for facilitating social change.

References

Bullard, R. (Ed). (2005). *The quest for environmental justice: Human rights and the politics of pollution.* San Francisco, CA: Sierra Club Books.

Eyerman, R., & Jamison, A. (1991). *Social movements: A cognitive approach.* University Park, PA: Pennsylvania State University Press.

Gedicks, A. (1993). *The new resource wars: Native and environmental struggles against multinational corporations*. Boston, MA: South End Press.

Gedicks, A. (2001). *Resource rebels: Native challenges to mining and oil corporations*. Boston, MA: South End Press.

Kimmel, M., & Ferber, A. L. (Eds.). (2010). *Privilege*. Boulder, CO: Westview Press.

LaDuke, W. (2005). *Recovering the sacred: The power of naming and claiming*. Boston, MA: South End Press.

Zorrilla, C., Buck, A., Palmer, P., & Pellow, D. (2009). *Protecting your community against mining companies and other extractive industries*. Boulder, CO: Global Response and the Minnesota Global Justice Project.

CASE STUDIES 3

Regional Research and Data Collection to Enhance Public Knowledge

Have you ever read a research article and found it difficult to follow? Students often ask, "Why is there so much jargon? Why is this so difficult to comprehend?" Public sociologists are particularly good at breaking down research so that it makes sense to the general public; they are skilled at peeling back the layers of academic jargon while preserving essential sociological analysis, ensuring that their research is understood and made accessible. In this section, five public sociologists share how their research enhances public knowledge by helping communities, policy makers, and local, regional, and state governments make use of sociological data and analysis to inform critical social issues.

In the first case study of this section, Garth Taylor describes the work of the Metro Chicago Information Center (MCIC), established in 1990 to collect demographic and baseline data on social policy and human needs in the greater Chicago area. Taylor shares research findings from MCIC projects designed to inform investment programs for urban neighborhoods. From these projects, MCIC developed extensive methods for understanding place-based investment strategies. As explained in this case study, an important distinction is made between investments that focus on *people* (e.g., job training, financial literacy) and investments that focus on *place* (e.g., housing development, business strip renovation). Using examples from several MCIC projects, Taylor examines key indicators critical to successful place-based initiatives: typology of contexts, connection to region, neighborhood stress, and resilience. Taylor offers a set of practices and six valuable lessons assembled from the expansive and innovative MCIC research to help practitioners and researchers make data useful for place-based initiatives.

The second case study describes *The Sacramento State Annual Survey of the Region*, a multi-unit collaborative housed at Sacramento State University.

Amy Liu involves undergraduate and graduate students in collecting data on residents' opinions about quality-of-life issues in California. Students conduct the annual surveys in a CATI (computer-assisted telephone interview) lab, analyze the data, and report the results. The findings and reports from this annual survey are used extensively by local and state organizations as well as by California policy makers. Liu describes the enormous benefit to students who have the opportunity to experience, firsthand, the many steps of the research process from identifying survey questions by talking to community leaders and residents, to data collection, analysis, and dissemination.

In the third case study, Michael Leachman describes his work at a non-profit research and advocacy organization, the Oregon Center for Public Policy (OCPP), tackling food security needs of low-income Oregon residents. Faced with an unusual challenge, Leachman describes the advocacy work of OCPP in addressing claims by the Oregon governor's office, who questioned the validity of a U.S. Department of Agriculture (USDA) report listing Oregon as having one of the highest hunger rates in the nation. OCPP began a media campaign educating the governor's office and other key policy makers of the accuracy and validity of the USDA findings and the need to improve the hunger rates on low-income Oregon residents. What followed was an anti-hunger campaign using state and national data, and grassroots organizing, to make OCPP's case and successfully redress Oregon's public food assistance system.

The last two case studies are both based in North Carolina. Leslie Hossfeld describes an interesting type of public sociology involving a poverty information project called PovertyEast.org. Faced with a dwindling budget, a nonprofit organization got together to figure out the best way to use their remaining resources. They developed a website that provides a host of data pertaining to quality-of-life indicators for 41 high-poverty counties in eastern North Carolina. The website makes available county profiles, research briefs, and downloadable PowerPoint presentations that can be easily accessed for community presentations, grant writing, and policy making. One of the outcomes of this project resulted in the development of the Poverty Reduction and Economic Recovery Legislative Study Commission by the State of North Carolina.

In the final case study in this section, Paul Luebke offers a different perspective on public sociology. Paul is both an academic sociologist and a state legislator in North Carolina. In this case study, Luebke describes his journey as a public sociologist and elected official and how his own research informed both his career as an activist-scholar and a lawmaker. He speaks candidly about the early tensions within his academic department, how he navigates his roles as researcher and elected official, and how he uses sociological data to inform both. This case study is particularly helpful to those interested in the relationship between sociological research and public policy.

Case Study 3.1. Neighborhood, Region, and Place: The Chicago Experience[1]

Garth Taylor

Organizations dedicated to community improvement make a distinction between investments that focus on *people* (e.g., job training, financial literacy) and investments that focus on *place* (e.g., housing development, business strip renovation). The difference is significant because philanthropy frequently wants to improve places by helping individual people, but when people develop more human, social, or cultural capital they become enabled to move to a new place, taking the value of the investment with them. The aim of place-based initiatives such as the New Communities Program (NCP; focusing on 18 Chicago neighborhood areas) or the Partnership for New Communities (PNC; focusing on several public housing transformation sites in Chicago) is to support investments that will sustainably improve the quality of life in targeted places (see www.newcommunities.org and www.thepartnershipfornewcommunities.org). Since the early 1990s, the Metro Chicago Information Center (MCIC) has conducted close to 1,000 projects that relate to designing, monitoring, or evaluating place-based initiatives.

Background on MCIC

The Metro Chicago Information Center was created in 1990 by members of the Commercial Club of Chicago to collect demographic and baseline data on social policy and human needs on a regular basis in order to create a more complete picture of the seven-county metropolitan Chicago region. The goal was to empower the nonprofit sector with critical information to make better strategic development decisions. In the past 20 years, MCIC has worked with hundreds of organizations locally and nationally, providing

[1]This case study is based on work funded by the John D. and Catherine T. MacArthur Foundation and the Chicago-based New Communities Program. The author thanks the many people who worked with him on these projects and have freely shared their ideas (many of which are included here). The list is long but includes Joel Bookman, Rob Chaskin, George Galster, Andy Mooney, Susan Lloyd, Taryn Roch, and colleagues on the MDRC evaluation research team.

solutions in data sourcing, preparation, and visualization, for turning data into action (see www.mcic.org).

The projects described here developed as the research/monitoring/evaluation component of extremely large-scale investment programs targeted for urban neighborhoods. The steering committees chose MCIC as the research partner, based on its long-established presence in the community as an objective, responsive social science resource. Grant and/or contract funds through local foundation partners and/or city government were provided to MCIC to undertake its activities.

The research process, in each case, began with a review of the goals of the investment program. A lengthy back-and-forth discussion of available data sources, potential metrics, and benchmarks for evaluating change followed. The social science of the project evolved as the development project itself increased in scope and implementation. It was important to base public sociology on a methodology that could expand, and occasionally retrofit, as community development projects evolved, primarily by building a substantial role for objective indicators from small-area databases with a long time series.

Funding provided to MCIC as a research partner for these projects included support to test the validity of indicators, develop new means for visualizing data and making them Web-accessible, and presenting these results at meetings of professional peers such as the National Neighborhood Indicator Partnership.[2]

This case study presents some of MCIC's methods for understanding place and ways that this understanding may be used to shape place-based investment strategies in these diverse sectors.

Typologies of Context

Understanding neighborhood context is key to knowing which kinds of investments have the best chance of success and which benchmarks ought to be applied for monitoring and evaluating change. Every neighborhood is unique. But there are also systematic forces in a neighborhood's social and economic context.

Until recently, the focus on context was about gentrification versus disinvestment: (1) in *gentrifying* neighborhoods, the dialogue was about

---

[2]The National Neighborhood Indicators Partnership (NNIP) is a collaborative effort by the Urban Institute and partner organizations from U.S. cities to further the development and use of neighborhood-level information systems in local policy making and community building. http://www2.urban.org/nnip/

whether it is a good or bad thing, whether it can be harnessed for "good," and whether residents who worked to improve the community will be displaced and lose the benefit of their efforts; and (2) in neighborhoods suffering *disinvestment*, population loss, and loss of the middle class, the dialogue was about how to deal with blighted buildings while respecting the rights of the remaining low-income population and how to attract outside investment—or even gentrification (albeit limited and controlled). Strategies used to improve the quality of life in communities undergoing gentrification are different from strategies used in neighborhoods facing disinvestment.

To understand which places are which, MCIC analyzed long-term patterns of economic change in Chicago's historically defined 77 community areas and developed an Index of Economic Diversity that classifies neighborhoods according to (1) whether the number of low-income families is increasing; and (2) whether the number of high-income families is increasing. The resulting fourfold classification is shown in Figure CS3.1.

Figure CS3.1   Neighborhood Context of Income Diversity

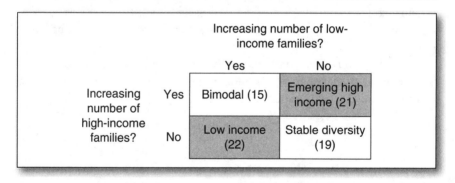

"Emerging High-Income" (gentrifying) areas are the 21 neighborhoods where the number of high-income families is increasing and the number of low-income families is stable or declining. Within this category, neighborhoods differed in the time of onset of gentrification: in the 1970s (2 neighborhoods), in the 1980s (12 neighborhoods), and in the 1990s (7 neighborhoods). There are 22 neighborhoods that show the opposite pattern: The number of low-income families is increasing, and the number of high-income families is stable or declining. In this group, 11 neighborhoods still have a significant number of high-income families, so they are described as "Emerging Low-Income" areas, whereas the other 11 neighborhoods have almost no high-income residents and are described as "Disinvested" areas. It was not anticipated that 19 areas—about one-quarter of the city's neighborhoods—would be characterized by "Stable Diversity"—that is, little change since the 1970s in the number of high-income families and the number of low-income families. These places tend to be off the radar screen, but they are important for understanding how neighborhoods change because stable economic diversity is an explicit goal of most place-based improvement strategies. There are 15 neighborhoods in which the number of high-income families and the number of low-income families are both increasing. The neighborhoods are statistically diverse, but on closer look these neighborhoods almost all have a spatially segregated pattern of change, with high-income growth in one part of the neighborhood and low-income growth in another part—an inherently unstable, bimodal situation, with substantial pressure for gentrification.

Connection to the Region

Place-based development usually places a priority on linking neighborhoods to outside economic resources (e.g., jobs) and on strategies to attract outside investment to communities (Katz, 2004). There are databases to track some regional linkages and outside investments: (1) Community Reinvestment Act (CRA) Business Lending data show the trend in small (up to $1 million) loans to businesses; (2) MCIC acquires data on local government spending on infrastructure and business strip improvement and recodes this data into tract scores; (3) Local Employment Dynamics (LED) data from the Census Bureau demonstrate regional labor market connections; for residents in a neighborhood, LED data show the tracts where they work. A regionally integrated neighborhood is one in which a large proportion of residents work in jobs outside the local area, as shown in Table CS3.1 for a typical Chicago community.

Table CS3.1   Neighborhood Connection to Regional Labor Market

Where people work who live in Humboldt Park		
Chicago	9,852	59%
Suburban Cook Co.	4,329	26%
Elsewhere	2,530	15%

Another way to analyze regional connection is to use LED data on the industry of jobs held by people who live in a neighborhood and compare this to the profile of jobs in the region. Table CS3.2 shows an Industry Concentration Index—the proportion among neighborhood residents divided by the proportion in the benchmark area. It is a version of the "location index" frequently used in regional economic research. A regionally integrated neighborhood is a place where the concentration indexes are close to 1.0.

Table CS3.2   Neighborhood Connection to Regional Industry Base

Industry	Employed Residents	Chicago	Concentration Index
Manufacturing	2,633	|||||||||||| ||||||||||	47.9
Retail Trade	2,064	||||||||||| ||||||||||	24.6
Accommodation, Food Svs	1,454	||||||||| |||||||||	6.9
Education, Public Admin	1,161	||||| ||||||||||	−31.7
Health Care, Social Asst	2,294	|||||||||||| ||||||||||||||	6.6
Arts, Entertainment, Rec	255	| ||	−6.6
Information	335	|| ||||	−31.8
Finance, Insurance	847	||||| ||||||||||	−36.0
Prof, Scientific, Technical Svs	861	||||| ||||||||||	−43.1

Neighborhood Stress

During the housing bubble, data on mortgage lending, speculator purchases, sub-prime lending, home sales, and foreclosures were typically combined into indexes of neighborhood market *strength*. Now these data are used to measure *stress*.

As Figure CS3.2 shows, the amount of stress has to do with the degree of downward inflection in the graph of market conditions—in this case sales volume and median sales price. In Chicago, the number of single-family home sales dropped by about 35% between 2006 and 2008, while the price dropped by about 4% (inflation adjusted). So for the average neighborhood, the stress in the market for single-family homes is that it has become very difficult to sell, and the price has declined a little. The market for multiple-unit dwellings is another story; between 2006 and 2008 the number of sales dropped by about 54% and the median sale price fell by about 46%.

Figure CS3.2   Neighborhood Market Stress

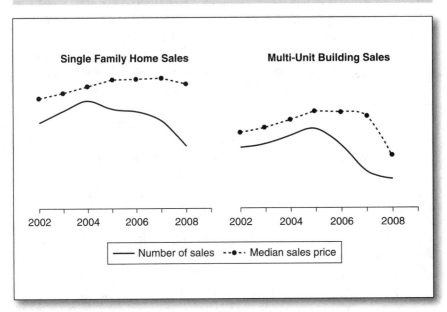

Citywide totals tell the average story. The need to adapt place-based strategies to context arises because *not all communities experienced equal amounts of stress*. Among the 77 Chicago community areas, the change between 2006 and 2008 in the *number* of single family home sales ranges from –56% to +11%—that is, a handful of neighborhoods had very little change, and some increased sales even though there was a regional downturn. A similar observation applies to the pattern of change in the price of single family homes.

Resilience

The most relevant aspect of neighborhood context is no longer the pattern of gentrification and disinvestment. Most relevant now is the level of stress in a neighborhood and the presence of assets that modulate stress—what many now describe as assets that support *resilience* in the face of adversity (Chaskin, 2008). Measuring the extent of neighborhood assets that modulate stress and support resilience can help target investments where they can do the most good.

The term *resilience* appears in the literature of almost every scientific discipline ranging from biology and ecology to political science and organizational theory. It refers to the ability of a system to bounce back from an external stressor or challenge and recover healthy functioning. Interesting, however, there is no consistent operational definition of the concept or how to measure it. To support place-based strategies, the most helpful definition of resilience might be one that distinguishes (1) neighborhood *features that promote resilience*—such as social capital—from (2) the *pattern of change* in a measure that shows how much a neighborhood has "bounced back and recovered"— such as housing prices.

A place-based theory of resilience might begin by asking why some communities are considered by their residents to be a pleasant place to live and raise children, even though the neighborhood is, by conventional standards, poor and run-down. A great deal of community research has focused on ways that place-based amenities, anchor institutions, and social patterns help overcome negative neighborhood features (Taub, Taylor, & Dunham, 1984):

1. The Project on Human Development in Chicago Neighborhoods found that the prevailing level of *collective efficacy* in a place predicts lower crime rates (Sampson et al., 1997).

2. Architects and planners argue that good urban design can lower crime and increase the perceived value of public space among residents by creating *defensible space* (Cisneros, 1995) increasing the number of *eyes on the street* (Jacobs, 1961), and following design practices that increase the accessibility and *use of public space* (Whyte, 1988).

3. MCIC found that low-income neighborhoods with many *opportunities for informal arts participation* (e.g., poetry reading, open mike performances, photography displays) tend to be safer, have better school performance measures, and are more likely to attract population than similar neighborhoods without such activity—suggesting that cultural participation contributes to resiliency (Taylor, 2008).

4. It is likely that because of the recent increase in crime rates (after many years of decline in American cities), there will be renewed discussion of *policing practices* that target public disorder as a way of modulating stress and increasing resilience (Kelling & Coles, 1996; Skogan, 2006).

Measuring Resilience

To monitor progress toward the goals of NCP, PNC, and other place-based initiatives, MCIC acquires data from national and local sources to develop 92 neighborhood indicators organized according to the seven topic areas shown in Table CS3.3. An Index of Community Change includes 19 measures of neighborhood *status* (concentration, rate) and 61 measures of neighborhood *trajectory* (trend, rate of change). Monitoring status measures alone would repeat again and again the finding that there are low-asset, disinvested communities. Measuring change adjusts for the level of *challenge* and shifts the focus to the *return on investment* by allowing each community to function as its own baseline.

Table CS3.3   Data Sources for Measuring Neighborhood Context and Resilience

Scale	Number of Scale Component Measures			Descriptive Use Only, not in Scale
	Trend	Concentration,	Rate	
1 Employment, Jobs	4	‖‖ ‖	1	1
2 Business in the Community	7	‖‖‖‖‖ ‖‖	3	5
3 Community Capital Flow	21	‖‖‖‖‖‖‖‖‖‖‖‖‖‖‖ ‖‖	4	4
4 Health, Ambience	10	‖‖‖‖‖‖‖ ‖‖‖‖	7	–
5 Social Participation	5	‖‖‖ ‖‖	3	–
6 Stable Income Diversity	4	‖‖‖	0	1
7 Education	10	‖‖‖‖‖‖ ‖	1	1
Community Change Index (all scales combined)	61	‖‖‖‖‖‖‖‖‖‖‖‖‖‖‖‖‖‖‖‖‖‖‖‖‖‖‖ ‖‖‖‖‖‖ 19		12

Table CS3.4 illustrates neighborhood differences in assets that modulate stress, based on a simple classification of Chicago neighborhoods by median income and percentage of homeowners: (1) assets that promote resilience vary by neighborhood context (the scores vary in each row), and (2) neighborhoods that are low on one type of asset can be high on another (each column has a "high score"). The patterns mean that place-based strategies to support resilience ought to vary depending on the level of stress in the neighborhood and the specific resiliency factors present.

Finding Meaning in Large Quantities of Data

Most researchers and policy makers would agree that more than a handful of indicators are required to understand the complexity of community change. But nearly everyone also agrees that more than a handful of indicators are too many to understand at once—the forest gets lost among the trees. MCIC has developed practices for tracking complex change and communicating results.

Humans are programmed to rely on *benchmarks* to help judge whether change is substantively significant or whether it is "about what we would expect." Potential benchmarks for place-based programs are nearby

Table CS3.4 Neighborhood Assets That Modulate Stress

Indicators	Neighborhood Context			
	High-Income Rental	Low-Income Rental	Low-Income Owner	High-Income Owner
Personal, Social Capital of Residents				
Presence of College Educated Population	47%	15%	10%	20%
Commercial/Non-Profit Infrastructure				
Cultural Business per 10K pop	22.7	8.2	6.7	18.5
Health Care Offices per 10K pop	10.1	46.4	33.8	15.7
Elderly and Social Services per 10K pop	29.3	98.0	57.9	30.1
Perceptions of Safety				
Annual % decline personal crime rate	5.4%	5.0%	1.0%	1.5%
Annual % decline property crime rate	3.7%	2.1%	1.9%	2.8%

Table CS3.5   Measuring Neighborhood Progress Versus Benchmark

	Rate 2008	Change 2002–2008 (%)	Rating
Near West Side	876.1	–30	Improving faster than benchmark: 2
South Lawndale	219.6	–20	
Quad Communities	458.8	–19	Improving at benchmark: 1
Chicago Lawn Area	481.6	–13	
East Garfield Park	745.5	–3	Little change: 0
Auburn Gresham	633.5	2	
Washington Park	806.6	9	Worsening: –1
Woodlawn	685.2	15	
Chicago total	**463.1**	**–13**	

neighborhoods, similar neighborhoods in the city that are not nearby, citywide patterns, regional patterns, and national patterns. Complex monitoring programs often use more than one benchmark, but they usually include a citywide benchmark because most people have a sense of how their city has been changing. Table CS3.5 shows an example of an indicator presentation using a citywide benchmark. The indicator is the trend in property crime—shown in the second column from the right. The citywide benchmark (–13%) is at the bottom of this column. The column all the way to the right is a verbal description of how the neighborhood change compares to the citywide pattern (e.g., "improving faster than benchmark") and also shows a numerical ranking (2, 1, 0, –1), explained in more detail below.[3]

A second practice that makes it easier to digest large amounts of neighborhood information is to present findings in a *dashboard* that focuses on the most important patterns and conclusions. For instance, the left-most column of Table CS3.5 shows the name of the neighborhood; the second column

---

[3]Determining whether the pattern in a neighborhood is "better" or "worse" than the benchmark requires a value judgment of what is "good" and what is "bad." Usually the value judgment is explicit in the statement of place-based strategy.

shows the most recent status measure (i.e., crime rate); the third column shows the year-by-year pattern of change in each community and citywide. These dashboard elements are assembled to focus on the most important neighborhood information and to avoid the most common presentation error, which is to make a graph that looks like a spaghetti bowl because overlapping trend lines are presented for several different places at once.

A third practice that makes it easier to digest large amounts of neighborhood information is to develop summary indexes. An index combines measures to provide a general sense of "how things are going" and a heads-up on what to expect for a drill-down to individual indicators. Figure CS3.3 illustrates hypothetical neighborhood-by-neighborhood variation in MCIC's Community Capital Flow index, based on 25 component measures scored (2, 1, 0, –1) depending on whether the neighborhood result is better, worse, or about the same as the citywide benchmark. The index score is the average of the 25 scores multiplied by 100.[4] The result is a scale score that is (1) near 100 if the 25 indicators are all near the benchmark; (2) well over 100 if the neighborhood pattern of change is more positive than the benchmark; (3) under 100 if the neighborhood is doing worse than the benchmark; and (4) well below 100 (or negative) if the neighborhood is performing well below the benchmark.

Lessons on Making Data Useful for Place-Based Initiatives

To help place-based initiatives figure out where to go, what to do, whether to make midcourse adjustments, and how to communicate results, one should

1. Create typologies of context: gentrification, disinvestment, stress, resilience

2. Measure neighborhood connection to the region: labor market, capital availability, industry

3. Measure neighborhood stress: that is, market downturn, capital loss

4. Measure neighborhood assets that modulate stress: institutions, social patterns, infrastructure

5. Use national and local data sources: advocate for data openness

6. Communicate data effectively: benchmarks, dashboards, summary indexes

---

[4]After experimenting with several ways to achieve the goal of better communication through the use of summary scales, we find it is best to use an intuitive, additive model for computing index scores and reserve complex multivariate techniques for the task of ensuring that the indicators are in the right groups.

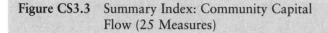

Figure CS3.3 Summary Index: Community Capital
Flow (25 Measures)

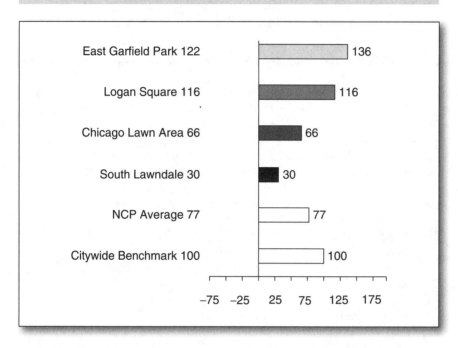

Lessons for Public Sociology

The publics involved in the projects discussed in this case study are primarily city and state government officials; decision makers in philanthropic foundations; private sector developers; and directors of nonprofit organizations specializing in community development. These public actors speak and think about their efforts in terms that are sociological but that are sometimes less conceptually defined and usually less operationally defined than the academic sociology usage. The tensions in these kinds of projects usually revolve around the choice of indicators and the use of benchmarks. Agencies tasked with implementation do not want their progress to be measured with indicators that they view as beside the point or benchmarks they consider unattainable or irrelevant. Developers who are asked to make targeted investments nearly always want indicator data for a geographic area that is too small given the granularity of the available information. The resolution of this issue usually involves a combination of indicators plus fieldwork and site analysis.

The role of the public sociology entrepreneur is to bring conceptual and operational clarity to the table while focusing on the substantive interests and informational needs of the client.

References

Chaskin, R. (2008). Resilience, community and resilient communities: Conditioning context and collective action. *Child Care Practice, 14*(1), 65–74.

Cisneros, H. (1995). *Creating defensible space: Deterring crime and building community.* New York, NY: Diane Co.

Jacobs, J. (1961). *The death and life of great American cities.* New York, NY: Vintage.

Katz, B. (2004). *Neighborhoods of choice and connection: The evolution of American neighborhood policy and what it means for the United Kingdom.* Washington, DC: Brookings Institute Research Brief.

Kelling, G., & Coles, C. (1996). *Fixing broken windows: Restoring order and reducing crime in our communities.* New York, NY: Simon & Schuster.

Sampson, R. J., et al. (1997). Neighborhoods and violent crime: A multilevel study of collective efficacy. *Science, 277,* 918–924.

Skogan, W. (2006). *Police and community in Chicago: A tale of three cities.* New York, NY: Oxford University Press.

Swanstrom, T., Chapple, K., & Immergluck, D. (2009). *Regional resilience in the face of foreclosures: Evidence from six metropolitan areas.* Building Regional Resilience Project, WP 2009-05. Retrieved from http://brr.berkeley.edu/publications/2009-05 .pdf

Taub, R., Taylor, D. G., & Dunham, J. (1984). *Paths of neighborhood change: Race and crime in urban America.* Chicago, IL: University of Chicago Press.

Taylor, D. G. (2008). *Informal arts and magnetization of urban neighborhoods.* Chicago, IL: Metro Chicago Information Center.

Whyte, W. H. (1988). *City: Rediscovering the center.* New York, NY: Doubleday.

Case Study 3.2. The Sacramento State Annual Survey of the Region[5]

Amy Liu

The Sacramento region includes Sacramento, Yolo, Placer, and El Dorado counties and is the major center of state politics and a fast-growing region in California. When we first started the Sacramento State Annual Survey of the

---

[5]This project is a great collaboration among many units on campus: data gathered through the Institute for Social Research, advice from the Center of Community Engagement, publicity from the Office of Public Affairs, and support from the Department of Sociology and Dean's Office, Social Science and Interdisciplinary Studies (SSIS).

Region in 2002, there was no systematic study of area residents' opinions on quality of life and other important issues in the region, the state, or the nation.

Background on the Survey

The Sacramento State Annual Survey of the Region was established in 2002 with the support from the Department of Sociology, the Institute for Social Research, and the College of Social Science and Interdisciplinary Studies at the California State University, Sacramento to

1. Offer opportunities for the residents in the region to voice their opinions and concerns on quality of life and various other social, economic, and political issues of local, regional, state, and national importance

2. Provide decision makers and the general public with current and objective information about the Sacramento region

3. Facilitate public discussion and debate on these important issues

4. Enable policy makers, the media, and the public to see the significance of social research in facilitating social and political engagement of the university and the community, and

5. Provide opportunities for graduate and undergraduate students to use their sociological methods and theories to carry out social research that would benefit residents, organizations, and communities in the region.

The annual survey is a year-round project. Each fall since 2002, we determine the topics and specific research questions for the survey. We spend a great deal of time researching how we can make sociological research an integrated part of life in the Sacramento region. To achieve this goal, we talk with leaders in the community and experts at the university, follow the media closely, and discuss these topics with students in my research methods classes and with other residents in the region. Each survey has about eight topics with roughly 70 questions, including issues important to the public in the region and to the policy makers in the state and the nation. Then the survey questions and topics are sent to the university's Human Subjects Review Committee for approval. This process has helped students in my research methods classes better understand how to develop and finalize research questions in a survey and how to make the voice of ordinary residents in the region heard.

Our data collection typically runs from February to March each year. For example, the 2008 Sacramento State Annual Survey of the Region is a computer-assisted telephone interview of 1,200 adult residents ages 18 and older from randomly selected households in the Sacramento region. More than 40 students conducted phone interviews in English and Spanish from February 16 to March 2, 2008, at the Institute for Social Research, California State University, Sacramento. Each year, about 25 students from my research methods classes participate in the data collection.

Disseminating Results

The results of our survey are important resources for the region. In 2008, for example, we worked closely with 14 graduate and undergraduate students in my methods classes to systematically produce eight applied reports on topics that were of particular interest to the public, the policy makers, and the media from March to July. These reports can be found at http://www.csus.edu/ssis/annual_survey.html.

Since 2002, we have systematically produced 54 reports. The moment a report is ready, we release it to the public, policy makers, and the media. We have worked closely with the College of Social Sciences and Interdisciplinary Studies (SSIS), the Office of Public Affairs, and the Office of Government Relations to make our results widely available. Media is also critical for sharing our results with the public and is one of the most effective strategies recommended by Gans (1989), Burawoy (2004, 2005), and Schwartz (2005) for public sociology.

Major newspapers, TV stations, and radio stations in the Sacramento region and northern California have extensive coverage of our research because of the broad dissemination process, the quality of our research, the importance of our topics, and the collaboration with the university's Public Affairs Office. Our studies have been reported by major newspapers and radio and TV stations, including the *Wall Street Journal*, the *Sacramento Bee*, the *Sacramento Business Journal*, the *World Journal*, Capital Public Radio, NewsTalk 1530 KFBK, KCRA Channel 3, Fox News, and KXTV Channel 10.

Since 2002, the annual surveys not only have been widely reported in the media, they have also become important vehicles by which the public can be heard by the media and by elected government officials. Our studies have provided the public and many organizations with important data to facilitate discussions and debates of important issues in the region. For example, 2008 was a very important election year for the city of Sacramento. Mayor Heather Fargo planed to seek a third term; no strong candidate challenged her until March 5, 2008, when former National Basketball Association star Kevin Johnson publicly entered the race. Residents and government officials did not know whom city residents would vote for—Heather Fargo or Kevin

Johnson? Our random survey of 380 residents in the city of Sacramento was released on March 5, 2008, to provide critical knowledge for the region: 28% would vote to reelect Fargo, and 29% would choose Kevin Johnson in a contest between the two. Moreover, 36% approved of the way Heather Fargo performed in the capacity of mayor. The remaining residents (64%) either disapproved (35%) or said they didn't know (29%).

The public knowledge produced by these surveys has also been used by various community groups and by officials in governmental organizations at both the state and local levels to deal with many important state and local issues such as flood protection, the war, housing, and a new arena for the professional basketball team, the Sacramento Kings. Over the years, the surveys have retained very high visibility in the Sacramento region, enhancing local, regional, and statewide awareness of California State University, Sacramento.

Since 2002, we have also presented our data at local, regional, and national conferences, and our studies have been widely used for creative teaching, scholarly research, presentations, and theses. Moreover, participation in this research project enables students to realize that social research can affect the social and political dialogue and/or policies in the region and the nation. Even though some students approach the service learning course with anxiety, many have left with a heightened sense of confidence in their own ability to carry out social research, a profound sense of accomplishment, and a deepened understanding and appreciation for sociological research and for our region. Students are also intrigued by the debate generated by their research and the attention garnered from the public, the media, and policy makers. This has also boosted their interest and confidence in carrying out important social research for the community, thus directly and indirectly facilitating greater social and political engagement in the region.

References

Burawoy, M. (2004). Public sociologies: Contradiction, dilemmas, and possibilities. *Social Forces, 82*(4), 1603–1618.

Burawoy, M. (2005). For public sociology, 2004 presidential address. *American Sociological Review, 70,* 4–28.

Gans, H. (1989). Sociology in America: The discipline and the public, 1988 presidential address. *American Sociological Review, 54,* 1–16.

Schwartz, P. (2005). Sociology as public practice: Toward a better utilization of research and theory, 2005 Presidential Address to the Pacific Sociological Association. *Sociological Perspectives, 48*(4), 423–431.

Case Study 3.3. Reducing Hunger in Oregon

Michael Leachman

In late September 1999, the U.S. Department of Agriculture (USDA) issued a report on hunger in the United States (Nord, Jemison, & Bickel, 1999). The report was based on a new survey conducted by the U.S. Census Bureau and included the "hunger rate" in each state.

I was working at the time for the Oregon Center for Public Policy (OCPP), a nonprofit research and advocacy organization, and we were very interested in this report. It ranked Oregon as having one of the nation's highest hunger rates. That was useful information. It added to the evidence that Oregon needed to do more to help low-income people get ahead. Since our organizational mission was to educate policy makers and the public about exactly this concern, the report presented a powerful potential tool for moving our agenda forward.

The information would not have been useful to us if it had been generated by an unreliable source or if the survey on which it was based were suspect. Our credibility as a research organization—and consequently our effectiveness as an advocacy group—depended on our integrity as researchers. This report and the survey that supported it, though, were highly credible. The survey, a set of 18 extensively researched questions, had been tested over several years by some of the nation's leading nutrition researchers and then conducted by the U.S. Census Bureau as a supplement to the same survey that is used to measure the monthly unemployment rate and other widely used statistics.

In its media response, Oregon governor John Kitzhaber's office questioned the report's validity without offering any evidence of methodological problems. The governor's office thought that because Oregon was a middling state on poverty and other measures related to low-income families, the state could not have one of the nation's highest hunger rates. They also emphasized that a state-run survey conducted a year earlier had found a much lower hunger rate.

Our first step was to write a report educating the governor's office, other key policy makers, our allies in the anti-hunger community, and the media about what the USDA report and the state survey told us about hunger in Oregon (Leachman, 1999). We explained why the findings from the national survey were more accurate than the state findings, which came from a single question on a phone survey. We also analyzed the state survey results, showing that these results—like the national survey results—suggested a serious food security problem in Oregon. Fewer than half of poor Oregonians in the survey, for example, said they always had enough to eat and were able to eat the kinds of food they wanted. The report concluded with recommendations for improving the state survey to better measure hunger by mimicking to the extent possible the national survey methodology.

We released the report as quickly as possible, to maximize our impact on the policy debate, and distributed it to our extensive list of state officials, legislators, media outlets throughout the state, allied organizations, and engaged individuals. We also wrote an opinion-editorial taking the governor's office to task for its careless response and defended the survey methodology against an inaccurate attack on it by the governor's staff in a meeting of policy makers.

Organizing to Address Hunger

We also coordinated closely with other organizations in the state that were concerned about hunger and the needs of low-income people. These included advocates at the Oregon Food Bank, Ecumenical Ministries of Oregon, and the Oregon Hunger Relief Task Force, a quasi-governmental group. They also included three community organizing groups—CAUSA, an immigrant rights group closely aligned with the farm workers union; the Rural Organizing Project, a group rooted in opposition campaigns to anti-gay ballot measures; and Oregon Action, the state's U.S. Action affiliate.

Our work with the community organizing groups benefited from the fact that we'd just received a three-year grant from the Ford Foundation to work in coalition with these three. The groups involved in this project were determining the coalition's first-year work plan when USDA issued its hunger report. In strategy meetings, we decided that an anti-hunger campaign using the report as a catalyst would be a good first coalition-organizing effort.

The efforts of this coalition and our other allies also benefited from having a forum available in which we could advocate effectively for policy improvements. In the early 1990s, the Oregon legislature had set a goal of eliminating hunger by 2000. The statute setting this goal established the Interagency Coordinating Council on Hunger (ICCH), a gathering of state department heads whose purpose was to coordinate anti-hunger policy among various state agencies. This council had been moribund for most of the 1990s but had recently begun meeting, in part to mediate a dispute between anti-hunger advocates and the state Department of Human Services (DHS). The dispute occurred after the department proposed to apply for a federal waiver that would have limited how much food stamp benefits Oregonians could receive. It ended with the department withdrawing its proposal, several months before the USDA issued its hunger report.

One of the first tasks of our coalition efforts was to determine specifically what policy improvements we wanted to pursue. This required research and fell primarily to us at the Oregon Center for Public Policy. What exactly should the state do to improve its anti-hunger policy infrastructure?

In deciding what to recommend, we drew on the advice of nationally recognized food policy experts at the Center on Budget and Policy Priorities (CBPP) in Washington, D.C. We had regular contact with these experts because our organization was (and remains) a member of a network of state policy research groups coordinated by CBPP. The center's experts recommended that Oregon increase the income eligibility limit for families to receive food stamps and eliminate a time limit on food stamp receipt for childless adults. They also described the technical process Oregon would need to follow to implement these improvements. We then gathered the Oregon unemployment data necessary for making the changes and wrote a report that described what Oregon needed to do to eliminate the food stamp time limit in 30 of its 36 counties (Leachman & Sheketoff, 2000). We later showed how Oregon could eliminate the time limit in every county. We also described in meetings with our allies what needed to be done to raise the income eligibility limit.

If these changes were going to be made, the state's Department of Human Services would need to implement them. Unfortunately, the department generally was hostile to suggestions for increasing state food stamp caseloads. Still absorbed in the mentality of welfare reform earlier in the 1990s, the department considered higher caseloads a measure of failure.

That's why we and our allies focused our energies initially on pressuring the Interagency Coordinating Council on Hunger to recommend various improvements in the state's food stamp program. At ICCH meetings, our coalition of advocates and organizing groups could force the DHS to consider our recommendations before a council of their colleagues statutorily obligated to find ways to reduce hunger in Oregon. Because we were armed with careful research about hunger in the state and specific, workable, and affordable policy solutions, the DHS couldn't easily dismiss our ideas. We were also fortunate that the council was cochaired by a leading member of the administration—the head of the state housing agency—who insisted on an honest policy discussion.

Coalition members who spoke during policy discussions at ICCH meetings were mostly advocates with significant knowledge of state policy, and low-income members of Oregon Action also testified. Outside of the ICCH meetings, the coalition's organizing groups employed direct action tactics to pressure the state to improve the food stamp program.

For example, Oregon Action organized a meeting of its members with the leadership of DHS at which the group pushed for a variety of food stamp policy improvements, including changing department policy to allow food stamp applicants to apply at any welfare office instead of only the one in their zip code. We at the Oregon Center for Public Policy helped Oregon Action members prepare for this meeting, primarily by coaching the membership's leaders to talk about Oregon's hunger problem and describe some of the more technical food stamp policy improvements our coalition sought. Similarly, the Rural Organizing Project organized its members to send to the ICCH and the governor hundreds of paper plates with messages urging the state to eliminate the food stamp time limit for childless adults.

Ultimately, the Department of Human Services agreed to use the approach we had recommended to eliminate the time limit for childless adults in every Oregon county. The department also used the method we proposed to raise the food stamp income eligibility limit from 130% of the federal poverty line to 185% of the federal poverty line, and it made a variety of improvements to the food stamp application process, including shortening the application and allowing applicants to apply at the nearest welfare office to their home, whether or not it was in their home zip code. And, the ICCH agreed to fund an improved set of hunger questions on a state health survey.

Success for the Coalition and Future Work

Over the next couple of years, the coalition continued to work for additional improvements. Working again with the national experts at the Center on Budget and Policy Priorities, we showed the state how it could increase the amount of food stamp benefits received by immigrant families containing an ineligible noncitizen adult. At the Oregon Center for Public Policy we wrote a paper detailing the process (Leachman, 2001). Our paper also called on the state to pay for legal immigrants in the country less than five years to receive food stamps, since the federal government would not pay for these benefits.

Our coalition organized a public meeting to push the DHS to adopt our recommendations. CAUSA, the immigrant rights group, organized some of its low-income members to speak at the meeting about how improving the food stamp rules would help their families.

The department did change its rules so that immigrant families with noncitizen adults could receive more in food stamps, but the state did not pay for food stamps for legal immigrant families in the country less than five years. The first proposal did not cost the state anything, since the federal government pays all of the cost of food stamp benefits. The second would have cost the state because federal law explicitly bars federal food stamps for recently migrated legal immigrant families. The cost to the state was the key difference.

Oregon implemented these changes in late 2000 and 2001, allowing many more Oregonians to access food stamps just as the economy slipped into recession. The food stamp caseload exploded, rising 85% from

September 1999 (the month the USDA report was released) to September 2003. Meanwhile, despite the economic decline, Oregon's hunger rate fell. Before the program changes, Oregon's hunger rate was 6%, meaning that in 6% of the state's households at least one member went hungry at times because they didn't have enough money for food. After the changes, Oregon's hunger rate fell to 3.8%.

There's more to solving Oregon's hunger problem than expanding the food stamp program, though. A study I cowrote used regression analysis to conclude that states with high annual unemployment spikes, large shares of renters with unaffordable housing, and much internal migration have high hunger rates (Tapogna et al., 2004). Studies we did at the Oregon Center for Public Policy revealed a link between hunger and depression, particularly among young mothers (Margheim & Leachman, 2003).

These problems suggest a range of policy solutions, most of which require revenue. Using rigorous research and working in coalition with a range of allies, we were able to improve markedly Oregon's public food assistance system. It was relatively easy to win these changes because they did not cost the state much money. Ending hunger in Oregon and the rest of the country will require a much stronger and more sustained coalition. By conducting and distributing credible research strategically, in ways that are timed and designed to influence policy decisions happening in the near term, public sociologists can help build this sort of coalition, using research to improve the public policies that shape our lives and the future of our communities.

References

Leachman, M. (1999, November 30). *How many hungry Oregonians? Measuring food insecurity and hunger*. Silverton, OR: Oregon Center for Public Policy.

Leachman, M. (2001, March 16). *Restoring food stamp benefits to immigrants and refugees in Oregon*. Silverton, OR: Oregon Center for Public Policy.

Leachman, M., & Sheketoff, C. (2000, February 23). *Helping rural Oregonians avoid hunger: Eliminating the three month food stamp time limit in 30 Oregon counties*. Silverton, OR: Oregon Center for Public Policy.

Margheim, J., & Leachman, M. (2003). *Empty cupboards, empty feelings: Food insecurity, depression, and suicide are intertwined*. Silverton, OR: Oregon Center for Public Policy.

Nord, M., Jemison, K., & Bickel, G. (1999, September). *Prevalence of food insecurity and hunger, by state, 1996–1998*. Washington, DC: U.S. Department of Agriculture, Economic Research Service.

Tapogna, J., et al. (2004). Explaining variations in state hunger rates. *Family Economics and Nutrition Review, 16*(2), 12–22.

Case Study 3.4. PovertyEast.org: Providing Information to Help Communities Address Critical Needs

Leslie Hossfeld

Povertyeast.org is a poverty information project of the Eastern North Carolina Poverty Committee (ENCPC). Truthfully, for all intents and purposes, ENCPC is now a defunct organization. But Povertyeast.org lives on as a resource for communities in eastern North Carolina. Of all the public sociology projects I work on, it remains one of my favorites.

In early 2001, I was approached by a friend, Nelson Reid, then chair of the Social Work Program at the University of North Carolina Wilmington. At the time, I was on the faculty at a neighboring institution, the University of North Carolina Pembroke. Nelson called to see if I would be interested in helping ENCPC revive itself and put to use some of its remaining funds toward poverty alleviation programming in our region. Nelson knew of my work on economic development projects addressing high-poverty counties in southeastern North Carolina. It was an easy decision to make—Nelson and I share similar passions and interests in social policy and our deep concern for North Carolina.

Some Background on ENCPC

ENCPC came out of the School of Social Work at East Carolina University in the 1980s. It was a small project developed by a faculty member who received seed money from the Z. Smith Reynolds Foundation, one of the few foundations in North Carolina that funds social justice projects. ENCPC made a few, small steps toward program development, primarily through providing small seed grants to social service organizations in the region. It then languished for many years until Nelson began making calls to pull a cadre of stakeholders together to breathe life into it and make some decisions about how to spend the remaining coffers of the organization. Representatives from the Department of Social Services, local housing coalition, and grassroots organizations in a five-county area were assembled to think through the best way to use funds to continue the mission of ENCPC.

Several very small projects emerged from that meeting: one was to help the housing coalition with a finance course for low-income families, another provided seed money for a homeless shelter in one of the 41 counties, and a third was to create a poverty information project to help communities address critical needs in their region.

Eastern North Carolina is historically one of the poorest in the state; some of the 41 counties that comprise eastern North Carolina stand out in the nation in terms of high pockets of persistent poverty. Persistent poverty is defined by USDA as counties with more than 20% of the population in poverty since 1970 (USDA-ERS, 2004). Since the mid-1990s, I have been examining poverty in our state and working with community partners on economic development projects in high-poverty counties hit by massive manufacturing textile job loss. The prospect of creating a central information hub for eastern North Carolina was very exciting to me. Over the years, I had been struck by local leaders' lack of knowledge on the most basic demographic variables in their counties: Few could describe the racial composition, median income, and poverty rates of their own constituents. Creating a central location that community people could turn to for assistance with data particular to meet their needs seemed like an excellent use of the dwindling ENCPC funds.

The Birth of Povertyeast.org

The core ENCPC group essentially turned the poverty information project over to me to develop. We had $6,000 with which to work. At that time, my younger brother was a Web developer, so I looked to him to help design and develop the Web presence of www.Povertyeast.org. I turned my attention to data collection. North Carolina has 100 counties that are divided up into economic development areas by the North Carolina Department of Commerce. Each year, the North Carolina Department of Commerce ranks all 100 counties on economic well-being and assigns a tier designation for each county: Most distressed counties in the state (40 in 2010) are designated as Tier 1; the next level of counties of distress are designated as Tier 2 (41 counties in 2010); and the least-distressed counties are designated as Tier 3 counties (19 counties in 2010) (North Carolina Department of Commerce, 2010). Within the 41 counties covered by ENCPC, 22 are considered Tier 1 counties (most distressed) and another 14 counties are designated Tier 2 counties. All but one of the counties is rural.

While I was aware of the high poverty levels in the counties I had been working in, the level of distress among the entire 41 eastern counties was disturbing. At the time, 17% of residents in the 41 counties lived in poverty (compared to 12.3% for the state of North Carolina). And the poverty gap between Whites and African Americans in these 41 counties was stark: 28% of African Americans in the region lived in poverty and 10% of whites lived in poverty; 40% of African American children lived in poverty (U.S. Census Bureau, 2000).

Helping residents, community organizers, and civic leaders gain an understanding of poverty through a central portal/website was very important to me and to the success of the poverty information project. Providing empirical data for the anecdotal stories of hardship told in these communities would be extremely valuable. Using sociology to do this was paramount.

In the introductory demography courses I teach, I always have students create county profiles as one of their projects. Over the course of a semester, students gather data on key demographic quality-of-life variables and create a profile of a county of their choice (typically their home counties). Students learn how to navigate census data, state vital records, health and human service datasets, Bureau of Labor Statistics data, and other important information to describe their counties. This is basically the strategy I took for Povertyeast. org: collecting key data for each county and compiling it in a way that is easily accessible for community people to use. Each of the 41 counties has its own county page, with tables and statistics that focus on important poverty indicators using current data.

I also wanted to provide visual mapping of key issues in the region so people could easily see the patterns of need and distress in our part of the state. Working with my brother, we designed a databank that has a map of the region highlighting shades and degrees of strength for select variables, such as per capita income, poverty rates (for children, families with female householder, elderly, and general population), income and wealth, unemployment, crime rates, education, voting, infant mortality, home ownership, percentage uninsured. When one moves a cursor across the map, data pop up for each county, highlighting specific variables and visually marking the severity of need in each county (see http://www.povertyeast.org/databank/default.html). Comparisons are made to the state rates and percentages, and one can see the differences between counties in the east and the rest of the state.

I also wanted to offer a tool kit for users that provides definitions and sources for each of the variables that are highlighted on the county pages and databank. The tool kit also has a Frequently Asked Questions page that answers questions like: "What is poverty?"; "How is poverty measured?"; and "Who are the poor?" There are links to interesting articles that discuss current trends across the state and nation. There are reports by the North Carolina Justice Center and the great work they do creating a Living Wage Index for North Carolinians, as well as articles on gender wage gap, poverty, and the environment, and other sociological studies that enhance one's understanding of the complexities of poverty in America (see http://www .povertyeast.org/toolkit/research/default.html).

As a public sociologist, I knew that it was important to help people break down the data in a way that makes sense to their lives. I wanted to help communities understand what the data and numbers mean and how to use these for their own purposes and community needs. I decided to create a Poverty Research Page in which I write short briefs on poverty in the 41 counties and across the region. Each brief examines inequalities in particular counties, focusing on income, poverty, unemployment, educational attainment, and homeownership. With each of these variables I provided analysis on the differences based on race and gender. Each brief contains graphs and narratives that tell a story tailored for a nonacademic audience. I also provide an accompanying downloadable PowerPoint presentation that people can use in their community meetings and workshops. To date, there are 15 poverty briefs with PowerPoint presentations on the website. I update these each year as new census data become available. The website also provides a links page that directs people to relevant websites related to poverty both in the state and nationally. Each year, as new American Community Survey data become available, I update the website and add new poverty research briefs.

The Impact of This Project

The Poverty Information Project culminated in a regional conference on Wealth and Poverty attended by more than 100 practitioners, academics, and community organizers in the region. We worked with community partners in the 41 counties to unveil the website. Our plan was to hold Web launch workshops in every county, but we simply didn't have the funding to do it. Instead, we sent mass emails to our community partners' listservs directing folks to the new site. In the beginning, we were never really sure of the impact of the site; as the calls and emails continued to come in, we began to feel confident that the information was being used. Soon, after the coffers were depleted, ENCPC stopped meeting regularly. But www.povertyeast.org continues to be updated, enhanced, and used by people across the state.

I receive several calls and emails a month from people across the region and state asking me questions about the website and requests to use the PowerPoint presentations and poverty briefs as handouts at their community meetings (even though the website states that these are for public use). Over the years, Povertyeast.org has generated many requests from a wide range of community partners asking me to speak to people on the critical issues of poverty in their communities. These have included a regional mayors' meeting, poverty alleviation workshops, press conference with state representatives, small town initiatives, food security coalition meetings, Latino migration conference, housing coalition conference, town hall convening, poverty reduction press conference with a North Carolina congressman, and Living Wage workshops, to name a few. I have also run workshops for community groups using the website to help them write grant proposals for various projects in different counties. Perhaps one of the more interesting results of the Poverty Information Project has been the development of the Poverty Reduction and Economic Recovery Legislative Study Commission created by the State of North Carolina House Bill 2687. Through my work on Povertyeast.org, I was asked to assist our state representative, Garland Pierce, to craft the bill that resulted in the creation of the study commission. This commission is charged to "study and develop a coordinated, integrated approach to poverty reduction and economic recovery across the State."

This project has been one of the most rewarding public sociology projects I have had the opportunity to work on. The partnerships that have grown from meeting people across the region and speaking to them on the issues of poverty and inequality have only helped my own economic development and community organizing projects grow and expand and help me gain a deeper understanding of the needs facing rural North Carolinians.

Though ENCPC is, in essence, defunct, www.Povertyeast.org remains a vibrant tool and resource for North Carolina, using sociology to reach multiple publics to expand the knowledge base and inform policy on the critical issues facing rural communities in our state.

References

North Carolina Department of Commerce. (2010). *2010 county tier designations.* Retrieved from http://www.nccommerce.com/en/BusinessServices/SupportYour Business/Incentives/CountyTierDesignations2010.htm

USDA-Economic Research Services. (2004). *Rural income, poverty and welfare.* Retrieved from http://www.ers.usda.gov/publications/aib710/aib710l.htm

U.S. Census Bureau. (2000). *Decennial census data.* Retrieved from http://factfinder .census.gov/servlet/DatasetMainPageServlet?_program=DEC&_submenuId=&_ lang=en&_ts=

Case Study 3.5. Sociology in Public Service

Paul Luebke

This case study differs from others in this volume because I simultaneously play the role of sociologist and public policy maker. In particular, since 1991, I have served as a Democratic member of the North Carolina State House from Durham while also being a faculty member in the sociology department at the University of North Carolina Greensboro (UNCG). My UNCG research, especially my books, *Tar Heel Politics* (Luebke, 1990) and *Tar Heel Politics 2000* (Luebke, 1998), has continually informed my work at the state legislature.

In turn, my political action has influenced my scholarship. In this case study, I provide examples of the interaction between sociology and political action. In particular, I show how, as a legislator, I have used sociology to effect state-level policy change, to work in tandem with citizen advocacy groups at the legislature, and to teach publics in my district and across North Carolina how to understand and navigate the general assembly.

Carving a Niche in the Sociology Department: 1976 to 1990

As a new member of the UNCG sociology department in the late 1970s, I discovered that some senior colleagues were troubled by my interest in both scholarship and progressive political change. Perhaps unsurprisingly in that time period, I faced the criticism of being too politically active. In fact, my citizen activism was the source of several peer-reviewed articles that were published in nationally recognized social science journals.

The first article analyzed why an African American candidate for lieutenant governor, Howard Lee, lost the September 1976 Democratic primary to a conservative White. I had been an active volunteer in the Lee campaign. When he lost, I took on the researcher role to delve into the voting returns, using race, region, and level of urbanization as key variables. My conclusion was that Lee's campaign failed to provide a convincing reason for Whites to vote for him. This contrasted with the voting behavior of Blacks, who appeared to support Lee because they hoped to have an African American in an important elected office. My article offered a policy suggestion: Blacks should campaign in North Carolina as economic populists, seeking to build a coalition between "have-little" and "have-not" Whites and Blacks.

This resulting article, "The Social and Political Bases of a Black Candidate's Coalition" (Luebke, 1979), piqued my interest in biracial political action. It is clear in retrospect that this sociological scholarship increased my interest, as a citizen, in helping to build a viable biracial political alliance in North Carolina. I was particularly motivated to do so in my home town of Durham and cofounded there an activist group, the People's Alliance.

In early 1978, the North Carolina Department of Transportation (DOT) threatened to destroy a Durham low-income Black neighborhood in order to extend a cross-town expressway. As a leader of the People's Alliance, I worked with the neighborhood residents to build the Black–White coalition that challenged both the DOT and Durham's city council, which had rubber-stamped the highway proposal. The coalition successfully saved the neighborhood, forcing the DOT to make concessions in order to build the highway.

My anti-expressway action led to another research article. I interviewed coalition members, Black and White, to identify their reasons for their commitment to the political battle. Their motivation overwhelmingly was the desire for racial justice. In the article, I also explained in detail the tactics used by the movement. For example, at government meetings, movement activists always followed the "dress-up" norms of their political opponent. Dressing in business attire rather than T-shirts neutralized the attempt by the city and state elites to marginalize the People's Alliance activists as disgruntled hippies.

The resulting journal publication, "Activists and Asphalt" (Luebke, 1981), became an important part of my tenure papers. In the UNCG sociology department's debate over my case, the issue emerged whether the interplay of scholarship and activism was acceptable behavior for a "professional sociologist." The consensus was that there was a place in the department for a sociological researcher who was also deeply committed to citizen activism. I earned tenure and promotion in 1982.

Questioning the Dominant Paradigm of North Carolina Politics

My experiences as a citizen-activist led me to question the commonly held view of state politics: that Democrats would be more beholden to the needs of the majority if only the majority would support egalitarian change, and that the impediments to a politics of equality were the state's Republicans. My research on state politics between 1968 and the late 1980s found that the two political parties should not be viewed as starkly different from one another. I concluded that ideology rather than political party label best explained state political dynamics. To maximize public discussion of my analysis, I avoided academic jargon in *Tar Heel Politics*. The book appealed to an audience of politically interested North Carolinians and urged readers to focus on the two prevailing belief systems, modernizers and traditionalists, instead of on Democrats and Republicans.

Urban-based modernizers welcomed economic change but opposed any effort to deny them political control. Modernizers were advocates of urban political control and sought to respond to national and global economic changes by welcoming large out-of-state corporations. Traditionalists, committed to preserving North Carolina's small-town Baptist belief system, were marked by opposition to both cultural and political-economic change. Small town–based traditionalists opposed both economic and cultural change but were seldom able to control the economic changes advocated by the modernizers. Mostly, the modernizers and traditionalists who dominated state politics were White men. The two groups shared an antipathy to an economically populist agenda that would promote the economic well-being of the less affluent. My conclusion was that state politics would become more progressive only when more Democratic progressive legislators, with the support of citizen movements, joined the battle for legislative power. This led to my decision in 1990 to run for a seat in the North Carolina State House.

Carving a Second Niche: 1991 to the Present

The North Carolina General Assembly is a part-time legislature but operates as a full-time body for about six months following a November election, beginning in January. This is the time when most legislation is proposed and passed. Thus, I had a conflict during the spring semester between my faculty role at UNCG and my legislative work. The department and I agreed that I would go on leave-without-pay during that time. This arrangement has been followed for each of my 10 terms in the North Carolina State House. Unlike in the late 1970s and early 1980s, my department colleagues saw a legitimate link between a sociologist and an activist. In my case, the role had evolved from a movement activist to that of an activist politician.

The Link Between Tar Heel Politics and My Legislative Agenda

I won my election in November 1990 and took office in early 1991, just as a recession hit both North Carolina's and the nation's economy. Faced with a significant budget shortfall, the majority Democrats debated how to raise the revenue that would allow the state to continue to fund public education and key social services. At this point, the research findings of Tar Heel Politics could and did inform political debate.

In Tar Heel Politics, I had pointed out how modernizers disliked the progressive income tax. During the 1991 session, in my role as a politician-activist relying on my own public sociology, I challenged, in intra-Democrat debate, the modernizer paradigm that advocated the sales tax as the preferred source of new tax revenue. Working with other progressive Democrats in the state house and the North Carolina AFL-CIO, I succeeded in passing my bill to raise the income tax on couples with taxable income above $100,000.

Subsequently, in 2001, during a second recession, I once again advocated for a progressive income tax increase, this time on couples making more than $200,000.

By 2001, the AFL-CIO had been joined by two other advocacy groups to support progressive taxation: the North Carolina Budget and Tax Center and Action for Children. Working with these organizations and with progressive Democrats, I succeeded in including the higher income tax rate in the overall tax package passed by the Democratic majority.

A third revenue issue emerged in 2005: the lottery. Consistent with my findings in *Tar Heel Politics* that modernizers favor regressive methods to raise revenue, Democratic modernizers pushed hard to pass the lottery legislation. But an unlikely bipartisan group of traditionalists and progressives opposed the bill. As expected, traditionalists viewed the lottery as gambling and labeled the bill immoral. They were joined in opposition to the bill by a few progressives who recognized that the lottery is played disproportionately by the poor and who opposed the lottery as a regressive "voluntary tax." On this issue, my closest ally, unusually so, was a traditionalist advocacy group, the Family Policy Council. I knew from *Tar Heel Politics* that we disagreed on almost every policy issue except the lottery, but I also knew that such an "unholy alliance" was the only way to defeat the lottery bill. With help from Republican modernizers, Democratic supporters passed the bill by one vote. The closeness of the vote supported a finding of *Tar Heel Politics*: that a cross-party alliance of traditionalists and progressives on certain issues could place great pressure on the usually dominant Democratic modernizers.

Beyond revenue issues, I have worked with advocacy groups and other legislators on numerous policies that relate to my research on North Carolina. Two examples are legislation against indoor smoking in all North Carolina buildings and anti-bullying legislation that identified LGBT (lesbian, gay, bisexual, and transsexual) persons as a protected category. For each issue, my background as a sociologist helped me to identify allies as well as opponents.

A ban on smoking inside buildings became law in North Carolina in 2009 because of a legislative coalition that argued that, even in the top-producing tobacco state in the United States, public health concerns should carry the day. My research suggested the core opposition would be Republican and Democratic traditionalists, who viewed the smoking ban as inappropriate big-government intrusion. In addition, urban Democrats from cigarette-producing districts could be expected to oppose the ban. Other legislators and I worked with advocacy groups such as the American Heart Association, American Cancer Society, and the Campaign for Tobacco-Free Kids to build a majority of Democratic progressives and of modernizers from both political parties. This vote supported a key finding of *Tar Heel Politics*: that ideology rather than political party best explained legislators' vote on the smoking ban.

A second issue from 2009 centered on an issue that I had discussed in *Tar Heel Politics 2000*: whether gay rights could in any fashion gain legislative support. Traditionalists of both parties are strongly opposed to any attempt to legitimate LGBT persons. But a bill that opposed bullying in K–12 schools provided a vehicle for a coalition of progressives and modernizers to grant legal protection to LGBT youth. The controversy centered on whether LGBT youth should be an enumerated category, along with racial minorities and the handicapped, to be protected from school bullying. The statewide gay rights advocacy group, Equality North Carolina, lobbied for enumeration. Traditionalists sought to code a Yes vote for enumerated categories as a vote for gay rights. Modernizers defended their vote as a means to protect all children by naming specific groups more vulnerable to being bullied. Not for the first time in a legislative body, a victory could be won (legal standing for LGBT youth) while many modernizer legislators could deny that their vote had anything to do with gay rights. My research had suggested that precisely such a strategy could be successful.

Sociology in the Legislative District and Beyond

As a legislator who is also a sociologist, I am often asked by constituents to help clarify the politics of the General Assembly. These meetings have been with voters concerned about public education or mental health funding as well as with fourth graders whose teachers want an "expert" to talk to the children about the process and politics of the General Assembly. Graduate students from around the state also single me out to help them with their legislative policy projects, primarily by asking me in interviews to explain the coalitions that would likely support or oppose their proposed legislation. Finally, I am asked regularly by various social science organizations and by college faculty across North Carolina to comment on the links between sociology and public policy. While combining sociology and legislative policy making in one person is unusual, I view it as a logical consequence of the interplay between research and activism that I first undertook in 1976.

References

Luebke, P. (1979). The social and political bases of a black candidate's coalition: Race, class, and ideology in the 1976 North Carolina primary election. *Politics and Society, 9*, 239–261.

Luebke, P. (1981). Activists and asphalt: A successful anti-expressway movement in a New South city. *Human Organization, 40*, 256–263.

Luebke, P. (1990). *Tar heel politics: Myths and realities.* Chapel Hill, NC: University of North Carolina Press.

Luebke, P. (1998). *Tar heel politics 2000.* Chapel Hill, NC: University of North Carolina Press.

CASE STUDIES 4

Inequalities of Race, Class, and Gender

The study of social inequality is central to the field of sociology. The work of Karl Marx and Max Weber was important in shaping our understanding about inequality rooted in economic, social, and political structures. W.E.B. DuBois and Jane Addams provided examples of how sociological research could provide insights into the structures of racial, ethnic, and gender inequalities in American society. As early public sociologists, they demonstrated how the knowledge acquired through such research could be applied to reducing social inequalities. Throughout the 20th century, countless sociologists have documented inequality and provided a deeper understanding of its causes and consequences through their research. As the case studies in this section highlight, public sociologists in the early 21st century continue to use their training and skills to improve opportunities and expand resources for those who have been marginalized by inequalities in our society.

Gender inequality is the focus of the first two case studies. Abby Ferber is a feminist sociologist committed to social justice and social change. As a member of the board of Girl-Smart, a national girl-serving organization based in Denver, Colorado, she has used her sociological training and women's studies background to help the board identify ideologically charged topics around single-gender programming and develop a common language for discussing and framing these issues. She has also found different ways for her university to serve this organization. These included recruiting university students to be mentors to middle school girls, creating credit-bearing courses relevant to mentor training, and involving other faculty in program development. What emerges from her case study is an example of how the work of public sociologists can be beneficial to both the university and the community.

The second case study demonstrates how personal experiences are important in shaping the work of public sociologists. After college, Melissa

Swauger worked with youth employment programs as an analyst for a county workforce investment board. There she learned firsthand that information and services offered by these programs did not always address the needs of communities of color and young women. Interested in learning how to address these deficits, she decided to pursue a graduate education, choosing to investigate the factors and conditions that influence adolescent girls' decision making about future careers. Working with a nonprofit, girl-serving organization in Pittsburgh, she recruited adolescent girls and their mothers to participate in focus groups and interviews. But as a public sociologist, she did not simply *extract information from* this community. Instead, she found ways to *work with the organization* to address the needs of these girls. This included conducting a career development needs assessment with girls and their mothers, providing career information workshops about nontraditional careers, and assisting in the development and implementation of a range of materials that focused on equity issues. Her involvement led to an appointment on the steering committee of a regional girl-centric coalition, where she has been involved in developing and conducting workshops.

The contemporary view of youth as "disinterested and disengaged" is being challenged by a project that engages young people in dialogues around race and ethnicity, the subject of the third case study. Since its inception, the program has involved youth from across the metro Detroit areas in intergroup dialogues, metropolitan tours, community action projects, residential retreats, and youth policy summits. Youth participate in all stages of the program, as participants, planners, leaders, and organizers. They engage in an evaluation research process that is intergenerational, with youth and adults working in partnership. One outcome is the production of an annual report of their activities. Using different media, youth participants have also produced a DVD, a theatre piece, and a book that give voice to their experiences growing up and living in communities that are at once both diverse and yet segregated. As a result of participating in this project, many of the young people have gone on to apply their community-based participatory research principles and skills in other projects in their communities. As Barry Checkoway and Katie Richards-Schuster observe in this case study, the effect on youth not only challenges contemporary negative media images of youth but also has tangible benefits for them, strengthening their substantive knowledge, practical skills, and civic competencies.

Madeline Troche-Rodríguez understood early in her educational career that the community voice is important to the research process. As an undergraduate research assistant she worked with various professors, observing the number of projects that started with community input but generally ended with the academic researcher in the "driver's seat" and the community left out of the process. In contrast, while a graduate student in the Center for Urban Research and Learning at Loyola University, she was part of a research team that partnered with a Chicago fair housing organization and a Latino advocacy organization to identify and document resources available to Latino families facing housing discrimination in selected suburban communities. Based on the researchers' findings that there were not many resources for Latino families, the partner organizations developed a plan to address the gap. For Madeline, this experience led to a job as a fair housing activist, designing and implementing a bilingual fair housing outreach and education curriculum in targeted municipalities experiencing substantial Latino population growth, as well as to a dissertation topic. While finishing the work on her dissertation, she returned to the fair housing field, this time as a community educator. In that capacity she collaborated with other fair housing advocates to create MoveSmart.org, a new tool to promote residential integration. The commitment she made several years ago, to make sure that the community remains engaged in the research on pressing social problems and the search for solutions, is reflected in all the work she has done. Like the other sociologists in this section, she shows how sociological knowledge can be effective in reducing social inequalities.

Case Study 4.1. Bringing Feminist Sociology to Smart-Girl: Building a University-Nonprofit Partnership

Abby L. Ferber

As a feminist sociologist committed to social justice and social change, I always try to tie my research and coursework directly into practice. I have served as director of the Women's Studies Program at the University of Colorado at Colorado Springs for many years and helped found the Matrix Center for the Advancement of Social Equity and Inclusion, which I also direct. The mission of the Matrix Center is "to foster an intellectual climate that supports inclusion and collaboration to examine the intersections of oppression and privilege and promote solutions to inequality" (www.uccs .edu/matrix). One of our central goals is to build connections among our faculty, students, and the community.

This combined focus on community outreach and practical solutions has led us to pursue various partnerships with community organizations. Perhaps our most extensive and well-institutionalized collaboration is with Smart-Girl (www.smart-girl.org). Our relationship involves both students and faculty working directly with the organization as well as a number of structural components.

I learned about the organization when I was approached by one of the founders after leading a gender-focused workshop for a church youth group. I was invited to join the board of the organization, which had only been around for a few years. That was in 2002, and I have served on the board ever since and have been chair of the program committee for about half of that time. Working with Smart-Girl, I have found a way to directly link my own passion for community service and dedication to improving girls' and women's lives with my academic career. It has been personally fulfilling as well as beneficial for both the organization and the university.

Smart-Girl

Smart-Girl is a nonprofit founded by a group of women in Denver, Colorado. The organization's mission is "to enable and inspire middle-school aged girls to make smart choices and become confident, capable, self-reliant women." The program consists of groups of about 12 girls being guided through the Smart-Girl curriculum by high school- or college-aged women.

Smart-Girl is unique in a number of ways. It is a community-based program, with the location, time, content, and leadership adaptable to and determined by the needs of the community that it serves. Unlike other programs that have a one-size-fits-all model, the Smart-Girl program is adaptable to serve all girls without diminishing the very real differences among them. It is research based and tested, reflecting the findings of current research; its outcomes are continuously tested and the program is modified as needed. It is activity and skill based, grouping girls of similar ages together, freeing them to be themselves and to learn from each other. These gender-specific groups validate girls and provide a comfortable space in which they are free from the objectifying gaze of boys. Overall, Smart-Girl promotes emotional and social intelligence development, a critical quality often overlooked by other organizations that cater more to athletics or academics.

PUBLIC SOCIOLOGY AS A FOUNDATION FOR A COUNSELING CAREER IN EDUCATION

Angie Jacobs, a high school counselor in Colorado Springs, heard about Abby Ferber and her work with the Smart-Girl program while working on an M.A. in sociology at the University of Colorado at Colorado Springs. But it wasn't until

(Continued)

(Continued)

2007, when she returned to the university to complete an M.A. in school counseling, that she got involved with the project. In a move that she calls "life changing," she went through the Smart-Girl training as part of a counseling internship; she immediately thought, "Why didn't I get involved in this sooner?"

Upon completing the training she served as a coach, working with near-peer guides (high school- and college-aged girls) who lead the Smart-Girl groups. She is now a program manager and conducts trainings for the guides and counselors so they can be involved in middle schools.

There are different reasons for Angie's continued involvement. Looking back on her own adolescence, she wishes that there had been something like Smart-Girl for her. Having previously been a middle school teacher, she knows adolescent girls struggle with forming their identities, managing their relationships, and thinking about their futures. Because Smart-Girl offers a program with proven results, she says, "It was just a no-brainer to get involved."

Becoming active in Smart-Girl also provided a chance to put into practice everything she had learned in her sociology classes and school counseling program. Angie's work on the project gave her affirmation that she had made the right career choice because it brought together her interest in body image and eating disorder research, counseling, and adolescent development.

Recent Smart-Girl program research shows that the guides and coaches, even more than the girls themselves, are reporting positive responses regarding their participation; Angie feels this has been true in her own case. She has also seen the impact that the program has had on near-peer guides. After working with middle school students, she has watched her own high school students come back excited and eager to continue their involvement when they move on to college.

Overall, the partnerships that form among local universities, middle schools, and high schools are viewed very positively by all participants. The school communities can see and feel the energy that university students have for the program and for these young women. They know that no one makes this kind of time commitment unless they really want to be there; this awareness creates a vitality and energy that filters through all of the school communities.

The program uses a "near-peer" model, with girl groups led by near-peer guides. These guides, who are usually between 5 and 10 years older than the participants, provide positive role models to girls who may be turning away from parental guidance. Likewise, guides report to coaches who are a generation older than them. In some cases, coaches are supervised by program managers who add another layer of experience. Smart-Girl's intergenerational methodology utilizes circle mentoring to its best effect.

Smart-Girl recognizes that girls have far more opportunities available to them today than did previous generations; however, it also takes seriously the challenges facing girls today. Girls face peer pressure, choices around sexual activity and sexuality, threats to body image, bullying, perceived need for boyfriends, threats to their self-esteem and self-worth, and high rates of eating disorders. The program provides a safe space, role models in whom girls can confide, and strategies for dealing with family and peer dynamics. The curriculum does not tell girls what to think but provides them with essential tools to make more informed and thoughtful decisions for themselves. The Smart-Girl program was established to serve all preadolescent and adolescent girls everywhere, in partnerships with schools, organizations, communities.

Substantive Framing

As a board member of an organization in its early stage of development, I was fortunate to help guide the board through a process of identifying our key positions. While I saw strong feminist perspectives invoked by many members of the board, others came from a wide range of political and ideological positions. Even the founders of the program occupied a range of political perspectives. It was important, therefore, to come to some shared understanding of the board's position on specific ideologically charged topics. This became especially apparent when board members or staff members were interviewed by the press and provided answers that some board members did not feel were consistent with their own values. As the organization grew beyond the involvement of the founders and new generations of board members moved in, it became increasingly important that certain issues be addressed explicitly.

My sociological and women's studies training helped me to identify issues that I knew had significant ideological implications. For example, the issue of gender differences: As a girl-serving organization committed to single-gender programs, board members would often be asked to explain why we offered single-gender programs. This decision could be justified in numerous ways, depending upon board members' and staff members' personal convictions. It is also an issue about which there are very real differences among publications in the field (Hutchison, 2001; Lee & Bryk, 1986, 1989; Marsh, 1989; Parker & Rennie, 2002; Simson, 2005; Stables, 1990). Having taught about this issue for many years, and having experience negotiating the minefields of our mythical "nature versus nurture" dichotomies, I knew the danger inherent in an individual answering that girls and boys are inherently different, even if this was his or her personal conviction (Butler, 1993; Fausto-Sterling, 1992, 2000; Hubbard, 1990; Tarrant, 2006). I was able to help identify this as an important issue for us to address and come to agreement upon.

In a retreat, I facilitated board dialogue around a number of key questions so that we could adopt a common language in the discussion and framing of potentially controversial issues.

What Is Our Position on Sex/Gender Differences at This Age?

Our response: "Smart-Girl does not have a position on the issue of sex differences, nor on the issue of single-sex schools. We recognize that research finds some differences between boys and girls in this age range, and how they learn best. The research is inconclusive regarding the origin of these differences, and it is irrelevant to the Smart-Girl program and its success." In our publications, we delve into this issue in far more detail. There we draw upon the body of research that emphasizes that there are far more similarities among boys and girls than there are differences at every stage of development. We discuss the rationale for gender-specific programs because girls and women face ongoing inequality and thus unique challenges. We also find that girls are more likely to speak openly and honestly in a girls-only setting. In addition, girl bullying is a central issue addressed in the program, and thus strengthening relationships among girls is a central goal that can only be accomplished in a girls-only group.

An ongoing point of contention for the organization is whether or not we should serve boys. This is an issue over which there are deep emotional divisions. Some of the differences I see mirror some of the historical divides I have seen taking place in the discipline of women's studies (Brod, 1987; Cranny-Francis, Waring, Stavropoulos, & Kirkby, 2003; Kimmel, 1987; Kimmel, Hearn, & Connell, 2004; Pilcher & Whelehan, 2004). On the one hand, there is a strong belief that because we live in a society that is still so unequal, in which boys and men continue to reap masculine privilege, we need to maintain our strong commitment to serving girls. Why should we dilute that commitment and our limited resources? On the other hand, there is the conviction that by serving boys we also serve girls. As the pro-feminist men's studies literature reveals, we know that in order to create a more equitable world for girls and women, we need to educate boys and men. We need to work on changing the behaviors of those who perpetuate the violence and sexual harassment against girls and women. We need to hold boys accountable for their behavior and counteract the detrimental messages they receive about masculinity and manhood. These ideological divisions parallel the debates that have occurred on campuses across the country as many women's studies programs have transformed into gender studies programs. At the moment we are evaluating the results of a pilot program for boys that uses a modified version of the Smart-Girl curriculum to aid our decision making.

What Is the State of Girls Today, and How Does It Compare With the Past?

Wary of the dichotomous portrayals of girls as either helpless victims, on the one hand, or, on the other hand, blind to ongoing gender inequality, this emerged as an important issue for consideration.

Response: "Much has improved; we don't like to use the language of girls in crisis. Yet, the reality is that girls still face many challenges today, many of them new and different from those of previous generations. Our organization is a proactive one, not reactive, empowering and equipping girls with the tools and skills they need to navigate today's world and grow into successful women."

Individual Versus Broader Systemic Change: How Can We Create Social Action on the Part of the Girls? How Can We Create Systemic Change? Is Smart-Girl Just an Individual Solution?

Response: "Smart-Girl touches individual girls, the schools/organizations serving them, and the communities they live in. As we evaluate schools implementing Smart-Girl we hope to show school wide results. In addition, Smart-Girl empowers girls to become agents of change to work for social justice." Here our position has been informed by C. Wright Mill's notion of the sociological imagination, seeing personal troubles in a broader social context, as well as the feminist conviction that the personal is political and intimately interconnected. This sociological perspective shaped my efforts to facilitate the discussion and articulate a position that reflects this insight.

I also had the opportunity to contribute to and edit the Smart-Girl curriculum and training books. This was another area in which my sociological training directly contributed to the program's development. I emphasized diversity and inclusiveness as areas for strengthening. I was able to add activities to the training course and content to the texts to help the program more fully address the goal of creating inclusive groups in which all girls feel welcome and valued, while at the same time increasing awareness and respect of the racial, ethnic, and religious diversity among them.

Structural Contributions

I developed an internship course for the Women's Studies Program when I served as its director and, when introduced to the Smart-Girl program, I immediately recognized it as a possible internship site for my students. One of the unique features of the program is its near-peer mentoring format. The program was fairly new; it employed high school girls as "guides" working with the groups of middle school girls. Once I became familiar with the program, I suggested we also allow college women to serve as guides. Each semester, a number of students enrolled in the internship class chose to intern with Smart-Girl and found it to be a profound experience. Most of them would write in their journals that they wished they'd had a program like this when they were in middle school. Many of them chose to continue volunteering for the program after the semester ended, and a number have decided to go on to graduate programs in school counseling as a result of this experience.

This model worked out so well that we developed a partnership between the program and the university. The Smart-Girl training course and the internship experience were established as courses available through our college's Extended Studies Program and housed in the Matrix Center for the Advancement of Social Equity and Inclusion. In this way, we were able to offer both high school and college students transferable academic credit for the training course and working with a Smart-Girl program. This has been a terrific arrangement, especially for the many high school students who participate and can now earn college credit. Many of the high school students recruited to work with Smart-Girl programs are recruited from the same communities as the middle school girls, and many come from low-income homes. Smart-Girl has created a scholarship fund to help pay for the academic credit for many of these young women.

This is one of the many ways in which my role as a faculty member in a university setting has structurally benefitted the Smart-Girl organization. I have introduced a number of faculty members from our school counseling program to Smart-Girl. They have contributed to enhancing the training course and running numerous programs. We have turned the training course into the Smart-Girl Leadership Institute, a rigorous training course with required readings. My students have found both the training and the internship experience incredibly beneficial. The training course provides hands-on skills with conflict resolution and mediation, verbal and nonverbal communication skills, diversity and cultural competency, and leadership skills that are widely transferable to all aspects of their lives.

The other faculty now working with the program have conducted Smart-Girl training courses at the American School Counselors Association for the past few years, and the association published an annotated version of the curriculum, introducing the program to school counselors around the country. In addition, a number of faculty members are conducting evaluation research for the program that has already led to a number of publications, benefitting both faculty and Smart-Girl.

We have created a lasting partnership that benefits both Smart-Girl and the university. This partnership has created a new institutional configuration for Smart-Girl that would look very different were the university not involved. At the same time, the partnership makes real our campus commitment to community outreach. Our students and faculty are learning from the Smart-Girl program; we are contributing to strengthening the organization itself in new and creative ways. This partnership is a model for how universities and nonprofit organizations can work together in ways that are mutually rewarding.

References

Brod, H. (1987). *The making of masculinities: New men's studies.* New York, NY: Routledge.

Butler, J. (1993). *Bodies that matter: On the discursive limits of sex.* New York, NY: Routledge.

Cranny-Francis, A., Waring, W., Stavropoulos, P., & Kirkby, J. (2003). *Gender studies: Terms and debates.* New York, NY: Palgrave Macmillan.

Fausto-Sterling, A. (1992). *Myths of gender: Biological theories about women and men.* New York, NY: Basic Books.

Fausto-Sterling, A. (2000). *Sexing the body: Gender politics and the construction of sexuality.* New York, NY: Basic Books.

Hubbard, R. (1990). *The politics of women's biology.* New Brunswick, NJ: Rutgers University Press.

Hutchison, K. B. (2001, June). The lesson of single-sex public education: Both successful and constitutional. *American University Law Review, 50*(5), 1075.

Kimmel, M. S. (1987). *Changing men: New directions in research on men and masculinity.* Thousand Oaks, CA: Sage.

Kimmel, M. S., Hearn, J. R., & Connell, R. W. (2004). *Handbook of studies on men and masculinities.* Thousand Oaks, CA: Sage.

Lee, V. E., & Bryk, A. S. (1986, October). Effects of single-sex secondary schools on student achievement and attitudes. *Journal of Educational Psychology, 78*(5), 381–395.

Lee, V. E., & Bryk, A. S. (1989, December). Effects of single-sex schools: Response to Marsh. *Journal of Educational Psychology, 81*(4), 647–650.

Marsh, H. W. (1989, March). Effects of attending single-sex and coeducational high schools on achievement, attitudes, behaviors, and sex differences. *Journal of Educational Psychology, 81*(1), 70–85.

Parker, L. H., & Rennie, L. J. (2002, September). Teachers' implementation of gender-inclusive instructional strategies in single-sex and mixed-sex science classrooms. *International Journal of Science Education, 24*(9), 881–897.

Pilcher, J., & Whelehan, I. (2004). *50 key concepts in gender studies.* Thousand Oaks, CA: Sage.

Simson, G. J. (2005). Separate but equal and single-sex schools. *Cornell Law Review,* 443.

Stables, A. (1990). Differences between pupils from mixed and single-sex schools in their enjoyment of school subjects and in their attitudes to science and to school. *Educational Review, 42*(3), 221–230.

Tarrant, S. (2006). *When Sex Became Gender.* New York, NY: Routledge.

Case Study 4.2. Feminist Research in Action: An Intersectional Approach to Girlcentric Programming

Melissa Swauger

Social scientists have long been criticized for engaging in research that is irrelevant to the everyday practical concerns of the individuals they study. Since the 1970s, however, the field of women's studies has pioneered a theoretical approach that explains the world through the eyes of those whom we "study" and calls for activist research that promotes social change. Adhering to the basic tenet that there is no one universal woman subject, women's studies encourages an *intersectional approach,* in which the researcher examines how other identities (race and ethnicity, social class, and sexual orientation) intersect with gender to produce various forms of disadvantage and privilege in the everyday lives of all people (Collins, 2000; Crenshaw, 1991).

Girls' studies draws from women's studies by moving away from gender-specific research toward an intersectional approach for recognizing and understanding girls' social identities. Yet a gap remains between academic theorizing about girls' diverse social identities and developing girlcentric programs using an intersectional approach.

This case study illustrates a process by which academic theories about the social identities of girls are being incorporated into girl-centered programs in southwestern Pennsylvania. The process began as a dissertation project in partnership with one organization but turned into a public sociology project that affects numerous girlcentric programs in the region.

Background

My research examines how poor, working-class, African American, and White adolescent girls in Pittsburgh, Pennsylvania, perceive their futures and how their mothers influence these perceptions. I approach the study of career aspirations from a sociological perspective examining how everyday life, including interactions with people, culture, and institutions, shape girls' sense of what is possible and how gender, social class, and race influence how girls construct their futures.

As is the case for many sociologists, my research is inspired by my upbringing. In the 1980s, I grew up in McKeesport, Pennsylvania, a small working-class town surrounded by what used to be several of the most profitable steel mills in the world. During this time, I saw steel mills and subsidiary businesses close, local economies crumble, and the viability of working families diminish. When I went to college, my sociology courses provided me a framework from which to understand inequalities and how to act to dismantle them. Today, armed with a Ph.D., and more important, a class conscience, I am fueled by a sense that the world has more opportunities to offer poor and working-class women and that poor and working-class women have more knowledge and skills to offer the world.

In addition to my class background, my research is inspired by my work as a program analyst within the Allegheny County government's Workforce Investment Board, which sets policy and funding requirements for youth employment programs. In Pittsburgh, these organizations struggle with a number of labor force concerns, including how to help young people make informed decisions about their future careers, how to better match student interests with labor market needs in the region, and how to attract and retain young people to live and work in the Pittsburgh area. In this work, I learned how policies are made and implemented and, in turn, how youth development programs operate under local, state, and federal governance. In my work with the Workforce Investment Board, I became disenchanted as I found that government and nonprofit agencies disseminated fragmented workforce information and that the corresponding career literacy tools assumed all families have equal access to information and resources. Moreover, career literacy efforts ignored the systemic racialized and gendered barriers that communities of color and girls encounter in education and labor markets, including the lack of information and resources mothers face in helping their children plan.

The consequence of this fragmentation and lack of attention to the challenges of a diverse youth population is that youth career development efforts do not account for how lived experiences of girls from poor and working-class backgrounds can result in limited education and career opportunities or how these girls bring specific strengths to careers. Seeking a way to mend the rift between youth development efforts and the available resources and needs of girls, I returned to school to earn a Ph.D.

Research

At the University of Pittsburgh, I began to investigate the possible relevant factors and conditions that influence how girls think about their futures. I found that I needed to draw on the spirit of symbolic interactionism to examine how girls' meanings about the future are derived from social processes, including interactions with people, groups, culture, and social structures (Berg, 2001). Under the guidance of the feminist qualitative researcher Dr. Kathleen Blee, I conducted focus groups and interviews, hoping to encourage girls to "tell their own stories of their lived world" and to devise ways that youth career development programs could account for that lived world (Babbie, 2004, p. 300).

The first step in the research process was to find a pool of available girls from which to recruit a sample. After several unsuccessful attempts to work with local schools, I decided to approach nonprofit organizations. Coincidentally, I ran into a former coworker who introduced me to Gwen's Girls, an organization that seeks to improve the quality of life for girls in the Pittsburgh region. I began recruiting at Gwen's Girls, which led me to other organizations and the use of a snowball sample.

After sampling, I conducted a career development needs assessment with girls and mothers, using focus groups and individual interviews. While my specific interest pertained to girls' career development needs, I wanted to talk to mothers who, in poor and working-class homes, are primarily involved in children's educational and career planning activities (Lareau, 2003). Care managers, nonprofit agency staff who worked directly with families, also assessed girls' and mothers' career development needs during their home visits. Working with care managers and education staff from the agency helped navigate several difficulties with girls returning consent forms and mothers' initial lack of participation; these connections also made it easier to gain trust and build rapport with girls and mothers. All of this work required staff to alter their schedules and, in some cases, take on extra work to see my project through to its completion. Simultaneously, I worked with the girls at Gwen's Girls by providing career information workshops about nontraditional careers. This helped me to learn more about the lives of adolescent girls and also to engage them critically in thinking about their futures.

Outcomes

The career resource needs assessment was funded by the Women and Girls Foundation of Southwest Pennsylvania. Once these needs were assessed I, in conjunction with Gwen's Girls, pursued additional funding from the Jewish Women's Foundation of Greater Pittsburgh to develop a career resource manual to be used by mothers with the help of their care managers or independently. These funds also allowed us to pilot materials that supplemented Gwen's Girls' current career exploration curriculum with "equity" activities. These equity-based career education materials included information, discussion, and activities that address issues of gender, social class, and racial inequalities in the workforce. For example, in the self-awareness component of the program, we added activities that teach girls about stereotypes and the ways stereotyping limits opportunities in the workforce. In the career exploration component, girls learn about disparities in education and the labor market, specifically in the Pittsburgh region.

Lynn Knezevich, the executive director of Gwen's Girls, also recommended my successful appointment to the steering committee of the Girls Coalition of Southwestern Pennsylvania. This organization addresses the needs of staff and leaders of girl-serving agencies in the region by sharing information about programs, new research, and training opportunities in a formal way. My work as a committee member has focused on encouraging the committee to challenge universal definitions of gender and acknowledge the diverse needs of girls from all backgrounds. For example, at past strategic planning sessions, girls' diverse needs were explored as we developed the coalition's mission, vision, and values, ensuring that our work is more equity focused. Last year we offered a workshop entitled, "Are All Girls the Same: A Conversation on Gender, Race, and Class" to staff and administrators of girls' programs; the workshop used data from my research project to examine how economic, social, and cultural resources vary and matter in the lives and futures of girls. At the end of this workshop, we worked with service providers to brainstorm tangible ways in which their organizations could address, in their programming, staff development, and administration and leadership, issues facing adolescent girls because of the complex and multifaceted ways gender, race/ethnicity, and social class interact in their lives. This year, the focus of the annual conference and yearly programming is economic empowerment.

Lessons Learned

My work with Gwen's Girls taught me the importance of aligning myself with organizations that share my research goals and then finding individuals within these organizations who are willing to work collaboratively and will champion our work. Gwen's Girls recognizes the unique needs and strengths of girls and understands that youth development programming must be approached from an intersectional perspective. Moreover, Lynn Knezevich supported my work because of our shared class backgrounds and related experiences, our past work together at a similar community-based organization, and because, as a leader of an organization, Lynn chooses to ground her organizational decision making in research. Lynn also encouraged me, in partnership with Gwen's Girls, to seek funding from two local foundations for this research.

Wanting to make my partnership and commitment worthwhile to Gwen's Girls while also adhering to the requirements of the grant applications, I learned that the research funding process is an example of how public sociology is symbiotic. As public sociology researchers we are asked to reflect on tangible discipline-based research goals while we also consider how our research will affect the lives of those with whom we work. As I wrote the foundation grants I began to conceptualize the practical and measurable ways in which the research could have an impact. Foundation funders look for organizations that match their interests and expect grantees to clearly specify the goals and objectives of a project. More important, grant seekers are required to establish clear and measurable outcomes for a project.

While we work not only to meet the goals of organizations and funders but also to contribute to knowledge in our discipline, we must have our participants' best interests as our main priority. That is, we must not treat them solely as subjects of research but become active participants in their lives. When I was honored with the Iris Marion Young Award by the University of Pittsburgh Women's Studies Department, I shared my monetary rewards with a study participant who, despite facing many obstacles, graduated from high school and went off to college this year. I continue to be a resource to this participant.

I also learned that if we are to do public sociology, our work has to contribute to a larger academic conversation about our role as academic researchers. In particular, in the course of doing this research I became aware of the social justice issue related to the ways institutional review boards (IRBs) limit social scientists in their research with disadvantaged and silenced populations. Before I began my project, some of my advisors at the university encouraged me to abandon work with girls, not only because my participants were under the age of 18 and were deemed "vulnerable subjects" but also because some of them were in foster care. IRB policies and procedures shaped my research approach as I adjusted my methods to fit established guidelines. For example, I couldn't include girls in foster care; I wrote long and tedious consent forms for these adolescent subjects and their legal guardians, who were generally unfamiliar with, and did not necessarily understand, why these were even necessary; and I had to change recruitment methods mid-study. However, I saw these limitations as an opportunity to become involved in a conversation about ethics in qualitative research through the International Center for Qualitative Inquiry at the University of Illinois at Urbana-Champaign. My work with girls has resulted in conference presentations and a publication that seeks to challenge IRB ethics and bring awareness to how IRBs undermine qualitative researchers' efforts to achieve socially responsible ethical standards.

Conclusion

Public sociology is driven by a passion often derived from lived experience that inspires us to use the tools of sociological analysis to transform institutional barriers into opportunities for activism. My quest to bridge the gap between academic theorizing about girls' social identities and implementing programs that incorporate intersectional approaches has been a long process, not a simple project.

This work incorporates my personal and professional backgrounds, feminist research methods, partnership with an organization that shares my vision for girls, foundation funders that recognize the imperative of understanding the diverse needs and strengths of girls, and my refusal to be stagnated by the confines of institutional review boards. When we do public sociology, we need to become involved in the lives of our participants in meaningful ways, form partnerships with organizations that share our vision, and provide concrete information that improves organizations and the lives of people with whom we work.

References

Babbie, E. (2004). *The practice of social research* (10th ed.). Belmont, CA: Wadsworth.

Berg, B. (2001). *Qualitative research methods for the social sciences* (4th ed.). Boston, MA: Allyn and Bacon.

Collins, P. (2000). *Black feminist thought: Knowledge, consciousness and the politics of empowerment.* New York, NY: Routledge.

Crenshaw, K. (1991). Mapping the margins: Intersectionality, identity politics, and violence against women of color. *Stanford Law Review, 43,* 1241–1299.

Lareau, A. (2003). *Unequal childhoods: Class, race, and family life.* Los Angeles, CA: University of California Press.

Case Study 4.3. Youth Participation in Community Research for Racial Justice

Barry Checkoway and Katie Richards-Schuster

What are some strategies for involving young people in community research that simultaneously develops knowledge, contributes to their social development, and strengthens racial justice? How can young people gather information in ways that enable them to challenge discrimination and increase dialogue in metropolitan areas that are characterized by both segregation and diversity? What is a racially just approach to community-based research?

These questions are significant for various reasons. While many metropolitan areas are increasing in their diversity, these areas remain highly segregated, with little interaction across racial and ethnic lines. These communities are being challenged to build capacity for solving problems, planning programs, and addressing issues arising as part of the process.

Young people are ideally positioned to become engaged in this work. Most of them reside in segregated areas, attend segregated schools, and have expertise based on their own experiences. Some of them are aware of segregation and open to opportunities to communicate and collaborate with people who are different from themselves. Young people generally hold attitudes toward racial justice that are different from those of earlier generations and would take action against injustice if encouraged to do so. They are future leaders, to be sure, but they also are leaders today, and if some of them were to step forward and speak for themselves, it might prod their teachers and parents to do the same.

This case study describes a program to involve young people in challenging segregation and creating change in metropolitan Detroit. The program features youth participation in community research as an instrumental element, and it is this that we emphasize here.

Youth Dialogues on Race and Ethnicity in Metropolitan Detroit

Metropolitan Detroit is among the nation's most segregated metropolitan area. According to the 2000 U.S. Census, the city is 80% African American, while the suburbs are 85% White. For years, the city has been losing employment opportunities, residential development has been suburban, and disparities have been widening.

Amid segregation, there also is diversity. While most suburbs are White European, the city is largely segregated in its African American population. However, some suburbs are undergoing changes as they experience increases in their population of African, Asian, Middle Eastern, and Latin American descent. Some communities boast of their racial and ethnic mosaic of students, their cultural roots in nations worldwide, and their numerous languages spoken at home as forerunners of emergent "micro melting pots" expected elsewhere.

Young people in metropolitan Detroit are open to discussion of race and ethnicity, but they live in segregation, with few opportunities to communicate with people who are different from themselves. Studies show that young people often understand the limitations of segregation, appreciate the benefits of diversity, and want to interact with other young people across boundaries, again with few opportunities to do so (Checkoway, 2009).

Youth Dialogues on Race and Ethnicity in Metropolitan Detroit was established by the University of Michigan and the Skillman Foundation to increase dialogue and challenge discrimination in the metropolitan area. Since its launch, the program has involved young people in intergroup dialogues, metropolitan tours, community action projects, residential retreats, and youth policy summits. Youth participation is central to all stages of the program. Young people are participants, program planners, policy leaders, community organizers, and also researchers and evaluators.

Youth Participation in Evaluation and Research

Youth participation in evaluation and research is a process of involving young people in knowledge development at the community level. In this approach, young people participate in defining the problem, gathering the information, and using the results. They serve as directors or partners in the work rather than as subjects in research in which adults take the lead.

Youth participation in evaluation and research provides information for making better program decisions. It also strengthens the social development of the participants, enables them to exercise their political rights as citizens, and builds organizational and community capacity in ways that can contribute to community change.

Evaluation is central to the Youth Dialogues on Race and Ethnicity in Metropolitan Detroit program and has a multilevel design that assumes that young people should assess the programs that affect them. On an annual basis, they and their adult allies form an evaluation team and employ quantitative and qualitative methods to assess the program. They define the problems, gather information, and prepare reports with findings and recommendations for future practice.

It should be emphasized that our approach to evaluation is community based rather than community oriented, intergenerational rather than adult led or youth led, and neither qualitative nor quantitative, but rather both qualitative and quantitative.

As part of their qualitative work, young people document a bus tour, residential retreat, and other activities; interview participants about their experiences of growing up in segregation and their involvement in the dialogues; and conduct focus groups with youth and adult stakeholders. They use photovoice as a technique to take pictures of images of diversity and discrimination in schools and communities in which participants reside and to discuss how young people "see" race and ethnicity in their own communities (see Wang & Burris, 1997, for a description of photovoice).

As part of their quantitative work, they help create a pre- and posttest questionnaire to assess attitudinal changes among participants using multiple scales, including Communications Scale, Multigroup Ethnic Identity Measure, Color-Blind Racial Attitudes Scale, and Collective Self-Esteem Scale. They also create and administer a post-test questionnaire at the end of the program to rate their overall experience and to make recommendations for the program itself.

A recent pre- and posttest questionnaire to 88 youth participants from 16 neighborhood groups, community agencies, and school districts resulted in a response rate of 92%. The findings showed that as a result of the program, young people increased their knowledge about their own racial and ethnic identity and that of others; increased their awareness and understanding of racism and racial privilege; and developed leadership skills and took actions to address issues of racism in their community.

Communications Outreach

Our evaluation team produces reports on an annual basis. Each report documents program activities and their various effects and features photographs and stories from participants in their own words to amplify their voices. Annual reports are hard copy, but one took the additional form of a DVD conceived, photographed, and narrated by the youth themselves. The video has been presented in classrooms, workshops, and conferences.

As an integral part of evaluation, we have collaborated with the Mosaic Youth Theatre of Detroit—a prominent youth theatre company whose members participated in the dialogues—in dissemination and outreach. Theatre members facilitated a special workshop with young people, gathered information from the participants, studied their journals, and prepared a script for public presentation. The outcome was *Speak for Yourself*, which has been performed in more than 100 school assemblies and community centers. Some of these performances have reached more than 1,000 young people. Following each performance is a "talk back" in which audience members shared thoughts about discrimination. Thus the evaluation has enabled young people to assess young people and for young people to perform their stories to large audiences of young people across the metropolitan area.

In addition, some participants took part in a special writing workshop and produced *Our Dreams Are Not a Secret: Teenagers in Metropolitan*

Detroit Speak Out,[1] a book written by young people about their experiences "growing up in segregated social worlds and living on the borders of change." At this writing, television producers have come forward with an agreement for a series of programs devoted to the dialogues.

Outcomes

Because of the work, young people have been approached to employ community-based participatory research principles in other projects. In the field of health, for example, young people have conducted community health assessments, interviewed community members about health needs, facilitated community meetings to gather information about health resources, and shared their findings with public officials. They compiled their findings in *Youth Participation in Neighborhood Planning for Community Health* and presented them to community leaders, public officials, and Michigan's surgeon general.

In the field of education, they conducted focus groups with students in neighborhoods and suburbs and gathered information and ideas from students about their present and future schools in coordination with community meetings and group discussions. Students answered questions about the curriculum, teachers and principals, safety and discipline, pathways after school, facilities and environment, and diversity. The publication *Voices of Youth: Metropolitan Detroit Students Speak Out on Their Schools* documented problems and issues that concern students across metropolitan Detroit and summarized improvements they want in their schools.

Sharing With Others

Young people participate in community evaluation research, but this approach is itself young as a field of practice and subject of study (Checkoway & Richards-Schuster, 2003, 2004, n.d.; Delgado, 2006; Sabo Flores, 2007). We cannot make broad generalizations from one example, but observations are possible.

Our observation is that young people are willing and able to participate in all stages of evaluation research, from defining the problem to gathering the information to sharing the results. They can join an evaluation research team and develop an evaluation plan. They can formulate questions and

---

[1]For more information about any of the projects or reports described in this section or to download a copy of *My Dreams Are Not a Secret: Teenagers Speak Out in Metropolitan Detroit*, please see http://www.youthandcommunity.org.

gather information through various research methods. They can make sense of information, analyze patterns and themes, draw conclusions, and make recommendations for action.

It is important to emphasize that this work is intergenerational rather than adult led or youth led, and, as such, youth and adults are partners in the process. They are not always equal in their influence, however, for there are stages and situations in which one or another might take the lead. For example, an adult evaluation team member might have primary responsibility for finding funds or providing transportation to and from an interview, whereas a youth member might take the lead in asking the questions and recording the answers. While young people are able to employ research methods that are standard among adults, they are also proficient with methods that are deemed more age-appropriate, such as using cell phones for photovoice, or conducting surveys on the Internet, or using youth-based media to communicate the findings. When young people provide their peers with a youth-authored document or perform their stories in a school assembly or community center, their age gives them a special advantage.

Young people can play various roles in the process. They can consult with their colleagues, provide them with guidance and feedback, and partner with them in questionnaire design, data collection, and report writing. Young people also are subjects of study in youth programs like these, but this is not their primary role as it normally is in evaluation research conducted by adults alone. At the same time, young people are not alone in this work. Adults are strong members of the evaluation team, and they collaborate with the young people at every stage of the process. There also are parents and teachers who support young people in their initiatives, of which evaluation research is only one.

We observe that youth participation in evaluation research has effects on the youth who participate by strengthening their substantive knowledge, practical skills, and civic competencies. When young people ask their own questions rather than the ones given by adult authorities, gather their own information rather than uncritically accept that of others, and formulate their own strategy rather than stay with the status quo, it benefits them and the communities of which they are part. There is no evidence yet about the duration of its effects or about what happens when they return to schools and communities that hold standard views of the roles of youth in society.

The notion that young people are willing and able to participate in evaluation research contrasts with portrayals of youth as problems in society who are withdrawn from participation or disengaged from democracy. Such portrayals are common in mass media, social science, and professional practice. When adults accept media portrayals of young people as disengaged, and youth accept these conceptions of themselves, this weakens expectations of their engagement.

Toward Racially Just Research

This case study describes a program that engages young people in all stages of research that promote equal opportunities and equal outcomes for all community groups regardless of their race, that challenges discrimination in the nation's most segregated metropolitan area. Their approach aims to create changes in the area in which they reside and contributes to their own social development and civic competencies as part of the process.

We are aware that this is only one example from which we are unable to draw generalizations, that we cannot claim that it overcomes the causes or consequences of metropolitan segregation, and that we cannot know whether its effects on the researchers continue over the long haul.

But we know that youth and adults are addressing a powerful social problem, that they employ research methods that are racially just in their content and process, and that their work is a story worth telling. If youth and adults in only one other metropolitan area were to read this case study and attempt a project of their own and to pass their own experience along to others, this work would be worth the effort.

References

Checkoway, B. (2009). Youth civic engagement for dialogue and diversity at the metropolitan level. *The Foundation Review, 1*(2), 41–50.

Checkoway, B., & Richards-Schuster, K. (2003). Youth participation in community evaluation research. *American Journal of Evaluation, 24*(1), 21–33.

Checkoway, B., & Richards-Schuster, K. (2004). Youth participation in evaluation and research as a way of lifting new voices. *Children, Youth and Environments, 14*(2), 84-98. Retrieved from http://www.colorado.edu/journals/cye/14_2/article5.htm

Checkoway, B., & Richards-Schuster, K. (n.d.). *Participatory evaluation with young people.* Battle Creek, MI: W.K. Kellogg Foundation.

Delgado, M. (2006). *Designs and methods for youth-led research.* Thousand Oaks, CA: Sage.

Sabo Flores, K. (2007). *Youth participatory evaluation: Strategies for engaging young people.* San Francisco, CA: Jossey-Bass.

Wang, C., & Burris, M. (1997). Photovoice: Concept, methodology, and use for participatory needs assessment. *Health Education and Behavior, 24,* 369–387.

Case Study 4.4. Building Resources to Create and Maintain Stable Diverse Communities

Madeline Troche-Rodríguez

In the tradition of C. Wright Mills, sociologists are called to *do* sociology by using our sociological imaginations and by connecting biographies, social contexts, and historical junctures. More recently, sociologist Michael Burawoy has renewed that call, encouraging us to do *public sociology* by engaging civil society in the work that we do. Today more than ever we are asked to evaluate our approaches to doing sociology. Most of our work remains confined within academic circles, out of reach of the people who need it to address pressing social problems (i.e., economic and social disparities) and to promote social change. We are asked to continue the conversations about racial/ethnic, economic, and political inequities in spaces beyond academia. We have a responsibility to engage communities (or those working with them) affected by such inequalities, providing a voice to those who are often silenced. I see this as an important call in metropolitan areas like Chicago, where subtle and sophisticated forms of racial and economic segregation persist. This case study traces my experience connecting the academic and the fair housing advocacy worlds.

Sociologist in Training

While working as an undergraduate research assistant at the University of Puerto Rico-Mayagüez Center for Applied Social Science Research (*Centro de Investigación Social Aplicada, CISA*) in the early 1990s, I had the opportunity to learn a thing or two about helping communities solve their problems. In the field, I witnessed many lively discussions between faculty mentors and community leaders trying to find the best solutions to community everyday problems. These conversations often resulted in the genesis of research projects designed to evaluate and provide recommendations to address residential segregation, the high rate of asthma and cancer in disadvantaged neighborhoods, or the effectiveness of community policing, for instance. In the end, applied social science research took the driver's seat; we studied community issues but did not always keep the community engaged in the research process. I reasoned that whichever direction I took in my academic career, it had to make sense to the community, not of fellow sociologists, but of those who were affected by the outcomes of our research.

Four years later, while working on my doctorate at Loyola University Chicago, I participated in a project with the Center for Urban Research and

Learning (CURL) and community partners Leadership Council for Metropolitan Open Communities (LCMOC) and Latinos United. The Leadership Council was the oldest and largest fair housing organization in Chicago's metropolitan area. It was established more than 40 years ago as a result of the Chicago Freedom Movement's campaign for open housing led by Dr. Martin Luther King Jr. Latinos United[2] was a smaller comprehensive housing organization with a very strong presence in the city. Latinos United was incorporated in the late 1980s with the support of the late mayor Harold Washington's Advisory Council on Latino Affairs (MACLA). In 1994, Latinos United and former members of MACLA successfully sued the Chicago Housing Authority (CHA), charging the government agency with discrimination against Latinos based on the lack of representation of eligible Latino families in public housing. As a result of the successful settlement of this lawsuit, millions of dollars were allocated for community outreach and education in the Latino community. During the 10-year consent decree, Latino families gained increased access to housing resources and CHA programs.

In 1998, the Leadership Council and Latinos United asked CURL to help both organizations list and document community resources available to Latino families facing housing discrimination in suburban Chicago. Since the mid-1980s, municipalities adjacent to the city of Chicago have been experiencing an increase in the Latino population. By the 1990s, the percentage growth of Latinos in suburban Chicago was significantly higher, and they were not always welcome in predominantly White areas. Fair housing specialists and community organizers at both LCMOC and Latinos United were receiving numerous complaints about families who felt discriminated against in those municipalities. My job was to create profiles of target municipalities (i.e., Northlake, Melrose Park, Franklin Park, Cicero, Elgin, and Addison) and compile a list of fair housing and community resources. I found that the community and fair housing resources available to Latinos were very limited or nonexistent in those suburbs. Most Latinos relied on the church and other faith-based organizations to address their concerns. Latinos United and LCMOC decided to devise a plan to address the gap.

The Fair Housing Activist

In the spring of 1999, Carlos de Jesús, then executive director of Latinos United, offered me a position as fair housing specialist. Having completed

---

[2]Since 2006, Latinos United expanded its scope of work and changed its name to the Latino Policy Forum. See http://www.latinopolicyforum.org/default.aspx for details.

my master's thesis, I put my graduate education temporarily on hold to enter the world of fair housing. In that position, funded by the U.S. Department of Housing and Urban Development (HUD)'s Fair Housing Initiatives Program (FHIP),[3] I was responsible for the design and implementation of a bilingual fair housing outreach and education curriculum in target municipalities experiencing a substantial Latino population growth. Latinos United set out to explore new territory, as this was their first FHIP grant. I received fair housing training from the John Marshall Law School's Fair Housing Clinic, the Leadership Council, and the National Fair Housing Alliance. I also learned a great deal about housing policy by networking with other housing practitioners and Latino leaders in Chicago. For the most part, my job consisted of traveling to the various suburban municipalities to meet with Latino community leaders, developing bilingual fair housing materials and facilitating fair housing rights workshops, and assisting families filing bona fide fair housing complaints with HUD and other enforcement agencies.

During that year I also became a fair housing tester. Testing is a legal tool used by fair housing enforcement agencies to uncover patterns of discrimination in the insurance, lending, and real estate industries. I developed close relationships with fair housing advocates from the only agencies doing that kind of work in the region: LCMOC, the Chicago Lawyers' Committee for Civil Rights Under Law (CLCCRUL), HOPE Fair Housing Center, Interfaith Housing Center of the Northern Suburbs, and the South Suburban Housing Center.

My 18-month HUD/FHIP contract with Latinos United ended, and I returned to Loyola University in the fall of 2000 equipped with a new set of skills, firsthand knowledge about fair housing policy, and many questions that I would later address in my dissertation. Most important, this experience informed the subsequent choices I made as a fair housing advocate and sociologist in training. In 2005, while working on my dissertation about the housing experience of Latino families in suburban Chicago, I received another call from Latinos United. They were creating a new position on community education and needed

---

[3]HUD FHIP grants are awarded to organizations with capacity to educate the community about fair housing rights. These organizations help clients file bona fide complaints and refer them to enforcement agencies. FHIP also provides funds to enforcement agencies with legal staff to carry out fair housing investigation, training, testing, and litigation activities under the Fair Housing Act of 1968 (as amended in 1988).

someone with my skill set in sociology and fair housing. I accepted the position.

Sociology, Advocacy, and the Birth of Movesmart.org

Although housing discrimination and residential and economic segregation were still pervasive in Chicago's metropolitan area (Frey & Farley, 1996; Lewis Mumford Center, 2001), the fair housing movement was struggling. Funding for community education and outreach was scarce, limiting the impact of organizations like Latinos United. My job, like that of many of my colleagues, was in danger. Fair housing enforcement was still HUD's priority, but only a handful of agencies in the region were receiving funding to do the work. Members of the Chicago Area Fair Housing Alliance (CAFHA), an association of fair housing organizations, lawyers, and real estate agents committed to fairness in housing, gathered regularly to discuss the future of the fair housing movement. That same year another event deeply shook the local fair housing community: The Leadership Council—the oldest fair housing organization in the region—closed its doors. In the wake of this loss, Justin Massa, then fair housing testing and outreach coordinator for the CLCCRUL, and Rob Breymaier, then director of the Community Relations Program at LCMOC, invited me to explore alternatives and identify next steps.

Our first coffee meeting was on September 14, 2006. By that time, I had accepted a full-time faculty position with the City Colleges of Chicago at Harry S. Truman College, and Rob Breymaier had become the executive director of the Oak Park Regional Housing Center in Oak Park, Illinois. Rob, Justin, and I initially envisioned either an online refereed journal or "virtual community" in which housing practitioners, advocates, and scholars could have serious discussions about policy and research on fair housing and diversity. We called it HARP—the Housing Advocacy Research Project. But perhaps HARP sounded too academic and removed from the people we intended to serve—the future beneficiaries of residential integration and stable diverse communities? Our discussions still centered on the fact that 40 years after the Chicago Freedom Movement, segregation remained virtually unchanged. Soon, the idea of a virtual community took hold. The future of fair housing was in using technology to further racial and economic residential integration.

Justin Massa is not only a dedicated and passionate fair housing and civil rights advocate but a visionary, innovator, and new technologies expert. The next time we met for coffee, he showed up with an extraordinary action plan and brand: MoveSmart.Org: Technology for Residential Integration. Next, we assessed the need of the organization by surveying housing counselors and senior housing personnel who could potentially use MoveSmart.org. Many counselors still find housing information via word of mouth, newspapers, or real estate listings. However, for home seekers with access to technology, housing searches have moved online (i.e., Craigslist). Given that face-to-face affirmative counseling programs can be very costly, it appeared that MoveSmart.org could be a very important tool to housing counselors, who experience high demand for their services in an environment short on funding. It would enable them to connect their clients to areas of opportunity, community amenities, and housing resources, saving the counselors a great deal of time and work.

In the fall of 2007, Justin, Rob, and I cofounded MoveSmart.org and incorporated it as a not-for-profit organization.[4] Since then, we have worked tirelessly to make this concept a reality. We recruited a very talented board of directors[5] that includes fair and affordable housing professionals, attorneys, and academics. Among the academics, early on, we counted on the support of Professor Janet Smith of the UIC Nathalie P. Voorhees Center for Neighborhood and Community Improvement, who lent us her expertise on equity issues and housing planning. We currently count on the expertise of Professor Maria Krysan, a sociologist at the UIC Institute of Government and Public Affairs. Her research focuses on residential segregation and examines barriers to integration in Chicago (Krysan, 2008). Clearly, our work is grounded on cutting-edge research from prominent scholars and practitioners in the field (Massey & Denton, 2003). We also have a dedicated team of volunteers and very talented individuals including Web developers, publicists, student consultants, geographic information system (G.I.S.) developers, and writers.

With the housing practitioners' and sociologists' insights in mind, we pitched the idea to funders and fair housing experts. As Aurie Pennick, executive director of the Field Foundation, said during one of our meetings, "This [MoveSmart.org] is where fair housing needs to go." We took her words very seriously. We have presented our concept at numerous professional meetings and conferences in Chicago, San Francisco, Washington, D.C., and Baltimore, just to name a few cities. We have participated in

---

[4]The organization received 501(c)(3) status in October 2008.

[5]Rob Breymaier serves as board president, I am the board secretary, and Justin is the organization's executive director.

competitions. We have written concept papers and crafted our mission statement, by-laws, and strategic plan. All along, we have received much support and encouraging words to move forward.

Our mission as stated on the website is to "foster vibrant and diverse neighborhoods by empowering housing seekers to move to opportunity."[6] MoveSmart.org uniquely positioned itself to use data and technology, thereby making it accessible to various publics. The goal is to encourage integration with a versatile and user-friendly platform. The website features guides in a variety of topics written at a level community members can understand. The Neighborhood Finder section creates profiles based on priorities the user chooses from a list of amenities (i.e., schools, transportation, grocery stores). The site also has tools for housing counselors and registered users. The data sets include information about amenities (i.e., transportation, health care centers), quality-of-life indicators (i.e., air quality, crime index, food deserts), and opportunities (i.e., maps, social services, affordable housing). The data come from various sources including the U.S. Census, the City of Chicago, FDIC, Board of Education, and HUD. With these tools we expect to mitigate residential, racial, and economic segregation in our region and to some extent bridge the digital divide. The site is designed to encourage integrative moves to neighborhoods that home seekers would have otherwise thought out of reach.

The Future of Movesmart.org

This has been an incredible journey. As a sociologist I have had the opportunity to see the impact of our work when working alongside community leaders and advocates. As fair housing advocates, we are committed to continue the legacy of the Leadership Council and Dr. Martin Luther King's call for open communities. But, like many other organizations struggling in this uncertain economy, we have not been able to get all the funding needed to fully launch our programs. Approximately 80% of the website's infrastructure has been built, with about 60% of the data and information we would like to have already into the site. We hope MoveSmart.org will live up to its mission to foster vibrant racially and economically integrated communities in our region. We need a fair housing model that benefits all kinds of people in our communities.

---

[6]See http://movesmart.org/about

References

Frey, W. H., & Farley, R. (1996). Latino, Asian and black segregation in U.S. metropolitan areas: Are multi-ethnic metros different? *Demography, 33*(1), 35–50.

Krysan, M. (2008). *Racial blind spots: A barrier to integrated communities in Chicago*. Critical Issues Paper. Urbana, IL: University of Illinois, Institute of Government and Public Affairs.

Lewis Mumford Center. (2001). *Ethnic diversity grows, neighborhood integration lags behind*. Albany, NY: Lewis Mumford Center.

Massey, D. S., & Denton, N. A. (1993). *American apartheid: Segregation and the making of the underclass*. Cambridge, MA: Harvard University Press.

CASE STUDIES 5

The Media

The mass media has become a powerful social institution in modern societies, encompassing a wide variety of different media—for example, newspapers, magazines, radio, television, books, new digital media— that communicate simultaneously to people within a local community, the broader society, and even around the globe. Sociologists have been engaged in identifying the various ways in which these media affect us, both on an individual as well as a societal level. Some of the areas of inquiry have included the processes and consequences of media concentration, how we consume media messages, how the media shape our behavior and perceptions, and even how the media contribute to or undermine our communities.

Demonstrating the power of the media to shape our perceptions about a story, Peter Dreier and Christopher Martin conducted research on the framing of stories by the media during the presidential campaign of 2008—specifically looking at alleged voter fraud perpetrated by the Association of Community Organizations for Reform Now (ACORN). ACORN, once the largest community organizing group in the country fighting to improve the living and working conditions of poor and working-class people, had become a frequent target of attacks by the George W. Bush White House and the Republican Party. These attacks, first voiced in marginal conservative media outlets, eventually found their way into the mainstream news. Dreier and Martin analyzed stories coming out of major news outlets from 2007 to 2009 to see how the story developed over the course of the presidential campaign. They found substantial evidence of negligence in reporting the news about ACORN. They demonstrate the power of the politically conservative media in influencing the mainstream media's framing of stories. As public sociologists, Dreier and Martin did not leave their report to gather dust on some shelf but distributed it to major news outlets, where it received considerable attention.

Media advocacy involves using different media to influence how and what people think about a social issue. In the second case study, David Jernigan describes his work with the Center on Alcohol Marketing and Youth (CAMY) researching and monitoring the marketing practices of the alcohol industry, especially practices that jeopardize the health and safety of the country's young people. CAMY analyzed audience data from advertising research databases and then used findings to build media and political advocacy campaigns to work for changes in industry practices. The research had a number of concrete achievements. These included forcing alcohol companies to move their advertising away from youth audiences; influencing the U.S. Congress to pass legislation requiring that the federal government annually report the rates of exposure of youth to messages encouraging alcohol use in the media, tightening self-regulatory standards for the alcohol industry, and playing a role in the passage of the first piece of legislation devoted solely to underage drinking.

Focusing on production and consumption of media content, the Reel Girls interdisciplinary project at the University of North Carolina Wilmington (UNCW) involved faculty and students in the areas of technical filmmaking, media literacy, feminism, and film studies. University women enrolled in the course studied these topics, then taught local middle school girls about media literacy, technical film production, and self-portrait documentary. The middle school girls produced their own short independent films under the mentorship of the university women. In the first year, the professors encountered an unexpected challenge involving age, racial/ethnic, and economic gaps between the two groups of students. The media literacy activities developed by the university women reflected their own perceptions about adolescence, their race/ethnicity, and their social class; they assumed a youthful innocence and naiveté for the middle school girls that they would be training that did not reflect these younger girls' lives. In the second year, there was a greater focus on the ways race, class, gender, and sexuality interact in exploring media literacy. Each year there was a final screening of the documentaries on the UNCW campus, which transformed Reel Girls from a personal video project to a community event. For the middle school girls, it was an empowering experience to be on campus speaking about the documentary and their experience.

The first three case studies focused on more traditional forms of media—print, television, and movies. In the final case study, Keith Hampton describes his work with i-Neighbors.org, an Internet website that is both a research project and an intervention. There is abundant research showing that neighborhood social networks are important to both individuals and communities. However, such networks are on the decline. This trend is particularly true for residential neighborhoods characterized by concentrated disadvantage. The i-Neighbors.org project is based on prior research suggesting that the Internet supports, rather than detracts from, the formation of social ties through networks, although this is less true for disadvantaged communities that do not have the same access to the technology. Offering a free service that allows people to create a virtual community for their geographic community, this project studied how Internet use affects neighborhood interactions. In particular, researchers were interested in learning whether residential areas of concentrated disadvantage would benefit from the Internet in the form of higher levels of local social cohesion. Data on users and usage patterns showed that the most active i-Neighbors communities were in middle-class suburban areas, but a significant minority was in neighborhoods classified among the most disadvantaged in the country. This finding represents a significant contribution to policy that addresses the poor/rich digital divide, making the case for more attention to and technological investment in low-income communities.

Case Study 5.1. The Media, ACORN, and Presidential Politics

Peter Dreier and Christopher R. Martin

In 2008, the Association of Community Organizations for Reform Now (ACORN) tried to steal the presidential election for Barack Obama through systematic voter fraud. After Obama's election, ACORN was rewarded with the promise of billions in government contracts. Finally, in 2009, undercover journalists posing as a pimp and a prostitute walked into several ACORN offices in the United States, where workers freely gave them advice on illicit businesses, revealing for all of America the fundamental corruption of the organization.

That's what most of America knows about ACORN, and all of it is wrong.

We sought to uncover why Americans had such a misleading view of ACORN by examining how the media reported—or misreported—the controversy over the so-called ACORN scandal. As this case study recounts, our research put us in the middle of a political firestorm.

Until 2008, ACORN, the largest community organizing group in the country, was well known primarily among liberal activists and the low-income people it has organized since it began in Little Rock, Arkansas, in 1970. By mobilizing poor people and their middle-class allies, it won major victories to improve the living and working conditions of poor and working-class people. It successfully fought banks that redlined and engaged in predatory lending, employers that paid poverty wages, and developers that gentrified low-income neighborhoods and refused to provide affordable housing. By early 2009, ACORN registered more than a million Americans to vote. At that point, ACORN also had about 400,000 low-income members in 70 cities and a $25 million budget, raised by a combination of dues, local fundraising events, and foundation grants.

During its four decades of community organizing, ACORN earned the ire of certain business groups (who opposed ACORN's efforts to raise wages for the working poor), banks and payday lenders (who were the target of ACORN organizing campaigns), and the Republican Party (who disliked ACORN's success at registering urban minority voters, who happen to be more likely to vote for Democrats).

Starting in 2004, Karl Rove (President George W. Bush's top political advisor) personally orchestrated an attack on ACORN. He insisted that a number of U.S. Attorneys prosecute ACORN for voter fraud, even if there was no evidence for it. When one of them, David Iglesias, the U.S. Attorney in New Mexico, investigated the situation and discovered ACORN had not engaged in any fraud, he refused to prosecute the group. Rove quickly got Attorney General Alberto Gonzales to fire him. The resulting scandal eventually forced Gonzales to resign in 2007, but he had already helped put the anti-ACORN campaign in motion. In 2006, during Bush's second term, conservatives and Republicans renewed their efforts against ACORN. Although there was growing dissatisfaction in public opinion polls with Bush and the Republican Party, if they could make their political opponents look worse by linking them to a controversial, even "radical," group, conservatives still might win in 2008.

Their attack on ACORN was part of a broader conservative effort to discredit Barack Obama—first as a candidate, then as president. This was obvious at the Republican convention in St. Paul in 2008, where former New York mayor Rudy Giuliani, former New York governor George Pataki, and newly minted vice presidential candidate Sarah Palin pointedly attacked Obama's experience as a community organizer. On October 15, in the third presidential debate, held at Hofstra University, Republican candidate Sen. John McCain (2008) said, "We need to know the full extent of Senator Obama's relationship with ACORN, who is now on the verge of maybe perpetrating one of the greatest frauds in voter history in this country, maybe destroying the fabric of democracy."

By the final few weeks of the 2008 presidential campaign, persistent attacks on ACORN by the conservative media and Republican politicians, which were repeated in the mainstream news, had clearly put the community organization on the public's agenda. A national survey conducted in mid-October by the Pew Research Center for the People and the Press revealed that 82% of Americans had heard about ACORN.

The mainstream news media's nearly uniform acceptance of those conservative attacks and their impact on public opinion, before and after a historic election, made us pause. Were the news media accurate and truthful in how they portrayed or "framed" ACORN? Did they fact-check allegations about ACORN's work?

How We Got Started

The project started when Peter Dreier, a professor of politics and director of the Urban & Environmental Policy Program at Occidental College, emailed Christopher Martin, a professor of journalism and communication studies at the University of Northern Iowa, in November 2008, just a few weeks after the presidential election. Dreier studies urban politics and community organizing and was familiar with the work of ACORN, while Martin researches how the news media cover labor and working-class issues. ACORN had become a significant political issue in the election and was likely to remain one. Our intent was to bring rigorous research to the question about how the mainstream news media portrayed, or "framed," ACORN. Our study received no outside funding.

We began by focusing on news media stories from two full years, 2007 to 2008, to see how the framing of ACORN had developed during the course of the campaign, peaking in October 2008. We limited our analysis to 15 major news media organizations, which yielded a total of 647 stories during the two-year period.[1] As the conservative allegations against ACORN continued, we broadened our analysis to discuss the stream of news stories that continued through the summer of 2009, including a false allegation from the Republican National Committee that the economic stimulus package held a special $8.5 billion set-aside for ACORN and a Republican congressman's report that accused ACORN of being "intentionally structured as a criminal enterprise." We completed the report in August 2009 (Dreier & Martin, 2009, 2010).

Releasing the Results Into Media Spectacle

As we prepared to release the study, we had no idea that in the summer of 2009, Hannah Giles and James O'Keefe, two young conservative activists posing as a prostitute and her friend, were walking into ACORN offices around the country and asking for advice on taxes and, in some cases, a business venture that involved underage undocumented immigrant girls

---

[1] This included four highest-circulation national newspapers—*USA Today, New York Times, Washington Post,* and the *Wall Street Journal*—and an analysis of the transcripts of reports from leading broadcast news organizations: ABC, CBS, NBC, Fox News Channel, CNN, MSNBC, National Public Radio (NPR), and *NewsHour With Jim Lehrer* (PBS). We also included stories from three metro newspapers representing cities in which ACORN has a long-time presence: the *Cleveland Plain Dealer, Minneapolis Star-Tribune,* and *Pittsburgh Post-Gazette.*

from El Salvador; they recorded their stunt with a hidden video camera. It is now clear that they selectively edited the tapes for release, later adding in video with O'Keefe dressed up in an outlandish pimp costume (hat, sunglasses, fur coat, and walking stick) with racist overtones.[2]

By the second week of September 2009, these edited videos became a national story. They were posted to the conservative website biggovernment. com and quickly became the top story on the Glenn Beck Show, the rest of Fox News, conservative talk radio, and CNN's Lou Dobbs Show. Throughout the fall of 2009 and winter of 2010, Beck paid special attention to ACORN, regularly ranting that it was part of a Marxist, socialist, Saul Alinsky-inspired left-wing conspiracy that includes President Obama, the Service Employees International Union, the Tides Foundation, and other liberal and progressive groups.

The controversy about the videos proved irresistible for the mainstream news media and compounded ACORN's troubles. Congress—including some of ACORN's long-term allies—quickly voted to rescind ACORN's federal funding, primarily for homeownership counseling. Although ACORN received no funds from the Internal Revenue Service or the Census Bureau, both agencies also removed ACORN as a partner in their efforts to help the working poor qualify for tax rebates and to encourage low-income households to fill out census forms. Some of ACORN's key foundation funders withdrew their support.

Our study was released in the midst of this spectacular media environment—and we use "spectacular" because the story was all about the spectacle that the videos presented and that seemed to be incontrovertible truth (if one ignored the videomakers' political agenda and the existence of selective video editing). The conservative push against ACORN had finally succeeded in making ACORN an outcast in almost every corner of the country. Even the University of Northern Iowa dropped its efforts to help publicize the report's release. Although Occidental College's media staff agreed to send out the press releases, it refused to feature the study on its website, despite (or perhaps because of) the likely national attention it would bring to the college.[3] While we were able to find an alternate method to send out the press releases on time, the episode reminded us how university bureaucrats who are scared of offending conservative patrons can quickly turn their back on public sociology.

---

[2]The complete original videos have never been released by O'Keefe, Giles, or their conservative media patron, Andrew Breitbart.

[3]The incident also reminded us of the value of tenure (which, fortunately, we both have).

The Results of the Study

We found substantial problems of negligence in news reporting on ACORN:

- More than half (55%) of all the articles about ACORN in the 15 major media outlets during 2007 and 2008 were about allegations of "voter fraud."
- 82.8% of the stories about ACORN's alleged involvement in voter fraud failed to mention that actual voter fraud is very rare (only 17.2% did mention this fact).
- 80.3% of the stories about ACORN's alleged involvement in voter fraud failed to mention that ACORN was reporting registration irregularities to authorities, as required by law.
- 85.1% of the stories about ACORN's alleged involvement in voter fraud failed to note that it was acting to stop incidents of registration problems by its (mostly temporary) employees when it became aware of these problems.
- 95.8% of the stories about ACORN's alleged involvement in voter fraud failed to provide deeper context, especially well-documented efforts by Republican Party officials to use allegations of voter fraud to dampen voting by low-income and minority Americans.[4]
- 61.4% of the stories about ACORN's alleged involvement in voter fraud failed to acknowledge that Republicans were trying to discredit Obama with an ACORN scandal.

Although the mainstream media framed ACORN in negative terms during the campaign, the spectacle of the hidden videos made our timely report a salient story for many news organizations. With so many political allies shrinking away from ACORN, we were one of the few information sources with an alternative story (and one backed by strong research) about what had happened to the community organization. In the first week after it was released, our report was discussed or mentioned in columns in the *Washington Post* and the *Chicago Tribune* (both columns were syndicated in other papers) and the *Philadelphia Inquirer,* as well as numerous other print and radio outlets. The report's visibility was heightened when Dreier twice appeared as a guest on segments of MSNBC's *The Rachel Maddow Show* devoted to the ACORN controversy. In addition, he wrote an op-ed, "The War on ACORN," in the *Los Angeles Times* (which was reprinted in other daily papers) and several articles summarizing the

---

[4]In August 2009 a House Judiciary Committee investigation released more than 5,000 pages of White House and Republican National Committee emails and transcripts of closed-door testimony by Karl Rove, former Bush senior advisor and deputy chief of staff, and Harriet Miers, former White House counsel, providing further evidence that Rove personally orchestrated an attack on ACORN, leading to the firing of U.S. Attorney David Iglesias and a scandal at the Department of Justice.

report (Atlas & Dreier, 2009; Dreier, 2009a, 2009b; Martin & Dreier, 2009).

In our interviews with the media, we recapped our report, explained why Republicans and conservatives were attacking ACORN, and defended ACORN's track record as an effective community organizing group. Inevitably, interviewers asked us about the controversy over the videos. We were at a disadvantage because neither the two people who made the videos nor their sponsor, Andrew Breitbart, made the original videos available to journalists, ACORN, or the public. Having examined the videos that appeared on Breitbart's website, and having interviewed several ACORN staffpersons, we concluded (and acknowledged in media interviews) that in at least a few offices, ACORN staff made serious misjudgments but apparently had done nothing illegal. We reported that ACORN had fired those staffpersons and had initiated a management review of its training program for staff members involved in providing housing and tax counseling.

The Conservative Response

In addition to getting many supportive emails, the study made us immediate targets of the conservative media and their devotees. Attacks on the report, and on us, quickly surfaced in conservative publications, websites, and the blogosphere, and we were soon deluged with negative emails—many of them clearly by people who had not read the study (many also did not sign their names).[5] The barrage of emails was not random. This became obvious when, after Dreier's op-ed column appeared in the *Los Angeles Times*, he received many emails from around the country that made the same

---

[5] One emailer insisted that Dreier "apologize to the American people and COMMITT [sic] SUICIDE!" Another wrote, "You are not academics at all, merely hacks." Wrote another, "Why would you lie about Acorn Pimpgate? The worst part is you know that you are lieing [sic], you just don't care." "Nice job dipshit," wrote another. "Is that how they do research over there at oxy.edu? . . . I guess that's what happens when you get tenure based on a mail order degree." Another wrote that he was "saddened that any child would have to sit in a classroom and listen to such a liar as yourself. Yes, liar, that is what you are. Oh, and Obama went to school there. Let's not forget that." A man named Paul Bernard from Goodyear, Arizona, wrote, "I am not a professor like you profess to be, Why don't you do your self [sic] and the college a huge favor and step down, saving the college from more humiliation than you already bring upon it. You sir are whats [sic] wrong with our country, your [sic] a bigot, a liar, and probably a closet racist and homosexual prevert [sic]."

points, often with similar rhetoric. These criticisms of Dreier and his column circulated on right-wing websites (including NewsBusters.Com and Patterico. Com) and were obviously picked up by readers who felt compelled (or were encouraged) to contact him. For example, a Los Angeles attorney wrote, "Drier [sic], you are a fucking liar, your latimes story was bs with lie after lie, is that how you teach. RESIGN NOW."

Breitbart, a one-time staffperson for the Drudge Report, whose biggovernment.com released the ACORN videos, emailed Dreier and Martin on the day of the study's release. On the phone with Martin, he suggested that he would give us a "forum" on his website. We politely declined and responded saying that the best thing would be for him to link to our study so his readers could read the entire report. Breitbart never did link to it, until a month later, when he devoted an entire blog post to attacking us as shills for ACORN and—oddly—accusing us of "trying to rebuild the media and the left elite, who use the poor and the downtrodden as their foot soldiers in order to maintain power in government, academia, the media and Hollywood." Breitbart sent the story link to Martin the same day, with no message except a threatening subject line that said "i'm giving you benefit of the doubt that dreier has used you."

We could take the browbeating by the right-wing bullies, but apparently the mainstream media could not. Encouraged by Glenn Beck and right-wing bloggers, many people waged a lobbying campaign accusing mainstream media organizations of liberal bias and demanding that they apologize for their failure to report about ACORN's corruption. At the *New York Times*, the pressure had an impact. Public editor Clark Hoyt (2009) responded in a September 27 column to charges that the *Times* had tuned in too late to the ACORN video story. He noted that "Jill Abramson, the managing editor for news, agreed with me that the paper was 'slow off the mark,' and blamed 'insufficient tuned-in-ness to the issues that are dominating Fox News and talk radio.'" At the *Washington Post*, ombudsman Andrew Alexander (2009) concluded in a September 20 column that his newspaper had also been slow to report the ACORN story.

NPR ran several stories and blog postings about the Breitbart videos and got criticized by conservative emailers. In contrast to the *Times* and the *Post*, however, NPR's ombudsman Alicia Shepard (2009) drew on our study in reaching her conclusions: "In this case, ACORN deserved intense—not halting—scrutiny from any reputable media organization. The same is true for the groups that have raised allegations against ACORN. Allegations need to be checked out—not just repeated." But neither the *New York Times* nor the *Washington Post* consulted our study, which offered the only available rigorous evidence of news media coverage of ACORN, the very issue they were addressing.

Being anti-ACORN is now an unquestioned tenet of right-wing conspiracy theorists and right-wing "Tea Party" activists, TV and radio hosts, and bloggers. Breitbart, O'Keefe, and Giles soon became heroes of the right-wing echo chamber, including Breitbart's appearance at the first National Tea Party Convention and at the Conservative Political Action Conference, both in February 2010 (Sun, 2010).

Outcomes

Our goal was to use historical research and social scientific methods to describe the conservative campaign against ACORN and document mainstream media framing of the organization. Although we were pleased that our study got some attention in the news media, it was no match for the relentless conservative media propaganda nor the full force of the Republican Party. Moreover, few Democrats or major funders were willing to stand up for ACORN; most Democrats timidly watched ACORN being attacked, assenting to the assertions of the videos before there was any conclusive evidence of wrongdoing.

Like all large organizations, ACORN is not without flaws. But the misjudgment of a few employees is hardly grounds for withdrawing federal or foundation funds. ACORN was embarrassed by its errant employees and fired them immediately. After Bertha Lewis took over as chief executive in July 2008, she improved staff accountability, financial safeguards, and internal communications. She brought in management experts, accountants, and lawyers to help ACORN establish new management practices.

By the time a December 2009 report by the Congressional Research Service exonerated ACORN of any wrongdoing, however, ACORN was already laying off staff, closing offices in many cities, and fighting for its survival. The damage to ACORN had already been done. When its federal funding was cut, ACORN had to end its counseling work helping low-income people with tax preparation and obtaining the Earned Income Tax Credit. But when its major funders withdrew their support, ACORN had to start laying off its much larger staff of organizers in cities around the country, closing its offices, and curtailing its work fighting foreclosures and investigating wage and hour exploitation of workers. By March 2010, ACORN no longer existed as a national organization.

For the poor, the attack on ACORN is a tragedy. ACORN's modest operation—run out of well-worn offices, using donated computers and torn furniture, paying low salaries for long hours—helped empower the poor to stop home foreclosures, increase wages through living wage campaigns, put up stop signs at dangerous intersections, rebuild parks, and save neighbor-hoods from decay.

After 40 years, ACORN no longer existed. One of its major legacies, how-ever, is the thousands of organizers and researchers it had trained, many of whom went on to work for, even found, effective political, labor, environmen-tal, policy, and community groups in cities around the country. Moreover, in early 2010, about 17 of ACORN's state chapters, including California and New York, quietly began to reconstitute themselves as separate, stand-alone organizations with their own names. Some of ACORN's key national staffers formed a nonprofit group to provide technical advice to grassroots organizer groups. Some of the nation's newspapers reported on this effort to rebuild a grassroots movement from the ashes of ACORN. None of those media outlets, however, acknowledged their own roles in ACORN's demise.

References

Alexander, A. (2009, September 20). Wrongly deaf to right-wing media? *Washington Post*. Retrieved from http://www.washingtonpost.com

Atlas, J., & Dreier, P. (2009, December10). The ACORN scandal offers lessons to all charities. *Chronicle of Philanthropy*. Retrieved from http://philanthropy.com/article/The-Acorn-Scandal-Offers-Key/57679/

Dreier, P. (2009a, October 22). The war on ACORN. *Los Angeles Times*. Retrieved from http://articles.latimes.com/2009/oct/22/opinion/oe-dreier22

Dreier, P. (2009b, December 8). ACORN, "not guilty." *Talking points memo*. Retrieved from http://tpmcafe.talkingpointsmemo.com/2009/12/08/acorn_not_guilty/#more

Dreier, P., & Martin, C. (2009). *Manipulating the public agenda: Why ACORN was in the news and what the news got wrong*. Retrieved from http://departments.oxy.edu/uepi/acornstudy/acornstudy.pdf

Dreier, P., & Martin, C. (2010). How ACORN was framed: Political controversy and media agenda-setting. *Perspectives on Politics, 8,* 761–792.

Hoyt, C. (2009, September 27). Tuning in too late. *New York Times*, p. WK12.

Martin, C., & Dreier, P. (2009, November 29). Have the media "falsely framed" ACORN? *Editor and Publisher*. Retrieved from http://departments.oxy.edu/uepi/publications/Have%20the%20Media%20Falsely%20Framed%20ACORN.pdf

McCain, J. (2008, October 15). The third McCain-Obama presidential debate. *Commission on Presidential Debates*. Retrieved from http://www.debates.org/index.php?page=october-15-2008-debate-transcript

Shepard, A. (2009, September 23). The ACORN videos: Did NPR ignore them? *NPR Ombudsman*. Retrieved from http://www.npr.org/blogs/ombudsman/

Sun, L. (2010, February 20). Breitbart rouses CPAC by criticizing news media, liberal politics. *Washington Post*. Retrieved from http://www.washingtonpost.com

Case Study 5.2. Pressuring Alcohol Companies to Reform Marketing Practices

David H. Jernigan

From 2002 to 2008, the Center on Alcohol Marketing and Youth (CAMY) combined secondary analyses of commercial advertising research datasets with media advocacy to reframe national debates and influence public policy regarding alcohol advertising and young people. During this time period, CAMY generated more than 2,500 news stories, including coverage in the *New York Times*, the *Wall Street Journal*, the *Washington Post*, *USA Today*, and major network television outlets including CNN and NBC. Aggressive dissemination of the center's findings through community-based partners and targeted briefings of policy makers complemented the news coverage and led to significant changes in the ways alcohol companies do business. As a result of CAMY's work, alcohol companies strengthened their self-regulatory codes and changed their advertising practices. Key policy makers in Washington and in the states adopted CAMY's policy goals. State attorneys general in particular undertook a variety of new actions on underage drinking, leading to the withdrawal of products from the marketplace and other changes in industry marketing practices.

Background

Underage drinking is a significant public health problem in the United States, responsible for 5,000 deaths of persons under 21 each year (U.S. Surgeon General, 2007). The earlier young people begin drinking, the more likely they are to suffer from a wide range of health problems, including alcohol dependence (Grant & Dawson, 1997), motor vehicle crashes (Hingson, Heeren, Jamanka, & Howland, 2001), and physical fights after drinking (Hingson, Heeren, & Zakocs, 2001), as well as cardiometabolic profiles putting them at risk later in life, no matter how much they moderate their drinking as they age (Fan, Russell, Stranges, Dorn, & Trevisan, 2008). Numerous longitudinal studies have found that youth exposure to alcohol advertising and marketing predicts early onset of drinking (Anderson, De Bruijn, Angus, Gordon, & Hastings, 2009). Reducing this exposure is an important public health goal.

Media advocacy is a health communications strategy built on social science research showing that the news media not only sets the agenda for policy debates (McCombs & Shaw, 1972) but also powerfully influences how and what people think about social issues (Iyengar, 1991). In addition to media effects literature, media advocacy draws on sociological analyses of social movements that have emphasized the critical role that framing plays in recruiting supporters, mobilizing "bystander" publics, and countering opposition in order to influence public policy and state action (McAdam, 1996; Snow & Benford, 1992). Defined as the strategic use of the mass media to support community organizing to change health policies (Wallack, Dorfman, Jernigan, & Themba, 1996), media advocacy has been successfully used in a wide range of communities and on a range of social and public health issues to promote policy changes (Jernigan & Wright, 1996).

Prior to 2001, efforts to change alcohol industry advertising practices were largely unsuccessful. For instance, in the early 1980s, the Center for Science in the Public Interest spearheaded the Stop Marketing Alcohol on Radio and Television (SMART) campaign. The campaign delivered to the U.S. Congress petitions containing more than 2 million signatures calling for federal action, but no action ensued. In the early 1990s, then-Rep. Joseph Kennedy sponsored the Sensible Advertising and Family Education (SAFE) Act, which would have mandated health warnings on both print and broadcast advertising for alcoholic beverages. The bill never came to a vote in Congress. In 2000, advocates tried to get the $140 million federal antidrug paid media campaign broadened to include alcohol. Instead, Congress created a $1 million public service advertising campaign telling parents to talk to their children about drinking.

In the absence of regulatory or other government action, youth exposure to alcohol advertising has been determined by the alcohol industry's own self-regulation. In 1999, the Federal Trade Commission (FTC) for the first time examined this self-regulation and found it to be woefully lacking. Soliciting data from eight companies that accounted for approximately 80% of the advertising spending, the FTC found that two companies had no data on whether their advertising was playing to majority underage audiences, while two others aired substantial percentages of their advertisements to majority underage audiences. For all three branches of the alcohol industry— beer, wine, and spirits—the self-regulatory codes stipulated no placement of advertisements before majority underage audiences. This was a weak standard (applicable to less than 1% of television programming), and the FTC encouraged adoption of a stronger one, as well as better monitoring procedures (Federal Trade Commission, 1999).

The Center on Alcohol Marketing and Youth

This regulatory conversation between the FTC and the alcohol industry provided an opportunity for public sociology to make a difference. In 2002, a representative from the Pew Charitable Trusts approached the author to inquire about the possibility of developing a project on alcohol advertising and young people. With assistance from experts in the alcohol and tobacco policy and advocacy communities, and inspired by the research findings from the FTC report, the Pew Charitable Trusts and the Robert Wood Johnson Foundation funded the Center on Alcohol Marketing and Youth at Georgetown University.

Leading CAMY were Jim O'Hara, a former journalist specializing in federal politics who had worked in communications for Dr. David Kessler when he headed the Food and Drug Administration and had served as Donna Shalala's deputy assistant secretary for Health when she headed the federal Department of Health and Human Services; and the author, a health policy sociologist with 15 years of experience translating research findings relevant to alcohol policy into advocacy campaigns. CAMY's mission was to monitor the marketing practices of the alcohol industry to focus attention and action on industry practices that jeopardize the health and safety of the country's young people. To do this, CAMY would combine analyses of secondary datasets—audience data from commercial research services such as Nielsen Media Research and Arbitron—with media and political advocacy designed to engage policy makers and mobilize public opinion to encourage change.

Sociological skills used in the project involved a marriage of basic statistical reasoning and analysis with an understanding of the influence of framing and media effects on political discourses. The foundations provided adequate resources ($11 million over three years) to gain access to and analyze the advertising research databases, the costs of which had historically left them accessible only to advertisers and never to the advocacy community.

Engagement of Other Publics

The foundation funding also supported the engagement of other key publics in dissemination of the research findings. CAMY hired organizers with political campaign experience and provided them to state and local coalitions working on underage drinking issues. These local affiliates were chosen based on the strength of their leadership, policy agendas, and state-level connections as well as the placement of their federal representatives on key committees of oversight in the U.S. Congress. They received early access to center reports, organizing and media advocacy training, full-color brochures and scripted PowerPoint presentations summarizing CAMY's findings, well-referenced fact sheets, model editorial board memos and op-ed pieces, legal memoranda and technical assistance, and access to an online gallery containing thousands of magazine and television advertisements for alcohol. Using these tools, they assisted with dissemination of the research and used it to support a variety of their own successful state and local campaigns. These included restricting alcohol billboard advertising, eliminating alcohol advertising in a college stadium, prompting withdrawal of merchandise encouraging excessive and underage drinking from leading department stores, reclassifying youth-oriented products ("alcopops") into a higher tax bracket to make them less available to young people, and eliminating alcohol advertising on public bus shelters. They also stimulated local legislative study committees, resolutions, legislation, and other forms of engagement in the issue by local and state policy makers.

There is an inherent tension between federal and state and local advocates, with federal advocates often calling on the states only when they need pressure placed on Congress or the federal government. In contrast, CAMY understood from the start that federal and state and local efforts could be synergistic. The national staff worked closely with state and local affiliates and shaped or commissioned resources to meet their articulated needs during the course of the campaign. For instance, close collaboration with activists in the African American and Latino communities contributed to the creation of reports comparing exposure of youth in these communities with the levels of exposure experienced by youth in general to alcohol advertising (Center on Alcohol Marketing and Youth, 2005, 2006).

CAMY's Contributions

Over the course of six years, the more than 2,500 news stories generated by CAMY in the U.S. news media contributed to a reframing of the debate over alcohol advertising from an anecdotal one focused on content to a data-driven one regarding placement. Faced with the spotlight of the center's reports, alcohol companies moved their advertising, and youth exposure to that advertising fell in magazines and on the radio. In 2006, the U.S. Congress passed legislation requiring the federal government to report to it on an annual basis the rates of exposure of youth to messages encouraging alcohol use in the mass media. As a result, CAMY now receives funding from the U.S. Centers for Disease Control and Prevention to continue its analysis and reporting of youth exposure to alcohol advertising.

Other CAMY accomplishments included tightening of alcohol industry self-regulatory standards; publication of far more detailed guidelines for advertising placements in broadcast, print, and digital media by leading alcohol industry trade associations; adoption of greater transparency by trade associations representing brewers and distillers; passage of the first legislation in Congress devoted solely to underage drinking; and the creation of a working group within the National Association of Attorneys General focusing on youth access to alcohol. The latter group convinced alcohol companies to stop advertising in magazines going to schools and libraries and to withdraw from the market several leading brands that mix alcohol and caffeine.

CAMY's principal contribution to social science was the development of a rigorous and replicable methodology for monitoring youth exposure to alcohol advertising (Jernigan & Ross, 2010). The center drew on and benefited from the expertise of Virtual Media Resources, a commercial advertising research firm with 25 years of experience working primarily with advertisers. Adapting the research methods of the advertising field to suit the goals of sociology and public health was innovative and critical to the project's success. The involvement of advertising researchers lent credibility to the center's findings in debates with alcohol companies and with policy makers, allowing the debate to center on reducing youth exposure and not on whose numbers were correct (not a single number published by CAMY was ever challenged by the alcohol companies).

Sociology in Action

CAMY exemplified sociology in action, and its practices illustrate both the strengths and some of the constraints of an activist sociological research enterprise. Early on in its history, CAMY employed social science research tools—polling and focus group research—to help shape and refine its message. The findings from this research influenced hundreds of presentations of CAMY's findings given over the period from 2002 to 2008. The master frame was one of fairness, with a moderate and reasonable policy goal (shifting alcohol advertising from any venue where youth were more likely per capita to be exposed to it than adults) supporting the notion that the practices of alcohol advertisers unfairly and unnecessarily expose youth to advertising for a product that by law they cannot purchase. The message of CAMY's reports, press releases, interviews, opinion pieces and editorial board memoranda, and other communications vehicles was consistent and focused: Youth see too much alcohol advertising, and alcohol companies can do a better job of preventing this.

However, unlike many social science research enterprises, most of the CAMY reports were not published in peer-reviewed journals (although some were) (Jernigan, Ostroff, & Ross, 2005; Jernigan, Ostroff, Ross, & O'Hara, 2004), because the timeline of peer review is often too lengthy compared to the timeline within which public policy debates occur. Instead, CAMY developed its own internal "peer-review" process, hiring advertising and public health research experts to critique its reports as part of the drafting process. Following this review, CAMY brought its reports directly to media and public policy audiences, relying on a steady stream of reports (at least three per year) to build and maintain the frame regarding unnecessarily high levels of youth exposure to alcohol advertising.

Aside from the core research staff, CAMY's staff were more likely to specialize in political and issue organizing than in sociological research. The research enterprise itself occurred within a "campaign" mentality, with the policy change as the "candidate" and an initial time frame of three years to "win" the desired changes. In democratic societies, significant social change generally requires very good organizing. There were numerous examples in the 20th century of social movements organizing large groups of people to change the course of history. Although CAMY's goals were far more modest than many of these movements, CAMY changed the landscape surrounding alcohol advertising in the United States. New standards, new players (for example, the state attorneys general, and better-informed and more effective and empowered state and local coalitions), and a new and sharpened focus on the industry's practices laid the groundwork for new possibilities in holding alcohol companies accountable for their role in underage drinking and the many negative consequences that may ensue from it.

References

Anderson, P., De Bruijn, A., Angus, K., Gordon, R., & Hastings, G. (2009). Impact of alcohol advertising and media exposure on adolescent alcohol use: A systematic review of longitudinal studies. *Alcohol and Alcoholism*, *44*(3), 229–243.

Center on Alcohol Marketing and Youth. (2005). *Exposure of Hispanic youth to alcohol advertising, 2003–2004*. Washington, DC: Center on Marketing and Youth.

Center on Alcohol Marketing and Youth. (2006). *Exposure of African-American youth to alcohol advertising, 2003–2004*. Washington, DC: Center on Alcohol Marketing and Youth.

Fan, A. Z., Russell, M., Stranges, S., Dorn, J., & Trevisan, M. (2008). Association of lifetime alcohol drinking trajectories with cardiometabolic risk. *Journal of Clinical Endocrinology & Metabolism*, *93*(1), 154–161.

Federal Trade Commission. (1999). *Self-regulation in the alcohol industry: A review of industry effects to avoid promoting alcohol in underage consumers*. Washington, DC: Federal Trade Commission.

Grant, B. F., & Dawson, D. (1997). Age of onset of alcohol use and its association with DSM-IV alcohol abuse and dependence: Results from the National Longitudinal Alcohol Epidemiologic Survey. *Journal of Substance Abuse*, *9*, 103–110.

Hingson, R., Heeren, T., Jamanka, T., & Howland, J. (2001). *Age of drinking onset and unintentional injury involvement after drinking.* Washington, DC: National Highway Traffic Safety Administration.

Hingson, R., Heeren, T., & Zakocs, R. (2001). Age of drinking onset and involvement in physical fights. *Pediatrics, 108*(4), 872–877.

Iyengar, S. (1991). *Is anyone responsible? How television frames political issues.* Chicago, IL: University of Chicago Press.

Jernigan, D., Ostroff, J., & Ross, C. (2005). Alcohol advertising and youth: A measured approach. *Journal of Public Health Policy, 26*(3), 312–325.

Jernigan, D., Ostroff, J., Ross, C., & O'Hara, J. A. (2004). Sex differences in adolescent exposure to alcohol advertising in magazines. *Archives of Pediatrics and Adolescent Medicine, 158,* 629–634.

Jernigan, D., & Wright, P. (1996). Media advocacy: Lessons from community experiences. *Journal of Public Health Policy, 17*(3), 306–329.

Jernigan, D. H., & Ross, C. (2010). Monitoring youth exposure to advertising on television: The devil is in the details. *Journal of Public Affairs, 10*(1–2), 36–49.

McAdam, D. (1996). The framing function of movement tactics: Strategic dramaturgy in the American civil rights movement. In D. McAdam, J. D. McCarthy, & M. N. Zald (Eds.), *Comparative perspectives on social movements: Political opportunities, mobilizing structures and cultural framings* (pp. 339–356). Cambridge, UK: Cambridge University Press.

McCombs, M., & Shaw, D. (1972). The agenda setting function of the mass media. *Public Opinion Quarterly, 36,* 176–187.

Snow, D. A., & Benford, R. D. (1992). Master frames and cycles of protest. In A. D. Morris & C. M. Mueller (Eds.), *Frontiers in social movement theory* (pp. 133–155). New Haven, CT: Yale University Press.

U.S. Surgeon General. (2007). *Surgeon general's call to action to prevent and reduce underage drinking.* Washington, DC: Department of Health and Human Services, Office of the Surgeon General.

Wallack, L., Dorfman, L., Jernigan, D., & Themba, M. (1996). *Media advocacy and public health: Power for prevention.* Thousand Oaks, CA: Sage.

Case Study 5.3. The Reel Girls Project: Self, Image, Adolescence, and Filmmaking

Shannon Silva, Susan Bullers, Mariana Johnson, Donna King, and Jean-Anne Sutherland

The "Reel Girls" project was a community project involving University of North Carolina Wilmington (UNCW) students and a group of local middle school girls. It was part of a joint women's studies/film studies/sociology course offered in the spring semesters of 2007 and 2008 that provided cross-training in technical filmmaking instruction, media literacy, feminism, and film studies. All aspects of media production, reception, and representation were included in our Reel Girls curriculum. The interdisciplinary foundation of the course ensured that critical awareness and creative expression would be equally valued and promoted.

In both semesters, students and faculty advisors worked together to plan and produce the project, in which UNCW students taught middle school girls about media literacy, technical film production, and self-portrait documentary. The middle school girls were then mentored in the production of their own short independent documentary films. The final projects were shown in a professional venue on the UNCW campus in the spring semesters of 2007 and 2008. Training and mentoring took place at many levels among faculty advisors, UNCW students, and Wilmington middle school girls.

In total, the Reel Girls projects involved 11 UNCW students, five faculty, one graduate student volunteer, and 38 girls from a middle school in Wilmington. Five professional writing students from UNCW were also involved in the development of promotional materials. The project was strongly supported by UNCW and community entities and garnered significant positive local press. The final screening brought a large audience of students, family, and friends of traditionally underserved middle school girls to campus. Funding from Academic Affairs allowed us to buy equipment that ensured the project's success. In addition, funding from the Honors Program allowed us to send the UNCW students to the Full-Frame documentary film festival in Durham, North Carolina.

The Reel Girls program was successful; we received positive feedback from the community, including press in local and university newspapers and requests to run the program in several community venues including the public school system and the YWCA. In addition, faculty supervisors organized and presented a workshop about the project at the 2008 Southeastern Women's Studies Association meetings in Charlotte, North Carolina.

Using Social Scientific Skills

Media Literacy

Media literacy is an important pedagogical tool by which women and girls can better understand themselves, their positions in society, and the persistent gender contradictions they inevitably face. The list of media available for analysis—film, fashion, music, television, advertising, magazines, comics, books, radio, the Internet, news programs—is virtually inexhaustible. A collection of learned skills, media literacy includes the ability to

- Recognize the ways that the media constructs messages
- Critically analyze the content of media messages
- Recognize that most mainstream media messages are commercial and are generated by profit-oriented media conglomerates
- Recognize power relations in contemporary society, specifically that most mainstream messages are generated by elite White men; women and ethnic minorities are grossly underrepresented as media executives
- Explore the influence of these media constructions on how we define ourselves and how others define us
- Create our own media messages in a variety of voices and formats

Incorporating media literacy in the Reel Girls project was an ongoing and dynamic activity. We began our first Reel Girls semester by introducing our UNCW students to the concepts of media literacy through informal discussion and content analysis of magazines and television shows. As sociology, women's studies, and film students, each had some experience in analyzing media in other coursework, and each had specialized knowledge to contribute to peers. Students were then assigned responsibility to explore the Internet for media literacy resources targeted to middle school girls.

This assignment highlighted one of the biggest challenges we encountered in the first year: recognizing and then bridging the age, ethnic, and economic gap between the college women and the middle school girls. All of the UNCW students participating in the first Reel Girls project were in their late teens or early twenties, White and relatively privileged. The middle school girls, for the most part, were early teens, relatively underprivileged and Black or Latina. When the UNCW students recollected their own middle school experiences in constructing their media literacy activities, they sometimes assumed a youthful innocence and naiveté for the girls they would be training. They assumed the girls might be watching Nickelodeon and Hannah Montana and might be overly concerned about body image and weight. Several reported surprise that so many of the middle school girls asked explicit questions about sex and seemed to relate, at first, with a cool sense of irony to their older mentors.

Armed with this knowledge and experience, the second Reel Girls project focused much more explicitly on the ways race, class, gender, and sexuality interact in exploring media literacy activities with these middle school girls and provided a complex look at the consumerism and positioning of women in hip hop culture. The pedagogical point was to avoid preaching or condemning.

Rather, the students were encouraged to consider the stereotypical sexist imagery and unreflective celebration of consumer excess.

Film Production

For the production portion of the course, the focus was on (1) equipping the UNCW students with basic camera operation and editing knowledge, and (2) teaching these students how to teach the younger girls, using equipment that the participating school had on hand (and would make available to its students once the project was over). Due to equipment availability issues, the UNCW students were unable to teach the younger girls how to use lighting or sound equipment, and the younger girls worked with consumer-grade cameras and editing software. Nevertheless, we felt that the younger girls benefited from learning on equipment and software that would be available to them when our involvement at the school ended.

Beyond basic equipment use, the production curriculum that the UNCW students developed focused on teaching the younger participants composition and framing for effect, the meaningful use of shot angles and sizes, proper exposure and how to conduct vox pop interviews, and how pacing, special effects, and sound can affect the mood one is trying to portray in a final project.

Film Studies and Pedagogy

Beyond media literacy, it was imperative that students understand the connection between media content and the formal strategies that affect gender representation in film and video. How does the way something is shot influence the message being communicated? To what extent do framing, lighting, or camera angle, for instance, encourage identification with a certain gender representation? These kinds of questions were relevant to the component of our curriculum that focused on documentary genre and form from a film studies perspective.

The UNCW students looked at a range of documentary works, examining observational, poetic, expository, performative, and self-reflexive techniques. The goal was to expose these students to the diversity of documentary filmmaking, especially in relation to identity-based projects that would be relevant to the middle school student participants. Also, personal documentary serves as counterpoint to the overly homogenous representations of gender, race, and class in the dominant media. We hoped that the UNCW students would feel encouraged to think creatively and aesthetically about personal expression and the infinite options available to the middle school students. However, implementing aesthetic diversity and experimentation while working with the middle school girls proved difficult during the first year. Given that the real value in the Reel Girls experience lies in the *process* of the experience as opposed to the *product*, this was not an overwhelming concern. During the second year, steps were taken to emphasize aesthetic and formal diversity.

A key strategy was to have our UNCW students each make her own 3-minute self-portrait documentary. By exploring the different kinds of techniques that appealed to them, they were better armed to "think outside the box" and come up with creative prompts and strategies that would encourage our middle school girls to embrace experimentation (using unusual props, for instance). The second year, instead of showing the middle school students clips from professional documentaries, the UNCW student-instructors showed their own unpolished video portraits. This was both a way to showcase the diversity of approaches evident in the UNCW students' videos and a way to celebrate the amateur and experimental nature of the project.

Another important aspect of the film studies curriculum was to make clear the potential link between nonfiction film and video and community activism. How do films *work* to build communities and inspire social change? How might communal filmmaking projects such as Reel Girls help to strengthen underserved communities or bring underrepresented perspectives into focus? Although we approached this challenge somewhat modestly, we do believe that the final screening event of the Reel Girls films, which took place on the UNCW campus in a 300-seat, state-of-the-art movie theater, played a major role in transforming Reel Girls from a personal video project into a community event. After the screening, all the participants came to the stage to discuss their experience in the Reel Girls project. Given that many of the middle students had never been on a college campus, the opportunity to screen and speak about their work to a packed house proved to be an empowering one. Important, too, the younger girls demonstrated that they had forged meaningful bonds with one another.

Conclusion

The Reel Girls project took the skills of UNCW faculty and students into the public. Faculty involved with the project equipped their students with expertise that enabled them to engage with middle school students. Local middle school girls were exposed to critiques of media, including representations of gender and beauty. These young girls then produced their own autobiographical alternative media, which they screened for the public. Throughout the development and implementation of this project, a relationship was forged between the university and the public school system. UNCW students learned how to engage with the community while working *with* and *alongside* them. In the process, the younger girls were exposed to alternative media messages about women while recognizing the importance of their own stories.

Case Study 5.4. The Internet as a Leveler Between Advantaged and Disadvantaged Communities

Keith N. Hampton

Some pundits suggest that new technologies such as the Internet have reduced the formation of local bonds. This public sociology case study challenges that statement. The i-Neighbors.org project is simultaneously a research project and an intervention. The project investigates in detail the specific contexts in which Internet use affords or detracts from neighborhood interactions and offers a free service that allows people to create a virtual community for their geographic community.

Neighborhoods matter—even in the age of the Internet and mobile phone. Although new information and communication technologies are increasingly a part of our everyday lives, we still live in a place. Our connections to local people provide an informal network of social support that affords safety, health, and happiness. Neighborhood ties need not be extremely intimate or close to be beneficial; relatively weak local ties formed through infrequent social contact facilitate local surveillance, the formation of community norms, and increase the likelihood of community collective action in dealing with local social problems (Bellair, 1997; Granovetter, 1973). Large, local friendship networks are associated with community attachment (Sampson, 1988), empowerment (Geis & Ross, 1998), low crime rates (Sampson & Groves, 1989), low levels of fear and mistrust (Ross & Jang, 2000), reduced mental distress (Elliott, 2000; Ross, 2000), and fewer instances of depression (Aneshensel & Sucoff, 1996). Individuals and communities benefit from a dense network of local social ties.

As beneficial as neighborhood ties can be, they are in decline (Guest & Wierzbicki, 1999; Putnam, 2000). A recent study by the Pew Internet and American Life Project found that more than 30% of adult Americans do not know the names of their neighbors (Hampton, Sessions, Her, & Rainie, 2009). In addition, people with few neighborhood ties are often clustered in the same residential areas. As a result, some neighborhoods have high social cohesion because of the many neighborhood ties, whereas others have low social cohesion because local ties are nearly absent.

These neighborhood effects can often be explained by the ages and life-styles of people who choose to live in an area. For example, the young and the childless tend to have very good extra-neighborhood social networks, but they move more frequently and have less interest in neighborhood relationships (Hampton, 2007; Michelson, 1977). Living in close proximity to people who move frequently and have little interest in neighboring makes it difficult for even a social butterfly to form local ties. This *fugacious instability*—residential instability that results from environmental and life-style choices—tends to change for individuals as they age, move, and change lifestyles. However, some neighborhood effects do not result from environmental choice. Social cohesion also tends to be low in areas of concentrated disadvantage. Areas of concentrated disadvantage experience *structural instability*—residential instability that is a result of the concentration of inequality, such as the presence of poverty, unemployment, and racial segregation. In these areas, individual levels of social support, safety, and health tend to be lower, whereas the need for collective action is often high.

Not only are local social ties in historic decline, but they are least likely to be present in residential areas that could most benefit from the informal network of social support afforded by local social cohesion. Although considerable sociological research has focused on identifying this trend and understanding its implication for community (Sampson, 2006), few sociologists have tried to reverse the trend or identify social forces that may undermine prevailing, community-level inequalities that result from a concentration of disadvantage.

Studying Neighborhoods With an Intervention

The i-Neighbors.org project is based on prior research that the Internet supports, rather than detracts from, local tie formation. A two-year ethnography and survey of residents who lived in the "wired" suburban Toronto neighborhood of Netville found that Internet users had three times as many local, weak ties as their nonwired counterparts and that Internet users communicated more frequently with neighbors on- and offline (Hampton & Wellman, 2003). Residents of Netville who used a neighborhood discussion email list also demonstrated unexpectedly high rates of collective action (Hampton, 2003). A U.S. national survey by Hampton et al. (2009) found that of those who use an online neighborhood discussion forum,

- 60% know "all or most" of their neighbors, compared to 40% of other Americans.
- 79% talk with neighbors in person at least once a month, compared to 61% of the general population.

- 43% talk to neighbors on the telephone at least once a month, compared to the average of 25%.
- 70% had listened to a neighbor's problems in the previous six months, and 63% received similar support from neighbors, compared with 49% who had given and 36% who had received this support in the general population.
- 65% had helped a neighbor with household chores or loaned a household item in the previous six months, and 54% had received this support, compared to the average 41% who had given and 31% who had received.

Although an online neighborhood discussion forum is associated with higher social cohesion at the local level, research on digital inequality suggests that disadvantaged communities are least likely to have the technology to benefit from this trend. In addition, in a longitudinal study of four neighborhoods in the Boston area, Hampton (2007) found that, although Internet users formed more neighborhood ties over time and use of a neighborhood email list amplified this trend, the trend was limited to neighborhoods of low fugacious instability: residential, stable, middle-class suburban communities. Prior research on the contextual effects of structural instability, as found in areas of concentrated disadvantage, further suggests that social cohesion is unlikely to develop in these areas. However, beyond interventions designed to bridge the "digital divide" by providing access to computers and the Internet to residents of low-income communities, no one had ever studied how the Internet would influence social cohesion in areas of concentrated disadvantage.

The i-Neighbors.org project sought to accomplish two goals. The first was to learn whether residential areas with concentrated disadvantage were likely to benefit from the Internet in terms of higher levels of local social cohesion. The second was to provide an intervention available to residents of any neighborhood that would help reverse the historic trend of declining neighborhood interaction.

The i-Neighbors.org project website was released in August 2004. An early version of the website was built with funding from the U.S. National Science Foundation (Hampton, 2007), with additional support provided by the Annenberg School for Communication at the University of Pennsylvania, Microsoft Research, L-Soft, and a Google Grant.

The i-Neighbors website allows anyone in the United States or Canada to use a series of Internet services for communication and information exchange at the neighborhood level. The website resembles a traditional commercial website, except that it is completely free and is operated by a faculty member and students at a university. Visitors to the website can enter their zip codes and view a list of digital neighborhoods that correspond to actual neighborhoods in their geographic area. If a visitor's neighborhood is not listed, they can add it to the list of communities. Within a digital neighborhood, a user can create a personal profile, send group and personal discussion messages, contribute to a shared calendar, post photos, review local services, share documents, survey group members, view a neighborhood directory, and invite other neighbors to join.

The project website provides an opportunity for researchers to identify and observe instances when the Internet is adopted as a means of local communication. To maximize generalizability, i-Neighbors was designed as a naturalistic experiment. No attempt was made to target the project website to specific users or geographic communities. No additional technology or training was given to participants. Adoption of the site was a result of word of mouth, Internet search, and mass media coverage of the site. With i-Neighbors, researchers can examine variation in the types of neighborhoods that use the Internet for local contact and learn how and whether the technology is used for local engagement and collective action.

Project Outcomes

i-Neighbors.org has attracted more than 75,000 users from neighborhoods in every state in the United States and every Canadian province. Thousands of new users join each month. In a typical month, i-Neighbors users collectively use the Internet to receive more than one million messages from neighbors (the typical digital neighborhood corresponds to a single apartment building or about 500 homes).

Findings from the first three years of the i-Neighbors project were published as a peer- reviewed article in the journal *American Behavioral Scientist* (Hampton, 2010). An analysis of the ecological context of the most active i-Neighbors communities revealed that the majority are located in middle-class suburban areas (72%), but a significant minority (28%) are located in neighborhoods that are classified as within the top 20th percentile for the most disadvantaged areas in the nation (Hampton, 2010). These truly disadvantaged neighborhoods, with concentrated levels of racial segregation, poverty, and unemployment, are located almost exclusively in inner-city areas. An analysis of 25,000 emails exchanged within the most active digital neighborhoods found indicators of high social cohesion and collective action. There were few differences in the levels of social cohesion and collective action between neighborhoods with concentrated disadvantage and more advantaged areas. Although areas of concentrated disadvantage represent only slightly more than one-quarter of the most active i-Neighbors communities, this level of involvement is many magnitudes higher than would be expected given levels of structural instability and digital inequality.

The i-Neighbors project revealed and supports the potential for the Internet to be used in areas of concentrated disadvantage to overcome contextual constraints on local engagement. Constraints resulting from structural instability that would otherwise limit opportunities for local tie formation and collective action can be overcome through the use of the Internet as a tool for local communication. A boost in local social cohesion and collective action of the magnitude observed through i-Neighbors may represent the start of a slow reversal in a trend of declining neighborhood interaction. In addition, the existence of collective efficacy among a population that would otherwise be unlikely to experience high local social cohesion may represent a significant decrease in social and civic inequality between the most advantaged and the most disadvantaged communities.

References

Aneshensel, C. S., & Sucoff, C. A. (1996). The neighborhood context of adolescent mental health. *Journal of Health and Social Behavior, 37*, 293–310.

Bellair, P. E. (1997). Social interaction and community crime. *Criminology, 35*, 677–703.

Elliott, M. (2000). The stress process in neighborhood context. *Health and Place, 6*(4), 287–299.

Geis, K. J., & Ross, C. E. (1998). A new look at urban alienation: The effects of neighborhood disorder. *Social Psychology Quarterly, 61*(3), 232–246.

Granovetter, M. (1973). The strength of weak ties. *American Journal of Sociology, 78*(6), 1360–1380.

Guest, A. M., & Wierzbicki, S. K. (1999). Social ties at the neighborhood level: Two decades of GSS evidence. *Urban Affairs Review, 35*(1), 92–111.

Hampton, K. N. (2003). Grieving for a lost network: Collective action in a wired suburb. *The Information Society, 19*(5), 417–428.

Hampton, K. N. (2007). Neighborhoods in the network society: The E-Neighbors study. *Information, Communication and Society, 10*(5), 714–748.

Hampton, K. N. (2010). Internet use and the concentration of disadvantage. *American Behavioral Scientist, 53*(8), 1111–1132.

Hampton, K. N., Sessions, L. F., Her, E. J., & Rainie, L. (2009). *Social isolation and new technology.* Washington, DC: Pew Internet and Everyday Life Project.

Hampton, K. N., & Wellman, B. (2003). Neighboring in Netville: How the Internet supports community and social capital in a wired suburb. *City and Community, 2*(3), 277–311.

Michelson, W. (1977). *Environmental choice, human behavior and residential satisfaction.* New York, NY: Oxford University Press.

Putnam, R. (2000). *Bowling alone.* New York, NY: Simon & Schuster.

Ross, C. E. (2000). Neighborhood disadvantage and adult depression. *Journal of Health and Social Behavior, 41*(2), 177–187.

Ross, C. E., & Jang, S. J. (2000). Neighborhood disorder, fear, and mistrust: The buffering role of social ties with neighbors. *American Journal of Community Psychology, 28*(4), 401–420.

Sampson, R. (1988). Local friendship ties and community attachment in mass society: A multilevel systemic model. *American Sociological Review, 53*(5), 766–779.

Sampson, R. (2006). Collective efficacy theory. In F. T. Cullen, J. P. Wright, & K. R. Blevins (Eds.), *Taking stock* (pp. 149–168). New Brunswick, NJ: Transaction.

Sampson, R., & Groves, B. (1989). Community structure and crime: Testing social-disorganization theory. *American Journal of Sociology, 94*, 774–802.

CASE STUDIES 6

Health

While an individual's health is linked to a host of biological factors, sociological research shows that social factors also play an important role in a person's health. Among these are socioeconomic status, cultural beliefs and traditions, religion, the quality of available medical services, and the ability to access those services. Public sociologists today are using the power of their research to identify practices and policies that can improve health outcomes. Authors of the five case studies in this section have helped to reduce the risk of early pregnancy, found ways for local ministries to use assessment in their HIV/AIDS prevention work, developed local food systems to make healthier foods available to communities, challenged the power of insurance companies, and campaigned against tobacco use. While the examples included here provide lessons on the power of sociology to make a difference, they also demonstrate that such campaigns need to be tailored to local conditions. One size does not always fit all in the endeavors of public sociologists.

Demographer Vandana Kohli used a research grant to study the motivational and technological dimensions of teen pregnancy prevention as well as develop an intervention project in her university's community. The project involved the creation of a mentoring program in partnership with a local family planning clinic. University students who were enrolled in teacher preparation classes were matched with high school youth most at risk for unplanned pregnancies and least likely to attend college, and together they participated in a variety of activities. The results of pre- and posttests showed that the youth involved in the project were more likely to say that they would postpone sexual intercourse, use contraceptives to prevent pregnancy and sexually transmitted diseases (STDs), attend college, and seek guidance from an adult when having to make a decision about a sexual matter.

In the 1990s, the AIDS Pastoral Care Network of Chicago created HIV prevention ministry outreach to congregations and religious leaders in the city's Latino and African American communities. The goal was to create self-sustaining HIV prevention programs located within the churches or through the clergy association in the neighborhoods. Sociologist Anne Figert evaluated the training and outreach of this HIV/AIDS ministry project and found that it was failing to establish a self-sustaining HIV prevention ministry in the targeted communities. In the Latino community reasons for this failure had to do with a lack of continued funding, while in the African American community they had to do with organizational and cultural resistance to evaluation projects and research by the academic community. After a series of internal changes in the organization, the original focus shifted from primary evaluation consultation to helping contribute to a national dialogue on faith-based programming and on steps for practically implementing an HIV ministry with evaluation in mind. Figert then worked with the organization to develop a tool kit that provided detailed descriptions of evaluation research to help ministers see that evaluation can play a role in their ministry work. The research led to a greater awareness of the conditions for implementing research evaluation in HIV/AIDS and ministry programs.

The third case study describes a project to develop a regional food system that would promote economic development in the struggling agriculture sector in southeastern North Carolina. A coalition of public and private sector representatives, including public sociologist Leslie Hossfeld and Mac Legerton, executive director of the Center for Community Action, identified market opportunities for limited resource farmers. In particular, their research identified institutional buying relationships with area schools, hospitals, colleges and universities, and restaurants. Since its inception in 2006, the coalition has developed programs to provide education to consumers on the economic and health benefits of buying local; training on sustainable agriculture and food-related occupations that support a regional food system; and schools with local produce and fresh foods.

When Blue Cross/Blue Shield of New Jersey increased insurance rates for small groups and individuals at rates greater than rising medical costs, a red flag went up for medical sociologist Donald Light. After doing some research, he discovered that this tax-exempt, quasi-public nonprofit insurance company was engaged in a practice of underpricing its big risk-rated commercial policies in order to outbid the commercial competition; it then misleadingly attributed the losses to the community-rated policies for small groups and individuals and filed for rate increases. Light further found that there were inequities in how the increases were being applied; the company used "demography community rates," which effectively led to charging higher rates to women, disadvantaged minorities, and older policyholders.

Light's case study is particularly helpful in highlighting how some public sociologists move between research and community activist roles. Light translated his research into action by organizing a campaign to fight Blue Cross. Linking up with a statewide public health association, he conducted further research and helped to mount a legal challenge to the discriminatory rate structure. Before Light and his partners were through, they had fought three campaigns: to rescind the discriminatory rates, to make rate increases equal to increases in medical costs, and to prevent the company from dropping seriously ill patients and cut critical benefits. The coalition was ultimately successful in achieving its original goals and winning passage of state legislative reforms to the small-group and individual market.

While sociologists are not necessarily trained to be community organizers, their research skills and perspectives can help them to identify effective community-based intervention strategies. Armed with an M.A. in sociology and a history of community research and interventions, Patricia Nichols set out to organize and implement tobacco prevention programs in rural Montana. What she soon learned was that the standard organizing methods did not translate well to the rural communities where she worked. So, she applied her academic training as a sociologist to do some research and develop new strategies better suited for her setting. The result was a series of partnerships with local schools and strategic contacts with a small number of local businesses throughout the different communities in her region of Montana. She became the hub of a wheel of prevention activities that attracted attention and built momentum for the antismoking campaign; along the way she was slowly changing the way tobacco prevention was taught. Nichols writes that her efforts showed that while building coalitions in the community is the best way to manage community adherence and participation in tobacco prevention work, the notion of community must be flexible enough to take into consideration the characteristics of rural regions and the groups represented there.

Case Study 6.1. Teen Pregnancy Prevention

Vandana Kohli

Applied research, designed to solve the practical problems of modern life by bridging the gaps between theory and practice, is a hallmark of the regional, comprehensive university. The social realities of an institution's service area can inspire researchers to ask the type of questions that may result in positive social change. For example, I work in a community where, in 1999, 18% of all persons lived below the federal poverty line, and the median household income was approximately $40,000. Only 19% of all persons over the age of 25 had a baccalaureate degree in 2000. In the 2000 census, approximately 32% of all persons living in this service region reported that they were Hispanic, and nearly 4% and 9%, respectively, reported that they were Asian and Black. Twenty-seven percent of all persons reported in their 2000 census response that they spoke a language other than English at home.

When I began my career in this community, I was challenged to think about ways in which my research expertise in the area of demography, particularly intergroup fertility differentials, could be used to address the needs of this community. In my early career, that assistance was mostly in the form of methodological assistance such as needs assessment and program evaluation but not social intervention per se. In the late 1990s, data produced by researchers at the University of California, Berkeley, showed that my university's community had the highest rate of pregnancy among teens under age 15 in the entire state of California, making it a "hot spot" for teen pregnancy. The reasons involved a combination of variables having to do with low socioeconomic status, low education, single-parent households, and residential instability.

It was at this time that I started to develop an emphasis on applied demography, particularly adolescent pregnancy prevention, because it addressed this urgent social need in the university's service region. I had already acquired a few small grants to support further research on adolescent pregnancy prevention when I received an invitation to discuss a grant opportunity in this area by the dean of the Office of Graduate Studies and Research.

Unlike other grants, this was a large grant of nearly one-half million dollars, spanning a three-year period. I was interested in using grant funds to apply a quasi-experimental research design that addressed both the motivational and technological dimension of teen pregnancy prevention. In this regard, previous demographic research pointed to two intervening variables: availability and use of contraception to prevent unwanted pregnancies, and motivation to delay childbearing (Bongaarts, 1982; Poston & Terrell, 2006). In the proposed model, I hypothesized that a mentoring program involving university students and at-risk youth in our service region should have a positive impact on a teen's motivation to delay childbearing by increasing teens' resiliency, future orientation, and prosocial values. I also reasoned that making contraceptives available to sexually active teens would result in a reduction of unwanted pregnancies.

The grant provided the funds to establish a well-rounded mentoring program matching our college students with local high school students. The program included participation in such things as plays, sports camps, artistic endeavors, and self-esteem-building exercises along with pregnancy prevention knowledge. Many of the activities were hosted on the university campus, and teens were introduced to the many cultural and academic opportunities the university had to offer. I also included a variety of financial aid workshops and guest presentations for teens so that they could see that a positive future that included college was possible even under tough economic conditions. This dimension of the grant was intended to address those factors that would discourage sexual risk-taking behavior and increase the motivation to delay childbearing.

The motivational side of pregnancy prevention worked harmoniously with the goals and missions of the university, which were to ensure that individuals maximize their chances for self-actualization through higher education and to improve the health and well-being of the residents in its service region. However, I needed and welcomed an opportunity that was afforded by the grant to work with a local agency to disseminate contraceptives to teens. The partnership that developed between the university and this family planning clinic made it possible to provide a two-pronged approach to preventing adolescent pregnancies. In this way, the grant became an experimental model for monitoring and analyzing changes in human fertility behavior that was grounded in demographic theory (Caldwell, 1976; Coale & Watkins, 1986; Easterlin & Crimmins, 1985). It started as applied research, using sociology to make sense of social problems, but it evolved into an agenda for social change.

Publics and Impact

The most significant goals of the project were to build client and agency capacity for preventing teenage pregnancies. Various publics were involved in the project. These included high school–aged teens 15 to 17 years old, a family planning clinic, university faculty, and university students.

Students were recruited from a local high school in the poorer part of the community. Some of these students were first-generation, English language learners, and all came from economically underprivileged backgrounds. All participants were asked to complete a short questionnaire on their sexual attitudes and behavior at the beginning (pretest) and end of the program (posttest). A comparison of pretest and posttest scores indicated that after participating in the program, all the teens, regardless of gender, were more likely to postpone initiating sexual intercourse; use contraception to prevent pregnancy and sexually transmitted diseases (STDs); attend college; and seek sexual decision-making guidance from a responsible adult. Posttest survey results also indicated that teens who had completed the program became aware of local agencies that disseminated contraceptives.

The only variable that remained unchanged at the end of the program was self-esteem.

Although the teens had some say about whether they preferred to play baseball or learn a new sport or whether they wanted to paint or sculpt, they were primarily the focus of the research and the ones who benefitted from it in the most direct fashion. However, indirectly, the lessons from the project diffused to other members of their families and strengthened them in their ability to make responsible sexual decisions. Siblings were greatly influenced by the positive impact the project had on the teen participant. Similarly, parents, especially those who actively participated in the project, became more active in encouraging a future orientation that did not include early family formation. In this way the project had a greater impact on the local community than was originally conceived by the project developers.

Another significant impact of the project was on the family planning clinic. This clinic had been providing contraceptive services to members of the local community at its various branch offices throughout the city. However, one of these branches was frequented more often by teen clients because it was close to a large high school. It was at this site that the agency opened a dedicated "teen clinic." Using project funds to defray the cost of its medical staff, the clinic elected to offer family planning services only to teens during the last two hours of each day. During these hours, the reception area and waiting room were converted to a more teen-friendly environment. Posters depicting images of happy young couples deliberating childbearing options were replaced with images of teens curious and concerned about pregnancy. The music in the waiting rooms was also changed to appeal to teenage sensibilities. Overall, this resulted in more teens visiting the clinic for information about human sexuality and abstinence as well as family planning services.

The improvements in the atmosphere in which these family planning services were provided to teens were a direct outcome of various applied research findings that had been documented and presented in journals and magazines that were not academic in nature. I was able to coordinate the efforts of the clinic staff by providing them with this information. I believe that clinic staff gained an appreciation for information sharing and knowledge development because they could see firsthand how small changes resulted in an increase in client satisfaction and an expansion in the scope of their service provision. Many clinic staff members, for example, had never attended any staff development workshops that addressed teen needs prior to their involvement in this project. The project was, therefore, critical in developing the clinic staff's capacity to offer services that suited client needs.

The staff was instrumental in recommending changes to project design. For example, they suggested changes with appointment-scheduling methods, summer outreach activities, and even worked with their administrators to acquire more teen-friendly informational brochures. Undoubtedly, the project was extremely successful in increasing this agency's capacity for reducing teen pregnancy by providing teens with access to contraceptives in a more user-friendly environment.

The last publics involved in the project were university faculty and students. I worked with my colleagues in the university to create a curriculum that would be engaging for teens. The goal was not to inundate teens with messages of responsible sexual decision making but rather to help them see another type of future in which early childbearing was an unattractive choice. Thus, we aimed to increase teen interest and involvement in college by providing a curriculum that focused on activities centered around sports and health and art rather than traditional college-level classes. There were at least two reasons for this final selection.

First, most of the students who were enrolled as mentors in this program were teacher preparation students. These students would be taking jobs in local schools upon graduation and would be in ideal positions to become ambassadors for propagating responsible sexuality messages. The mentor experience with this project was folded into the requirements for the students' major and substituted for their culminating experience course if their emphasis in the teacher preparation program was either physical education or art. These students worked closely with their faculty mentors to develop a meaningful curriculum in their areas of expertise for the teen pregnancy prevention project. To this extent, these students and faculty were co-researchers, along with the principal investigator. They were instrumental in defining key issues that were to be addressed by the curriculum. Three faculty members remained closely connected to the project for the entire three-year period. Together these faculty members trained nearly 200 college students about issues related to teens' positive engagement and resiliency development. In turn, these college students became mentors for the local high school. Thus, even though the curriculum was designed for high school students, the practice of using the curriculum was training for college-level teacher preparation students.

Conclusion

Applied research requires working outside of the academic "comfort zone." Usually this type of research poses a predictable set of challenges and obstacles. However, what I had not expected was how risky applied research can be for securing tenure and/or promotion. Some university faculty do not recognize applied research grants—even large ones—as a significant part of a retention, tenure, and/or promotion record. Thus, it is imperative before embarking on an applied research project to understand institutional priorities as they play out in rhetoric as well as in precedent-establishing tenure and promotion practices. In my case, it was a battle that was eventually won in the form of a promotion. However, the road was rocky, and colleagues' reservations were extremely discouraging.

Apart from occasional setbacks because of different schedules between the university and high school and the like, the project had a long-term and lasting impact on the community, partly because the university's leadership advertised project achievements in media clips and news coverage. News of the project also reached the popular teen magazine *Seventeen,* and I was interviewed by a reporter for the magazine about any advice I could give its readers on how to deal with questions related to sexuality. The family planning clinic associated with this project became identified as a teen-friendly place, and teens continued to frequent it to avail themselves of its services even after grant funds were depleted and the clinic could no longer afford to set aside teen-only hours.

Finally, the project had a lasting impact on my colleagues and me. First, it increased our reputation in the local area, and we were able to secure more local grants that dealt with children's health issues such as immunization, teen alcohol and drug use prevention, and factors influencing teen resiliency. Additionally, securing a large grant improved the institution's sense of its own capacity to handle large-scale grants and projects. When I secured the grant for this project, it was the largest grant the school had ever received, but now it is mentioned as one of many. This was a remarkable outcome, particularly since the project began as a social intervention strategy. I encourage anyone who wishes to make a change in his or her community to try out an applied research project. It can test the relevance of more abstract and complex ideas and be infinitely rewarding.

References

Bongaarts, J. (1982). The fertility-inhibiting effects of the intermediate fertility variables. *Studies in Family Planning, 13,* 179–189.

Caldwell, J. C. (1976). Toward a restatement of demographic transition theory. *Population and Development Review, 2,* 321–366.

Coale, A. J., & Watkins, S. C. (Eds.). (1986). *The decline of fertility in Europe.* Princeton, NJ: Princeton University Press.

Easterlin, R. A., & Crimmins, E. A. (1985). *The fertility revolution: A supply demand analysis.* Chicago, IL: University of Chicago Press.

Poston, D. L., Jr., & Terrell, H. K. M. (2006). Fertility. In B. Turner (Ed.), *The Cambridge Dictionary of Sociology* (pp. 201–203). Cambridge, UK: Cambridge University Press.

Case Study 6.2. Doing God's Work and Doing Good Work(s): Unique Challenges to Evaluation Research in Ministry Settings

Anne E. Figert

Pre-Collaboration History

In the United States, HIV infection and AIDS continue to have a disproportionate effect in urban communities of color. The Centers for Disease Control and Prevention (CDC) and researchers have established that religious leaders and institutions are key gatekeepers to HIV prevention in low-income, primarily minority communities (Mertz, 1997). As a disease, HIV/AIDS can engender both stigma and fear that often results in denial of the problem by religious leaders. In the 1990s, nonprofit AIDS/HIV agencies like the AIDS Pastoral Care Network (APCN) in Chicago began to shift their mission and focus from primarily serving gay men to work with the more diverse communities affected by the spread of the disease. APCN started the West-Side Religious Initiative with Latino faith communities to create a two-track HIV prevention ministry outreach to religious leaders and their congregations (hereafter referred to as the Centro project) on the West Side of Chicago. APCN then began a second project in the predominantly African American neighborhoods on the South Side of Chicago in collaboration with the local clergy association. The ultimate goal of both projects was to create a self-sustaining HIV prevention program located in the churches themselves or through the clergy association in the neighborhoods.

AIDS Foundation of Chicago Collaboration and Partnership Narrative

Through a competitive grant program funded through the AIDS Foundation of Chicago in 2000, a collaborative partnership was formed between APCN and an academic social scientist with experience working with HIV/AIDS agencies (Figert). Loyola researchers (Figert and a graduate student trained in social work and ministry) embarked on a mission to evaluate the training and outreach of the HIV/AIDS ministry projects. APCN staff had previously conducted some initial evaluation of the training programs, focused upon measuring HIV knowledge, attitudes, and facts before and after the APCN training. Loyola researchers analyzed these data and found that the results contradicted some of APCN's early assumptions about the degree of ministers' knowledge about HIV and their activities in the targeted communities. For example, the researchers found that most clergy began the trainings with a significant degree of knowledge regarding HIV/AIDS and did not have initial attitudes about the illness that would prevent them from being personally or professionally involved in HIV prevention ministry. In the Centro Project, even though more than 6,000 people in faith congregations received HIV prevention information, the failure to reach the goal of establishing a self-sustaining HIV prevention ministry with churches in the community was not because of ministers' inattention but because of the lack of continued funding for the project.

Similar to the Centro Project, the South Shore project was also successful in bringing HIV education and prevention information into the local communities through established religious congregations. However, this project also did not transition into a locally based permanent HIV/AIDS ministry through local clergy associations, as had initially been planned. The reasons for this failure had less to do with funding and more to do with organizational and cultural resistance to evaluation projects. As many social science researchers and government officials have found, there continues to be substantial resistance to anything called "research" in African American communities. The specter of the Tuskegee Syphilis Study is very much alive and well (Brandt, 1978; Gamble, 1987; Jones, 1993). APCN staff wanted to determine how they could address this specter and at the same time change ideas found within the culture of ministry itself about program evaluation.

This project was funded for two years with the hope that APCN itself would be prepared to conduct evaluation research. In the second year of the project, the Loyola researchers refocused their attention from primary evaluation consultation to that of helping APCN staff design both a theoretical model and practical instruments for conducting the evaluation of HIV ministry programs. This decision was made due to the many organizational changes occurring at APCN, including its merger with a local community health organization, the departure of all APCN staff involved with both the Centro and South Shore projects, and the partnership difficulties faced in light of these personnel changes. Together, the Loyola researchers and the new APCN staff and leadership had to learn how to be flexible and agreed that we needed to change the nature of the project from being a primary evaluation project to one in which we could contribute to the national dialogue on faith-based programming and how to practically implement HIV ministry programs, with evaluation in mind, in faith communities.

Unique Challenges to Evaluation Work in Ministry Settings

Evaluation work can be challenging in many different settings, but the ministry setting brings its own unique challenges. By its nature, ministry's goals are beyond "helping others" as many social services are. Ministries' goals can also include recruiting new members and doing "God's work." Due in part to these goals and assumptions, the question of the ministry's overall effectiveness may go unasked. Often there is a higher value placed on a minister's ability to be charismatic and relational than being structured and detail oriented.

Together, the Loyola researchers and APCN staff constructed a manual or tool kit in order to guide the agency's work. This manual consisted of templates of evaluation surveys for HIV programs; a step-by-step outline of HIV ministry evaluation processes in the context of the city of Chicago, for example, knowing the ministerial alliances or aldermen (city council representatives) in a neighborhood; and a pamphlet connecting ministry and evaluation titled "Evaluation as Ministry."

In this pamphlet, we discussed evaluation research in terms of push/pull factors. As push factors, we suggested that the good thing about doing an evaluation is that a ministry can find out whether it is meeting the needs of the community and accomplishing the things it set out to do. In other words, we tried to show how evaluation takes the guesswork out of "So how did you think that went?" We provided a scenario about an HIV ministry program in a church and how evaluation may have helped the program be successful. We also addressed the issue of how the term *evaluation* can provoke feelings of mistrust and suspicion and provided some questions and examples of non-threatening evaluation and how it could be used in ministry settings. The pamphlet became more of a living document as opposed to something set in type so that APCN was able to tailor and change parts of the pamphlet for different groups, for example, Pentecostal ministers versus American Baptist ministers.

The pull factors for evaluation may be even more important and compelling. Because of the church/state separation tradition in our country, churches and congregations until recently have not been able to access government funding whenever there is a question about proselytizing as a part of the program. This lack of familiarity with funders, most of whom insist on evaluation, puts ministries at a disadvantage in the larger social service market. While there are advantages to getting some outside help to support different church ministries, there is often the expectation by the grant giver that program evaluations be done and reported back to them. From their standpoint, this is an important tool for monitoring whether or not the money they have given is making the hoped-for difference in a community. From a ministry's standpoint, evaluation can be more work and seem like a hassle at times. However, we tried to portray evaluation as a win-win situation. With evaluation tools, pastors and ministers can find out whether their ministries are making a difference. Also, by including evaluation in these ministries, HIV/AIDS ministry programs can broaden their funding possibilities, and in the end, be able to help more people.

Recommendations

It would be naive to suggest that all ministers are, or will be, receptive to reframing the evaluation process as an important part of ministry work. Like anyone, ministers may not want to know whether their programs are effective or not. For many, ministry programs are part of what ministers feel is their calling, and maybe for them just having the program is enough. How do you measure the "Spirit" or "God's Love"? There are multiple challenges to introducing evaluation in ways *that make sense to ministers and congregations*. Agencies and researchers need to find ways to engage willing and not-so-willing ministers and congregations in dialogue. This can make more transparent the ways those congregations already evaluate their ministry and methods by which they can formalize that process and maintain its consistency with the mission of each of the local congregations.

Stemming from this project, there are four recommendations for implementing research evaluation in HIV/AIDS and ministry programs:

1. Recognize that the focus of many ministries is on the group of people in the world who are in desperate need and have run out of places to turn.

HIV/AIDS is just one of many social and personal problems faced in the low-income and primarily minority communities. The ability of local congregations to turn on a dime and marshal resources with zero or limited requirements or restrictions on clients and programs has been crucial in the battle against HIV/AIDS. Helping people and communities who are affected by HIV/AIDS can be an overwhelming experience for ministers and congregations. At the same time, there is still a fair amount of authority granted to ministers that goes unquestioned in congregations. This authority often leads to a lack of accountability for ministry programs and leaves unanswered congregational interests and desires to integrate HIV/AIDS programs into the mission of the church. The lack of familiarity with funders who require evaluation puts ministries at a disadvantage in grant applications. In the end, any kind of good evaluation training can help ministers and congregations be sure of the effectiveness of their programs and may even help them be competitive for future funding opportunities.

2. Understand and address the long-standing tension between ministry culture and social science research and social service programs.

Social science research is often seen as uncaring and inadequate in measuring spiritual transformation of people and communities. In Christian ministries especially there is often an attitude that the very idea of evaluation is contrary to the central teachings of the church. The question of ministry's measurable, earthly effectiveness is often asked and answered by considering abstract or ambiguous qualities like being charismatic rather than looking at qualities that are measurable, such as being organized or attentive to details. Theological education teaches, legitimately, that simply by being present to others' needs and representing God's will and presence in the midst of that need is sufficient for mutual transformation. Even among the most professional ministers, there is an absence of theological language that supports outcome measures and evaluation. This supports the functional belief that to simply "show up" for ministry is blessed. The subsequent rationalization, "Well, at least I'm here" can be helpful *in sustaining ministries* but is not conducive to *evaluation questions about the effectiveness of ministry*. If evaluators and social scientists can begin to understand this tension, then they can begin to address this tension in a way that is supportive rather than dismissive of ministries.

3. Recognize that the ministries of most congregations are staffed by volunteers with scant training or evaluation background.

Working with ministers is hard, but working with volunteers is even more challenging. Volunteers in faith communities generally measure their success on the following intangibles: recruiting new members and doing "God's work"; how consistent they feel their work is with their faith or values; and how "graced and blessed" the ministry is. As with work in social service agencies, it can be difficult to see what difference volunteers are making. For researchers, working with volunteers means learning to effectively communicate in a non-challenging manner. For instance, we have to find ways to explain why we may want to ask for people's names and addresses on a sign-in log or why we might want to know why a person is attending a workshop beyond the call from God to do so. When volunteers are also helping in the evaluation, researchers need to be prepared for things to go wrong or be less systematic than the protocol demands. At the same time, by helping in the evaluation, the volunteers begin to understand why researchers ask the kinds of questions that they do.

4. HIV/AIDS ministry programs must have a progressive theological message in order to have effective outreach into the community.

Pastors, ministers, and congregants are both part of the problem and part of the solution to creating better and more just HIV/AIDS ministries. In addition to helping pastors and ministers learn about evaluation techniques, they must acquire a different theological perspective to help them effectively minister to all people in their community who are affected in some way by HIV/AIDS. It is not enough to conduct social scientific or medical programs about HIV/AIDS to clergy and lay leaders. We found that contrary to what was thought, ministers did have a basic understanding of medical and scientific knowledge about HIV transmission or AIDS. Ultimately what is going to help more people in the community is the progressive, non-damning theological message of love, acceptance, and knowledge. Not all ministers or ministries are willing to do this.

References

Brandt, A. (1978). Racism and research: The case of the Tuskegee Syphilis Study. *Hastings Center Report, 8*(6), 21–29.

Gamble, V. N. (1997). Under the shadow of Tuskegee: African Americans and health care. *American Journal of Public Health, 87*(11), 1773–1777.

Jones, J. H. (1993). *Bad blood: The Tuskegee Syphilis Experiment.* New York, NY: Free Press.

Mertz, J. P. (1997). The role of churches in helping adolescents prevent HIV/AIDS. *Journal of HIV/AIDS Prevention & Education for Adolescents & Children, 1*(2), 45-55.

Case Study 6.3. Feast on the Southeast: Creating a Sustainable Local Food System in Southeastern North Carolina

Leslie Hossfeld and Mac Legerton

The Southeastern North Carolina Food Systems Program (SENCFS) began in 2006 as an offshoot of the Jobs for the Future project based at the Center for Community Action (CCA) in Lumberton, North Carolina. Mac Legerton, executive director of CCA, and Leslie Hossfeld, director of Public Sociology, University of North Carolina Wilmington (UNCW), had been working on economic recovery in Robeson County, North Carolina, where CCA is based. Robeson County lost more than 10,000 textile manufacturing jobs from 1993 to 2002 due to the implementation of NAFTA (North American Free Trade Agreement) (Hossfeld, 2010; Hossfeld, Legerton, & Kuester, 2004). Since then, our overall focus has been on economic recovery for the region and for rural America in general. While our initial concern was on the manufacturing job loss, we wanted to approach economic recovery in as comprehensive a way as possible, and we began to examine our region, sector by sector.

Our research in southeastern North Carolina identified the growth sectors of health and education; the challenged sectors of agriculture, forestry, and manufacturing; and the emerging sectors of entrepreneurship and small business and recreation and tourism. Based on these findings, one of our strategies focused on the challenged agriculture sector through an economic development initiative around a regional food system. This involved identifying market opportunities for limited resource farmers[1] through institutional buying relationships with our schools, hospitals, colleges and universities, and restaurants. SENCFS is a local food movement that emphasizes buying local and keeping a greater percentage of food dollars within the local economy, providing healthier and more nutritious food for communities, and also reducing our carbon footprint.

The Region and Foundation for SENCFS

The rural, small-town South captures much of what southeastern North Carolina has traditionally been and still is today. Enduring, persistent poverty defines many of the counties in eastern North Carolina. Indeed, four adjacent SENCFS counties are designated as persistent poverty counties by the USDA-ERS.[2] These counties have experienced significant manufacturing job loss, and given their close proximity, it has been difficult for residents to

---

[1]Limited resource farmers are defined by the USDA as socially disadvantaged farmers who have a total household income at or below the national poverty level for a family of four, or less than 50% of county median household income in each of the previous two years.

[2]Persistent poverty counties are defined by USDA as counties with poverty rates over 20% since 1970.

find employment in neighboring counties—a traditional strategy in coping with job displacement. Robeson County has remained in the top five poorest counties in the nation (for counties with populations of 65,000 and over) since 2005 and in 2008 ranked fourth highest in the nation for counties its size (U.S. Census Bureau, 2008). The average percentage of poverty for SENCFS counties is 19% (U.S. Census, 2009), compared to North Carolina and U.S. poverty rates of 14% in 2009.

SENCFS counties comprise more Native Americans than any region east of the Mississippi River and are homes to the Lumbee, the largest tribe in the eastern United States, and the Waccamaw Siouan. In addition, the African American population comprises 24% of the six-county population; the poverty rate for this population is 30%. Black and Latino poverty in the SENCFS counties is approximately 2½ times higher than White poverty. About 15% of the SENCFS region's population 25 and older holds a bachelor's degree or higher.

In a region with remarkable growth and a growing affluent coastline, the enduring problems that have characterized rural North Carolina for generations have simply not gone away. High pockets of rural poverty, low educational attainment, and a racial divide in income and access to resources linger and aggravate embedded social and economic problems in the region.

There is extensive farming in the rural counties, but farming continues to serve the export economy rather than local food needs. Small-scale farmers face enormous hurdles: food imports and competition from large-scale agribusiness make it increasingly difficult for small-scale farmers to maintain a livelihood and sustain their farms. In 2006, North Carolina lost more farms than any other state in the nation. Limited resource farmers have been hardest hit: Based on 2007 U.S. Agriculture Census data, there was a 15% decline in African American farmers in North Carolina from 2002 to 2007. In southeastern North Carolina, there was an 8% decrease in African American farmers from 2002 to 2007 (U.S. Department of Agriculture, 2007).

With rising poverty and the massive loss of manufacturing and agricultural jobs, the entire rural economy of southeastern North Carolina is in need of reconstruction. The establishment of local and regional food systems is a key component in developing vibrant and sustainable local and regional economies.

Building a Movement

In late 2006, SENCFS held our first meeting at a community college in Columbus County, North Carolina, a central location in the six-county area.

It is incredible to think back to that meeting and to reflect upon how far along we have come in a relatively short period of time. We remember being unsure of how many people would turn up to the meeting.

Rural sociological research points to key elements of the agrifood system that should be included in creating a sustainable movement around local foods; these include the environment, the community, food industry workers, farmers, consumers, and livelihoods (Allen, 2007). This research informed our outreach to public and private sector representatives in the six-county area. We also drew upon the community partnerships we had developed in the Jobs for the Future Project. We extended invitations to key constituents in the region, ensuring diverse representation based on race, gender, and geography (rural/urban). We sought support from all our Cooperative Extension agents, the U.S. Department of Agriculture (USDA), the North Carolina Department of Agriculture (NCDA), farmers' markets managers, farmland protection advocates, community colleges, small business technology and development centers, elected officials, farmers, students, conservation groups, researchers, food cooperatives, 4-H, Future Farmers of America, and community organizers. The 12 core people who attended the first meeting, and the agencies they represent, are still working hard on our local food systems initiative. The monthly meetings have grown in capacity and strength. We have now extended to eight core counties. Today, we have more than 100 public and private sector organizations and individuals involved in SENCFS. And we still feel like we are just getting off the ground!

Using Sociology to Inform Regional Food Systems

While we focused on community organizing and bringing people to the table, we also turned our attention to data collection. We needed baseline data to tell us the critical needs surrounding agriculture in our region: We immediately began a community food assessment, county by county, to identify farmers' needs, institutional buyers' needs, and food security concerns. We partnered with several institutions to assist in data collection. Undergraduate and graduate students began to work on SENCFS research: A public sociology undergraduate class at UNCW conducted a survey of restaurants in one county to determine potential demand and opportunities for local food-buying practices. Raven Bruno, a UNCW M.A. in public sociology student, focused her research and thesis on farm-to-school to determine barriers, challenges, and opportunities for increased farm-to-school practices in three SENCFS counties. SENCFS partnered with M.A. graduate students at the University of North Carolina Chapel Hill Department of City and Regional Planning program to examine farm-to-school challenges and opportunities in the other three SENCFS counties. Another UNCW public sociology undergraduate class conducted a food security assessment in a public housing community in the one urban county in the SENCFS region. And we have worked with UNCW, North Carolina State University, North Carolina Agricultural and Technical State University, and Duke University on farmer surveys identifying limited resource farmer needs, barriers, and challenges in participating in local food systems. In addition, SENCFS has surveyed institutional buyers (all hospitals, schools, colleges, and universities) in the region on their local food-buying practices and opportunities to expand and increase local food purchasing. We have also created county profiles of agricultural production in each county along with USDA census data detailing the number of farms and farmers and the market value of agricultural commodities (see http://www.feastsoutheastnc.org/research for all SENCFS research reports).

Our research has helped us understand the serious needs in the region surrounding our challenged agricultural sector and, more important, helped shape the program initiatives of SENCFS.

DOING PUBLIC SOCIOLOGY

Raven Bruno holds an M.A. in public sociology and is an alumnus of the University of North Carolina Wilmington.

My work in public sociology started with a graduate assistantship in which I served as coordinator of the Southeastern North Carolina Food Systems Program (SENCFS)—a community organization working on the creation of a local food system. Coordinating this group meant working closely with key stakeholders across southeastern North Carolina on the development and implementation of a local food system.

My experience with SENCFS enabled me to truly engage in public sociology, and my relationship with SENCFS members proved essential to my graduate research. My research focused on farm-to-school as a potential institutional buying program that would benefit both small farmers and local schoolchildren, along with improving the local economy, environment, and community relations. My research developed out of a need identified by SENCFS, and the information it generated benefited the organization.

I utilized a collaborative research design adapted from Randy Stoeker's project-based research model whereby members of SENCFS and the community at large served as primary informants for my research. Data were collected to identify the needs and challenges of local school districts in participating in a farm-to-school program as well as the successes of the statewide North Carolina farm-to-school programs. An important part of my research was to create and nourish relationships as data were collected. All interviewees were informed of the work of SENCFS and invited to join the organization.

My research did not end with a professionally bound thesis. I synthesized the results of the research into a presentation for SENCFS. The presentation proposed potential models of farm-to-school program implementation in southeastern North Carolina and policies that would support the implementation of a local food system, specifically through institutional purchasing from schools, at the local, state, and national levels. This information was used by SENCFS in their pursuit of developing a local food system.

Working with SENCFS opened the opportunity for extending academic research into the community to bring about positive change. Informed by my graduate research, SENCFS has now established a processing and distribution center that will provide local agricultural products to schools.

Building Partnerships to Ensure Success

Our research has helped provide the important data we need to write grants and find funding to support SENCFS programming. SENCFS has received more than $650,000 in grant funding and more than $300,000 in technical assistance from community partnerships to carry out its work. While this may sound like a lot of money, it really isn't! To date, we have only two staff members and a remarkable corps of volunteers that manage SENCFS programming through working committees (see http://www .feastsoutheastnc.org/committees). Expanding and deepening community partnerships have been mainstays of our organization's success.

SENCFS focus is on limited resource farmers who have been neglected by the traditional agribusiness model. Our priorities include (1) strengthening local economies in economically distressed counties and encouraging economic development; (2) implementing agricultural and food system development strategies focused on job creation, market expansion, and alternative crop production; and (3) increasing access to affordable food and encouraging the consumption of healthy foods both in public institutions and at home.

SENCFS has created a Buy Local campaign that educates consumers on the importance of buying local to support their local economy, as well as educating consumers on the health and environmental benefits of purchasing local foods from sustainable agricultural producers in their region. We also have a vibrant farm-to-chef program that links limited resource farmers to local chefs, featuring local foods and local farmers, educating consumers about the importance of knowing the source of their food and eating seasonally, following menus prepared from local foods in season.

SENCFS has a workforce development committee that supports training through local community colleges on sustainable agriculture and food-related occupations that support a regional food system. This committee also focuses on youth mentoring for new farmers as well as entrepreneurial enterprises for young farmers and community garden projects.

SENCFS works with child nutrition directors in eight counties to develop and strengthen the farm-to-school program, ensuring that more local produce and fresh foods are purchased and served in our local schools. We have an extensive community and school garden program, providing education to low-income communities and to public school children on the importance of preparing and eating healthy nutritious foods from the garden. In addition, SENCFS has worked to support electronic benefit transfer (food stamp) use at our famers' markets so that low-income families can buy fresh fruits and vegetables.

One of our grandest projects to date is SENC Foods (Southeastern North Carolina Foods) Processing and Distribution Center. We received funding from the Golden LEAF Foundation and the North Carolina Tobacco Trust Foundation (both tobacco settlement foundations) to support a processing and distribution center for limited resource farmers. We have created a farmer LLC/cooperative to process and distribute local produce to institutions in the region. This provides a mechanism for limited resource farmers to be competitive in institutional-buying procurement bids to ensure new markets for their agricultural production.

While SENCFS is leading the southeastern part of North Carolina in the local food movement, we know that we are part of a much bigger movement that is taking place at the state, national, and global levels. To this end, we have been instrumental in the statewide movement to expand sustainable agriculture and local food production in North Carolina. SENCFS joined forces with other local food systems organizations in North Carolina to help establish and pass North Carolina Senate Bill 1067 that created the North Carolina Sustainable Local Food Advisory Council mandated by the North Carolina General Assembly to regulate the development of a sustainable local food economy in North Carolina; SENCFS cofounder, Mac Legerton, along with another SENCFS member serve on this council. SENCFS is also a lead partner with the Center for Environmental Farming Systems (CEFS) at North Carolina State University on the newly created 10% Campaign that encourages North

Carolina consumers to commit 10% of their existing food dollars to support local food producers, related businesses, and communities (http://www.cefs .ncsu.edu/whatwedo/foodsystems/10percent.html).

We learned long ago that none of our work can happen without working with others; developing these partnerships takes time, yet they are essential to the success of any sustainable community-based work (see http://www .feastsoutheastnc.org/partners).

Using Public Sociology to Make a Difference

The work we do through SENCFS focuses on the inequalities in race, gender, and geography surrounding local food production. Sociology gives us that particular lens with which to view our world to illuminate the critical issues in our region—and to make meaningful social change. From the presentations we give to program development, we are informed by and inform others using the tools of our trade to make a difference.

References

Allen, P. (2007). *Together at the table: Sustainability and sustenance in the American agrifood system*. University Park, PA: Pennsylvania State University Press.

Hossfeld, L. (2010). Why don't we do something about it? Response to job loss in rural communities. In K. Korgen & J. M. White (Eds.), *Sociologists in action* (pp. 243–248). Thousand Oaks, CA: Sage.

Hossfeld, L., Legerton, M., & Kuester, G. (2004). The economic and social impact of job loss in Robeson County North Carolina 1993-2003. *Sociation Today* 2(2). Retrieved from http://www.ncsociology.org/hossfeld.htm

U.S. Department of Agriculture. (2007). *The census of agriculture*. Retrieved at http:// www.agcensus.usda.gov/Publications/2007/index.asp

Case Study 6.4. Challenging Discrimination Against Women, Minorities, and the Sick in Health Insurance

Donald W. Light

One kind of public sociology aims to demystify claims promoted by elites that work against the common good and social justice. These same claims often mislead the public, the press, and policy makers. Sociological methods can clarify what is happening, or might happen, while sociological concepts can be combined with ethical ones to formulate more just reforms. This kind of public sociology is critical to showing which practices or strategies by mainstream organizations are not working, will not work, or have deleterious effects. It can be most effective when combined with clear reform ideas. However, this kind of public sociology can harm one's career if powerful corporations and interests bite back. I do not recommend doing this work before having tenure, unless the issue is in political fashion.

A major four-year campaign that exemplifies this kind of public sociology concerned New Jersey Blue Cross and Blue Shield (Blue Cross). Providing affordable, community-rated policies (i.e., the same premium regardless of health profile or risk) to individuals and small groups was a major reason for creating Blue Cross plans across the country in the 1930s. As tax-exempt, nonprofit, quasi-public bodies, they were required to structure their policies in this way (Law, 1974; Starr, 1982). In New Jersey in the mid-1980s, the company tried to abandon its 1938 founding mandate. Blue Cross mounted a large lobbying campaign to persuade the legislature and public that it was going bankrupt. It blamed its losses on these equitable risk-blind "community-rated" policies for individuals and small groups.

But when a plan raises premiums 2–3 times more than the increase in medical costs year after year, this raises questions. It threatens small group and individual policyholders who have no choice—"no exit," as A. O. Hirschman (1970) famously put it in *Exit, Voice and Loyalty*. They are left with two choices: either "voice," that is, complain, or "loyalty," that is, stay put and be quiet. But most policyholders do not know how to voice their objections other than to complain about the sharp increases in their premiums. When insurers explain they have to raise premiums to cover rising medical costs, policyholders cannot question this explanation, even though it is suspect.

What Hirschman did not consider is how consumers with no option to exit can organize their voice. I call this "No Exit and the Organization of Voice" (Light, Castelblanch, Arrendondo, & Socolar, 2003). In the aftermath of Blue Cross's application to the state for large "community-rated" increases in premiums, we organized a coalition representing one-sixth of the population in New Jersey to voice our objections and fight the rate increases.

Background of the Campaign

The original vision in the 1930s was to create nonprofit state and area Blue Cross plans that offered fair community rates to all enrollees. To promote itself as a caring social institution, the name "Blue Cross" was chosen to benefit from the hallowed reputation of Red Cross. Since that time, Blue Cross plans have dominated many state markets, and most small groups or individuals have few other affordable options.

Things began to change in New Jersey when the separate Blue Cross and Blue Shield companies merged in 1986 to form Blue Cross and Blue Shield of New Jersey, with a combined surplus of $62.2 million (not bad at the time). Within in a year, however, it reported a loss of $0.2 million and lost another $177 million the next. As an expert on health insurance, I was suspicious, especially when Blue Cross filed for rate increases of 20–25% a year. The company claimed that it was hemorrhaging from its community-rated policies for small groups and individuals. How could the state's oldest and largest health insurer be losing so much money all of a sudden when it instituted premium increases much greater than the rising cost of medicine? Statistically, this stable population of small groups and individuals could not be getting cancer, heart disease, or other conditions that could explain such increases. Something else was going on.

Based on related research for the state legislature, I began to see that Blue Cross's losses were not coming from its community-rated policies for small groups and individuals but from its big, risk-rated commercial policies. In New Jersey, Blue Cross dominance of health insurance had begun to erode as risk-rating commercial insurers came in and siphoned lower-risk groups off. They started a "death spiral." Blue Cross plans were left with increasingly higher-risk enrollees whose conditions required the insurer to charge more than the commercials, which led to still more of its better risks switching to the commercials. The result was an ever-widening gap between Blue Cross premiums and those of the commercial insurers. Although Blue Cross claimed that the losses were coming from its mandatory community-rated policies for small groups and individuals, the losses were really the result of the company's policy of underpricing its big, risk-rated commercial policies in order to outbid the big commercial companies and gain market share.

This is a way in which an insurer can lose a great deal of money very fast. However, if the company could successfully make the case that it was the fault of its mandatory community-rated policies, then the commissioner of insurance (almost always a former executive of an insurance company) would grant it the right to extract several million more from small policyholders with "no exit."

Why was Blue Cross, an organization that strongly promoted itself as a caring social institution, behaving this way? Further research revealed that the false campaign was being orchestrated by a new generation of ambitious executives who wanted to transform Blue Cross into a large commercial insurance company and get rid of its historic nonprofit mission. Executives at Prudential and Metropolitan Life had chauffeured cars and a helipad— why didn't they? A similar change in corporate culture had transformed Blue Cross Blue Shield plans across the country.

In the case of Blue Cross and Blue Shield of New Jersey, the sleight of hand it chose was to impose rate changes selectively. Blue Cross applied to the state for large "community-rated" increases in premiums, but they discriminated by zip code (social class and race), gender, and age. The company called them "demographic community rates." It was at this point that our campaign kicked into gear.

Dynamics of the Campaign

Initially, a research assistant and I translated our research into press packets to inform legislators and the news media that Blue Cross was violating its public mandate, creating a false crisis of bankruptcy, and using this to charge higher rates to women, disadvantaged minorities, and policyholders who were older or poorer. Since Blue Cross had long, deep ties with the Department of Insurance, the governor's office, and the legislature, it was not accustomed to incisive challenges with counter-facts and figures by a well-informed public sociologist. Within weeks, my dean called me in and informed me that that the governor's office had spoken to the university president about getting me to stop making trouble. He told me not to conduct research or related activities on this project during work or to mention my academic position as a professor of health care policy.

That seemed reasonable to me and, in fact, rather tolerant. I complied and turned to the New Jersey Public Health Association as a new base for the campaign, reasoning that I could work on it after hours and weekends. Its board of New Deal Democrats quickly understood the issues, and together we built a large, statewide coalition that included the NAACP, NOW, AARP, Common Cause, and the New Jersey Council of Churches—organizations that together represented about 1 in every 6 adults throughout the state. Getting such a large and diverse coalition together was difficult and benefited from sociological studies of social movements. We created, in effect, a new issue-based public. Granted that much public sociology, as Burawoy (2004, p. 1608) writes, "focuses on solutions to specific problems defined by clients," most of my campaigns alert and mobilize a public to a personal problem with hidden roots in exploitation and structural inequality.

Because of my training at the University of Chicago and Brandeis, I did most of the research. The key findings were translated into simple bar graphs and phrases for TV and press conferences. With the help of the NAACP Legal Defense Fund, we also began to mount a legal challenge to the discriminatory rates as a violation of Blue Cross's enabling legislation and charter. We then appealed to the New Jersey public advocate to use taxpayers' money for the costly court case to defend the public interest by suing Blue Cross for violating its legal mandate. When the public advocate realized the breadth of our coalition and heard its legal team's arguments, he agreed to prosecute; it was public attention and organized voice that led to the public advocate taking the case and suing Blue Cross for violating its legal mandate. The result of this lawsuit was the first appellate court ruling against the increases, which rolled back premiums for about 600,000 people. The campaign took three years.

Blue Cross responded next by simply increasing premiums for everyone 4 times more than medical expense increases. That was much easier to oppose, and we persuaded the commissioner of insurance to hold premium increases to the same percentage as medical cost increases. Next, having been stopped from increasing revenues by risk rating or sharply increasing premiums across the board, Blue Cross turned to cutting costs by dropping seriously ill patients and cutting critical benefits. This led to a campaign centering on finding sick patients who would go on camera and describe how life-sustaining services were being threatened. The commissioner forced Blue Cross to restore the cuts.

The work was exhausting, especially so because Blue Cross used a fail-safe tactic to minimize any opposition—file in mid-November for a change in January, so citizens' groups had to organize during Thanksgiving and the December holidays as well as New Year's. Initially, the commissioner of insurance also chose not to hold public hearings, eliminating that vehicle. When he did hold meetings, the location was changed the day before they were held. These kinds of tactics make organizing voice especially difficult, and one has to be ingenious to counter them. Nevertheless, we prevailed.

Accomplishments and Next Steps

This campaign, with its three victories, laid the groundwork and raised awareness for the New Jersey legislature to pass a sweeping reform of the small-group and individual market that was reasonably fair and required all insurers in the state to participate in proportion to their market share. We could say this is the end of the story, though several adjustments and changes had to be made subsequently. These reforms never worked very well because they were surrounded by insurers competing in a commercial market based on, to some degree, risk discrimination. Insurers have developed several techniques to discriminate most against those who most need insurance, what I call the "inverse coverage law" (Light, 1992): In competitive health insurance, the more you need coverage, the less you are likely to get and the more you are likely to pay for it. And now New Jersey Blue Cross and Blue Shield is converting to a for-profit corporation, just as the new generation of ambitious executives wanted to in the 1980s.

I used this lesson and my experiences in this campaign for another campaign in Ireland to stop a large external plan from eroding the base of Ireland's Blue Cross equivalent and to close loopholes that allowed demographic rates (Light, 1998). Ministers realized that competition from commercial insurers would divide the Irish and their families by risk. Once this happened it would be difficult to restore equitable, community-rated insurance.

With the 2010 national health insurance reforms in the United States, this dilemma is likely to occur again as states organize insurance exchanges in which dominant insurers sell policies to individuals and small groups at community rates. Some of the widespread discriminatory techniques can still be used by insurers after the 2010 reforms, especially selective marketing and policy design. Thus, this case holds lessons for discriminating against older, sicker, and female policyholders in the coming years. But the new reforms greatly reduce risk selection, making health insurance unaffordable to the poor and vulnerable who need it most.

Finally, I continue my work as a public sociologist in two large campaigns that aim to demystify central claims of the pharmaceutical industry. One is focused on pricing practices; my intent is to show why their prices do not have to be so high. The other is about why new drugs are causing an epidemic of adverse side effects; drugs are the fourth leading cause of death, and adverse reactions are prevalent, about 46 million a year in the United States alone (Light, 2010).

References

Burawoy, M. (2004). Public sociologies: Contradictions, dilemmas, and possibilities. *Social Forces, 82,* 1603–1618.

Hirschman, A. O. (1970). *Exit, voice and loyalty.* Cambridge, MA: Harvard University Press.

Law, S. A. (1974). *Blue Cross: What went wrong?* New Haven, CT: Yale University Press.

Light, D., Castelblanch, R., Arrendondo, P., & Socolar, D. (2003). No exit and the organization of voice in biotechnology and pharmaceuticals. *Journal of Politics, Policy and Law, 28,* 437–507.

Light, D. W. (1992). The practice and ethics of risk-rated insurance. *Journal of the American Medical Association, 267,* 2503–2508.

Light, D. W. (1998). Keeping competition fair for health insurance: How the Irish beat back risk-rated policies. *American Journal of Public Health, 88,* 745–748.

Light, D. W. (Ed.). (2010). *The risk of prescription drugs.* New York, NY: Columbia University Press.

Starr, P. (1982). *The social transformation of American medicine.* New York, NY: Basic Books.

Case Study 6.5. Tobacco Use Prevention in Montana's Frontier Communities: Developing New Rural Strategies

Patricia G. Nichols

It was 2000 and I had completed all the coursework for a master's degree in sociology. Combining my academic background and history of community research and interventions, I took a job as a tobacco use prevention education coordinator with the Montana Tobacco Use Prevention Program (MTUPP) of the Montana Department of Health and Human Services (MDHHS). This program developed an annual action plan that was in accordance with Centers for Disease Control (CDC) Best Practices for Comprehensive Tobacco Control Programs and that would, in time, yield changes in prevalence of youth tobacco use, changes in policy, and in the long term reduce death from tobacco-related illnesses. There were some expectations that the education coordinator could teach and work with schools. What wasn't obvious was that the position would require organizing communities, building coalitions for social change, producing policy, and growing "self-enforcing" restrictions such as secondhand smoke ordinances. That came later.

The environment in rural Montana in 2000 was virgin territory for tobacco control. Exposure to secondhand smoke was a common occurrence in all places, except the county offices that had implemented a state law to prohibit smoking in government buildings some years earlier. The advent of the MTUPP, funded after the Master Settlement Agreement (MSA) with the tobacco industry, changed all of that.

The state program was aimed at reducing tobacco use and subsequent disease, which has medical implications but relies more on social change and environmental change than simply medical intervention. Funding was provided by the CDC as well as by the MSA. In most cases, county health departments were charged with staffing the project, but the project would entail community assessment, education, and policy promotion to change the manner and degree of tobacco use and bring about an environment that would deter future tobacco use and subsequent harm.

I did not live in the community, but I would be allowed to work from my home in a nearby county. Most of my life I'd lived in huge metropolitan areas, and I'd lived in Montana only a few years, but I would learn all about finding my way in rural communities. Grounded theory would help.

Standard Training and Methods

The MDHHS provided MTUPP staff with training about related health topics and the CDC-recommended best practice of coalition building. Organizers from major health advocacy associations shared their strategies at these trainings. Foremost among these was the strategy to assemble a group of local citizens who would volunteer their efforts to assist the tobacco use prevention program staff in implementing strategies and achieving goals. A primary tactic would be to ally with doctors and medical providers in the community whose voices could legitimize the changes required to impact tobacco disease and death. The voices of concerned citizens would punctuate the need, tell the story, and stimulate decision makers to act on policy.

These organizers from the health advocacy associations seemed well acquainted with this strategy for organizing communities and building coalitions. They suggested that sharing coalition lists would be helpful in furthering attendance and donations for their health-related causes and suggested these lists were the "mother lode" of citizens who could and should be recruited to our coalitions. The names of these lists epitomized the notion of upstanding citizens who donate time and money for the good of the social order. They reflected respectability, had an idea of how government worked, were currently in or retired from the workforce, and agreed that good health practices were part and parcel of the healthy future. In fact, all of the strategies we discussed during the trainings seemed to fit this group exactly.

These trainings were conducted quarterly in different locations across the state, and the program employees were required to use money from their small budgets to travel and attend. Grant recipients from across the state would often meet at these trainings, thus allowing peer-to-peer networking and discussions. This provided opportunities to hear the experience of other similar communities, big and small. Those situated in larger communities seemed to have better success at coalition building. I looked closely at their experiences and advantages.

Montana's communities are small in comparison to metropolitan areas in other states. Even the larger communities rarely exceed 100,000 people. But larger and smaller had vast differences. The notion of population density best captures this. According to the U.S. Census, population density in the United States is 79.6 persons per square mile, but in a major city such as Atlanta, Georgia, may be as high as 4,000 persons per square mile. In Montana, population density averages 6.2 persons per square mile. A larger city in Montana may have 1,000+ persons per square mile; however, rural and frontier counties skew the state's density by counting 0–4 persons per square mile. My county was one of the four.

So, given the low density of my county, I soon discovered that having a meeting of any type was challenging. And asking people to get involved in an unpaid venture to rally for health policy or change the behavior of their very few neighbors did not meet with rounds of happiness. This was a common experience of the MTUPP personnel working in rural communities. The strategies promoted at trainings seemed an ill fit, so I began to study a nearby community to find out who attended meetings, how often, and what could be expected.

I visited coalition meetings in two larger communities (population density of 1,000 or more per square mile). Each community had a greater assortment of people and career specialization and thus more options to recruit coalition support from within the population. Often, these were people with occupations in medicine, education, law enforcement, or chemical dependency; they had a work-subsidized interest in the tobacco prevention activities and could easily fit this activity into their workdays. Proximity was not an issue in these communities. Driving to a meeting was a short travel investment that had the perk of providing social time as well as a chance to develop connections and obligations for reciprocal favors over time.

Going back to the community I was charged to improve, I began to look for the same citizen base. I began in the county seat where my contract originated. There, I expected to find the most developed group from which to choose. We made a plan for a first coalition attempt. We ran a display ad to attract the appropriate people. Nobody responded. So I made directed phone calls and invitations to the usual representative group, as I had learned from the trainings and seen played out in the larger towns.

The public health nurse would attend. That seemed right; she was my administrator. A doctor, the only doctor in that town, would also attend. We invited people from the schools, but none attended. The meeting was scheduled for after school hours for their advantage, but that still didn't help. A judge agreed to attend but had another appointment at the last moment and couldn't attend. One person who did work with chemical dependency was interested, but couldn't attend. She did agree to another phone call with me. A businesswoman from Main Street attended. She had been invited to talk about her smoke-free tea shop.

When she arrived to meet with the other advocates, there weren't many. I opened the discussion to share the goals of the program, but I didn't know what to ask of this small group. There didn't seem to be much time or energy available to become advocates for a county that was nearly 3,000 square miles large. The doctor also seemed pretty down about the possibilities. He had noticed that "when people are concerned about their hearts, they are only interested in watching cholesterol. They don't want to hear about tobacco." Doctors were supposed to be my champions. I was losing hope.

Within the next couple of months, I completed a state-requested assessment of county features. I realized that this might be key to understanding how to locate the advocates who would make this project work.

The county is a large territory of 2,762 square miles. According to the 2000 U.S. Census, the population was 10,200 people. There were no metropolitan areas but instead a dozen separate small towns. In this county, each of the towns had an individual school district and similarly distinct community cultures. There were no colleges or universities. With a population density of approximately four persons per square mile, the county was classified as "frontier."

The population was primarily White (92%) and American Indian (5%). The county also included a portion of an open American Indian Reservation. Only 15.5% of the population held bachelor's degrees or higher. Sixteen percent of the population was living below the federal poverty level. The State Health Profiles (2002) designated the county as medically underserved. The only hospital was a critical access hospital (16 beds); there were nine primary care providers and two dentists.

This area remains mostly wild and unsettled. Timbered mountains, clear rivers, and wild game animals dominate the environment. There were few obvious avenues for employment but many obvious outlets for outdoor sports and recreation. The small towns had supply and service businesses but no large chain stores or national brand restaurants. Large industries, invisible at the town level, included trucking, logging, ranching, rock quarrying, forest management, and railroad operation and maintenance. There were some ranches and open range but few wealthy landowners. Each town was likely to have a single grocery store and had several bars and cafes, or combination bar/casino/restaurants, almost all of which allowed smoking. As a universal feature, all communities relied on convenience stores (C-stores) for small orders of food and beverage.

Developing New Strategies

The original coalition group didn't stay involved. The first time we met was also the last time we met. Armed with new demographic information from the state-requested assessment, I changed strategies. I began to visit the communities during working hours and interviewed the most active citizens during that time. Finding folks who had even a mild interest was not easy, as this was a fully new endeavor for the area. Tobacco use was everywhere, and nobody wanted to alienate family or peers over "some moralistic stance on tobacco."

Each community was totally disconnected from the next. I was discovering that each was a different situation, with slightly different tobacco policies, unique town cultures, and an overall community identity than the others. But I quickly learned that schools were rich sources for community information. They all seemed to have an interest in tobacco use prevention to teach the children and teens, but they weren't interested in working with neighboring communities.

Sports rivalry dominated the relationship between schools. And tobacco policies had entered into that. If one community had expelled a teen for tobacco, parents would intercede to protect a budding athlete. They'd transport the teen to another town where the high school would gloss over the tobacco issue and admit that student to their school, and their team. Even the schools that had a strong stance on tobacco couldn't seem to stop parents from dropping off the teens at school while both parent and teen were smoking. It was family bonding, and the jurisdiction of the school wouldn't start until the teen left the car.

Recognizing the schools could become strategic partners in my work despite the fact that they wished to remain separate rather than join together as a coalition, I established a plan with them, and we began to work together on a one-to-one basis. The CDC regulations included a caveat that tobacco prevention personnel not teach in classrooms. That language was very specific. So the school worked with me to do presentations in large assemblies and in special workshops away from classrooms. We were changing the way that tobacco prevention was taught, but it would take years to make a change in the whole county. The tobacco prevention community was officially a party of one.

Individual business owners couldn't provide much time for even an introductory discussion, so I visited three different Chamber of Commerce meetings. For this county, that meant three separate meetings given during a breakfast, lunch, or dinner in the three different segments of the county. As a planned speaker, I was allowed five minutes at each of these meetings to introduce myself and discuss the new county program. I would solicit their support and questions. The acquaintances I made at these chamber meetings were probably some of the best I would make in the business community, but they were sparse. I was able to connect with one person in each of the two distant communities, and a group of five at the remaining chamber. Seven people for all the planning and time it took to meet. None of them could commit to attending meetings but would do what they could when next I needed some help. I did attend some meetings for a second time as a spectator, but this was a huge investment for a half-time employee just to get introduced to the community.

Lessons Learned

The work went slowly, and over time, the way I was operating seemed to offer the hope of someday establishing a community coalition. The only way I was able to knit the communities together over tobacco prevention was to maintain a solid presence by regular phone calls and visits to the schools and progressive businesses throughout the community. I'd write health articles whenever the newspapers decided to focus on a health-related topic or drug prevention event. When events such as the annual Great American Smokeout would come about, I'd encourage the whole community to post notices and share the word by electronic signs or whatever routine announcements they made. And I became the hub of a large wheel of prevention activities to elicit attention and build momentum.

I did feel like the Lone Ranger. I didn't have enough money to hire an extra person or travel to areas more than twice per year, but what I couldn't do in travel or energy I did through the newspapers and telephone contact. We did make progress in those early days. Eventually I was hired by the state to do training for other tobacco prevention personnel to help them manage the stress of coordinating a team in rural areas. As part of that effort, we brought together the community of tobacco prevention persons across the state by a weekly email newsletter and sharing the same goals, awareness, and efforts. The state program has become the hub of statewide activity that, when joined by media or other analysis, appear as a large community movement.

In 2005, the State of Montana adopted a Clean Indoor Air Act to make all public places in Montana smoke-free by the year 2009. And by the year 2009, the state had systems in place to deal with the wide variety of rural and frontier prevention issues. Community coalition building remains the best way to manage community adherence and participation in tobacco prevention work and maintenance of secondhand smoke restrictions, but we have learned that community must be redefined regularly to take into consideration the characteristics of rural regions and the groups that are present.

CASE STUDIES 7

Crime, Reducing Violence, and Promoting Justice

Sociological research has made significant contributions to understanding the nature and extent of crime and providing strategies to reduce violence; indeed, the scope of sociological research in this field is vast. The public sociologists in this section demonstrate how important it is to disseminate their research to inform and guide the work of a variety of practitioners who seek to reduce violence and restore justice. Tackling issues such as homicide, racial disparities in the justice system, domestic violence, and hate crimes, these scholars are actively engaged in connecting sociological research to multiple publics to effect change.

The first two case studies in this section provide excellent examples of the importance of data collection and dissemination to inform critical issues related to crime. In the first case study, Carolyn and Richard Block describe the Chicago Homicide Dataset (CHD) project, an ambitious and successful 40-year-long project that offers researchers and practitioners detailed information on Chicago homicides from 1965 to the present. The authors describe this project as "a long-term commitment to make information accessible to academics, public agencies, community groups, and citizens." This commitment has resulted in one of the most recognized datasets in the nation and serves as a model for other homicide datasets in the United States and abroad. The CHD is used widely and serves as a testing ground for new academic techniques to analyze crime; its development of mapping techniques has been used to train undergraduate and graduate students and is used as a tool for police work. The Blocks describe the many collaborative partnerships needed to develop, expand, refine, and strengthen the CHD over the years, working closely with practitioners in the field and agencies such as the Chicago Police Department. They describe the struggle in securing funding for their work, often a challenge for long-term projects such as this one.

Pam Oliver describes the development of a public sociology project that brings attention to the problems of racial disparities in the criminal justice system in Wisconsin. In this case study, Oliver describes how her work evolved from attending a community meeting as a "person" to later providing research "as a sociologist." What developed is an extensive advocacy project using descriptive data to visually present the racial disparities in Wisconsin prisons. Oliver has compiled and analyzed statistical data, created a PowerPoint presentation and website, and makes frequent presentations to criminal justice professionals, advocacy groups, and the general public. She chronicles how this organic public sociology project unfolded, how she was able to secure funding for this work, and how she has incorporated both undergraduate and graduate students into the project. Most important, she describes how sociological data have made a major contribution to bringing awareness to, and helping shape policy on, racial disparities in criminal justice in Wisconsin.

In the third case study, Christine George describes the collaborative partnership that developed between Apnar Ghar, a South Asian social service agency, and the Center for Urban Research and Learning (CURL), on a research and dissemination project examining services, policies, incidence, and trends of domestic violence among the South Asian population in Chicago. George describes how the dissemination of the Apnar Ghar research influenced a subsequent collaborative project with the City of Chicago Mayor's Office on Domestic Violence. This partnership grew into a two-year collaborative evaluation of the City of Chicago Domestic Violence Help Line funded by National Institute of Justice, examining the overall features of the help line as well as its effectiveness in serving domestic violence victims from diverse populations. In this case study, George emphasizes the importance of creating trust and team building as critical steps in laying the groundwork for effective collaborative partnerships. In a thoughtful section on lessons learned, George argues that an essential part of one's research methodology as a public sociologist should include the process of relationship building.

In the final case study in this section, Jack Levin and Jack McDevitt discuss their research on hate crimes. The authors analyzed case files collected by the Boston Police Department and developed a typology of offender motivation identifying four types of hate crime offenses: thrill attacks, defensive attacks, retaliatory attacks, and mission attacks. Theirs was the first attempt to systematically characterize hate crime motivations and has been used extensively to train law enforcement personnel both within the United States and abroad. Their work has been incorporated into the National Hate Crime Training Curriculum and is used by the FBI. Both Levin and McDevitt have each founded research centers at Northeastern University that address issues related to hatred based on group differences. They describe their public sociology work with practitioners, faculty from multiple disciplines, and interested stakeholders on programs and research projects that seek to reduce violence and restore justice.

Case Study 7.1. Forty Years of Codifying and Mapping Homicides in Chicago: Impacts on Policing, Research, and Community Well-Being

Carolyn Rebecca Block and Richard Block

The Chicago Homicide Dataset (CHD), one of the largest and most detailed datasets on violence ever collected in the United States, contains detailed information on every homicide in Chicago police records from 1965 to 2000—more than 200 variables and more than 27,000 homicides. Data collection began in 1968 and continues today, with the coding of all variables consistent back to 1965. The CHD is organized so that questions about victims, offenders, or incidents (and interrelationships among them) can be answered, and each case is geo-coded to Census tract. It is archived in the National Archive of Criminal Justice Data (ICPSR 6399). (A Google search for the name of the archived CHD yielded 14,300 hits.) Because of its wide availability and use, its consistent detail over a long historical period, and its model for other homicide datasets, the CHD is often called a national resource.

The Formation of the Chicago Homicide Dataset Project

How did the Chicago Homicide Dataset project begin? How has it been sustained for more than 40 years? The CHD was not the result of a finite research project but rather a long-term commitment to make information accessible to academics, public agencies, community groups, and citizens. It began with the huge increase in homicides from 1965 to 1968 in Chicago and nationally. Franklin Zimring and his graduate student, Richard Block, at the University of Chicago Law School, wanted to explain that increase. Frank told Dick to emulate Marvin Wolfgang's pioneering study of Philadelphia homicide (Block & Block, 1991; Wolfgang, 1958) and improve upon it. With the close cooperation of the Chicago Police Department and its Murder Analysis Unit, Frank and Dick were able to use the MAR (Murder Analysis Reports) as a basis for collecting basic data from 1965 to 1968. Because of security and privacy issues, the coding had to be done at

CPD headquarters in the midst of the Violent Crime Division. Homicide investigators provided a space to work and access to the MAR files and answered questions when they arose. Dick did the coding on a simple paper code sheet that was modeled after the code sheets Marvin Wolfgang had provided the project. The information was then keypunched on cards that could be fed to a mainframe computer. Since each punch card (representing a case) had room for only 80 columns (including ID) with 12 categories each, the initial CHD contained limited information. Still, that was an improvement over the Philadelphia project, where all the analysis was done by hand.

Though the CHD began when Frank Zimring and Dick Block noticed a steep increase in homicide, their vision was broader than a one-time research project. Frank insisted that any valid explanation of homicide increase must also explain homicide decrease, which meant that it would be necessary for the project to compare patterns over a long period of time. Frank and Dick envisioned a project that would collect detailed crime data consistently for many years. In the late 1960s, no long-term detailed study of any crime had yet been done, though there were more limited datasets of official data such as the FBI's Uniform Crime Report data.

Second Wave of Data Collection

The second wave of data collection brought the CHD up to 1971. In what became the rule for the CHD, any new MAR information for previously coded cases was coded, and any changes or additions to the codes were made consistent back to 1965. Inspired by Chicago's history of using handmade maps for community analysis (Lashly, 1929; Residents of Hull-House, 1895) and by CPD detectives and crime analysts who were using "pin maps" to better understand crime patterns, Dick added specific street address to the CHD. At the time, no easily available automated mapping system existed, but Dick envisaged that a mapping system would someday become available. In the meantime, he produced Chicago homicide maps using a spreadsheet.

Long-Term Partnerships

The CHD project would not have been possible without the Chicago Police Department's long-term collaboration. The initial collaboration was built upon earlier cooperation between the CPD and Frank Zimring on a project conducted responsibly and with respect for privacy and security of victim identifiers (Zimring, 1967). This laid a foundation of trust between the CPD and the University of Chicago Law School. Over the years, this trust was tested many times, as the CPD was rocked by scandals and police chiefs changed. Sometimes it seemed as if whenever we had assembled the funds, the resources, and the time to conduct another wave of homicide data collection, the CPD wasn't ready for us; and whenever the CPD was ready for us, we didn't have the resources. Yet we persevered.

The CHD required not only a long-term relationship with the CPD, but also long-term scrounging for money. CHD project funding has been precarious and opportunistic over the years. The Ford Foundation provided initial funding to Frank Zimring. When Dick graduated in 1970 and moved to Loyola University Chicago, the project went with him. Limited support for coders came from a small university fund for student research interns. The CHD contained 10 years of data in 1975, when Carolyn Rebecca Block (Becky), a research analyst at the Illinois Criminal Justice Information Authority (ICJIA), was looking for a dataset to use to test a graphics program for descriptive time series analysis. Through ICJIA, she applied for and received support from the Bureau of Justice Statistics (BJS) to use the CHD to develop the time series program, including funds for the continuation of CHD data collection through 1981. From that time on, the CHD was housed and maintained at ICJIA. In 1987, Becky applied again to BJS, this time for a grant to develop an accessible spatial analysis program for identifying "hot spot areas," and wrote CHD data collection into the grant proposal. This second BJS grant supported data collection through 1987.

Learning From and Expanding on CHD

With the CHD housed at ICJIA, its audience expanded from academic researchers and the CPD to public agencies at every level, community organizations, legislators, policy makers, and citizens, as well as the CPD and academia. Making the CHD accessible to everyone was a priority, and the project did several things to fulfill that goal. First, the project archived the CHD (with identifiers removed) in the National Archive of Criminal Justice Data, so that it became easily available to anyone. Second, the project produced publications, reports, and presentations that focused on improving public awareness and understanding of the dataset. Third, the project handled a continually increasing number of requests for information about the CHD, from students, community agencies, legislative staff, the media, and academic researchers. We helped them understand the data and come to their own conclusions about the meaning, sometimes by walking them through the analysis and other times by sending them some crosstabs and a short review of definitions. Fourth, the project published reports that analyzed the CHD, to demonstrate how to use the dataset and to show how much could be learned from it. In the 1980s, the project focused on using victim-level, offender-level, and incident-level demographics and on patterns over time of the number of people killed with a firearm, a subject that drew tremendous attention from policy makers and the media. By the late 1980s, the CHD was archived through 1981, the data were being used by a wide variety of people, and we had written and published or presented many CHD analyses.

The long collaboration with Margo Wilson and Martin Daly began with a chance meeting at the American Society of Criminology in 1987. Becky was presenting about intimate partner homicide, and Margo and Martin were presenting analysis that would soon be published in their book, *Homicide* (Daly & Wilson, 1988). Margo and Martin caught Becky's and Dick's excitement about the potential of the Chicago Homicide Dataset and wrote a proposal for a Harry Frank Guggenheim Foundation grant that supported data collection through 1989. For two years, Margo Wilson traveled from Hamilton, Ontario, to Chicago to stay with Dick and Becky for a week or two and collect CHD data. At her suggestion, we added variables to the CHD that previously did not exist in most homicide datasets, including co-reside, sexual jealousy, and sexual rivalry.

As the project continued, we realized that, in addition to those added through the collaboration with Margo and Martin, there were questions we did not originally ask that should be added. Although gangs had existed in Chicago for many years and had been the subject of many Chicago School of sociology studies, because of the technical limitations of punch cards, the original data collection had not included gang affiliation. Other research was showing that the relationship of drugs and violence required the capture of more complex information than had originally been collected. In both cases, CPD homicide detectives worked closely with the CHD Project to develop valid variables and codes. In our analyses, we discovered that "weapon" was much too simplistic, and we created more specific "cause of death" variables and codes that made it possible to study arson and strangulation. Working closely with CPD crime analysts, we added and revised "causative factor" variables and codes. Realizing that a homicide is sometimes connected to another in mass killings, serial killings, or retaliations, we added variables to link the cases and capture the type of connection. As always, each CHD edit or addition was coded consistently back to 1965.

When desktop mapping became available in the late 1980s, the CHD immediately became a test ground, because it contained Census tract and address data (to maintain victim confidentiality, only Census tract data are available to the public). Like most police departments, Chicago had used pin maps for many years and quickly saw the value of pin maps that could be generated and regenerated in a few minutes. In addition to pin maps, however, analysis of the CHD demonstrated that mapping could be used for analysis and as a tool for police work, community presentations, and academic research. Most large police departments now map crime patterns for tactical analysis. The Chicago Police Department also pioneered the use of maps on the department's website to provide detailed, up-to-date information about crime to the general community through the ICAM (Information Collection for Automated Mapping) website. A map is worth a thousand words. It puts into context the problems neighborhoods are experiencing on a daily basis, helps people communicate better with each other and with city agencies, and supports neighborhood-level decision making. The current CLEAR (Citizen Law Enforcement Analysis and Reporting) website (http:// gis.chicagopolice.org/CLEARMap/startPage.htm), which includes much more local information as well as crime, continues that purpose.

Finding Funding

Resources, always a problem in long-term research, continued to challenge the CHD project. The National Institute of Justice provided funds for investigating change over time of gang and drug-related homicides and for investigating spatial patterns of gang-related violence. Both grants included money to collect CHD data, extending the dataset through 1992. Potential funders often want answers to short-term questions and don't understand the value of long-term data collection and analysis. An exception was the Joyce Foundation, which provided money to continue the CHD through 1995 and then provided additional money to clean and archive the data and to collect geographically linked hospital data on firearm injuries and firearms data.

The Impact of CHD and Lessons Learned

The graduate and undergraduate students and ICJIA intern staff members who worked as coders received valuable experience in community collaboration and good data management practices, but they often found that coding a grizzly subject—especially killings of young children—in a difficult environment was hard to take. Several decided that they did not want to continue. Others, however, became interested in the data, and we encouraged them to write and publish or present their analyses, often collaboratively with Dick or Becky.

Because the data have always been readily available and Chicago has such a tradition of crime research, many researchers have used the data. To our knowledge, at least 300 published research papers, books, and agency reports have been based on the CHD. Because the CHD was available through ICPSR on a CD and later online, it became a source of numerous theses. College teachers commonly choose the CHD as the basis of an inter-active tool to train students in analysis and mapping techniques. As the only available long-term data set on homicide, the CHD is regularly reported in media and has been cited by Congress, the U.S. Department of Justice, and the U.S. Supreme Court.

The CHD project began with a model, Marvin Wolfgang's (1958) study of Philadelphia homicide. In turn, the CHD has become a model for count-less homicide data collection projects in U.S. states and cities and in many other countries, including Canada, Australia, the Netherlands, Japan, and South Africa. The CHD continues to provide a testing ground and example for new academic techniques to analyze crime.

Aside from being based in Chicago, many aspects of the CHD Project represent a continuation of the Chicago School of sociology. The Chicago School and the CHD project were both built on close and prolonged collabo-ration between academic researchers and practitioners; they meticulously compiled detailed, geographically grounded information and presented that information in maps that were accessible to nonacademics; and they did not constrain data collection within the boundaries of the statistical methodolo-gies and computational tools currently available.

You learn many lessons from a project lasting so many years, including the importance of intercoder reliability, the grant writing skills to keep the CHD going, the development of computerized crime mapping beyond sim-ple pin maps, the spatial linking of crime data with other datasets, and techniques to archive data to make them available to the public (ICPSR). However, one of the most important things we learned is not only that the CHD demonstrated the value of a consistently collected long-term dataset, but that creating and maintaining such a dataset takes the collaborative efforts of many people over many years. The CHD would not exist were it not for the long-term cooperation of the Chicago Police Department, par-ticularly the Homicide Division's consistent data coding and willingness to allow us access to their files. Far from passive partners, the Homicide Division took an active, hands-on interest in making sure that the research-ers understood the meaning of the legal terms and departmental phrases they were coding and that we respected confidentiality. In turn, our work was occasionally helpful to the department, and our spatial analysis pointed the way to better access to crime information for both the police and the public.

We learned that collaborations evolve and that it is necessary to be patient with the process (see Block, Collier-Goubil, Moore, & Reed, 2010). The

CHD collaboration began as a simple short-term agreement for data collection but grew into a true collaboration, continuing through difficult times, many, many changes of participants, and perennial lack of resources. Along the way, we learned that mutual respect, communal trust, the value of each other's perspective, and a shared vision of the ultimate importance of maintaining the CHD are just as important as statistical skills in building and maintaining practitioner-researcher collaboration.

References

Block, C. B., & Block, R. L. (1991). Beginning with Wolfgang: An agenda for homicide research. *Journal of Crime & Justice, XIV* (2), 31–70.

Block, C.R., Collier-Goubil, D., Moore, A., &. Reed, W. L. (2010). Collaborating with practitioners. In E. Lenning, S. Brightman, & S. Caringella (Eds.), *A guide to surviving a career in academia* (Chap. 8). New York, NY: Routledge.

Daly, M., & Wilson, M. (1988). *Homicide.* Hawthorne, NY: Aldine deGruyter.

Lashly, A. (1929). Homicide (in Cook County). In J. H. Wigmore (Ed.), *1929 Illinois crime survey*, Chap. 13, Illinois Association for Criminal Justice, Chicago. Retrieved from http://homicide.northwestern.edu/pubs/icc

Residents of Hull-House. (1895). *Hull-House maps and papers.* New York, NY: Thomas V Crowell. Retrieved from http://homicide.northwestern.edu/pubs/hullhouse

Wolfgang, M. (1958). *Patterns of criminal homicide.* Philadelphia, PA: University of Pennsylvania Press.

Zimring, F. E. (1967). Is gun control likely to reduce violent killings? *University of Chicago Law Review, 35*(4), 721–737.

Case Study 7.2. Racial Disparities in Criminal Justice in Wisconsin: Analysis, Graphs, and Engagement

Pamela Oliver

This project is complex and multifaceted. It was not planned but evolved as I interacted with organizations of various types over time. I first became involved with the issue of racial disparity in criminal justice in 1999. The core of my work has involved compiling and analyzing statistical data on the criminal justice system in Wisconsin and presenting this information graphically in PowerPoint slide shows to a wide variety of audiences.

I first wandered into this project because I was actively looking for a way to re-engage my community involvement now that my children were older.

I volunteered to be on the planning committee for a six-part forum series on prison issues to be presented by Madison-area Urban Ministry (MUM), a faith-based progressive social change organization, after attending a conference called Money, Education and Prisons put on by local activists close to MUM. I had been attending MUM meetings, looking for a way to get involved. I volunteered as a "person," not as a "sociologist," and much of what I did for the planning committee was not sociological. But because I was a sociologist, I volunteered to research the issue and develop a presentation on imprisonment patterns. I thought that people would want to know why people were sent to prison and how our local patterns compared to national patterns.

It was the work I did for this initial presentation that led to its development as a public sociology project. When I started the project, it was not easy to find state-level information on imprisonment rates by race nor to find state-level comparisons of the offenses of prison inmates by race. Because of my data analysis skills and the resources available through my university (the University of Wisconsin at Madison), I was able to download and analyze data from the National Corrections Reporting Program, the Census Bureau, and other sources. My first calculations revealed what nobody else seemed to know: that Wisconsin's racial disparity in imprisonment was much higher than the national average and that the disparity in Dane County (home of Madison and the University of Wisconsin) was much higher than that of Milwaukee, the state's largest Black population center. I prepared a handout and made a presentation at a forum. I tried to draw people's attention to my handout and to the racial disparities in a variety of subsequent meetings but got relatively little response. One exception was a state senator, now Congresswoman Gwendolyn Moore, who made an angry statement in the legislature based on the information in my handout.

The project unfolded on several initially unrelated tracks. In addition to the MUM forum planning committee, I began attending meetings of the advocacy group Money, Education and Prisons (MEP) formed around the conference and sat through many meetings and programs on a wide variety of criminal justice issues put on by MEP and other formal and informal groups concerned about social justice issues. MUM decided to put on a second year of forums on juvenile justice for 2000–2001, and for that forum I was asked to analyze data that had been collected on hundreds of sheets of paper from local police through freedom of information act petitions. I involved students in a freshman research opportunity program to help with entering that material into spreadsheets and then analyzing it. In addition, I periodically was asked to generate some statistical information in support of grant proposals by various nonprofit organizations.

On the research front, I applied to and obtained seed money from Wisconsin's Institute for Research on Poverty (IRP) for a research assistant to help me download and analyze data from federal sources on imprisonment and arrest across states as part of a sociology project to determine the predictors of high incarceration rates. I also extracted data about Wisconsin from the national data and prepared Wisconsin-specific charts and graphs. In 2001, I applied for federal grants to support creation of a longitudinal data set of imprisonment; these were initially turned down, but in 2002 I received a small planning grant from the National Science Foundation.

Three events in 2001 moved the project in a public sociology direction. The first was becoming front-page news in the local paper. Although I had spoken with reporters several times about racial disparities without making the news, an emailed handout after a presentation to an informal political group was forwarded (without my permission) to a reporter who turned it into a story that headlined on a Saturday. (The story of the story is interesting in itself: Rather than the regular metro reporters who had talked to me at length but never published anything from our interactions, the reporter who broke the story usually wrote gardening columns.) This story fed into an ongoing dispute between the mayor and the police about racial profiling and precipitated a political crisis in some circles. As a consequence of the news story, I made a presentation to city officials and met with the police several times.

The second 2001 event was obtaining a copy of the Wisconsin Department of Corrections data file from Senator Moore, who had received six floppy disks and a code book in response to her Freedom of Information petition for information about prisoners sent out of state. Her aide asked whether I could do anything with that. I could. The dataset included every person who had been in a Wisconsin prison between 1990 and 2001. A graduate student, James Yocom, volunteered his time to write the hundreds of lines of code to read the ASCII files into a statistical dataset. He and another graduate student paid by IRP built on the work of the previous graduate student paid by IRP to code offenses and other variables for analysis. Jim Yocom wrote the Stata programs and the Excel macros that merged population numbers and turned the counts into rates and exported them to tables.

Finally, it was in 2001 that I shifted to presenting my results graphically rather than numerically. Graphs could tell a story quickly and with much greater impact than words or a table of numbers. This became a central feature of the project. I developed a PowerPoint slide show that I presented to many audiences, including community groups, public officials, and conferences on criminal justice issues. I also started posting my results—first tables of numbers, and then spreadsheets and graphs and reports and

PowerPoint presentations—on my web page. These materials have been downloaded and used in classroom lectures and by community and advocacy groups all over the country.

Public Engagement

My public engagement has taken many forms. I have shown my PowerPoint presentations on racial disparities in imprisonment more than 80 times in the past 10 years to criminal justice professionals, advocacy groups, and the general public. This slide show originated on my own initiative to analyze and present data in a way to make a compelling case that there was a serious social problem that needed to be addressed. This slide show is fundamentally descriptive, although its detailed disaggregation by offense, race, year, type of admission, and so on provides much more information than had previously been available. Although most audiences are predominantly White, I have presented to integrated and predominantly Black groups. I show the trends and engage the audience in a discussion of the factors that have produced the trends. In these discussions I have learned a great deal from others about the complexity of the problem and the many different processes and factors that feed into the observed patterns, and I try to tell audiences what other groups have said. I am passionate about the issue— I think the mass incarceration of Black people is a tragedy—but I work hard to be careful about the facts that I know and the limits of the data. I have also tried to avoid partisan politics and attacks on individuals. I try to emphasize unconscious discrimination and the unintended consequences of seemingly race-neutral policies, but I have also stressed (based on the data) the way the racially biased so-called war on drugs beginning in the late 1980s sent huge numbers of Black men to prison and the way high rates of revocation from probation and parole churn people in and out of the system.

In addition to giving talks, I have been a member of a variety of groups working on these issues. I have been a member of an advocacy group for many years, although my work typically is not the center of its focus. After dozens of public presentations and several major news stories, I became known locally as an expert on racial disparities in criminal justice. This led me to be appointed in 2003 to the advisory board for the county's juvenile justice Disproportionately Minority Contact project; in 2007 to a special commission on racial disparities in criminal justice appointed by the governor; and in 2008 to a county task force charged with implementing the recommendations of the governor's commission. These three quasi-governmental groups have included criminal justice professionals, politicians, social service providers, and community advocates. I have been a full member, not a consultant, of these groups, and I enter into discussions and debates along with everyone else. I have done special data analysis for all three groups and played a major role in writing the reports for the governor's commission and the county task force, although in neither case was I the lead writer. The reports for the governor's commission and the county task force are public documents that have been posted on government websites. Both reports have been picked up as "best practice" models.

Participating in these groups has entailed sitting through a very large number of meetings (averaging two a month most of the time), often listening to presentations by others on some dimension of the problem, other times participating in discussions or debates about key issues. My own work on statistical analysis of racial disparities is only occasionally the central focus of these meetings. In short, engagement often means attending to others or "showing the flag" and being present at a meeting that one might otherwise not be interested in.

I have done special data analysis and presentations for all the groups I have worked with. Sometimes I have been given data and asked to analyze them. Other times I have asked to have access to data to analyze them. In addition to the imprisonment patterns that form the core of my PowerPoint presentation, I have analyzed official records of court cases, Uniform Crime Report arrest counts, individual police department arrests and citations, detention center intakes, surveys of youth at state penal institutions, prosecutions of juvenile referrals, traffic stops, and drivers' license revocations. In some cases over the years, I have been able to involve undergraduates in the data analysis. For the Governor's Commission, with the assistance of Jim Yocom (who by then had finished his degree and was paid as a consultant by the state), I analyzed probation and parole revocations, "time served" in prison, and generated specific calculations such as the proportion of prisoners who had been convicted of drug offenses. I always bring my professional insight to bear on what questions ought to be asked and how to analyze the data to reveal patterns not immediately apparent.

This project has contributed to bringing attention to the problem of racial disparities in criminal justice in Wisconsin and to using data to determine which factors and processes need the most attention. There are substantial ongoing efforts to address these issues in the state, and I have had an impact on how people think about the issues and the way to solve them.

Public Sociology and the Academy

I have been and continue to work on the sociology side of this project, in which I link theories of repression to theories of social control and seek to identify the factors that affect arrest and imprisonment rates across states and metropolitan areas, but progress on that work has been slowed by my intensive public sociology work. The link between public sociology and one's professional advancement is different for each person. For many people, their public work flows directly from their professional expertise, but this is not the case for me. I am not a criminologist, and this work did not build on the work in collective action and social movements that is the basis for my professional reputation. The data I have analyzed could be the basis for professional sociology articles in criminology journals, but such articles would require literature reviews and engagement with hypotheses and theories of more general criminological or sociological interest, not just the descriptive summaries I present in my public work. I was able to divert my attention into a public sociology project without immediate professional payoff because I already had tenure at a major university. I did not have to worry about getting fired, and I had access to resources including research grants and data archives.

Linking and balancing public and professional sociology raises important issues of priorities and tradeoffs. Sometimes professional sociology and career advancement can be yoked to good public sociology work, but other times they pull in different directions even though they draw on a common intellectual core. Some jobs give professional credit for public work that does not result in peer-reviewed publications, and other jobs do not. People who want to do this kind of work need to be honest with themselves and others about their situations and goals.

Case Study 7.3. The Role of Relationship Building in Research Partnerships

Christine George

- How do domestic violence survivors experience various societal systems as they attempt to build safer lives for themselves and their families?
- How do the various public policies that these women encounter in societal systems intersect, and how does this intersection facilitate or hinder the ability of survivors to build safer lives?
- What programs work best for diverse groups of domestic violence survivors? Does one size fit all? What about immigrants? Women living in poverty?

These are some of the questions that other researchers and I at Loyola University Chicago have been examining in research partnerships with domestic violence (DV) advocates and providers for the past nine years at the Center for Urban Research and Learning (CURL). CURL pursues its main goal of promoting equality and improving people's lives in communities throughout the Chicago metropolitan region by building and supporting collaborative research partnerships and education efforts. These partnerships connect Loyola faculty and students with community and nonprofit organizations, civic groups, and government agencies. This case study examines the development of these partnerships in two specific instances, highlighting the role of relationship building between researchers and community partners as they develop their research agenda and bring information into play in the policy process. It underscores the dynamic and continuous nature of building research partnerships ("mini-networks," if you will) to bring information based on a sociological analysis of the experiences of domestic violence survivors and the advocates serving them into the policy process.

Building a Research Agenda: The Apna Ghar/CURL Partnership

The Community Partner

In 2002, Apna Ghar, a South Asian social service agency serving women who are domestic violence survivors, contacted CURL for assistance in an evaluation of a joint program that they were conducting with a local community social enterprise/job training program named "The Enterprising Kitchen." Five Asian American women activists had conceived Apna Ghar in 1989. These women were aware that due to cultural differences in language, dress, food, religion, family structures, and values, many Asian American women and families were reluctant to avail themselves of the services offered by mainstream existing shelters and other organizations. Examining the situation, the activists found that existing shelters and service providers were not familiar with the South Asian culture, family systems, and immigration laws. They concluded that what was needed was a South Asian social service agency to provide translation, counseling, legal services, and other supports to women from the South Asian community who were victims of violence. Apna Ghar became the first transitional shelter and social agency in the United States serving Asian victims of domestic violence.

Apna Ghar was housed in a community adjacent to Loyola University's Rogers Park campus, and staff from the program often served as speakers to various sociology classes. In 2001, after a presentation in an introductory sociology class focusing on the urban Chicago community, the presenter, in an aside to the faculty member, asked for assistance in finding someone to provide research assistance for a program evaluation. Through the faculty member, Apna Ghar was connected to CURL.

Building a Mutual Partnership

In the first meetings the executive director of Apna Ghar was hopeful about working together, and she was very frank about problems the organization had encountered in the past with academic researchers. She described working with various researchers and not receiving any information back that could help Apna Ghar in its programmatic or policy work. She recounted instances of receiving books or articles long after the study occurred ("Not very helpful to us now") or no feedback at all. So, with little money for the evaluation, she was concerned that any "volunteer" research assistance might not be committed or attuned to the organization's needs.

The timing was perfect. CURL had just recently received a grant through the U.S. Department of Education FIPSE (Fund for the Improvement of Postsecondary Education) program to both train graduate students in participatory research and increase the capacity of community-based organizations to conduct their own research. Not only did this grant provide resources for student research assistants but also for "community fellows." The program directors could become fellows, and a portion of their time would be underwritten by the grant so they could work with the research team and participate in trainings and seminars.

The project commenced, and together the researchers and community fellows from the program agreed to use survey methods, focus groups, interviews, participant observations, and analysis of administrative data to evaluate Apna Ghar's program. This led not only to an assessment of the program's process and outcomes but also to an improvement of the program's records measuring client progress and programmatic modifications. Equally important, the researchers and leadership of Apna Ghar formed a strong mutual working relationship and started discussing a wish list of research questions. This wish list grew into a research agenda. This agenda was informed by (1) the researchers' observations of immigrant domestic violence survivors' experiences negotiating their communities, the social welfare system, the court system, the immigration system, and the employment system; and (2) the questions, tentative deductions, and/or theories the domestic violence advocates had formed working with victims. "Wouldn't it be great if we could work together more?" the Apna Ghar executive director mused. She talked about how she had wished since beginning her tenure at Apna Ghar to have the time and resources to systematically look at these questions in order to inform policy makers and advocates about models for service delivery and policy implementation issues.

Staff of CURL and Apna Ghar kept in touch after the evaluation happened, keeping this goal in mind. Thus, when a few months later a longtime funder of Loyola University and CURL announced that they were looking for projects focused on women and policy, the executive director and I developed a proposal. The result was funding for an 18-month research and dissemination project that would do the following:

- Identify effective models of service and outreach that are used to address the needs of domestic violence survivors within the context of South Asian immigrant culture and circumstance
- Analyze the current status of policies and laws affecting immigrant women who access social services, focusing on immigration, criminal justice, and social welfare policies
- Document the incidence and trends of domestic violence in metropolitan Chicago, particularly with respect to the South Asian population

Utilizing the Partnership to Strengthen the Research and Inform Policy

The strong partnership facilitated and strengthened the data collection and the dissemination of the data. Apna Ghar connected CURL researchers to a national conference of South Asian domestic violence organizations. The meeting was closed, but Apna Ghar included in their delegation a CURL researcher (a graduate student who ultimately based her dissertation on this research). The graduate student introduced the study to the participants in a workshop, met individually with many organizational representatives, and was able to pilot the proposed interview. From the contacts made at this conference and the assistance of the association in identifying South Asian organizations, the CURL researchers were able to conduct a series of in-depth phone interviews (three hours in total) on administrative capacity, services, and legal policy issues with a sample of 30 of the 50 domestic violence organizations in the United States and Canada. A research report based on these interviews was subsequently disseminated nationally through the national conference structure.

A key aspect of this research partnership was the focus on local dissemination of findings to policy makers and advocates within the domestic violence community. Steps for this were laid early on by the partners. An advisory board made of domestic violence stakeholders in the city, from organizations that served minorities and victims from a range of ethnic groups, and the more mainline domestic violence organizations and public agencies was developed and provided critical feedback, especially on issues related to dissemination and policy implications.

Expanding Research Partnerships

Among the members of the advisory board was the director of the City of Chicago Mayor's Office on Domestic Violence (MODV). As she and other MODV staff took on active roles on the advisory board and discussions about the implication of the Apna Ghar study to Chicago's DV programming, a relationship developed between MODV staff and CURL research staff. A result of this relationship was the development of a collaborative relationship between the MODV and CURL researchers.

Toward the end of the Apna Ghar project, the National Institute for Justice (NIJ) issued a call for proposals for a VAWA (Violence Against Women Act) research initiative, "Broadening Our Understanding of Violence Against Women From Diverse Communities." MODV did not have the in-house capacity to conduct the rigorous research project required by the request for proposal, yet at the same time MODV staff wanted a close working relationship with researchers through which findings could be utilized to inform local policy and to examine the needs of diverse domestic violence victims, an issue central to the discussions in the Apna Ghar working conference that had been held earlier that year.

MODV housed and supported the City of Chicago Domestic Violence Help Line, a unique public–private venture that had grown out of a citywide assessment of domestic violence services. All city domestic violence services, private and public, could be accessed through the help line. The help line number was included in information that police gave to any person they engaged when called to a domestic dispute. A key part of this unique model was a data collection component, with detailed case-level data on each caller served by the help line. Yet with their limited research staffing (one person) and demanding programmatic agenda, MODV had only been able to do limited descriptive analysis of the help line calls. Yet an intention of the MODV oversight was to use the help line data to further strategic planning and policy development related to domestic violence within the city. If funded, the NIJ project would allow for this kind of analysis. The resulting proposal was funded, and in January 2004, the Mayor's Office of Domestic Violence and Loyola University Chicago Center for Urban Research and Learning initiated a two-year collaborative evaluation of the City of Chicago Domestic Violence Help Line. The National Institute of Justice funded this study to assess the effectiveness of the help line's operation in meeting the needs of diverse victims of domestic violence under its initiative. The evaluation accomplished three main goals: (1) it assessed the effectiveness of the help line's operation in serving domestic violence victims from Chicago's diverse populations; (2) it described the unique needs of domestic violence victims from diverse populations and their experiences using the information, referrals, and linkages received; and (3) it examined key features of the help line model. Three hundred and ninety-nine victims who had called the help line and 74 domestic violence providers were interviewed for the study. In addition, 1,202 Chicago police patrol officers and 326 community residents were surveyed, and the help line administrative data were analyzed.

The role of the CURL researchers did not end with completion of the research report. Together with MODV they disseminated the findings to city and state policy makers and domestic violence system stakeholders, ranging from police commanders to community shelter providers. An ongoing formal and informal working partnership between MODV and CURL researchers was developed and strengthened. A key aspect of this was the willingness of Loyola researchers to volunteer for various policy and dissemination efforts and the comfort level the MODV staff had developed with the Loyola researchers. For example, I was appointed to the City of Chicago Mayor's Domestic Violence Advisory Coordinating Council. On a less formal level, discussions continued on outstanding questions about what was happening in Chicago: just who was going into shelters, what happened to women after they received services, and why (a finding of the help line study) was shelter utilized more by African American victims than by Whites and Latinas? Discussions also sought to determine how what had been learned could be used to inform public officials and foundations in the midst of budget cuts and questions about the efficacy of the current domestic violence system of shelters. Out of this discussion another research project was proposed by CURL with two additional researchers from the School of Social Work at Loyola, in collaboration with MODV. It was funded in 2008 by the Illinois Criminal Justice Information Authority to answer some of these questions. This project, completed in 2009, included interviews with 57 women in the first few weeks of their stay in one of four domestic violence shelters in Chicago. A second round of interviews was conducted six months later with 17 of the women whom we were able to locate from this initial group. Quantitative analysis of administrative data from the help line and from a statewide system tracking domestic violence service utilization was also conducted to determine on a larger scale, the characteristics and needs of women seeking shelter services.

THE PROCESS OF PARTNERING IS AS ESSENTIAL AS THE FINAL PRODUCT

Leslie Landis is currently the chief court administrator of the Domestic Violence Division of the Circuit Court of Cook County. Ms. Landis is the former director of the City of Chicago Mayor's Office on Domestic Violence. She worked with the Loyola University Center for Urban Research and Learning on multiple research projects, most notably a National Institute of Justice funded evaluation of the City of Chicago's Domestic Violence Help Line, which uses trained operators to connect domestic violence victims with supportive service providers.

The collaborative evaluation of the Domestic Violence Help Line benefited the city of Chicago, the help line operation itself, and all of the victim service entities that received referrals from the help line. It demonstrated that we were meeting the needs of the majority of victims using our system. We already knew the number of victims and the kind of referrals that we were making each year. But what we did not know prior to the collaboration was whether or not victims found that interaction useful; whether victims followed up on the referral that was made; and whether the referral provided the help that they needed.

We also did not know if we were responding to the needs of diverse communities—communities that had different needs and different ways of accessing help in stopping domestic violence. Once we had those findings, our office shared this with the domestic violence service community, government funders, and others in an effort to remove barriers and challenges as identified by the victims interviewed by Center for Urban Research and Learning (CURL).

The project outcomes had a reach beyond Chicago. Before the research, the Centers for Disease Control and Prevention (CDC) was already encouraging us to document and evaluate what were seen as Chicago's innovative practices. After the research, we answered inquiries from other jurisdictions seeking to develop a help line. I sent the report to the National Domestic Violence Hotline; they were very interested in it.

The evaluation ultimately led the State of Illinois to using our help line instead of developing its own. The state ultimately invested in the expansion of the City of Chicago's Help Line to become the State of Illinois Help Line. The city still runs it, which is unprecedented in most municipal-state service connections. It was the positive outcomes of collaborative research that led to this decision.

I felt really supported in CURL's participatory approach. In my past experience, a lot of researchers did not allow community partners to share in the research process.

The CURL style was about not interfering and not dictating. It was about making the research useful to the community as opposed to just making it useful to other researchers.

Christine George and her team were very respectful of the help line call staff in soliciting their input on the interview script and other parts of the research design. This participatory approach improved the quality of the research. Help line operators recognized that what they said to the researchers was not something that was going to hurt them as a call taker—a fear that staff in many organizations feel when "outsiders" run the evaluation process. In our case, those being interviewed and evaluated welcomed the feedback and knew it was about improving the system.

People in my area of the service community often fear that academic researchers will come in and assume they know best without seeking input or ongoing research guidance from community. When community members or organizations give up their data or when they partner on research, they fear that they will not be able to control it. This can make community members so guarded in their responses that the information they provide is not helpful. This further reinforces their feeling that they have no genuine impact in the evaluation and policy-making process.

In contrast, it is the participatory character of CURL research that taps into the knowledge and experience of staff and community members to produce insightful, highly relevant research outcomes that are of real use to us. The process of partnering is as essential as the final product. It is a process through which we learn alongside researchers and are able to adapt our programs and policies based on this new knowledge.

While that research was taking place in 2008 and 2009, MODV started planning a summit of stakeholders and policy makers to discuss a plan for the next 10 years of Chicago's response to domestic violence. Loyola researchers continued to remain involved in this process and advised and assisted MODV researchers in the preparation of data for the summit. The preliminary findings from the just completed shelter study were featured in the five-day summit.

Discussion

Obviously this case study only briefly summarizes the development of these two research partnerships; its main purpose is to illustrate how these relationships developed and how an ongoing collaboration developed over time. In both these partnerships three key factors are evident. First, team building was an essential part of the public research process. All these meetings and interactions take time, but it was essential that time was earmarked in the research process for developing these relationships. Time was needed not only to build trust but also to build a common understanding and agenda of what was needed. Each partner needed to know that his or her agenda would be met. And that meant lots of discussions, interactions, and working together. This took place in a number of different settings, ranging from more formal advisory boards in both projects and structured working partnership meetings to informal discussions and brainstorming sessions. Researchers have to understand that these tasks are not "extra," taking away from data collection and analysis, but an essential part of their research methodology. Conversely, there has to be a commitment by community partners to build time for these interactions into their work plans. Often this means finding the resources to underwrite the time for the partners to do this important work.

Second, in the partnerships both with Apna Ghar and MODV, the community partners needed to trust that the researchers understood that feedback to a public was going to be an essential function of the research process. Again, this meant a process in which a common understanding is developed of just who the audience was and how to best inform them. This entails joint development and writing of presentations and public reports. In addition, in the case of MODV, there were public deadlines for the dissemination of information. It was a challenge, but it was critical that the researchers could adhere to this public, as opposed to academic, time. So, while technical reports, presentations for various professional conferences, and submission to various journals are obviously on the professional agenda for faculty and graduate students, it has to be clear that the researchers understand that the development of public presentations and reports in which the information was presented in an accessible manner is a central task in any collaborative research partnerships.

Third, it is important to engage in continuing dialogue after the product of the project is completed. In any public discourse, it is rare that one event captures the decision-making process. Again, a continuity of formal and informal relationships facilitates the continued input of the researcher in the policy process when needed. And for this to occur, the supporting resource of time and organizational (department or research center) support is essential.

In conclusion, there are many aspects to the practice of public sociology, but as this case study illustrates, one essential component is the process of relationship building over time and the allocation of time for this process. In order for sociology to get into play to bring social change into community settings, an essential part of one's research methodology must be the process of relationship building.

Case Study 7.4. Hate Crime Motivation: The Practical Consequences of an Offender Typology

Jack Levin and Jack McDevitt

In 1993, we coauthored a book entitled *Hate Crimes: The Rising Tide of Bigotry and Bloodshed,* in which we focused on offenses committed, at least in part, because a victim is different with respect to certain characteristics including race, religion, national origin, gender, sexual orientation, or disability status. Our collaboration on this project seemed to make sense given Jack Levin's background in the area of prejudice and discrimination and Jack McDevitt's in the area of bias crimes and criminal justice.

Developing the Offender Typology

In our book, we examined the basis of victim selection, but we also developed and presented a typology of offender motivation. We asked, "What was the driving force underlying the attack?" Originally, we proposed three types of offender motives for hate crimes: thrill, defensive, and mission. Later on, we added a fourth motivational category: retaliatory.

To provide empirical grounding for the typology, we analyzed case files collected by the Community Disorders Unit of the Boston Police Department. At the time, this unit was headed by Deputy Superintendent William "Billy" Johnston, a pioneer in the field of hate crimes, who provided the authors with access to the files of the unit and invaluable insights into the characteristics of hate crimes. The final sample of 169 cases constituted the total number of cases in which the offender was known and represented: 47% of the 358 hate crimes reported and investigated by the Boston police during the 18-month period, July 1991 through December 1992. The review was limited to cases involving either a known suspect or an offender who was arrested.

Thrill Attacks

Based on our analysis of Boston Police Department reports, we found that nearly 3 out of 5 hate crimes in that city were committed for the thrill. More than 53% of these thrill offenses were perpetrated by two or more offenders looking for trouble, often in the victim's neighborhood. Perpetrators were predominantly White teenage males, the vast majority of whom—some 91%—did not know the person they were attacking.

Thrill hate crimes are committed by offenders who are looking for excitement. In the same way that some young men get together on a Saturday night to play a game of cards or go to a cinema, youthful hatemongers gather to destroy property or to bash minorities. In a thrill hate crime, there need not be a precipitating incident. The victim does not necessarily "invade" the territory of the assailant by walking through his neighborhood, moving onto his block, or attending his school. On the contrary, it is the assailant or group of assailants, looking to harass those who are different, who search out locations where the members of a particular group regularly congregate, such as a gay bar, a temple, or a convenience store run by Arab Americans. In addition to gaining a sense of importance and control, the youthful perpetrators also receive a stamp of approval from their friends who regard such acts of harassment as "hip" or "cool."

Some advocacy groups were, at first, less than happy with our use of the term "thrill hate crimes." They argued that conceptualizing an attack as recreational serves only to trivialize the offense. Their criticism fails to distinguish motive from consequences. Thrill hate crimes may have given the perpetrators little more than bragging rights and a feeling of power, but the impact of a thrill attack, especially a violent thrill attack, can be brutal in its consequences for the victim. Additionally, as we read police reports and spoke to investigating officers, we noticed how often offenders had described their attack as consisting of a group of friends who were "bored and just looking for some fun or excitement."

Defensive Attacks

In defensive hate crimes, the hatemongers seize on what they consider to be a precipitating or triggering incident to serve as a catalyst for the expression of their anger. They rationalize that by attacking an outsider they are in fact taking a protective posture, a defensive stance against intruders. Indeed, they often cast the outsiders in the role of those actively threatening them, while they regard themselves as pillars of the community.

As with thrill hate attacks, most defensive hate offenses in our study of incidents reported to the Boston police involved White offenders who did not know their Asian, Latino, or Black victims. In defensive crimes, however, the majority were committed by a single offender who was more often an adult than a teenager.

From the point of view of the perpetrators, it is *their* community, means of livelihood, or way of life that has been threatened by the mere presence of members of some other group. The hatemongers therefore feel justified, even obligated, to go on the defensive. They tend to target a particular individual or set of individuals who are perceived to constitute a personal threat—the Black family that has just moved into an all-White neighborhood, the White college student who has begun to date her Asian classmate, or the Latino who has recently been promoted at work.

Another element of defensive hate crimes is their escalating nature. The offenders often begin with simple acts of harassment such as phone calls in the middle of the night; when the victim does not respond as desired (e.g., move out of the neighborhood), the hatemongers escalate their violent attack until the victim "gets the message."

Retaliatory Attacks

Retaliatory offenses occur in reaction to a perceived hate crime, causing the victims in a targeted group to become the villains. In a number of communities, police have recorded specific hate crimes that were perpetrated against victims because of a perceived prior hate-motivated attack. The thinking is "You got one of us, we will get one of you." In such cases, particular victims are seldom singled out for abuse; offenders look to attack, on a random basis, any member of the targeted group.

In some cases, the original hate crime takes the form of a terrorist attack that creates the conditions for retaliation in kind. For example, many communities witnessed a dramatic increase in anti-Arab and anti-Muslim retaliatory hate crimes in the aftermath of the September 11, 2001, attacks on the World Trade Center in New York City and the Pentagon in Washington, D.C. For the year 2001, there was a 1,600 percent increase in anti-Muslim hate crimes reported to local police departments.

Mission Attacks

On rare occasions, hate crimes go beyond what their perpetrators consider thrilling, defensive, or retaliatory, at least in the narrow sense. Rather than direct their attacks at those individuals involved in a particular event or episode—moving into the neighborhood, taking a job at the next desk, attending the same party—the perpetrators are ready to wage "war" against any and all members of a particular group of people. No precipitating episode occurs; none is necessary. The perpetrator is on a moral mission: His assignment is to eliminate the "enemy" from his community (or the face of the Earth), making this life better for the people in his circle of friends and family.

Those who perpetrate a mission crime are convinced that all out-group members are bent on destroying *our* culture, *our* economy, or the purity of *our* racial heritage. The offender believes that he has a higher-order purpose in carrying out his crime. He has been instructed by God or, in a more secular version, by the Imperial Wizard or the Grand Dragon to rid the world of evil by eliminating all Blacks, Latinos, Asians, or Jews; and he is compelled to act before it is too late. Mission hate crime offenders are likely to join an organized group such as the Ku Klux Klan or the White Aryan Resistance. They often make careers, rather than hobbies, out of hate.

In our study of hate crimes reported to the Boston police, we uncovered only one mission hate offense among our 169 cases (Levin & McDevitt, 1993). This result is consistent with recent estimates that no more than 5% of all hate crimes in the United States directly involve organized hate groups.

The Public Use of Our Sociological Research

Perhaps because it was the first attempt systematically to characterize various hate crime motivations, the categories in our typology have been criticized by some academics for being non-mutually exclusive and unrepresentative of all types of hate crimes. But practitioners have a totally different take on our work, applying it widely for the purpose of training thousands of law enforcement personnel and government attorneys in the investigation and identification of hate crimes.

Police officers have reported using the categories of the typology to help identify offenders. In one case, an officer explained that he had responded to an incident that he believed was a defensive hate attack because of a pattern of less serious incidents targeting a Black family who had recently relocated into a previously White neighborhood. Thinking the latest incident was perpetrated by a local skinhead group, other officers in the department wanted the investigation to focus on members of that group. But canvassing the neighbors on the block for an eyewitness, the original officer was able to identify the offender as a young man from the neighborhood who had no ties to any organized hate group and who resented the presence of a Black family on his block.

Our typology has become part of the National Hate Crime Training Curriculum, the website of the National Institute of Justice, and hate crime training for national police departments in Bosnia and Herzegovina, Hungary, Poland, Northern Ireland, Croatia, the Ukraine, and the Czech Republic. In addition, it is taught by the FBI's Training Academy located in

Quantico, Virginia, and has been presented to law enforcement personnel affiliated with the International Association of Chiefs of Police, the White House Conference on Hate Crimes, and police officers from 59 countries who attend training conferences sponsored by the Office of Democratic Institutions and Human Rights in Europe. Overall, tens of thousands of police officers, prosecutors, and victim service providers have been trained to recognize offender motivations using the typology we developed.

Our typology has been adopted widely because it is based on sociological theories of intergroup conflict and solid social science research. Moreover, it was developed in conjunction with those in the field most familiar with hate crimes and hate crime offenders.

In 1998, Jack Levin (along with Jack McDevitt, who served on the center's advisory board) founded the Irving and Betty Brudnick Center on Violence and Conflict at Northeastern University in order to seek solutions to problems of hostility and hatred based on group differences. Involving faculty from a range of disciplines, the center has initiated research projects and educational endeavors. Its associates have communicated their research findings to a broad audience by writing for major newspapers as well as for academic journals and books. In addition, the center has held several conferences on campus in order to bring together researchers and practitioners from around the country as well as other relevant parts of the world. In May 2010, for example, the Brudnick Center collaborated with the Interfaith Action's Youth Leadership Program to organize a diversity education conference attended by more than 100 high school students from around the country. What separated this conference from most others in the area of diversity was that all of the workshops and lectures were developed and organized by the teenagers themselves rather than by experts in the field. Another recent event in which the Brudnick Center played a role was a seminar on disability hate crimes that took place at De Montfort University in Leicester, England. Serving as a keynote speaker, Jack Levin collaborated with practitioners in the field, including those from the Crown Prosecution Service and advocates for people with disabilities, to highlight the offender motivation typology and the lack of support and guidance given to disabled victims of hate offenses.

In 2001, Jack McDevitt (along with Jack Levin, who served as a member of the institute's steering committee) founded the Institute on Race and Justice at Northeastern University. The mission of the institute was to conduct policy research in areas where race (and broader issues of diversity) collides with the criminal justice system. The philosophy of the Institute on Race and Justice was that traditional academic research was improved when the stakeholders in the research participated throughout the research process. This philosophy developed in part from the research we had conducted to understand hate crimes and to develop our hate crime offender typology. Under the auspices of the institute, we offered training to hundreds of law enforcement officers on how to identify and investigate hate offenses and technical assistance to law enforcement agencies that sought to improve their policies regarding the investigation of hate crimes. Additionally, staff from the Institute on Race and Justice has conducted research on racial profiling by law enforcement and, more recently, on trafficking of human beings for sex or labor. As in the case of our hate crime research, both of these efforts have resulted in publications that have been utilized by practitioners and trainings to help improve current practices.

The model of research that we employ (sometimes referred to as "action research") attempts to bring practitioners into the research process in an iterative process, in which findings are shared and then refined with the expertise of practitioners. The result, in many cases, tends to be more helpful to those who operate in the field than an approach based only on armchair theorizing. We believe that our hate crime offender typology represents just such an approach. We hope that it has advanced the thinking generally about hate crime motivation among both academics and practitioners.

We have determined from our work in the area of hate crime research that it is necessary but hardly sufficient to publish our findings in academic and policy outlets. In order to assure that our research serves a useful purpose outside of academia, we have also attempted, wherever possible, to incorporate the thinking of interested stakeholders who are experts by virtue of life experiences, even if they lack the academic credentials. Using a collaborative framework, we believe that our research is more likely to serve as a bridge from ideas to action whereby community members are able to see how they might apply our findings within their own organizations. We hope that this approach has enhanced our ability as public sociologists to inform and influence public policy.

Reference

Levin, J., & McDevitt, J. (1993). *Hate crimes: The rising tide of bigotry and bloodshed*. New York, NY: Plenum Books.

CASE STUDIES 8

Community Organizing

C ommunity organizing represents the collective effort by a group of people with shared interests to resist change in some cases or, more often, to bring about positive changes. When the powerless come together they create a powerful force in society. Sociologists have studied many aspects of community organizing, from identifying who is involved and why they are involved to uncovering the strategies and identifying goals of community organizers. In his call for a renewed commitment to public sociology, Michael Burawoy suggested that the fate of the discipline lies in forging a strong relationship to vibrant reform groups, activist organizations, and social movements. The case studies in this section profile contemporary sociologists whose work speaks to this call.

An ongoing debate in public sociology is how far the sociologist goes in his or her work. Does she just do the research and hand it over, or does she become involved in the movement or change organization itself? Does he remain neutral or become an agent for change? There is no easy answer, but there are lessons to be learned from the case studies included not only in this section but throughout the book.

Since 1998, Peter Callero has been teaching a series of courses in community organizing at Western Oregon University. Students in these classes not only learn about organizing, but they also go on to apply these lessons through their involvement in a tenants union. His very first class of students identified concerns over rental housing as an issue of importance to them and around which they wanted to organize. They read the sociological literature, researched the history and practice of community organizing, and investigated the legal, political, and economic dimensions of the landlord–tenant relationship. Collectively they decided that a tenants union would be the most effective way to advance the interests they shared with other community members who struggled with the problems of rental housing. Each year since then, students in the class continue the project, acting as community organizers for the tenants union and sustaining a community power base in the face of a transient student population. The student-tenant organizers have been able to influence city government to adopt policies and programs that extend the rights of tenants and protect them from the practices of unscrupulous landlords. This project provides an example of how public sociology can be promoted in the classroom, with students and faculty working together not simply to improve the conditions of local housing but also to fortify the more egalitarian elements of civil society.

Walda Katz-Fishman, Rose Brewer, and Jerome Scott were founding members of Project South, a community-based organization in Atlanta committed to social change. In 2007, they participated in the first U.S. Social Forum (USSF), a gathering of activists and activist organizations for the purposes of building a broad-based movement to transform this country and change history. The USSF provides a space in which to explore solutions to the economic and ecological crises. In this case study focusing on USSF, Katz-Fishman, Brewer, and Scott discuss how they were not only political activists engaged in the movement-building process, but also how they were able to use their sociological knowledge and training to analyze the historical moment and political framing of the USSF process. They served on the book committee, producing an edited volume that included analysis and writings by organizers, movement builders, and front-line fighters at the center of the process. In their work as public sociologists, they demonstrated that sharing power, cooperating in movement struggles, and co-creating knowledge are powerful tools of movement building and social transformation.

The third case study turns from building community organizations and social movements to sustaining one. Catherine Willis, Crystal Anders, and Randy Stoecker profile a research project that helped a nonprofit organization do a better job organizing and growing its membership. Community Shares of Wisconsin (CSW) is a social action fund made up of member nonprofit organizations that are oriented to social change. Like other social action funds across the nation, CSW raises awareness about its local member organizations and also helps to raise funds for them through workplace giving campaigns. Crystal Anders of CSW approached Professor Randy Stoecker about the possibility of having his students do some research to evaluate the effectiveness of a new CSW member recruitment strategy. Stoecker recruited Catherine Willis, a graduate student in a research methodology class. This was a truly collaborative project in which CSW drove the focus of research and the academics provided technical information on research methods. While the research found that the new membership recruitment strategy was effective and led to changes in how CSW organized and integrated new members into the organization, the process of presenting the findings also generated further discussions about the ways in which fundraising served as an important strategy for building solidarity and a community of support among the different organizations working for social change.

Reacting to the alienating environment of the typical post-World War II housing developments, Ray Oldenburg set out to research the qualities and functions of those places that were missing—places that had traditionally served as "hangouts" or centers of a community's social life. In this final case study Oldenburg describes the initial research—field work in a tavern and library research on anything written about these places—that led first to an article for *Psychology Today* and later a book about "third places." The idea of third places that he introduced has been adopted and integrated into many new developments and the redevelopment of existing developments, as well as office structures, churches, and libraries. The concept has spread globally and has been used to promote democracy in Siberia, to discourage gambling in Australia and New Zealand, and to encourage community gardens in Australia.

Case Study 8.1. Cultivating Public Sociology From the Classroom: The Case of a Student-Organized Tenants Union

Peter L. Callero

In his presidential address to the American Sociological Association, Michael Burawoy (2005b) argued that public sociology should be understood as a "double conversation" between two generic publics. The first public is defined by the diverse work of professional sociologists. The second public encompasses all of civil society—including fraternal organizations, neighborhood associations, sports clubs, communities of faith, and other voluntary groups. While this dialogue of mutual education has many possible forms and lines of exchange, Burawoy believes it is the particular relationship between sociology and vibrant reform groups, activist organizations, and social movements that is most critical to sociology's fate. This is because sociology's "object and value are civil society and its resilience" (Burawoy, 2005a, p. 318). Civil society is the "home ground" from which our perspective emerges. When civil society is constrained, smothered, or forced into a frail, underground status, sociology is also deprived of energy, banned, or transformed into a tightly controlled arm of the state. Conversely, when sociologists are in dialogue with activist publics, sociology contributes to the fortification and expansion of civil society.

Burawoy is to be commended for his leadership in advancing this understanding of sociology's public role. And I believe he is correct in recognizing the fundamental commitment of sociology to sustaining civil society and its democratic tendencies. There are no doubt times when sociologists have been instrumental in sustaining civil society. We can think, for example, of a faculty engaged in critical analyses of the state and market, public forums on salient social issues, or students who organize and agitate for civil rights. On the other hand, given the foundational principles of our discipline, it is both surprising and disappointing that sociologists in the United States have not been more active agents of civil society or served as stronger bulwarks against its enemies.

One area of particular neglect has been the classroom. We all recognize the classroom as a space reserved for teaching and learning about sociology's standpoint, but we rarely consider its secondary potential as a site for enhancing and enabling civil society. There are multiple reasons for this negligence—historical momentum, institutional barriers, and personal philosophy are key variables—but another factor may well be the dearth of practical case examples. What does public sociology look like in the classroom? Is it possible for students and faculty to work together to enhance democracy and fortify the public sphere? There are certainly many examples of sociology courses that foster civic engagement through service learning and community volunteerism. But these interventions usually have weak ties to reform movements and typically involve short-lived actions that rarely push back against the dominating forces of the state and market. If the sociology classroom is to defend civil society in a more forceful manner, a more radical strategy is required, one that goes beyond the traditional service model. In the following section of this case study I review a decade-long project that has spawned a local tenants union and in the process has assisted in the expansion of a more democratic civil society.

THE POWER OF COMMUNITY ORGANIZING

Ellen Keithley was a student in the Western Oregon University (WOU) sociology department's community organizing program and graduated in spring 2010. She currently is a community organizer in Tualatin, Oregon, and continues to work with the Monmouth Independence Tenants Union (MITU), an organization developed through the work of WOU students.

I am currently a community organizer for Sally's Kids, a Tualatin, Oregon, organization that secures sports scholarships to allow low-income youth to join local sports clubs. I am also the volunteer chair of the Salem-Keizer chapter of Stand for Children, a national grassroots advocacy organization that promotes public school reform and improved educational funding. We are doing a lot of work with legislative races and have put together a gubernatorial endorsement committee.

Although I have always been politically inclined, my experience in the community action program at Western sparked my interest in community activism. I had done canvassing and other political work, but nothing like the dedicated issue work we did in the courses and related work outside the university.

While I was participating in the WOU program, we worked with renters in challenging a contentious proposal by landlords to have city council pass an ordinance allowing landlords to increase tenant utility deposits. Ostensibly the suggested legislation was to protect property owners from paying bills left unpaid by some tenants after they moved. However, this was really an added burden for renters and something that we felt was unjust.

We did canvassing, distributed flyers, and held mass meetings. Some of our representatives sat down with the landlords' coalition to try and work out a proposal that would benefit all sides. The students, many of whom were tenants themselves, and other renters gave presentations to city council, talked with individual elected officials, and talked to the city manager. Through our research and this direct hands-on experience, we learned how the system is set up, the way it is structured, and said, "We don't agree with this. This is what we want."

We were not able to stop this particular ordinance from passing. Although we did turn what would have been routine passage of an ordinance into a one-year battle highlighting tenants' rights issues and raising community awareness. Through other organizing activities, MITU has been successful in protecting renters on a number of other fronts.

For someone who perceives that they do not have a lot of currency—either social or economic—it can be difficult to stand up against the power holders, the people who make the decisions. Being able to voice those concerns with what I felt was a great deal of support from tenants and fellow organizers gave me a lot of confidence. That has translated into the work I do now. Now I speak with legislators in their offices about the issues that Stand for Children is working on for stable funding for schools. Before, I would have been more timid. It would have been more difficult for me to disagree with a legislator when sitting in his or her office.

(Continued)

(Continued)

When you are in college you can be in this insulated bubble. Stepping out of that into the community and talking with tenants and renters who have no connection with the university makes the work we do particularly important for the community and for us as students. The core of this work is building participatory democracy, which is paramount to a liberal arts education.

The Tenants Union

In the fall of 1998 the sociology department at Western Oregon University (WOU) in Monmouth, Oregon, initiated a new course sequence on community organizing. The goal was to establish a sustainable praxis component in the curriculum that was student centered, emphasized critical analysis, and contributed to the advancement of participatory democracy in the local community. We wanted to create opportunities for community-based education that went beyond service learning and internships in which students typically serve as volunteers for "other people's" projects. Our aspirations were ambitious— facilitate both individual and social transformation by fostering the development of social capital with a grassroots community justice organization organized by students.

From its outset the project was guided by principles of critical pedagogy and a neo-Marxist critique of formal education in modern society (Apple, 1990; Freire, 1973, 1974; Mayo, 1999; McLaren, 2003). Accordingly, we sought to challenge a culture of individualism, expose the hidden curriculum of class interest, avoid an authoritarian classroom, and promote a more democratic and just counter-hegemony. But this philosophy of education posed a dilemma: How does one transform the traditional classroom, with its institutional constraints and undemocratic form, into a larger community space for radical democracy?[1] The first year of our experiment proved to be the most challenging in this regard.

As the course instructor, I began with a set of guiding principles—encourage dialogue, focus discussion on the link between personal troubles and public issues, and promote collective action. A limited reading list was prepared in advance but other than this, there was very little in the way of a predetermined

---

[1]For a more detailed overview of the project from a critical pedagogy perspective, see Braa and Callero (2006).

structure. Once the general goals of the course were explained, students were asked to identify an issue or problem in need of remedy that was common to all of their lives. To facilitate the process, the class of about 30 students was divided into small groups in which they were instructed to identify various topics and concerns for discussion. Small-group findings were then reported back to the entire class for review and consideration. The most common issues were taken up again in additional small-group discussions. This iterative procedure continued over several class meetings until a consensus emerged. In the end, after a relatively open and free dialogue among student participants, all agreed that rental housing concerns would be the focus of the course. Most students were tenants, and those who were not currently tenants either expected to be a tenant someday or had experience as a tenant at earlier times in their lives.

As a consequence of this decision, students spent the rest of the term researching the history and practice of community organizing and investigating the legal, political, and economic dimensions of the landlord-tenant relationship. Along the way, my role as professor was gradually transformed into that of facilitator as students were given a single guiding objective: Develop a collective strategy to address the core problems faced by tenants in their community. After approximately eight weeks of reading, research, and discussion, it was decided that the establishment of a tenants union would be the most effective way to advance the shared interests of community members who struggled with the problems of rental housing.[2] Armed with their new understanding of community organizing and inspired by a democratic deliberative process, the student-tenants set out to organize their community.

Western Oregon University operates on a quarter calendar, and at the conclusion of the fall term students who had completed the initial community organizing course were encouraged to enroll in a follow-up course called "Community Action." Approximately 20 students continued with the sequence into winter term, where regularly scheduled class time was transformed into organizing meetings for the new tenants union. Although I was listed as the instructor for the course, my practical role was that of an advisor. Student-tenants elected their own leaders, established meeting agendas, developed an organizing strategy, and deployed various tactics in support of the union's interests. The course sequence continued to follow a similar structure into spring and summer terms. However, at this point the union

---

[2]As the professor/facilitator for the course, I did not mandate this particular solution. However, given that the assigned reading relied heavily on Saul Alinsky (1989), the decision to form a tenants union is not surprising.

activists called the time and place of all meetings. Students could earn independent study credit if they desired, but by now the tenants union was for all practical purposes on its own.

The second year of the project was more structured. A decision was made at the outset to continue the work of the first-year students by cooperating with the nascent tenants union. A few veteran organizers were still active from the first-year experience, and they agreed to assist me in the community organizing course sequence. Fall term provided a basic introduction to the philosophy of community organizing, an overview of the history of the tenants union, and a primer on landlord-tenant law in Oregon. Winter and spring terms were once again praxis oriented as the student members transformed the classroom into a meeting space for their community organization.

This basic structure has continued for more than a decade. New students receive training in the fall from the instructor and a few veteran activists. A core group continues with the project for a year before assisting the next cohort of community organizers. A unique advantage of this arrangement is that student-tenant actions are structurally linked from year to year in a manner that sustains a community power base. Tenants, especially those in a small university town, tend to be transient, relatively young, and therefore difficult to organize over the long term. The sociology classroom assists with organizing by providing a stable, democratic space for recruiting and training activists. With this continuity of partnership, students have the time and support necessary to build and develop a community activist identity, and the tenants union is able to sustain its longer-term strategy despite high turnover from year to year.

Actions and Reactions

The material accomplishments of the tenants union have been impressive. These include (1) an expanded city housing code that includes recognition of mold as a health hazard, (2) the adoption of a formal procedure for the reporting of landlord violations, (3) the establishment of an administrative position with authority to review tenant grievances, (4) increased enforcement of code violations, and (5) granting code enforcement personnel the power to issue citations to landlords for code violations. In addition, tenants of particularly egregious apartment complexes have successfully organized to fight negligent property managers and irresponsible landlords. Strategy and tactics in winning these victories have varied from the ordinary and comfortable to the disorderly and disruptive. Actions have included the distribution of informational flyers, the coordination of mass meetings, the gathering of petitions, direct lobbying of city councilors, packing city council meetings with tenants and allies, confrontations with recalcitrant landlords, organized letter-writing campaigns, and the public shaming of persistent code violators with stories in print and cable media.

These collective acts of engagement with power holders have at times provoked retaliation. In one case a local property management company threatened to pull its advertising from the campus newspaper over a regular column written by the tenants union. The article was titled "Dump of the Month," and it featured the worst rental housing offenders in the area. In another instance, an out-of-state property owner filed a tort claim notice asserting that her reputation had been defamed. The legal document named top university administrators and the faculty advisor to the student-tenant activists as liable for damages. But contrary to their intent, these acts of reprisal were not effective in dousing the fire of the tenants union (nor did they prove to be successful). In fact, as a rule, I have found that threats from opposition groups have only energized the community to fight more fiercely.

Conclusion

This example of public sociology is not entirely fungible. Monmouth, Oregon, is a small college town (population ≈ 10,000) where more than half of the residents are renters. Tenants, therefore, have a relatively strong base of power from which to organize. In addition, the Western Oregon University faculty is represented by an active and muscular labor union with a notable tradition of defending academic freedom. Sociologists on other campuses may not enjoy similar protections. Nevertheless, the basic framework of the project should be transposable—a sequence of praxis-oriented courses though which students establish a community organization that is sustained by subsequent cohorts of sociologically trained activists. The unique strength of this course structure rests with its advancement of a more aggressive public sociology—one that goes beyond traditional models of volunteerism and service learning. Here students and faculty are not simply working to improve the conditions of local housing but are also engaged in a cooperative effort to fortify the more egalitarian elements of civil society. Along the way they cultivate the soil of participatory democracy and taste the first fruits of their collective labor.

References

Alinsky, S. (1989). *Reveille for radicals.* New York, NY: Vintage Books.
Apple, M. (1985). *Education and power.* Boston, MA: Ark Paperbacks.

Apple, M. (1990). *Ideology and curriculum*. New York, NY: Routledge.

Braa, D., & Callero, P. (2006). Critical pedagogy and classroom praxis. *Teaching Sociology, 34,* 357–369.

Burawoy, M. (2005a). The critical turn to public sociology. *Critical Sociology, 31,* 313–326.

Burawoy, M. (2005b). For public sociology. *American Sociological Review, 70,* 4–28.

Freire, P. (1973). *Education for critical consciousness*. New York, NY: Continuum.

Freire, P. (1974). *Pedagogy of the oppressed*. New York, NY: Seabury.

Mayo, P. (1990). *Gramsci, Freire, and adult education*. New York, NY: Zed.

McLaren, P. (2003). *Life in schools: An introduction to critical pedagogy*. New York, NY: Pearson.

Case Study 8.2. The Unity of Theory and Practice: The U.S. Social Forum and Movement Building for Social Transformation

Walda Katz-Fishman, Rose M. Brewer, and Jerome Scott

Public Sociology and the Historical Moment

Public sociology is, for us, a bottom-up project in which we are organically grounded in social struggles and social movements, and theory and practice are dynamically interrelated in ongoing movement-building processes of the late 20th and early 21st centuries. As we have written elsewhere (Katz-Fishman & Scott, 2006):

> The bottom-up path brings activists, organizations and movements to social analysis and social theory out of their social practice and as a necessity for social transformation. The analytical and methodological tools of social analysis are not the "private property" of academics and the academy. Rather, theory and practice are two aspects of a powerful, dialectical unity coming out of and continuously tested in the social struggle to end all forms of exploitation and oppression. Neither can exist without the other. (pp. 71–72)

Our bottom-up public sociology work began in the 1980s and 1990s through our involvement as founding members in Project South: Institute for the Elimination of Poverty & Genocide—a community-based organization in Atlanta, Georgia, that brings together grassroots, scholar, and student activists to conduct popular political and economic education for leadership development and developing consciousness, vision, and strategy for movement building and social transformation (Katz-Fishman, Brewer, & Albrecht, 2007). Like hundreds and thousands of grassroots organizations in the

United States and around the world, we were responding to the economic, social, ecological, and political crises of the historical moment. This was the period of capitalist globalization and growing domination by global corporations and financial institutions. Labor-replacing electronic technology was being applied more widely to production and distribution of goods and services, to capital flows, and to financial speculation. It was a time marked by the rise of neoliberal policies that dismantled the reforms of the social contract and welfare state and social democracies globally. In their wake, the gap between rich and poor has widened, un/underemployment and poverty that is gendered and racialized has increased, militarism and war has expanded, and vast social and ecological destruction is threatening our future.

The crises of the late 20th century also gave rise to a developing consciousness of global capitalism and neoliberalism as the systemic root causes of the problems plaguing grassroots communities and oppressed and exploited peoples. Electronic technology networked emerging struggles and movements through the Internet. The Zapatistas rose up on January 1, 1994, in Chiapas, Mexico, to oppose the North American Free Trade Agreement (NAFTA) and helped spark a global justice movement. The Battle of Seattle in 1999 brought together activists and movements nationally and internationally to challenge negotiations of the World Trade Organization (WTO).

Rooted in this context of resistance, social struggles and movements converged in Porto Alegre, Brazil, in January 2001, for the first World Social Forum (WSF). The WSF convened in opposition to the World Economic Forum meeting at the same time in Davos, Switzerland, where economic and political elites gathered to plan their corporate and military domination of the world's peoples. The WSF slogan—"Another world is possible"—expresses globalization from below and the developing global social struggle for humanity and the Earth. The WSF has created a convergence space and process for social movements around the world, including hundreds of local, national, and regional forums, in the past nine years (Blau & Karides, 2009; Santos, 2006).

Since 2003, the International Council of the WSF had asked grassroots organizations in the United States who were participating in the WSF to hold a U.S. Social Forum (USSF). These organizations (including Project South) said we needed time to make sure the voices, struggles, and visions of the grassroots sector would be central to the USSF. It was critical that those on the front line of struggle—working-class people, people of color and indigenous, women, youth, LGBTQ (gay, lesbian, bisexual, transsexual, queer), disabled—be at the center of the process.

In April 2004 we convened a consultation in Washington, D.C., with a broader grouping of social justice organizations. Setting in motion a powerful and historic process, we made a collective decision to hold the first USSF in Atlanta, Georgia, in summer 2007. We came together in all our diversity of history, experience, and perspective. We sang, shouted, laughed, cried, and, most important, we struggled with each other to deal honestly with our differences and to move our movement to a new place of convergence, solidarity, and vision.

Public Sociology From the Bottom Up and the U.S. Social Forum Process

The focus of this case study is our participation in that first USSF and the road from Atlanta to Detroit and the second USSF in June 2010. Because the grassroots sector convened the social forum process and we entered this process as Project South, our participation has not been an expression of "outside" or "expert" knowledge and praxis but rather of an organically connected theory and praxis from inside the movement and at the grassroots. This broader public sociology project involved analysis of the historical moment and political framing of the USSF process—from site selection to programming, from envisioning another world and another United States to discussing strategic directions, as well as documentation of this movement-building process through video and book.

"Another world is possible. Another United States is necessary." This was the call to the first USSF in 2007. It speaks to the energy, excitement, commitment, passion, and power of those of us who organized the USSF and of the 15,000 activists, organizers, and movement builders who gathered there. The USSF 2007 was and remains grounded in the realities of the early 21st century—the crises of global capitalism, war, and oppression—that require a global bottom-up movement to vision and create another United States and another world.

In reflecting on the USSF 2007 in Atlanta, two key points are most relevant: the social forum was grounded in U.S. history, and the social forum process was used for movement building. In planning for the first USSF, those of us in Atlanta took the lead in putting forward a proposal to bring it to our city. We understood the importance of grounding movement building in the United States in the context of the history of social struggle in this country and the significance of the U.S. South in that process.

The South has been and remains the site of the most intense repression and exploitation in the United States—for example, genocide of Indigenous peoples, enslavement of African peoples, Jim Crow and white supremacy, gender oppression, and crushing workers' movements. But the people of the South have also demonstrated immense resilience, resistance, and struggle. Many powerful movements that have won nationally have been rooted in southern struggle and won first in the South. Two powerful examples are offered by the abolition movement that ended chattel slavery and the modern civil rights movement that ended Jim Crow legal structures.

The USSF 2007 in Atlanta lifted up and built on this history of movement struggle and reflected a new moment, as well. Like today's South (and United States), it was multiracial, multinational, and included a rich diversity across gender, sexuality, and generations, coming together around the deepening economic crisis in struggles for the basic necessities of life, for peace, and for the planet. We added to the slogan "Another world is possible" that "Another United States is necessary," indicating the critical role of U.S. social movements in global movements and transformation.

The convergence, energy, power, and vision of the USSF 2007 in Atlanta strengthened the mass struggle and offered a process to begin to create a political direction toward fundamental transformation. We developed relationships that are ongoing and a Peoples Movement Assembly process to coordinate programs and actions for the emerging movement. Several alliances formed: National Domestic Workers Alliance, Right to the City Alliance, and Solidarity Economy Network. We got practice in struggling in a principled way around our differences. We came away with a greater sense of our capacity to pull this off with virtually no money but with political commitment and a vision of what could be for our movement, for humanity, and for the Earth.

Public Sociology From the Bottom Up and the USSF Book Documentation Project

The specific aspect of the broader public sociology project that we share here is the book documentation process. Public sociology from below embodies an organic relationship to social movement organizations. Integral to this is a co-creative process for knowledge and analysis that informs social struggles in response to today's multifaceted economic, social, political, and ecological crisis.

It is within this context that we volunteered to serve on the USSF Book Committee following the USSF 2007; our objective was to document the social forum and social movement process in an edited volume. We were joined on the book committee by Alice Lovelace, a poet, cultural worker, and organizer and the national lead organizer for the USSF 2007; and Marina Karides, a scholar activist in Sociologists Without Borders and sociologist at Florida Atlantic University.

The USSF book documentation project was important both sociologically and politically. A cottage industry has grown up around the social forum process in which scholars and scholar activists participate in, research, and write about the WSF and USSF. But few, if any, include analysis and writings by organizers, movement builders, and front-line fighters at the center of the process. In contrast, the methodology we used for the USSF 2007 edited volume was the co-creation of analysis, knowledge, and the documentation itself. This is unique among research, monographs, and edited collections on the social forum process. This is, to the best of our knowledge, the only volume written by those organizing on the ground and telling their stories in their own words.

As public sociologists, we brought framing, writing, and editing skills to this documentation process. We developed framing questions for the various chapters and the overall organization of the volume. We worked with grassroots organizers on writing where necessary. We also did a large amount of editing and developing text from other documentary materials such as video and reports. Finally we identified and dealt with the small movement press that published the book.

We also brought historic relationships and a trust factor because we entered the process through our involvement with Project South, the Atlanta anchor organization for the USSF. This organic connection to the movement as public sociologists from the bottom up was essential for developing the trust and access that was necessary to bring the documentation project to a conclusion. It is also worth noting that the book documentation project involved no university sponsorship or participation, though three of us (Rose, Walda, and Marina) are scholar-activists and have university affiliations.[3]

The volume, *The United States Social Forum: Perspectives of a Movement* (Karides, Katz-Fishman, Brewer, Lovelace, & Scott, 2010), was published in March 2010 and tells the story of the USSF organizing process in our own voices.[4] The first section, "The Political Moment: Movement Building, Structures, and Processes of the first United States Social Forum," lays out our overall political goals, assessment, and lessons learned. It is about the nuts and

---

[3]The book documentation project was unfunded or in-kind. We received no grants to do the work to gather the articles, edit the volume, and bring the project to closure. The USSF itself did receive some foundation funding as well as funding from registrations and grassroots donations.

[4]The incredible organizers and participants carved out time in our busy schedules to document what we did. We share our stories, analyses, visions, challenges, pitfalls, tensions, and triumphs, and what this all means for where we are in building our movement.

bolts, developing capacity and infrastructure for the USSF process. We created a "city within a city," a space and process that was grounded in the moment and place, but also reflected the realities of the U.S. South, especially the history and struggles of oppressed and exploited peoples. Sections 2, "Creating Convergence: Building a Movement from the Bottom Up," and 3, "Voices of Resistance and Struggle: Workshops and Reflections," capture the reflections, the struggles, the organizing models, and the strategies of the USSF organizers and activists to create movement convergence from the bottom up.

Public sociology from below in this historical juncture is an integral aspect of the unity of theory and practice. It is embodied within our praxis as part of the U.S. Social Forum and the book documentation project.

> The location of a bottom-up public sociology organically within social movements for fundamental change is essential in this moment. Scholar and student activists who come to movements through the academy, must eventually cross the divide between campus and community and all the power and privilege of the "top-down," and locate themselves within community-based movement building spaces. At the same time, scholar and student activists who are connected to social struggle are a bridge from the community to the classroom through curriculum transformation reframing our teaching and learning spaces and putting movement building at the center. . . . Bottom-up public sociology means that whoever we are, we immerse ourselves and our analysis in a social practice that embraces organizations in many fronts of struggle linked in a coherent movement that calls for fundamental and qualitative social change, and is central to our historic struggle for human liberation in the most inclusive sense. (Katz-Fishman & Scott, 2006, p. 72)

The social forum and book documentation project demonstrates that sharing power, cooperating in movement struggles, and co-creating knowledge are powerful tools of movement building and social transformation. Through praxis we are modeling and sharing a different way of envisioning and doing sociology in the 21st century. This is critically important not only for students and colleagues but also for oppressed and exploited communities who are too often studied and written about but have no power within the process. Long-term trust-building processes organically connected to a much broader social movement arising in this moment and a transformative vision and politics are what this historic moment demands.

References

Blau, J., & Karides, M. (Eds.). (2009). *The world and U.S. social forums*. Lanham, MD: Rowman & Littlefield.

Karides, M., Katz-Fishman, W., Brewer, R. M., Lovelace, A., & Scott, J. (2010). *The United States social forum: Perspectives of a movement.* Chicago, IL: ChangeMaker Publications.

Katz-Fishman, W., Brewer, R. M., & Albrecht, L. (2007). *The critical classroom: Education for liberation and movement building.* Atlanta, GA: Project South.

Katz-Fishman, W., & Scott, J. (2006). A movement rising: Consciousness, vision and strategy from the bottom up. In J. Blau & K. I. Smith (Eds.), *Public sociologies* (pp. 69–81). Lanham, MD: Rowman & Littlefield.

Santos, B. D. (2006). *The rise of the global left: WSF and beyond.* New York, NY: Zed.

Case Study 8.3. When the Community Leads

Catherine Willis, Crystel Anders, and Randy Stoecker

One critique of public sociology is that it remains academically driven and consequently replicates the power imbalances that accompany sociological research (Brewer, 2005; Gaventa, 2008; Stoecker, n.d.). The case we present here is just the opposite. While we usually think of universities as reaching out to community groups (Mihalynuk & Seifer, 2002; Stoecker & Stillman, 2007), in this case it was Community Shares of Wisconsin (CSW) that reached out to the University of Wisconsin (UW)-Madison. This case study focuses on how this community-driven model worked.

A Chance for Collaboration

Community Shares of Wisconsin was established in Madison in 1971 as the first social action fund in the country. Social action funds are composed of member nonprofits and are organized to raise public awareness of local grassroots organizations focused on system change and raise funds for them through workplace giving campaigns. CSW member organizations serve on the CSW board of directors and actively engage in the work of the fund. Today CSW is part of a national network of 27 social action funds representing 1,000 local nonprofit organizations.

In 2004 CSW identified developing stronger university relationships with students and increased visibility on area college campuses as goals within its strategic plan. Initially, CSW found it challenging to reach out to the university, in part due to the size of the university and the absence of an established system for developing partnerships between community organizations and university personnel. CSW also found, like others (Robinson, 2000a, 2000b), that there was less interest among students to be engaged with advocacy organizations compared to service activities. Professor Randy Stoecker arrived at the university in 2005, already familiar with the Community Shares (CS) model from his work with Community Shares-Northwest Ohio in Toledo, Ohio. Crystel Anders, CSW executive director, and Randy first met in 2006 to discuss the needs of local nonprofits and determine whether university students might have skills that could assist local nonprofits. That conversation led to an initial project providing tech support to nonprofits. It was due to this established relationship that Crystel approached Randy to explore a research project that could benefit CSW and perhaps its sister funds across the country.

The project focused on studying a new member recruitment strategy used by CSW in 2004. Up until that time, CSW had increased its membership by a couple of organizations every year. The number of nonprofits applying for membership increased, and the old model of accepting only a few new groups each year began to challenge the organization's core value of supporting new emerging issues in the community. Thus, the board voted to add a block of 22 new member nonprofits in 2004. CSW board members' biggest concern was that the increased number of member organizations would reduce the annual funding distribution to each organization. But in fact CSW doubled the amount of funds raised in private sector campaigns.

CSW was consequently planning another bloc recruitment for the fall of 2009. They wanted to test the validity of their initial conclusion that bloc recruitment caused the fundraising increase. CSW had data on donations for the previous 15 years but, like many nonprofits, lacked the capacity to conduct in-depth data analysis (Stoecker, 2007). A research partnership with the university could provide a more accurate understanding of the bloc recruitment–fundraising relationship and refine the recruitment strategy.

Randy brought this research opportunity to a graduate research methodology class that he taught in the spring of 2009. For the main course assignment, students could either work with CSW to develop a community-based research design (Strand, Marullo, Cutforth, Stoecker, & Donohue, 2003) or develop one for their own thesis or dissertation projects. Only one student, Catherine Willis, took up this option. She had been reading *The Revolution Will Not Be Funded* (INCITE! Women of Color Against Violence, 2007), which raised many challenges faced by nonprofits working for social change and the disorganizing impact of the hunt for funding. From what she knew of CSW at the time, Catherine believed that they were successfully using fundraising to build strength and solidarity among nonprofits, and she wanted to learn more.

Collaborative Research Design

We designed the research over three months in parallel with Randy's research methods course. At meetings with the CSW research subcommittee we developed and refined research questions to produce valid research that would be useful in improving the impact of CSW's mission. In later meetings we finalized the research design and developed interview and survey protocols.

These meetings were tremendously important for designing the research project. The CSW subcommittee drove the focus of the research, while the researchers provided technical information on the research methods. CSW staff members' expertise on their own work, along with the researchers' expertise in research design, provided a balanced collaboration.

In contrast to traditional research, this research had to pass two sets of ethics approval. The researchers needed approval from the university's institutional review board (IRB), and CSW needed approval from its executive committee and board of directors. The different priorities of these two institutional settings posed challenges. The researchers' challenge with regards to the IRB was twofold. First, we were working closely with the CSW research subcommittee, but too close a collaboration would require subcommittee members to complete an arduous IRB certification training. Second, we needed to address the IRB interest in protecting individuals from harm in scientific research while also ensuring that doing so did not undermine the activities of CSW or its member organizations. The consent form that we submitted to the IRB balanced these concerns by assuring the CSW member organizations that we would discuss identifiable research results only with the research subcommittee and executive committee and would not release identifiable data beyond those committees without that organization's permission. In addition, we agreed that no results would be released without review by the CSW executive committee.

The second ethics review involved CSW submitting the research project to its 52-member board of directors for approval. To prepare for this, the researchers and CSW staff crafted a presentation outlining the goals and methods of the research project as well as the confidentiality statement. Discussions occurred regarding member organizations' access to findings about their own organizations, and the board passed the resolution.

Almost a Typical Research Project

Over the summer of 2009, the researchers collected and analyzed data. The goal was to have preliminary results for the fall, at which time CSW would be welcoming its new members. Catherine analyzed the donation dataset and received summer independent study credit. Randy conducted the interviews and analyzed the survey results. CSW staff members had expertise in handling the organization's data and were able to provide a de-identified donations dataset. They also encouraged members to complete a survey.

If any part of the project resembled a typical sociology research project, the data collection stage was it. The researchers worked relatively independently of CSW at this time. This was partly the result of a lack of planning on how to collaborate on this part of the project. It was also due to our IRB strategy, which placed all responsibility for data analysis in the hands of Randy and Catherine to avoid CSW staff having to submit to the IRB training. In evaluating the project we have considered whether, in future collaborations, it would be helpful to work more closely together at this stage of the project. While more time consuming, intermittent discussions would have been helpful in refocusing research questions as details were uncovered.

Working With Results

In the fall of 2009 the researchers resumed meeting with the CSW research subcommittee to draft a final report and presentation for the board of directors. These meetings provided an opportunity for the researchers to answer questions and clarify tables and results and allowed subcommittee members to share what the results meant to them. The discussions and the results demonstrated many of the ways in which CSW went beyond fundraising as a necessity for organizational survival to fundraising as a strategy for building solidarity and a community of support among organizations working for social change.

To prepare a final report for the board of directors we needed to identify the most relevant information from among the research findings. We felt that the information presented should help make CSW a stronger organization and help member organizations understand what was unique about the work they did together. We decided to focus on three key discoveries. First, the previous expansion of CSW had an invigorating effect on donations; this was due in part to an increase in worksites that held CSW giving campaigns. Second, the research pointed to the important role played by CSW members' internal workplace fundraising campaigns. Employees of CSW member organizations gave money to other member organizations as well as their own, and often increased their contributions in difficult years! Finally, the research demonstrated the limited role that worksite size played in total donations, important information for CSW's efforts to grow the number of workplaces that hold giving campaigns for CSW.

We then worked on how best to present the information. Randy produced a summary sheet to highlight these three key discoveries and a PowerPoint for presentation at the CSW board meeting. CSW staff edited both documents, providing insights that are not common to academic presentations. These ranged from the suitability of graphics for the size of the conference room where the board meeting would take place to the amount of information that can be adequately conveyed in a board meeting setting. The collaborative fine-tuning contributed to a successful presentation. The board meeting discussion that followed the report demonstrated both a critical interest in the project results and a desire for more research.

Project Outcomes and Future Work

The research results informed changes within CSW. Specific changes included adjustments to how new member orientation is conducted, increased focus on new campaign development for a full 12 months after a bloc recruitment, and expansion of activities to increase relationships among the member nonprofits.

The results obtained to date, while helpful to CSW, are also incomplete. We were able to provide a clear description of the different ways in which the bloc recruitment success played out. It has been harder, however, to tease out the causal mechanisms at play. In order to advance this we have proposed two next steps. The first is to research the 2009 CSW bloc recruitment in order to compare it to the 2004 data, and we have received funding to complete this work. The second is to compare our data with those from other CS agencies. We recently presented the results at the nationwide Community Shares USA conference. This provides a forum for other CS funds to have their common questions answered and built interest among the other funds for designing comparative research projects to identify and understand other growth strategies that have been successful.

A New Model for Public Sociology?

We have presented a project that we feel was both very successful and unique. It was particularly unique in that CSW was in the driver's seat. CSW was able to develop (even if by chance) the connections with the university that allowed us to cooperate on a research project. They had quality data and were aware of its utility for strengthening the organization. While these elements are not unique to CSW, we were lucky in that they all came together successfully so that we could collaborate on a research project that contributed to the solidarity and strengths of CSW. Three main issues arise as we think about how we could replicate this model in the future.

First, we need to ensure that university-community connections are more than chance occurrences. This requires opportunities for community partners and academic staff to meet and share common interests and build community organization capacity to design and carry out projects. The European science shop model (Leydesdorff & Ward, 2005) provides one way of accomplishing this.

A second critical condition involves finding ways to push back against curricular and disciplinary pressures. In our case, Randy has a rare tenured position that is shared with UW-Extension and is thus expected to engage in community work. His design of the research methods course, with the specific goal of facilitating students working with the community, was essential in creating the opportunity for Catherine to participate in this project. We were, however, admittedly limited in what we could accomplish with only one graduate student opting to work on the project. The culture of the UW-Madison sociology graduate program implicitly and occasionally explicitly discourages community engagement. Consequently, the potential academic rewards for students that would come from participating were not clear. In addition, the socialization of graduate students emphasized they should control the research questions and research design; this was to be a participatory action research project, which meant that it would be led by CSW. Consciously creating both the opportunities for community engagement and a culture supporting it are essential to help students contribute their skills in community research.

Finally, we need to find ways to work beyond the typical term schedule of the higher education institution. Catherine's involvement with the project lasted more than a year, well beyond the initial classroom assignment. Despite her continued involvement, it became harder for Catherine to find the time to commit to the project as the demands of the new fall semester took over. The problem of the semester schedule in community-university collaborations and service learning is well recognized (Wallace, 2000). Fortunately, Randy was able to commit much more time in the fall to ensure the project continued to move forward. Organization staff in general desire more faculty involvement in community engagement projects (Blouin & Perry, 2009; Sandy & Holland, 2006), partly because they can provide continuity across semester transitions (Tryon, Hilgendorf, & Scott, 2009), as in this case. While faculty lives are also governed by term schedules, they are nonetheless available year-round.

This collaboration shows how the ingredients of a strong community organization initiating a project, along with a consistently engaged graduate student and faculty member, produce successful project outcomes. It suggests a new model for public sociology. It has been fun.

References

Blouin, D. D., & Perry, E. M. (2009). Whom does service-learning really serve? Community-based organizations' perspectives on service-learning. *Teaching Sociology, 37,* 120–135.

Brewer, R. (2005). Response to Michael Buroway's commentary: The critical turn to public sociology. *Critical Sociology, 31*, 353–360.

Gaventa, J. (2008, July 28–31). *Public sociology and participatory action research.* Presented at the Rural Sociological Society annual meeting, Manchester, NH.

INCITE! Women of Color Against Violence. (Ed.). (2007). *The revolution will not be funded: Beyond the non-profit industrial complex.* Boston, MA: South End Press.

Leydesdorff, L., & Ward, J. (2005). Science shops: A kaleidoscope of science-society collaborations in Europe. *Public Understanding of Science, 14*(4), 353–372.

Mihalynuk, T. V., & Seifer, S. D. (2004). *Partnerships for higher education service learning* (expanded). Retrieved from http://www.servicelearning.org/instant_info/fact_sheets/he_facts/he_partners/expanded.php

Robinson, T. (2000a). Dare the school build a new social order? *Michigan Journal of Community Service-Learning, 7*, 142–157.

Robinson, T. (2000b). Service-learning as justice advocacy: Can political scientists do politics? *Political Science and Politics, 33*, 605–612.

Sandy, M., & Holland, B. (2006). Different worlds and common ground: Community partner perspectives on campus-community partnerships. *Michigan Journal of Community Service Learning, 13*, 30–43.

Stoecker, R. (n.d.). *Rethinking public sociology.* Unpublished manuscript. Retrieved from http://comm-org.wisc.edu/drafts/pubsoc.htm

Stoecker, R. (2007). The data and research practices and needs of non-profit organizations. *Journal of Sociology and Social Welfare, 34*, 97–119.

Stoecker, R., & Stillman, L. (2007). Who leads, who remembers, who speaks. Constructing and sharing memory community informatics, identity and empowerment. *Selected papers from the 3rd Prato International Community Informatics Conference; Community Informatics Research Network 9–11 October 2006.* Newcastle upon Tyne, UK: Cambridge Scholars Publishing.

Strand, K., Marullo, S., Cutforth, N., Stoecker, R., & Donohue, P. (2003). *Community-based research in higher education: Methods, models and practice.* San Francisco, CA: Jossey-Bass.

Tryon, E., Hilgendorf, A., & Scott, I. (2009). Communication: The heart of partnership. In R. Stoecker & E. Tryon (Eds.), *The unheard voices: Community organizations and service learning* (pp. 96–115). Philadelphia: Temple University Press.

Wallace, J. (2000). The problem of time: Enabling students to make long-term commitments to community-based learning. *Michigan Journal of Community Service Learning, 7*, 133–142.

Case Study 8.4. The "Third Place" Project

Ray Oldenburg

Sometimes research topics are pursued for personal reasons, and so it is with this one. It all began in January 1972 when this writer first moved into a newly developed subdivision; into what the architect Raymond Curran

(1983) described as the "open order . . . with a high level of mobility, personal isolation, and independence from a communal context" (Curran, p. 9). There was no center, no gathering places, no stores, and nothing to walk to. As a friend from Norway observed, "You people have to get in the car for everything!" One could imagine that if General Motors were in charge of urban planning and had nothing but profit in mind, things would look pretty much as they now do. Our plight, I knew, was widely shared, for the United States had become the first and only suburban nation in the world.

Experiencing the abject stupidity and deleterious consequences of American urban planning in a personal way caused me to set aside my training in symbolic interaction and focus on urban sociology. The postwar American city, it seemed to me, promoted a home-to-work-and-back-again shuttle linked by the stress of automobile commuting and too little else. Smaller families moved into ever-larger houses as the home was called upon to meet unprecedented needs to supply opportunities for entertainment and relaxation once found in the public realm. The postwar American city struck me as an ill-conceived disaster that begged remedy. As the Polish architect Adolf Ciborowski (1971) observed, a third kind of destruction of cities has been added to nature and men at war—we now destroy cities in the process of building them, and there's no better example than our own.

Getting Started

My research focused on that which I missed most—those "hangouts" that I had enjoyed all my life until my wife and I became expatriated in a cul-de-sac, in surroundings that could transform us from citizens into mere consumers. I dubbed them "third places" (following home and work) and came to realize that urban planners seem to regard them much like pedestrians—more of a problem than a desideratum in their distorted views of how a city should function.

To have appreciable impact, any publications on third places would have to appear in plain English to be understood by those who can effect change. My thesis advisor warned me that the profession would not approve. Invoking James Joyce, he said, "They like the scholarly stink," and well I knew it. The dominant figure in sociology in my graduate school days was Talcott Parsons. His prose was barely readable, and if his voluminous abstractions have had any positive effect on our society I have yet to hear of it. The decision to communicate as clearly as I could was not a difficult one to make.

My research efforts were twofold: field research and a broad range of library searching that took me outside the discipline for the most part. Travel magazines, environmental psychology, newspapers, diaries, bar studies, association journals, and whatever else spoke to third places in both domestic and foreign cultures were eagerly devoured. I chose midwestern taverns for field research because of their number, ease of access, and popularity. A 4-by-5-inch, eight-page booklet was developed for observation in 84 neighborhood taverns. It elicited data on the physical dimensions, ambience, number and types of seating, customer demographics, customer "draws," prices, number and sizes of conversational groups, noise level, customer and staff attire, and type of license.

Based on the library research and the field data gathered, it was possible to create an ideal-typical model of third places, to identify their sine qua non features and the several important social functions they serve. If this information were clearly presented, I reasoned, it would be difficult to dismiss the importance of third places in a democratic society.

In 1980, a colleague and close friend, Professor Dennis Brissett called me with news that an editor at *Psychology Today* was seeking articles and asked whether I had anything to suggest. "The Essential Hangout" (Oldenburg & Brissett, 1980) was published in their April 1980 issue; it reappeared eight times in various books and magazines. The water had been tested, so to speak, and no more encouragement was needed to proceed with a full, book-length treatment of the subject. *The Great Good Place* (Oldenburg, 1989) received a full-page rave review in *The New York Times*.

The Impact of the Third Place Research

Early publication counts showed 116 feature articles on and reviews of the book in the nation's major newspapers, 52 in American periodicals, and 37 radio or television appearances by the author. I subsequently made 39 speaking engagements across 19 states and the District of Columbia and in Austria, Canada, Japan, and Sweden. The concept of the third place, I noted, was entering the language without attribution and gaining currency as time passed.

Many of the nation's developers have adopted the concept and proceeded to implement it. Outstanding among them is Ron Sher in Seattle, who is presently involved in his third rescue of planning disasters. The first of these is the Crossroads Commons in Lake Forest Park, a failed shopping mall that Sher turned into a vibrant community at the heart of which is his Third Place Books. A resolute believer in the necessity of face-to-face interaction, Sher is convinced that too much time spent on the Internet and watching TV breeds ignorance.

The corporate world has commandeered the concept of the third place in response to sweeping changes in the workplace. Both employee training programs and optimal workplace design have very short life spans. The old notion that productivity equates with time spent in the office has proven wrong. Attention has turned to optimizing conditions for the creative class of knowledge workers. "Collaborate and they will innovate" has become the new mantra. Where and when work is done has changed to an extent unimaginable a few decades ago.

New office structures encourage collaboration and collaboration also occurs well away from the office. Architect Siamak Hariri's creation of "The Hive" for McKinsey Consultancy's new building in Toronto is illustrative of the former. This centerpiece suggests an upscale café with cappuccino bar, pool table, stone fireplace, cabaret-style tables, easy chairs, chess sets, and a library. Affecting more knowledge workers, however, is the projection that 30% of their work time will be spent in third places in the near future. The availability of these places has become a major factor in worker recruitment.

The third place concept has also caught the attention of some of the largest YMCA branches in the nation. In 2003, the Central Florida YMCA Annual Report booklet had only the following on its cover: "Central Florida YMCA: The New Third place for the Twenty-First Century." The leadership informed me that it had abandoned its old "service for fee" posture after surveying the members and finding what was most important to them. I also visited the Y in greater Los Angeles and found that they, too, had decided to shape their operation as a third place. Houston, Texas, I learned, had also "converted," as had smaller branches here and there.

Churches the country over are announcing themselves as third places. High residential mobility and urban sprawl find many of them no longer serving a cohesive neighborhood and being a natural gathering place for their members. They now seek to offer far more than traditional services. When I consulted with the Community Christian Church in Naperville, Illinois, I remarked that most church entrances aren't very inviting. That, apparently, struck a note, for the entrance to a new church they built the following year is the "Ground Level Café." Most churches adopting the third place approach view it as a way to both increase membership and interaction among members.

Outnumbering third place churches are libraries, which, threatened by the Internet, are now devoted to becoming vital community centers. Both here and abroad libraries are being radically reshaped for that purpose. The once pervasive "Rule of Silence" has given way to a few quiet study rooms. There is space for community meetings, public performances, and comfortable seating in living room-like areas. Carrels and cubicles are being replaced with "kitchen" tables conducive to conversation. I have spoken to library associations in Colorado, New Jersey, and Ohio, where interest has been particularly high. In Evergreen, Colorado, a new library resembling an upscale lodge was built, complete with stone fireplace, easy chairs, and picture windows from which patrons can watch wildlife bedding down for the night.

North America and Australia have taken the lead in transforming their libraries with the Nordic countries and United Kingdom proceeding more slowly. There are developments in China as well, particularly in the university libraries such as the one in the Nanjing University of Science and Technology. It has adopted the third place model and is one that students can afford. Also in China are the Bookworm English language lending libraries in Chengdu, Beijing, and Suzhou. These combine library, bar, restaurant, and events spaces with jazz and blues featured on Friday and Saturday nights.

In Novosibirsk, the informal capital of Siberia, the third place concept has been employed to promote democracy and creativity. Traditionally, professional people gathered in kitchens or *Kuhnya*, hence the Third Place (Kuhnya) Project in that city of 1½ million where there had been few places for people to gather outside of the workplace.

The pubs in Ireland are currently threatened by a vigorous anti-alcohol campaign, and efforts are being made to defend them. Traditionally considered as little more than "watering holes," they are now being reassessed. Research is focusing on their social merits in light of the third place model.

In both Australia and New Zealand, gambling is a national pastime and a national problem. The gambling venues are doubly attractive because of the lack of other places for relaxation and enjoyment in the public realm. Thousands of people become addicted to gambling and with dire consequences. This has prompted the Third Place Project, which seeks to create safe alternatives to the poker machines. Chrysalis, Inc., in partnership with the Swinburne University of Technology, has taken the lead.

Also in Australia, community gardens are being encouraged to provide more public gathering places. These can be low-budget ventures with some protection from the rain, a simple means of cooking such as a small, portable gas barbecue, a long table, and some chairs. There is encouragement to find reasons to celebrate at these gardens, such as the equinox, solstice, or the seasonal arrival of migratory birds. The third place criteria are stressed—conviviality is considered more important than the condition of the garden.

Not all uses of the third place concept are laudable, however. As Americans got more and more into electronic communication, the concept of the "virtual third place" emerged. There is no place, of course, and there's little mix. "Virtual private networks" would be far more accurate. Also, corporations have appropriated the concept to "warm" their products. The corporate colonization of the public realm seems to continue unabated.

The most obvious case of corporate cooptation is Starbucks; so much so that many think that the owner coined the term. He felt it necessary to distance his places from McDonald's, hence the concept and the easy chairs. Bryant Simon, who has taken a hard look at what Starbucks sells and what it actually delivers concludes that it isn't a third place but it looks like one (Simon, 2009). There is, he determined after visiting some 400 of them, no community building going on there.

Closing Thoughts

This concludes a brief and incomplete summary of my work with third places. It was done without funding and the advantage to that has been the absence of deadlines and pressure to produce premature reports. A second book, a reader presenting accounts of third place establishments, was published in 2001 (Oldenburg, 2001). Many other publications bearing on the subject followed the first book, all of them invited and including encyclopedia essays, book chapters, journal articles, and articles for electronic media. It has been an interesting pursuit and, as it now seems, a worthwhile one.

References

Ciborowski, A. (1971). Foreword. In K. R. Schneider, *Autokind vs. mankind.* New York, NY: W. W. Norton.

Curran, R. J. (1983). *Architecture and the urban experience.* New York, NY: Van Nostrand Reinhold.

Oldenburg, R. (1989). *The great good place: Cafes, coffee shops, bookstores, bars, hair salons, and other hangouts at the heart of a community.* New York, NY: Marlowe & Company.

Oldenburg, R. (2001). *Celebrating the third place: Inspiring stories about the "great good places" at the heart of our communities.* New York, NY: Marlowe & Company.

Oldenburg, R., with Brissett, D. (1980, April). The essential hangout. *Psychology Today, 13*(11), 82–84.

Simon, B. (2009). *Everything but the coffee: Learning about America from Starbucks.* Berkeley, CA: University of California Press.

Conclusion

The Case for the New, Engaged, 21st-Century Scholarship

Throughout this book we have emphasized the variety of ways in which sociology "gets into play," taking sociology beyond the academy and to various publics. The case studies in this book provide rich examples of sociologists engaged with community partners in using the tools of the discipline to bring about social change.

Of course, this type of sociological praxis is not new—indeed it is the very foundation of American sociology and has been, and continues to be, widely practiced. Nevertheless, there has been a very real shift toward the hyper-professionalism of American sociology today that sets the standard for what is considered mainstream and marginal (Burawoy, 2004). We have argued that there is nothing marginal, nothing secondary, in the work being done by public sociologists. In fact, this type of research is probably more grounded in the discipline than much of the professional sociology that is produced. The reality is that there is a wealth of knowledge in the field of sociology that simply *does not get communicated* to those who could use that knowledge. Sociologists create and generate a body of knowledge that, ideally, should flow back into the community. Engaged scholars provide this bridge, connecting sociology to publics producing greater opportunities to put that body of knowledge into play. We make the case for a new, engaged, 21st-century scholarship that works in collaboration with, not in opposition to, professional sociology.

What we learn from the sociologists in this book is that when research is conducted in partnership with community, sociology becomes more "nimble on its feet." In their active engagement with various publics, sociologists become more aware of emerging issues and responding to those issues in their research. This elevates the field of sociology in the eyes of the 99.99% of the world outside of our field. The involvement of collaborative partners often improves the quality of research through the contributions and ideas of those most affected by the issues. Because of their direct and immediate proximity, collaborative partners often raise questions and concerns based on local knowledge that researchers may not even know about. Making these adjustments strengthens the research by making it more relevant to the publics involved. In Case Study 2.1, by Alissa Cordner, Alison Cohen, and Phil Brown, the Contested Illness Research Group (CIRG) at Brown University beautifully illustrate this nimbleness in adapting and changing projects and research based on local circumstances and needs, ultimately leading them to "new, innovative, and fruitful avenues of research." It is this type of organic public sociology that provides the flexibility necessary to ensure "rigor, relevance and reach." Armchair theorizing takes a back seat to a sociology that makes active and relevant connections to users of research.

The public sociologists in this book are in the business of building communities through relevant research. When new knowledge is disseminated to various publics, it strengthens community-based efforts by sharing information and avoiding costly "reinvention of the wheel." The primary goal of Garth Taylor's work at Metro Chicago Information Center (Case Study 3.1) is to empower the nonprofit sector with research that helps it make better development decisions. Synthesizing data from numerous place-based studies and making this research available helps communities avoid the pitfalls of earlier projects and steer clear of duplicating those that were unsuccessful or potentially irrelevant. Public information projects, such as PovertyEast. org (Case Study 3.4, Leslie Hossfeld), that provide poverty data and analysis for community groups, allow constituencies to access data so they can address critical issues in their communities and build on existing research and findings and tailor projects to meet their needs. Struggling communities can ill afford to reinvent the wheel.

The technology of the 21st century, with effective national and international communication systems (social networking sites, email, Internet, etc.), provides a new potential to link multiple grassroots collaborative research projects directly with each other and improve local knowledge aimed at social change. So many of the case studies in this book provide examples of how social networking, email, and Internet use have expanded projects and created networks, partnerships, and shared resources that otherwise would not have been available to community organizations. Perhaps one of the best examples is the U.S. Social Forum in Atlanta and more recently in Detroit demonstrating how 21st-century communication brings together thousands of grassroots organizations to address social change (Case Study 8.2, Walda Katz-Fishman, Rose M. Brewer, and Jerome Scott). David Pellow's public sociology work informing anti-mining campaigns in developing nations links activists in Europe, Canada, East and West Africa, Latin America, Asia, and the United States (Case Study 2.3). The ease of communication, particularly communication from one local grassroots project to another local grassroots project, means that public sociology (typically organic public sociology) that is anchored to local communities has been enhanced in its potential reach. In the past, only researchers connected with formal national or international organizations and government agencies would have had access to these connections; now there is broader, more democratic access.

If we are to think seriously about a new engaged scholarship, the training of future sociologists must be addressed. Preparing sociologists for engaged scholarship means rethinking the academic programs we currently offer to ensure graduates have the skill set needed to work outside academia, creating a curriculum that reflects the growing needs of the 21st-century sociologist. It also means recognizing that there is more than a single career model, embracing a diversity of sociological work beyond the academy. Key to this is a tenure and promotion model that recognizes and values the work of engaged scholarship and the establishment of clear standards for evaluating public sociology.

The sociologists in this book are those who are out in the field, in the trenches, and engaged with their publics. They are in the business of *doing* sociology, bringing their students along to ensure a new generation of engaged sociologists. The impressive body of scholarship presented by these sociologists makes the case for a new, engaged 21st-century scholarship that seamlessly integrates research, action, and change.

Reference

Burawoy, M. (2004). Public sociology: South African dilemmas in a global context. *Society in Transition, 35*(1), 11–26.

Index

About the Editors

Philip Nyden, Ph.D., is currently Distinguished Research Professor of Sociology and director of the Center for Urban Research and Learning (CURL) at Loyola University Chicago. CURL is a nontraditional research center that involves community partners in all stages of research, from conceptualization and research design to data analysis and report dissemination. From 2004 to 2009 Nyden cochaired the American Sociological Association Task Force on Public Sociology. He has done extensive research on the factors that produce stable racially, ethnically, and economically diverse communities in the United States. With colleagues at CURL and the University of Technology Sydney Shopfront (Australia), he coedits the e-journal, *Gateways: International Journal of Community Research and Engagement.*

Leslie Hossfeld, Ph.D., is Associate Professor of Sociology and Director of the Public Sociology Program at the University of North Carolina, Wilmington. She served as cochair of the American Sociological Association Task Force on Public Sociology. She received the 2005 Faculty Fellow in Public Policy and Public Engagement at the Institute for Emerging Issues at North Carolina State University. Her research and activism addresses poverty and economic restructuring in rural North Carolina and she has made presentations to the U.S. Congress and to the North Carolina legislature on the subject of job loss and rural economic decline and recovery.

Gwendolyn Nyden, Ph.D., is Professor of Sociology at Oakton Community College in Des Plaines, Illinois. She directs the college's service learning program and has been working with the American Association of Community Colleges in a national, multiyear initiative to enhance service learning at community colleges throughout the United States. In 1990, Dr. Nyden coauthored *Promises Made, Promises Broken*, an early report that highlighted the often unseen population of homeless women and children in Chicago and presented policy recommendations that were subsequently used by nonprofit and government service providers.

About the Contributors

Crystel Anders is Executive Director of Community Shares of Wisconsin, a grassroots fundraising organization that provides financial support and technical assistance to more than 64 nonprofits. She has nearly 30 years of experience with nonprofit organizations, including 20 years as an executive director.

Carolyn Rebecca Block, retired Senior Research Analyst at the Illinois Criminal Justice Information Authority, continues to maintain the Chicago Homicide Dataset as well as the CWHRS (Chicago Women's Health Risk Study) dataset, and to help citizens use the data. In addition to the Homicide Research Working Group, she continues to maintain networks and working groups for practitioners and academics, such as the CWHRS Forum, the Working Group for Criminologists Outside of Academia, and the Working Group on Research Collaboration Between Researchers and Practitioners.

Richard Block, Professor Emeritus of Sociology at Loyola University Chicago, has studied the relationship among violence, victimization, and community for more than 40 years. He participated in the development of the public computer mapping facility of the Chicago Police Department and has advised many other departments on computer mapping and the spatial analysis of crime patterns. Along with Carolyn Rebecca Block, he founded the Homicide Research Working Group.

Rose M. Brewer, Ph.D. is a scholar-activist and Morse Alumni Distinguished Teaching Professor of African American & African Studies at the University of Minnesota–Twin Cities. She writes extensively on inequality, gender, race, class, and social change.

Phil Brown is Professor of Sociology and Environmental Studies at Brown University. His research interests are in environmental justice, biomonitoring and household exposure, individual and community responses to environmental contamination, and health social movements.

Susan Bullers is a sociologist working in the areas of health and gender in the Department of Sociology and Criminology at the University of North Carolina, Wilmington.

Michael Burawoy is Professor of Sociology at the University of California, Berkeley. As President of the American Sociological Association in 2004, he created substantial new interest in public sociology within the discipline. His writing, speaking, and activism have continued to stimulate the growth of public sociology. Much of his research has focused on industrial workplaces as well as on how "globalization" can be studied from below through understanding the lives of those who experience it.

Peter L. Callero is Professor of Sociology at Western Oregon University. His most recent book is *The Myth of Individualism: How Social Forces Shape Our Lives.*

Fernando Cázares is currently working in Washington, D.C. At the time of this project, he was working at the Homeless Services Division in the City of San Jose's Housing Department, where he oversaw homeless outreach and service delivery coordination.

Barry Checkoway is Professor of Social Work and Urban Planning at the University of Michigan, where he teaches courses in community organization, neighborhood development, and youth empowerment.

Alison Cohen is a Master of Public Health candidate in epidemiology at the University of California, Berkeley. Her research interests include community-based participatory research and policy analysis; she has published on school siting and chemical policy implementation.

Alissa Cordner is a doctoral student in the sociology department at Brown University. Her research interests include environmental sociology, environmental health, environmental justice, the sociology of risk, and the sociology of science.

Julie Davis was formerly a Senior Researcher at Center for Urban Research and Learning (CURL) and has done work on the center's two-year evaluation of Chicago's Plan to End Homelessness.

Peter Dreier is E. P. Clapp Distinguished Professor of Politics and Chair of the Urban and Environmental Policy Program at Occidental College, where he teaches community organizing and urban politics. He writes regularly for *The Nation, American Prospect, HuffingtonPost, Talking Points Memo,* and the *Los Angeles Times* and is coauthor of *Place Matters: Metropolitics for the 21st Century,* and *The Next Los Angeles: The Struggle for a Livable City.*

Emily Edlynn coordinated university-community research projects for the Center for Urban Research and Learning at Loyola University Chicago. Dr. Edlynn currently works in Los Angeles as a pediatric psychologist.

Abby L. Ferber is Professor of Sociology and Women's and Ethnic Studies at the University of Colorado at Colorado Springs. She also directs the Matrix Center for the Advancement of Social Equity and Inclusion, home of the Annual White Privilege Conference and the Knapsack Institute: Transforming Teaching and Learning.

Anne E. Figert is Associate Professor of Sociology at Loyola University Chicago. She is a medical sociologist who has been actively working with HIV/AIDS organizations for the past 15 years.

Christine George is Assistant Research Professor at the Center for Urban Research and Learning, where she develops and leads a number of university-community research projects. Her most recent research has focused on informing public policy and/or program and public services evaluations related to homelessness, domestic violence, and the integration of public services.

Duane A. Gill is Professor and Head of the Department of Sociology at Oklahoma State University, where he conducts research on disasters and the environment. He is currently conducting research on social impacts of the 2010 BP oil gusher in the Gulf of Mexico.

Diane Grams, an Assistant Professor of Sociology at Tulane University, served as the Associate Director of the Cultural Policy Center at the University of Chicago (2003–2007) and Executive Director of the Peace Museum in Chicago (1992–1998). Among her publications: *Producing Local Color: Art Networks in Ethnic Chicago*, and *Entering Cultural Communities: Diversity and Change in the Nonprofit Arts* (Grams & Farrell, 2008).

Keith N. Hampton is Assistant Professor in the Annenberg School for Communication at the University of Pennsylvania. His research interests focus on the relationship between information and communication technologies, social networks, and the urban environment.

David H. Jernigan, Ph.D., is Associate Professor in the Department of Health, Behavior and Society and Director of the Center on Alcohol Marketing and Youth at the Johns Hopkins Bloomberg School of Public Health, where he teaches courses on social and behavioral aspects of health, media advocacy, and alcohol policy. He has worked as an adviser to the

314   Public Sociology

World Health Organization and the World Bank and was the principal author of WHO's first *Global Status Report on Alcohol* and *Global Status Report on Alcohol and Youth*, and coauthored *Media Advocacy and Public Health: Power for Prevention*.

Mariana Johnson is Assistant Professor of Film Studies at the University of North Carolina, Wilmington. She received her Ph.D. in cinema studies from New York University and specializes in Latin American cinema and documentary.

Walda Katz-Fishman, Ph.D., is a scholar-activist and Professor of Sociology at Howard University. She was a founder of Project South: Institute for the Elimination of Poverty & Genocide and serves on the National Planning Committee of the U.S. Social Forum.

Donna King is Associate Professor of Sociology at the University of North Carolina, Wilmington, where she teaches courses in media and popular culture. She is author of *Doing Their Share to Save the Planet: Children and Environmental Crisis* and is coeditor of the forthcoming book *Men Who Hate Women and the Women Who Kick Their A@#$!: Feminist Perspectives on the Stieg Larsson Millennium Trilogy*.

Vandana Kohli is Professor and Chair of Sociology at California State University, Bakersfield. Her teaching and research areas include demography, research methods, and spatial analysis. Dr. Kohli has conducted applied research in the areas of public health and adolescent pregnancy.

Anthony E. Ladd is Professor of Sociology at Loyola University New Orleans, where he teaches courses in both the Department of Sociology and the Environmental Studies Program, as well as conducting research on environmental controversies and disasters. He is currently conducting research on the sociopolitical roots and impacts of the BP oil disaster in the Gulf of Mexico.

Michael Leachman, currently Senior Policy Analyst at the Center on Budget and Policy Priorities, worked previously as an analyst at the Oregon Center for Public Policy. In both positions he has conducted timely research aimed at improving public policies that affect lower-income people.

Mac Legerton is Executive Director of the Center for Community Action (CCA) in Robeson County, North Carolina, and cofounder of the Southeastern North Carolina Food Systems Program. For his contribution to the enhancement of rural life and rural people, he received the Distinguished Service to Rural Life Award in 2007 from the Rural Sociological Society (RSS).

Jack Levin is the Irving and Betty Brudnick Professor of Sociology and Criminology at Northeastern University, where he codirects its Center on Violence and Conflict. His publications include 30 books and numerous articles and opinion columns in the areas of hate crimes, prejudice, and murder.

Donald W. Light is Professor of Sociology and Social Medicine at the University of Medicine & Dentistry of New Jersey who has done a series of campaigns against injustices in health care. He is a founding fellow of the Center for Bioethics at the University of Pennsylvania and a visiting professor at Stanford University.

Amy Liu is on the faculty in the Department of Sociology at California State University, Sacramento.

Paul Luebke is Associate Professor of Sociology at University of North Carolina Greensboro and the author of *Tar Heel Politics*. He has represented Durham in the North Carolina State House since 1991.

Christopher R. Martin is Professor of Communication Studies and Journalism at the University of Northern Iowa. He is coauthor of *Media and Culture: An Introduction to Mass Communication* and author of *Framed! Labor and the Corporate Media*, an award-winning book on how labor unions are covered in the news media.

Jack McDevitt is the Associate Dean for Research and Graduate Studies in the School of Criminology and Criminal Justice at Northeastern University. His areas of research focus on the intersection of race and crime in our society, specifically concentrating on hate crime, gang violence, racial profiling, and human trafficking.

Daniel Monti is a member of the Department of Public Policy Studies at Saint Louis University. His efforts to assist small businesses in urban areas is part of a larger body of work detailing the civic contributions of businesspeople in American urban history.

Dan E. Moore is the principal in GivingInsight, a consulting group that helps people and organizations increase their capacity to achieve their goals, especially through strategic giving. Dr. Moore is founder of NCGives, an innovative initiative for inclusive philanthropy that celebrates and inspires giving, particularly within and among communities of color, women, and young people. For nearly 20 years he was vice president for programs at the W. K. Kellogg Foundation in Battle Creek, Michigan. Before going to Kellogg, Dr. Moore was a faculty member at Cornell University, Pennsylvania State University, and the University of Wisconsin–Madison.

Laura Nichols is Associate Professor of Sociology at Santa Clara University.

Patricia G. Nichols of Superior, Montana, holds an M.A. in sociology from the University of Montana and is the owner of a private consulting firm, An Ounce of Prevention. Since 1992, she has worked to address public health issues as a policy advocate, program manager, writer, and service provider.

Ray Oldenburg received his Ph.D. in sociology from the University of Minnesota, taught in the Wisconsin and Nevada systems, and retired from the University of West Florida as Professor Emeritus. He has served as consultant, speaker, and writer in the field of community building for the past 30 years.

Pamela Oliver is a Conway-Bascom Professor of Sociology at the University of Wisconsin–Madison. She has given more than 80 public presentations on racial disparities in criminal justice and has served on a number of boards and commissions addressing these issues.

David N. Pellow is Professor and Don A. Martindale Endowed Chair of Sociology at the University of Minnesota, where he teaches courses on social movements, environmental justice, globalization, immigration, and race and ethnicity. He has published a number of works on environmental justice issues in communities of color in the United States and globally.

Steven Redfield is Managing Director of Training and Related Services at Coro, a national organization promoting leadership skills necessary to assure that government, nonprofits, and businesses more effectively meet the needs of the nation's citizens. He is the founder and former executive director of the Chicago office of STRIVE, an organization focusing on job training and career services for low-income, unemployed adults.

Katie Richards-Schuster is Assistant Research Scientist and Lecturer in the School of Social Work at the University of Michigan. She is also Director of the Community Action and Social Change Undergraduate Minor and teaches courses in Community Organization and Youth Empowerment.

Angelica M. Rodriguez graduated from Santa Clara University in December 2007. She is currently working on her Master of Public Health in health and social behavior at the University of California, Berkeley School of Public Health.

Jerome Scott is a labor and community educator and writer in Atlanta and was the founding director of Project South: Institute for the Elimination of Poverty & Genocide. He serves on the National Planning Committee of the U.S. Social Forum and is active in Grassroots Global Justice.

Shannon Silva is Assistant Professor of Film Studies at the University of North Carolina Wilmington, where she teaches courses in experimental and documentary film production. She received her M.F.A. in film production from the University of Iowa, and her principal areas of interest are gender, celebrity, fan culture, and organizing community-building creative initiatives.

Randy Stoecker is Professor of Community and Environmental Sociology at the University of Wisconsin–Madison with a joint appointment at the University of Wisconsin Extension Center for Community and Economic Development. He has written extensively on higher education civic engagement.

Jean-Anne Sutherland is Assistant Professor in the Sociology and Criminology Department at University of North Carolina, Wilmington. Her primary research areas are the sociology of mothering and sociology through film.

Melissa Swauger, Ph.D., is Assistant Professor of Sociology at Indiana University of Pennsylvania. Her research interests include gender, race, and class inequalities in education and work, public sociology, and feminist qualitative research methods.

Garth Taylor is Senior Research Fellow at the Metro Chicago Information Center, an independent public policy research firm. He is the founding chief executive officer and has worked there for 20 years. He is also the parent of a 16-year-old son, an organic gardener, an amateur musician, and rides a bicycle or walks to work every day of the year.

Madeline Troche-Rodríguez, Ph.D., teaches social science and sociology at Harry S Truman College, one of the City Colleges of Chicago. She is a cofounder of MoveSmart.Org and vice president of the board of directors of the Latin United Community Housing Association (LUCHA), where she focuses on racial and economic integration, neighborhood stabilization, and fair housing.

Catherine Willis is a graduate student in the Department of Community and Environmental Sociology at the University of Wisconsin–Madison.